HOW TO UNITE THE LEFT ON ANIMALS

HOW TO UNITE THE LEFT ON ANIMALS

A Handbook for Total Liberationist Veganism and a Shared Reality

John Tallent

How to Unite the Left on Animals: A Handbook for Total Liberationist Veganism and a Shared Reality (ɔ) 2022 by John Tallent is licensed under Attribution-NonCommercial 4.0 International. To view a copy of this license, visit http://creativecommons.org/licenses/by-nc/4.0/.

This book is dedicated to my marvelous and beautiful wife, my eternally-supportive parents, my mom's side of the family, my friends, and all my past and present companion animals. These are people anyone would want by their side.

Special thanks to Jillian Fischer for editing this book. I also want to thank those folks who I have had many great conversations with over the years, despite our geographic distances: Benny Malone, Nathan Poirier, Richard Twine, Nathan Nobis, Helena Chen, and many others!

CONTENTS

DEDICATION v

Introduction 2

Part I

1 | The Problem 12

2 | That's Fallacious! 17

3 | Plants are not Sentient, but Nonhuman Animals Definitely are 26

4 | Thinking More Clearly about Nonhuman Animals 33

5 | Speciesism is Real 41

6 | Nonhuman Animal Exploitation 68

7 | Ethics—How Should We Respond to All This? 123

8 | We have All Been Misled about Veganism 132

| vii |

CONTENTS

9 | Plant-Based Diets 146

Part II

10 | "There's No Ethical Consumption under Capitalism" 163

11 | Indigenous Rights & Traditions 181

12 | Entanglements and Analogies 203

Part III

13 | A Proposal 242

Conclusion 271

Notes 272

Bibliography 283

Do what you feel you must, but as for me, I was not put upon this earth to subjugate or serve.

—Propagandhi, from the song "Supporting Caste"

Liberate this world.
Liberate your mind.
Liberate the animals.
Liberate yourself.

—Cherem, from the song "Trapped in Torment"

The reasons for white supremacists, homophobes, patriarchs, and patriots to fear people like me is beyond identity politics; I am a sworn enemy of their control and order. The societal castle they seek to build and maintain will always be the target of my sabotage!

—Flower Bomb (2020)

Introduction

I have a traumatic memory that is still vivid in my mind from around 1990 or so when I was about five years old. On a sunny day in the middle of summer (if I remember correctly), my cousin and I were at my house in Wendell, North Carolina, and we were playing in my backyard. Growing up, my family always had at least several different types of pets at any given time. We had at least a few chickens and ducks at this particular time. We didn't ever kill them or use them for food. They were all treated like any other person would a dog or cat, except we had a horse for a few years that we rode very infrequently.

My cousin and I filled up a blue kiddie pool, putting 6 or 8 ducklings in to watch them play. After just a few minutes, we decided to go back inside my house to play Nintendo. I don't remember how we found out, but it turns out that the ducklings were too small to be able to get out of the pool themselves. All those baby birds drowned that morning.

I've always been considered an "animal lover" by those that know me, including myself. As we stood there outside later, looking down at the small, lifeless bodies, stunned at what we had done, I remember feeling sadness, guilt, and anger at myself. I remember thinking about how horrible it was for me, an "animal lover," to have killed these baby ducks, all because I was careless. The memories of that morning and those feelings have stayed with me throughout my life. And I still feel pain in my stomach each time I remember it.

When I was about 12, I remember going into my bedroom and seeing a tiny, young mouse cowering under my CD tower. I can't recall what went through my head or my justification for doing so, but I went to the bathroom, got a thick wad of toilet paper, picked the tiny mouse up, and promptly flushed this innocent and terrified animal down the drain. This memory still haunts me today, even though I didn't think twice about it until I started learning more about animal rights.

Now, there are a couple of aspects of all this that are interesting to me. First, why did I have such guilt about having a hand in the accidental deaths of the ducklings but not for having a direct hand in killing the mouse? Second, how could I kill that mouse by drowning them alive without so much as a tinge of remorse for so long?

I wrote this book about animal rights and veganism with the complete understanding that my hands aren't clean of the blood of so many animals. I ate meat, dairy, eggs, and honey until my twenties. I bought and wore leather and wool; I don't know if I've ever bought anything made of silk, but I wasn't opposed to it morally. I've visited aquariums and zoos many times. I've purchased animals from pet stores, including hamsters, gerbils, guinea pigs, and many fish species. I've harmed and killed many fish while fishing. Innumerable animals have suffered and been killed by my very existence simply because I wanted them gone or they had something I wanted from them.

Contrast this with the many pet dogs and cats that have died throughout my life and which tore my heart in two. Or when TV commercials about endangered wildlife induced so much anger in me, I wished all poachers and trophy hunters to receive a taste of their own medicine.

What can make us so unbothered by the suffering and deaths of some but simultaneously bothered by others? Is simply knowing an animal a good enough reason for why some deaths matter to us, and others can be directed at our will? Is killing endangered animals utterly different from killing other animals? Like most other people, my life is full of these contradicting ways in which we view and treat animals arbitrarily and based on seemingly random beliefs and traditions.

I have harmed animals throughout my life, and I currently harm animals because I exist and because we now live as a part of this capitalist, human-centered system. There is no escaping one's harm to others in a system built upon the broken backs and the countless unmarked and forgotten graves of people just trying to survive. But is that the whole story?

In this book, I want to convince you that the system has sold us too many lies and half-truths, and almost everyone we have ever interacted with has been an unwitting contributor to these lies. I want to persuade you that you are not helpless to change the world. You are not ineffective in a society of unbelievable cruelty. What you believe and what you do have real effects on other people and the intangible systems that order and are patterns of social life. Ultimately, I assure you that you have the agency to control your life. Not total agency, but enough agency to overcome this capitalist nightmare and bring about a world in which all people have intrinsic value that each of us determines for ourselves, but not at the expense of anyone else—value that goes beyond what can be appropriated from us through exploitation.

I work at an animal sanctuary dedicated to rescuing animals commonly used in animal agriculture. It's the most fulfilling job I've ever had. All the time, my bonds with so many of the animals grow and grow. Often, while at work, I will see logging trucks loaded down with freshly-cut timber out of my window speeding by on the road in front of the house where my office is. Truck after truck, all day long, every day. Whole ecosystems destroyed. Trees slashed. Diesel engines carry them away at breakneck speeds to be used for capitalist exploitation and expansion.

It's heart-wrenching to think about all the animals in animal agriculture. Still, there are these fucking trucks, day after day, carrying away the habitats, homes, or even family and friends of countless wild animals, who are now grieving for lost relationships and forced to find new shelter in ever-shrinking amounts of undeveloped ecosystems. The fact that I work at a place that cares for just over a hundred animals, but I am witness to the destruction of thousands of other animals' homes and lives, is not something that I am unaware of. On the surface, it might seem like a waste of time to some. After all, some systems need to be dismantled for the sake of all life on this planet, and some of us are so concerned about this relatively small number of farmed animals. It sounds so ridiculous, right?

But it's not ridiculous. Imagine if we used that same logic toward humans. What if we considered saving individual humans "ridiculous" simply because there are systems to dismantle? If you think that's a good idea, this book isn't for you because there will be no devaluing of any person's life in this book.

But, for those who disagree with such heartless logic, you may see how these situations, saving individual humans and individual animals, are not entirely different. Yes, you may value humans more than animals, but that's beside the point right now. You can see the logic I'm using here: no matter what oppressive systems threaten us, we shouldn't dismiss the suffering and deaths of individuals. We understand the intrinsic value of each person and that each person assigns a value to their own life.

So, yes, the wild animals that are harmed by the lumber companies I see every day deserve great attention and concern as a group, but that doesn't mean that each animal is not important to consider. And that's one of the significant points I will attempt to explain throughout this book: we can act to affect both systems and individuals, which is commonly unacknowledged, especially on the Left. We tend only to see oppression and change in binary ways: we work to change individuals *or* dismantle overarching systems. But why can't we do both?

I credit my introduction to radical politics to my high school best friend, Frank. We would listen to mixed CDs in his truck when we were hanging out, and within those mixes were always punk bands, like Anti-Flag, NoFX, Against All Authority, and, most importantly, to this story, Propagandhi. If you are unfamiliar, Propagandhi is Canada's amazing vegan anarchist punk band. They were crucial in my transition from a politically apathetic teenager into a politically conscious vegetarian socialist in 2007. In 2009, I started working on my undergraduate political science degree at a North Carolina university. There, I became familiar with the infamous ethics philosopher Peter Singer and began reading anything I could from him. Through social media discussions, I soon found my way into the online vegan abolitionist movement and the works of Professor Gary Francione. Francione differs from many other philosophers in that his ideas are straightforward and do not usually necessitate extensive prior knowledge of philosophical concepts to comprehend his message: if you care about animals, you must become vegan.

Furthermore, one of his main talking points about animals is that because they are sentient beings, they should be granted moral personhood and, thus, should not be considered the property of anyone. These realizations sparked my vegan identity and passion for animal rights. I began seeing myself as a motivated evangelizer of Francione's veganism and animal rights ideas.

Several years go by, and I'm deeply enmeshed in the vegan abolitionist movement. I joined several other activists in starting the world's first abolitionist vegan organization, The Abolitionist Vegan Society (TAVS). Abolitionist veganism, which uses an animal rights approach, sees the liberation of animals as its ultimate goal and rejects the more dominant form of animal advocacy that seeks the "small steps" approach that focuses on legislative reforms of animal use to make animal use supposedly more "humane." There is a common analogy that explains the difference between animal rights and animal welfare reform: those that want animal rights and liberation seek "empty cages, not bigger cages" (Regan 2005:10). At that time, vegan advocacy seemed so clean-cut: repeat some talking points about the moral obligation of ending the property status of animals and boast of the benefits and necessity of veganism. Several years passed, and our original group of dedicated and loyal activists began to fracture. Issues of white supremacy, ableism, sexism, transphobia, and attempts at apoliticization of the movement effectively pushed us all in different advocacy directions. Nuance was not well tolerated, and cultish behavior was normalized. The hierarchical group structure was also a significant problem for me because one (or three) people were calling all the shots and demanding complete ideological and behavioral allegiance within the organization. There also were almost no critiques of capitalism within the group. Furthermore, though his ideas on veganism can often be helpful, Francione is no longer someone I support or admire.

My fellow vegan Leftist friend Casey and I then started a Facebook page centered around veganism and anarchism called Veganarchist Memes. We had a lot of fun interacting with a few hundred followers on the account, but content creation fell off after a few months, and the page was forgotten for several years.

I don't remember what motivated me to reboot the page back up, but I did in early 2019 and renamed it Veganarchist Memes: Breaking Leftist Speciesism. Its focus tends to be critiquing and poking fun at how speciesism appears and is perpetuated within the political Left. The page has grown significantly in "followers" in the last few years. And, through several years of interacting almost daily on it, I have witnessed an incredible amount of nonsense from non-vegans and vegans. The first controversial thing on the page was when I ran a poll for a few days. This poll asked people what they thought about a theoretical scenario in which someone, for whatever reason, could not survive on a plant-based diet due to poverty or some disability. Would this person still be considered vegan if they did everything in their power to "be vegan" as much as they could in every other part of their life but had to continue eating animals? The poll received over 500 votes and hundreds of comments. When the poll finally ended, the results were that roughly 50% of respondents believed that the theoretical person could still be considered vegan. Roughly 50% of the other respondents voted in opposition. The comments were often vicious. Some vegans denounced the inclusion of the theoretical person into the vegan community as "speciesist"; the other side considered it "ableist" not to include them in the vegan community. This shows how divided the vegan community can be, even on the Left, and how beliefs and opinions are not monolithic. For me, this also shows how both shitty and misinformed the vegan community can be. As I will argue in this book repeatedly, every ethical claim is based upon the idea that only people who can fulfill an ethical claim are obligated to do it. And with veganism, if someone circumstantially cannot eat a plant-based diet, that does not necessarily prevent them from being vegan. The history of the vegan movement suggests this, as we shall see.

Friends, family, and other people we meet throughout our lives shape our worldviews, beliefs, values, and behaviors. Often unbeknownst to us, these worldviews, beliefs, values, and behaviors are defined by our daily interactions. They are also affected by the larger social structures we live under: patriarchy, capitalism, religion, white supremacy, hetero- and cisnormativity, governments, and more. At some point in our lives, we shield ourselves from challenging or complex forms of information. Social media uses algorithms that show us content they think we want to see (or they want us to see), thereby invisibilizing everything else. Many of us laugh at the people that believe in ridiculous things like a Flat Earth, Scientology, and the belief that dinosaurs never existed. How can anyone believe something that is so obviously false and has so much evidence to prove otherwise? The people that believe in a Flat Earth mostly only see content that supports their ideas, and they crowd themselves in their social lives with people that believe similarly—and the same goes for Scientologists and biblical creationists. This is a problem with social media corporations attempting to maximize their profits by advertising things they think we will be interested in. Though, we cannot just blame these companies. We each should seek out expertise and reliable information as best we can. This requires endeavoring to guard ourselves against misinformation and the clever ways in which discourse and reality can be twisted for biased or nefarious purposes.

This book will argue that both the mainstream vegan movement and the non-vegan Left are seemingly at odds with one another due to miscommunication, misinformation, and psychological, social psychological, and sociological reasons that are not easy to spot. Because of these issues, the non-vegan Left doesn't understand or actively support veganism and animal rights. Conversely, the mainstream vegan movement does not know how to show real solidarity with marginalized humans, nor does it understand the necessity to critique and dismantle capitalism. This book's underlying assumptions are that you care for other animals, believe in justice, and that you believe that evidence-based science is essential.

Another main point of this book is to express the urgency that is needed from all of us. The planet is burning. Trillions of animals are killed every year. Marginalized humans are oppressed and dying. And the only thing that will address all of these things in any significant way is a revolutionary and militant vegan anarchism, where we act *now*; where we stop with the fantasy that we have time and that we can go on about our normal lives; where we stop with the useless logic that some of us can just stand by and watch others try to change the world because we have various forms of oppression working against us; where we leave it up to those with more privilege to begin the process of liberating the world. Waiting for others to do something is one of the ways in which the status quo continues. Should the more privileged be doing most of the work of liberation? *Of course*. But they will not, in large part, start it or even engage in it. Privilege has a way of placating us into accepting this fantasy of normalcy. But, like so many cases throughout history, it will be the workers, the vulnerable, the severely oppressed who will lead the way and get us on the track to something better. So, we must accept this fate, this burden. If we do not, we die and so many others die on behalf of capital and hierarchy. If we do not accept the fact that we all have work to do in this, we have given up.

You may notice quite a few extended quotes from others throughout. I sometimes do some interpreting, especially if the selection is overly academic or jargon-laden, but other times I just let the paragraph or section end on the quote. I believe in letting others speak for themselves. I also sometimes make up my own citation rules. I'm used to the American Sociological Association's citation rules, so I mostly use those; sometimes, I find them arbitrarily nonsensical and I substitute my own rules. I hope that it is not too much of a nuisance. I am not an academic. Also, please refer to my endnotes in the back of the book when you can. There's some neat stuff in there.

Disclaimer: This book does not endorse any illegal acts.

☺

Part I

FACTS, LOGIC, AND THE IMPORTANCE OF A SHARED REALITY

1

The Problem

Allow me to state this as plainly and frankly as possible: it's not just right-wingers that do not accept or understand reality. Leftists are also perfectly capable of ignoring or suppressing scientific facts from ourselves. Indeed, most of the planet denies reality about certain things or has not been informed well enough about them.

I will argue four overarching points throughout this book:

1. We have been extremely misled about nonhuman[1] animals, veganism, and basic science and logic—no wonder we have so many competing views of reality. We must address these competing views, or we will never find common ground enough to come together concerning other animals. As I will show, this directly affects our efforts for liberation for all. If we can't agree on basic facts about the world—facts that can be determined through methods open to everyone—how can we ever hope to agree on other things, like ending capitalism?
2. When we finally have a shared reality in which basic, evidence-based facts are understood and acknowledged, we must come to the same conclusion that veganism is essential, necessary, and attainable by *every human on the planet with moral agency*.
3. Though mostly of good intentions, the non-vegan Left is misinformed about veganism and nonhuman animals, environmental

science, diet, and health. It must reckon with its oppression of nonhuman animals (and the destruction of the environment) if it wishes to liberate humans. Equally true, if vegans wish to liberate nonhuman animals, we must reckon with the fact that this also requires us to seek the liberation of humans and the Earth's ecosystems.

4. Finally, I offer a primarily bare-bones framework for what I term "Total Liberationist Veganism"—a veganism that sees all oppressions (nonhuman animal, human, and environmental destruction) as entangled and equally as reprehensible. Total Liberationist Veganism has its roots in the original interpretations of veganism. It exists not as a diet or "personal choice" and lifestyle but as a combination of radical political commitments of beliefs, social practices, and actions. It is anarchist. It is engaged. It is embodied. And it is holistic.

Like the Right, the Left has an essentially bankrupt view of nonhuman animals and our relationships with them. Most people care about nonhuman animals; I don't think anyone could dispute that. But *how* we care about them is the issue. What do we even mean when we say, "I care about animals"? Within the Left, some believe that we shouldn't unnecessarily harm nonhuman animals when we consume and use them; this group believes that nonhuman animal welfare is very important (i.e., It is OK to eat other animals if we treat them "humanely"). A tiny percentage probably couldn't give two shits about nonhuman animals because they are only concerned about humanity (or themselves). Likewise, some couldn't give two shits about human issues because they are only concerned about nonhuman animals. Lastly, there is a group, which I hope we will all eventually agree is the side of true liberation, that believes we must liberate humans, nonhuman animals, and the environment if we wish to free the world from all oppression. But,

|13|

keeping us from this last position are our common problems in logic, our misunderstandings of science, our twisted views on ethics, and how we all refuse to acknowledge and exist within the same *shared reality*.

We live in a world of differences: different cultures, different experiences, and different understandings. Obviously, this can often be a good thing; however, it can also often create confusion and conflict. One of the best examples of living among different realities is where I live, in the United States. Despite the overwhelming evidence for the anthropogenic climate emergency (IPCC 2023; NASA 2022; UN News 2022), an unfortunate portion of the population does not believe it is a problem. According to *The Washington Post* (Fears and Guskin 2021),

> [T]he share of Republicans who say climate change is a serious problem fell by 10 points, to 39 percent, [between 2014 and 2021]. The Republican decline in Post-ABC polls tracks with the findings of annual Gallup polls in which Republican concerns dropped after 2017, when Donald Trump took office as president.

Because of social media misinformation and its spread, a small yet growing percentage of the US population is convinced that the Earth is flat (Branch and Foster 2018); a poll in 2021 found that it was around 10% of the US population (Hamilton 2022). Research (PRRI-IFYC 2021) regarding the QAnon conspiracy theory found that '[a] nontrivial 15% of Americans agree with the sweeping QAnon allegation that "the government, media, and financial worlds in the US are controlled by a group of Satan-worshipping pedophiles who run a global child sex trafficking operation."' In another study of the US population's beliefs, 20% believed in at least one COVID-19 vaccine myth (Ognyanova et al. 2021). An NPR/Ipsos poll (Newall 2020) found that almost half of the respondents believed either that vaccines cause autism or that they were not sure either way. Miller et al. (2021) found that, while most of the US from 1985-2007 did not believe in evolution, only in 2008 was there a shift in public acceptance to the majority of the population accepting the scientific theory as fact. In a YouGov poll (Orth 2022), more than a quarter of the US population believes in astrology[2], and more than 20% responded that they were "unsure" if they believed in it. According to a Pew Research poll (Gecewicz 2018), 41% of US adults believe in psychics. In a UMass Lowell Center for Public Opinion survey (2020), over 40% of respondents believed that Black people and white people are treated the same by the police in the US. Most people in the US believe that the "acceptance" of transgender people in society is either "bad" or "neither good nor bad" (Brown 2022). These statistics show that misinformation is rampant, and most people do not always know or understand scientific and social realities.

Rectifying these gaps in understanding can be a difficult task. Take, for example, the issue of the global climate catastrophe. Despite its consensus in the scientific community as being real and greatly influenced by human activity (as noted above), there is widespread disbelief in it. So, how do organizations, activists, and policymakers change people's minds on this issue? The most obvious, common-sense solution should be to give people the correct information, right? That would be my guess, and it has been my approach to trying to change people's anti-science beliefs for as long as I can remember. But it's not always that simple. For instance, Brulle, Carmichael, and Jenkins's (2012) research suggests that more information-based advocacy had little effect on influencing concern for the global climate catastrophe overall. That's incredibly disheartening and counter to what many of us assume is how the world works.

There is other evidence, however, that correcting myths can lead to a reduction in belief in misinformation (Ullrich, Sharkey, and Briony Swire-Thompson 2023). So, in this book, I will attempt to overwhelm misinformation and disinformation with reliable research and data. Maybe some context will be provided about something you previously believed, and it will sway you to a different way of thinking. Perhaps a seed in your mind will begin to blossom in a few weeks, months, or years. One thing that I ask of you: if my explanations still leave you with a "But what about..." question, don't stop reading. Instead, write the question down and push forward. Your question might be answered later in another section. If it is not answered in this book, Google that exact question. Or make a social media post with the question. Or send me an email. As seen above in the surveys, false information can be widespread and difficult to detect and change. Keep these surprising statistics in mind. The following few sections will detail how many of our beliefs are created, influenced by, and maintained in ways we are not always conscious of. And it is our duty as Leftists to sift through the oppressive manners in which society, institutions, capitalists, our friends and families, and even our minds have affected reality for us. If we are to overturn how capitalism, hierarchy, and domination have oppressed so many people worldwide for ages, it is necessary to have a fundamental, shared reality of what is and is not true.

2

That's Fallacious!

Logical fallacies can make discussions and debates unproductive at best and impossible at worst. They are defined as "[misconceptions] resulting from a flaw in reasoning, or a trick or illusion in thoughts that often succeeds in obfuscating facts/truth" (Logical Fallacies 2022). Rather than facilitating fruitful discourse, fallacies impede the flow of discussion by various means. Most importantly, fallacies add a certain "fog" to a discussion that requires clearing up before the central topic can be dealt with. This "fog" can be purposeful or accidental, deceitful or unintentional. Fallacies in dialogue regarding veganism and non-human animal liberation are prevalent, and they happen regardless of position. The following is a non-exhaustive list of some of the more common fallacies around these subjects. It's essential to recognize the fallacies that we all frequently use as you read this book so that we can stop arguments from spreading that are unnecessary and harmful.

Appeal to nature

- "Eating animals is natural."
- "Lions eat meat, so humans can, too."

- "Humans have always eaten animals, which makes it acceptable now."
- "Humans have canine teeth for eating flesh."
- "Humans are omnivores."
- "Circle of life."
- "Vegan food is processed garbage."
- "Humans are at the top of the food chain."
- "Eating meat is what made us human."

I consider this type of argument to be one of the most, if not *the* most, used against nonhuman animal liberation and veganism. An **appeal to nature** is an argument that relies on basing what is ethically/morally "good" on what is commonly seen as "natural" and what is "bad" on what is "unnatural." In this form, the use and consumption of nonhuman animals by humans are automatically "good," "natural," and "acceptable" because humans (or other animals like lions) have done it historically. The primary purpose of this type of reasoning is an attempt to set a precedent for current behavior. However, something having a long historical existence in the past does not provide enough justification in and of itself for it to be continued currently. For example, as Leftists, none of us would argue that murder, violation, oppression, discrimination, violence, or domination would be currently acceptable just because human history (and, in some instances, throughout the animal kingdom) is littered with examples. Similarly, we would never argue that anthrax, a potentially deadly infection caused by a bacterium, is "good" just because it is "natural," even though it has been in existence for thousands of years (D'Amelio et al. 2015).

HOW TO UNITE THE LEFT ON ANIMALS

```
So I was at the                    But then I realised that
store the other day,                    lions eat meat.
buying some vegetables.
```

```
So I put the                       Because I'm basically
vegetables back, and                   a lion when you
had to buy meat instead.               think about it.
```

www.vegansidekick.com

Image created by Vegan Sidekick (2022) and published with full permission from the author.

The appeal to nature also extends to arguments against veganism that use reasons involving human teeth structure and the supposed "eating meat gave humans big brains" theory. Human evolution did result in humans having some interesting and useful characteristics, but that fact does not justify any and all behaviors in the here and now. Humans have a long history of using and consuming nonhuman animals, but, as we have seen, it is faulty logic to take that fact and apply an ethical or moral claim without regard for current circumstances and knowledge. As we will see in the later chapter on plant-based diets, a plant-based diet is perfectly suitable for humans, and current teeth structure does not carry much importance when considering ethical choices. Likewise, whether the early consumption of nonhuman animals aided in human brain size evolution or not has no bearing on how we should behave now.

One should also consider that the prevailing theories regarding early humans' consumption behaviors do not conclusively point to humans having eaten lots of or mostly nonhuman animals. As I write this, new research regarding the earlier accounts of nonhuman animal consumption being a large part of early humans' diet shows that this may not be true. Barr et al. (2022:1) describe the results of their research:

> Here, we present a quantitative synthesis of the zooarchaeological record of eastern Africa from 2.6 to 1.2 [million years ago]. We show that several proxies for the prevalence of hominin carnivory are all strongly related to how well the fossil record has been sampled, which constrains the zooarchaeological visibility of hominin carnivory. When correcting for sampling effort, there is no sustained increase in the amount of evidence for hominin carnivory between 2.6 and 1.2 [million years ago]. Our observations undercut evolutionary narratives linking anatomical and behavioral traits to increased meat consumption in H. erectus, suggesting that other factors are likely responsible for the appearance of its human-like traits.

In other words, due to sampling errors in previous research, the degree to which humans relied on consuming nonhuman animals was overestimated. Increases in brain size, body size, and differences in the gut were not due to increased consumption of other animals but rather from other factors. Recent research by van Casteren et al. (2020) also suggests that early humans could have consumed harder plant material than previously assumed, such as nuts, seeds, and tubers. This can point to a more significant amount of protein being consumed outside of nonhuman animal consumption.

Thought-terminating clichés

- "Eating animals is a personal choice."
- "Morality is subjective."
- "To each their own."
- "Live and let live."
- "Agree to disagree."

Phrases such as these are a type of rhetoric, which R.J. Lifton (2014) describes as when '[t]he most far-reaching and complex of human problems are compressed into brief, highly reductive, definitive-sounding phrases, easily memorized, and easily expressed." As Malone (2021:4-5) explains, these statements "aim to stop any further inquiry, development, or criticism of the thought. [Users of this fallacy] want to use the phrase and for that to be an end to the conversation before it can even begin."[3] While some of these phrases might, at first glance, seem to be excellent ways of thinking in specific situations, they do not provide sufficient justification for everything in life, especially when harm is the subject of debate.

Within this rhetoric, an issue as wide-ranging as the use and consumption of nonhuman animals can be reduced to a matter of "personal choice," and seemingly, the discussion ends there. Many things in our lives are a matter of personal choice: the type of clothing we wear, our hobbies, who we want to date, and what planet is our favorite.[4] It is true that whether we decide to consume and use nonhuman animals is a choice we have made. This preference, nevertheless, is disguised and couched within language that alludes to images of freedom, self-determination, and autonomy. But is this an accurate portrayal of what the "personal choice" to consume nonhuman animals entails?

For the person eating or using nonhuman animals, it is an act of "personal choice" to do so. Still, the other side to this issue is made invisible through the reductive language of the statement: the nonhuman animal side. There are *your* "personal choices," but there are also *their* personal choices; and *their* personal choices are, in every respect, being omitted from the equation. Humans' ability to consume unrestricted is fully appreciated when consuming nonhuman animals. Still, the nonhuman animal's personal choice to continue living, and their bodily autonomy, are not being respected. And we are under the assumption in this hypothetical, and in most situations throughout our society, that eating and using this nonhuman animal is unnecessary for human survival. When we look closely at this situation, the human is eating or using the nonhuman animal *only* out of "habit, convention, amusement, convenience, or pleasure" (Francione [2000] 2007:xxiv). Therefore, rather than this being a "personal choice" for humans, a more accurate appraisal would be that it *denies* "personal choice" for nonhuman animals. And every thought-terminating cliché listed at the top of this section ignores the "personal choice" and bodily autonomy of the beings consumed and used; instead, an ambiguous, contextless aphorism stunts further discourse.

Tu quoque fallacy

- "Vegans kill animals, too."
- "Vegans also have blood on their hands."
- "Factory farming is bad, but vegans harm human farm workers."

This argument relies exclusively on pointing to assumed hypocrisy in vegans or veganism. Called a ***tu quoque* fallacy** (pronounced "too qwō-qwē)—or an **appeal to hypocrisy**—the main topic of the discussion is typically derailed so that the vegan advocate must defend their own behaviors. It sometimes seems like a good-faith tactic to show how "we are all the same" and that "nobody is perfect," but it redirects *away* from the original subject and stops fruitful and logical debate. Avoiding this type of fallacy requires the person being asked a question to answer it before changing the topic or asking a question of the other person.

Red herring

A vegan says, "Harming other animals is wrong," and someone else responds with:

- "What about plants, though?"
- "What about Indigenous rights, though?"
- "What about humane meat, though?

This fallacy, intentionally or unintentionally, derails from the original topic. It can be a difficult tactic to spot because the response can be either *kind of* related or *entirely* off the original subject, but it ultimately directs the discussion elsewhere. Other issues should not be brought up until the original statement or question has been acknowledged and responded to.

Perfect solution fallacy / nirvana fallacy

- "No one is 100% vegan."
- "Veganism won't solve all the world's problems."

Unfortunately, there are no easy solutions to complex issues like human and nonhuman animal exploitation. The **perfect solution fallacy**—also known as the **nirvana fallacy**—rejects a proposed solution as not fully fixing a problem. Indeed, veganism won't solve all the world's problems; however, veganism, as a philosophy and a way of life, does not present itself as a total solution to every issue in the world.

But, as I will argue throughout this book, it can fix many problems if applied correctly. To show how unhelpful logic like this truly is, change the word "veganism" to "feminism" or "anti-racism."

Strawman fallacy

- "Vegans put animals over humans."
- "Vegans want to tell everyone what to eat."
- "Letting all domesticated animals go free overnight will create many problems."
- "Vegans think that they are morally superior."

A straw man fallacy occurs when, for example, vegan beliefs are presented as something they are not in order to make the beliefs more vulnerable to criticism. Vegans don't typically put nonhuman animal interests above human interests; vegans don't want to dictate what others should eat; and vegans don't normally think that they are morally superior. But when vegans' beliefs are described this way, they are much easier to denounce because it seems like they have scary or bullying motives. Beliefs are usually more complex and nuanced than when they are presented in this unflattering way.

Ad hominem

- "Vegans are pretentious."
- "Vegans are preachy."
- "Vegans are militant."
- "Vegans are [insert any other insult here]."

When all else fails in a discussion, calling someone an "asshole" might feel good in the moment, but it does little for the discourse itself. An **ad hominem** attack directs the conversation to insult or question the character or underlying motives of someone. It can be difficult to stay focused on the relevant facts and arguments in a debate about an important topic that has you worked up or emotional. No matter how much Mark Zuckerberg looks like a space alien or Donald Trump's mouth looks like an opening anus when he talks, bringing that up in a discussion about surveillance capitalism[5] or Trump's fascism[6] doesn't move the conversation along. In the context of veganism, it's important to remember that any person, vegan or non-vegan, can be "pretentious," "preachy," "militant," or an "asshole"; this fact has very little to do with the substance of any person's argument, however. Someone can be both pretentious and factually correct; they can also be factually correct, and the other person may just be *assuming* pretentiousness (De Groeve and Rosenfeld 2022; De Groeve et al. 2022).

Keeping these fallacies and others[7] in mind, refer back to this section if a counterargument pops up in your mind while reading the rest of this book. Does your argument commit any of these fallacies? I know I've had to refine my arguments many times over the years because I inadvertently used a logical fallacy. It happens to everyone, but the sooner we accept it, correct it, and move on, the discussion can progress, and the closer to positive change we can get.

3

Plants are not Sentient, but Nonhuman Animals Definitely are

The claims that plants are "sentient" (Angier 2009), "feel pain," "can hear you when you eat them" (Fang 2014), and "scream when you cut them" (Lanese 2019) are widespread arguments within discussions about veganism and nonhuman animal liberation. But, as we will see, claims of plant sentience are highly disputed.

But first, let's get on the same page about sentience versus consciousness. DeGrazia (2020:17-8) does an excellent job explaining sentience:

> Sentient beings are capable of having pleasant or unpleasant experiences. This capacity entails having a quality of life or experiential welfare, from which it follows that sentient beings have interests. The possession of interests, I assume, is both necessary and sufficient for moral status. So sentient beings have moral status.

Contrasted with this is consciousness—"[having] subjective experience." These two concepts are often used synonymously but are two distinct ideas with important subtleties. Sentience is concerned with the *ability* to experience positive and negative experiences (or "any feelings"), while consciousness is having an *inner life or mind* (Jablonka and Ginsburg 2022:402).

In 2007, 33 scientists wrote a letter (Alpi et al. 2007) in the journal *Trends in Plant Science* where they criticized the drift in the plant sciences to use phrases like "plant neurobiology," as well as the suggestion that plants have similar physiologies to humans and nonhuman animals. This habit of equating plants with animals is seen when plants are said to have so-called "neurons," "synapses," "intelligence," or their equivalents. Early in the letter, the scientists declare bluntly, "We begin by stating simply that there is no evidence for structures such as neurons, synapses or a brain in plants" (136). Another group of scientists (Taiz et al. 2019:677) state that,

> Although 'plant neurobiologists' have claimed that plants possess many of the same mental features as animals, such as consciousness, cognition, intentionality, emotions, and the ability to feel pain [sentience], the evidence for these abilities in plants is highly problematical. Proponents of plant consciousness have consistently glossed over the unique and remarkable degree of structural, organizational, and functional complexity that the animal brain had to evolve before consciousness could emerge. Recent results of neuroscientist Todd E. Feinberg and evolutionary biologist Jon M. Mallatt on the minimum brain structures and functions required for consciousness in animals have implications for plants. Their findings make it extremely unlikely that plants, lacking any anatomical structures remotely comparable to the complexity of the threshold brain, possess consciousness. (Bracketed text is mine)

The case against plant sentience and consciousness is robust (Ginsburg and Jablonka 2021; Mallatt et al. 2021a; Mallatt et al. 2021b), even when pop science articles (Klein 2018) report about anesthetizing plants (Draguhn, Mallatt, and Robinson 2021). Likewise, Robinson and Draguhn (2021:8) show a bit of disdain for the idea of "plant neurobiology." They say, "One can only conclude that plant synapses are a product of the over-fertile imagination of plant neurobiologists." Robinson, Draguhn, and Taiz (2020:1) also take a swing, albeit with a bit of diplomacy: "We agree that plants make an indispensable contribution to homeostasis in the biosphere and that they are highly complex organisms featuring multiple interactions with their environment. We maintain, however, that the plant science community is not benefited by the approach taken by plant neurobiologists and that it is highly misleading to the general public."

But let's engage in a hypothetical for a moment because it's not inherently disingenuous to be concerned about whether plants may be sentient or conscious. Imagine, one day in the future, the scientific consensus is that plants are, in fact, sentient and/or conscious. Would that put a nail in the coffin of veganism? After all, if vegans are eschewing the use and consumption of nonhuman animals but still eat these now confirmed-sentient plants, wouldn't that mean veganism simply arbitrarily changes who the "victims" are? For, if plants think and feel, and so do other animals, wouldn't it be true that vegans don't have a logical basis for choosing to care about nonhuman animals over plants? *Absolutely not*. This issue won't be covered in depth in this section—but it will be expanded later in the section dedicated to plant-based diets and the environment. However, I can briefly explain why a theoretical plant sentience would not be a good counterargument to veganism. Raising nonhuman animals for consumption is resource-intensive—land, water, energy, *and crops*. When a nonhuman animal, such as a cow, is turned into flesh and dairy "products," they are raised by consuming massive amounts of plant material. So, consuming nonhuman animal "products" does not just involve a singular nonhuman animal—it also involves all the plants and other resources that went into growing that being. When humans consume plant material directly, the resources necessary are (generally) much less resource intensive. Despite common understanding, nonhuman animal consumption *increases* required plant cultivation and resources. If we ever must be concerned with plant "sentience," a plant-based diet would limit the number of plants cultivated compared to the current status quo of food production. In short, plant "sentience" would be another argument *for* veganism and a plant-based diet because *far fewer plants are "harmed" and killed for plant-based foods than nonhuman animal-based ones.*

Nonhuman animals are sentient and conscious

[W]here there is feeling, there can be hurt.

—Stevan Harnad, Editor-in-Chief of the journal *Animal Sentience* (Gray 2022)

King Lear, late at night on the cliffs, asks the blind Earl of Gloucester, "How do you see the world?" And the blind man Gloucester replies, "I see it feelingly." And shouldn't we all? Animals must be off the menu because tonight, they are screaming in terror in the slaughterhouses, in crates, and in cages. Vile ignoble gulags of despair. You see, I heard the screams of my dying father as his body was ravaged by the cancer that killed him. And I realized I'd heard those screams before. In slaughterhouses, their eyes stabbed out and their tendons slashed; on the cattle ships to the Middle East; and the dying mother whale, as a harpoon explodes in her brain as she calls out to her calf. Their cries were the cries of my father. I discovered that when we suffer, we suffer as equals. And in their capacity to suffer, a dog is a pig is a bear is a boy.

—Philip Wollen[8]

It's not too often in this day and age to come across someone who honestly believes that nonhuman animals aren't sentient beings capable of experiencing pain and pleasure, at least from my own experience. There is evidence to suggest, however, that most people *underestimate* the minds of nonhuman animals (Leach et al. 2023). René Descartes (1596-1650), a French philosopher and mathematician, greatly impacted how people viewed nonhuman animals, which has some effects today. He claimed that nonhuman animals do not possess consciousness. Nonhuman animals, to him, were merely mechanical entities—like we would think of robots without artificial intelligence today (Massey and Boyle 1999). Essentially, to Descartes, turtles and horseshoe crabs were like Roomba vacuum cleaners.

Let me be explicit: **nonhuman animals are sentient and conscious** (Bekoff 2008; Low 2012; Proctor, Carder, and Cornish 2013). This includes fishes (Braithwaite-Read and Huntingford 2004; Lambert et al. 2022; Mason and Lavery 2022; Sneddon et al. 2018; Sneddon, Wolfenden, et al. 2018).[9] There is "very strong" evidence for octopi sentience, "strong" evidence for true crabs, and "substantial" evidence for squids and cuttlefish (Birch et al. 2021). This includes both vertebrates and, probably to a large degree, invertebrates (Mikhalevich and Powell 2020). Research suggests this could include insects (Baracchi and Baciadonna 2020; Gibbons et al. 2022a; Gibbons et al. 2022b; Lambert, Elwin, and D'Cruze 2021). Reptiles are also suggested to be sentient (Lambert, Carder, and D'Cruze 2019) and amphibians (Lambert, Elwin, and D'Cruze 2022). Snails, bivalves, jellyfish, sea sponges, starfish, sea cucumbers, sea urchins, coral, clams, oysters, and many other nonhuman animals don't have brains. Still, they do have different characteristics that could be signs of sentience (Animal Ethics 2021). The precautionary principle should be used for nonhuman animals with no current scientific consensus regarding sentience. This principle insists that when there is uncertainty, it is better to err on the side of caution with respect to harming them (Birch 2017). Nonhuman animals without brains listed above should be included in this precaution, as they have some semblances of a nervous system. It has even been suggested that "perhaps it is time to accept as a working hypothesis in the cognitive science of consciousness studies that all animals are sentient. This premise will promote research into a range of sentience dimensions across the animal kingdom" (Andrews 2022).

Beyond basic sentience and consciousness, many nonhuman animals also experience rich emotional lives (Bekoff 2008; de Vere and Kuczaj 2016; de Waal 2020; de Waal and Andrews 2022; Kret, Massen, and de Waal 2022; Marcet Rius et al. 2018). Some of these nonhuman animals have been shown to exhibit grief (Daley 2018; Nuwer 2012; Pierce 2018), have friendships (Hooper, Delphine De Moor, and Siracusa 2022), create and use tools (Seed and Byrne 2010; Visalberghi et al. 2017), have cultures (Allen 2019; Haslam, Falótico, and Luncz 2018; Schuppli and van Schaik 2019; Whiten 2021). There is also some evidence that a few species may be able to comprehend some amounts of mathematics (Agrillo 2014; Beran, Perdue, and Evans 2014). It is even theorized that (some?) nonhuman animals could exhibit moral behaviors (Rowlands 2020). And, as Sarat Colling (2020:51) notes, nonhuman animals often engage in resistance to their domination by humans:

> Animals resist through escape, retaliation, liberation of other animals, and everyday defiance. This resistance may be active, as in a horse throwing a rider, or passive, as in a tiger refusing to perform tricks at a circus. Animals may also resist in ways that humans don't comprehend. While self-reflective intentionality isn't required for resistance, animals' resistance entails a desire for freedom from an individual oppressor or larger oppressive system or occupation.

These behaviors and abilities are fascinating because we are constantly told that humans are distinct in many of these capabilities. However, when it comes to how we treat nonhuman animals and what fundamental legal and moral rights they are given in our society, should having a rich emotional life, or having the ability to grieve, or creating and using tools, or having a culture, or doing math be prerequisites for not being abused, exploited, or killed without necessity? That is to say, what capacities do nonhuman animals need to possess to be exempt from being resources and commodities for humans?

4

Thinking More Clearly about Nonhuman Animals

Revenge ain't no solution
To the inevitable pain
Every single one of us must face in losing
The kindred spirits in our lives;
Lives so brief, so disappointing, so confusing.
As Cronie slipped away,
I held her in my arms,
Reduced to
"Please don't leave me.
What will I do?"
This cosmic sadness
Is just here to remind you
That without love,
Breathing is just the ticking of an unwinding clock,
Counting down the time it takes
For you to comprehend the sheer magnitude of
Every single precious breath you've ever wasted.

—Propagandhi, from the song "Without Love"[10]

Differences between humans and nonhuman animals are often assumed to be so clear-cut that human domination over the planet is "deserved" or "only natural." But, as we have seen so far, humans and nonhuman animals are not all that dissimilar. With the ability to experience pain and pleasure and containing a spectrum of various cognitive and emotional capacities, other animals stand not as diametrically opposite from humans. Instead, we can understand them as other beings within the kingdom of Animalia with varying paths along the way to the present. Humans have built skyscrapers and quantum computers, flown to the moon, have written languages, and have had so much of an impact on the planet that we are on the cusp of a complete climate disaster. But do all these characteristics, though only seen within the human species, demand the supremacy of humanity? After all, not all humans can build a skyscraper or a quantum computer, took part in the Apollo 11 mission to the moon, can read or write, or can be considered as having made a significant contribution to our current climate crisis. And nonhuman animals have infinite abilities and behaviors beyond what any human could do. So, when we view humans and nonhuman animals, it shouldn't be as two separate, competing, dissimilar entities; it should be an overlapping Venn diagram—acknowledging a vast range of similarities and differences. Humans and nonhuman animals are viewed by society as distinct and hierarchical, with humans on "top" and all nonhuman animals subordinated to a much lower level, where they are viewed as only existing for human purposes.

This relationship is interesting for many reasons. We humans generally see ourselves as "above" and "superior" to nonhuman animals categorically. It is not out of the ordinary to eat them, wear them, experiment on them, or see them as entertainment. Even though it is known that nonhuman animals can experience pain and suffering, we capture them from their homes and lives. We confine them to often tight and pain-inducing cages. We violate and exploit their bodies' natural functions. We forcibly breed and impregnate them. We disfigure and genetically alter their bodies. We sometimes kill whole communities of a particular species of nonhuman animals to make way for our civilization. We deny them self-determination and bodily autonomy. We torture them. We kill them. We dominate them in all ways possible. They are things, not persons, of *total human domination*.

We even impart this kind of hierarchical valuing *within* different nonhuman animal species. Elephants, dolphins, and chimpanzees are valued morally higher than bees, eels, mice, cows, pigs, and chickens. This hierarchical valuing is so stark that those we value higher are often spared from the drudgery, hunger, and lifelong terror and agony of those considered "farm animals." Contrast this with even how we view and treat dogs and cats. We often sleep with them in our beds. We take them to the vet when they may be sick. Some of us allow them to lick our faces and hands. We take them to the park or dance a string in front of them for play. We might hold them close when we are afraid or sad, and they might seek comfort from us for the same reasons. Sometimes just seeing them brings a smile to our faces. We watch their bodies and personalities grow and change as they get older. We buy them their favorite foods or treats. We protect them from would-be predators, and we would bring Hell upon those humans that may harm them in any way. We see in their eyes that they are not emotionless and thoughtless objects but individuals who can think, feel, care, hurt, experience the pleasures of sex with one another, get sick, tremble with fear, run with excitement, become depressed, and give us unconditional love.

Then, tragically, in the end, after having done as much as we could to save their failing bodies, they are taken from us so cruelly and without mercy. We hope their passing brings no added pain or prolonged suffering for them, but we will always wonder—and we can never be sure. And as they lie there, lifeless, and we can no longer experience a mutual and loving embrace with them, they take a part of our hearts with them. Read the Propagandhi lyrics above again. Would it surprise you that "Cronie" was one of the band members' cats that had passed? The song has always had the power to move me, no matter how many times I've heard it over the years. I know all too well the heartbreak that comes with the death of companion animals. They are those who we once loved and now we grieve. With time, the sting of losing them begins to diminish, but only because our memories with them slowly fade. Not because they did not mean as much to us as we had thought; rather, it is because time is the only true reliever of pain in losing a *person* in our lives.

We are, of course, personally attached to our companion animals in incredible ways. Though similarly, we are also personally connected to our human families and friends—and this doesn't lead us to consider our personal friends and family morally different from any other humans on the planet (unless through xenophobia, racism, etc.). We must also refrain from allowing our beliefs to influence how we view nonhuman animals of different species, depending on whether we consider them close friends or distant objects in the media. We don't take advantage of and consume human people who we may not personally know just because we don't know them as well. We don't believe it to be just to exploit and consume other humans—they are people; they are sentient; their lives matter to them; they have interests. So, why do we generally treat and view our companion animals differently, morally speaking, from other nonhuman animals? And why do we treat and view nonhuman animals as *things* rather than *people*?

It might be weird to think of nonhuman animals as "persons" or "people" initially; after all, we typically think of "person" and "people" as synonymous with "human." And when we are referring to both humans and nonhuman animals, we conventionally say something like "people and animals." However, a couple of things about this conventional terminology don't make much sense. First, humans *are* animals (Lombrozo 2016). When we make a distinction between "humans" and "animals," we are essentially portraying humans *outside* of the animal kingdom. Humans are different from all nonhuman animals in that we are our own species, and we have some characteristics that are special to us. But those facts do not remove us from the kingdom Animalia. After all, every nonhuman animal species is different from every other species in unique ways. When we pretend otherwise, we engage in a manner that is, at best, misrepresentative of the scientific theory of evolution. This terminology is, of course, habit and tradition. Still, I think it is essential to understand how this type of differentiation contributes to the devaluing and material harm of all nonhuman animals. This is manifested in the form of *speciesism,* which is the arbitrary bias and discrimination against other species in favor of humans, and *anthropocentrism,* the belief system that puts humans at the center of everything (more on these concepts later). Second, since words for our species already exist ("humans" / *"Homo sapiens"*) but no standard way of combining humans and other animals into a single word, "person" and "people" make perfect sense. When it comes to "the law," a "person" is someone that has legal personhood, which entails official standing in a court (Wise [2005] 2010). But how does one obtain "personhood" status? Wise ([1998] 2010:1) explains, "one who possesses at least one legal right is a legal person." However, this is a steep uphill battle because nonhuman animals are not currently recognized as "legal persons." To gain legal rights as a person, Gary L. Francione ([2000] 2007), an academic of nonhuman animal rights, law, and philosophy, explains his view of how personhood for nonhuman animals should come about:

> [M]y argument [for nonhuman animal rights] focuses on the legal status of animals as property. I argue that as long as animals are regarded as property, they will be treated as things without moral status and without morally significant interests. I argue that animals have only one right—a right not to be treated as property or resources…[M]ost important, I argue that the basic right not to be treated as property may be derived directly from the principle of equal consideration and does not require the complicated rights theory upon which [other nonhuman

> animal ethicists rely]. Indeed, it is my view that the requirement that we abolish animal exploitation must be part of any theory that purports to accord moral significance to animals. If we really believe that animals are not merely things and that they have morally significant interests, then whether we otherwise endorse rights theory or not, we are committed to the view that we can no longer treat animals as our resources. (P. xxxiv)

However, reconciling current legal systems with the Leftist society we desire in the future is beyond the scope of this book. If we believe in extending rights and protections to marginalized human groups in this society in the here and now, there is no reason not to extend this current path of rights-seeking for nonhuman animals, as described by Francione above. In other words, we may desire a different system of ensuring our freedoms than our current legal system. But just as we do for humans right now, we have little choice but to do the same for nonhuman animals—seeking rights for their protection. And in addition to this, the current legal system should dismantle its anthropocentric biases in the interest of all persons. An anthropocentric legal system can never accurately or effectively represent nonhuman animals in matters of justice. If the basis of anthropocentrism is that humans matter more than everyone and everything else, the interests of humans, no matter how trivial, will forever trump those of other animals (Tabios Hillebrecht 2017). This should not be interpreted as viewing the legal system as the *only* way to bring about justice for nonhuman animals, though it is currently one of many necessary methods (including direct action, sabotage, confrontation, etc.).

The consequences of language cannot be understated, especially considering how it can negatively affect vulnerable and marginalized people. One prevalent way language negatively affects nonhuman animals is when we call them "it" instead of other pronouns that do not directly or indirectly mask their subjectivity. When we use "it," we typically refer to some*thing*, like a chair, body part, plant, sport, a pile of poop, or the infinite other *objects* in the world. Calling humans "it" is most often considered inappropriate and even offensive. A person is not a *thing* but rather a *someone*.

There is also a growing debate regarding the sexing and gendering of nonhuman animals. Generally, the best way to avoid assumptions of gender and sex, for both humans and nonhuman animals, is to refer to them as "they" and "them" unless otherwise specified by the individual. Categorizing nonhuman animals in this way, based in assumptions, mirrors the cisnormativity[11] in many human societies (Merskin 2022). Language might seem like it can't have material effects in society, but it can transform, maintain, and dismantle how we interact and make sense of things. Take a look at the following table (originally titled "Appropriate Terminology" from Merskin (2022:13)) to see how we can avoid the language we often use for nonhuman animals and our exploitation of them that further removes their individuality and personhood:

Instead of these terms	Use these more precise and neutral terms
It, that, which or something	He, she, they, who, whom, someone or somebody
Pets	Companion animals, nonhuman family members
Objectifying industry terms	**Animated species names**
Livestock	Cows, sheep, pigs, donkeys, etc.
Poultry	Chickens, turkeys, geese, etc.
Pork	Pigs
Veal	Calves
Seafood	Fish, salmon, shrimp, etc.
Game	Deer, rabbits, foxes, etc.
Passive terms that conceal human control	**Active terms that reveal human control**
Farm animals	Farmed animals, animals raised for food
Dairy cows	Cows used for their milk/dairy
Beef cattle	Cows and bulls killed for beef/meat/flesh
Lab rat	Rats used as research subjects
Circus elephant	Elephants kept in circuses; elephants trained to perform for humans

Source: https://animalsandmedia.org/project/selecting-appropriate-terminology/.

Republished with full permission from the author.

Language is an excellent way to promote action or to stifle it. For instance, the term "climate change" was created in 2003 by Frank Luntz, a Republican consultant to then-US President George W. Bush. Luntz, in a now infamous memo, suggested that the way Conservatives could "win" their pseudoscientific war against the science of global warming was to change the common word "global warming" to "climate change." He claimed that the words "global warming" were "frightening" to the public, which would, in turn, incentivize them to action against greenhouse gas emissions; on the other hand, "climate change" made the issue seem less scientifically certain (Burkeman 2003). Likewise, when we refer to nonhuman animals in ways that we often refer to objects and things, it can have real psychological effects on how we relate to and treat them.

As we've seen, humans are not so different from the rest of the animal kingdom. Despite this fact, humanity still consumes, uses, exploits, and harms nonhuman animals seemingly without much restraint, unnecessarily, and in unimaginable ways. Given that nonhuman animals are sentient and often even possess those qualities and capacities that we believe solely belong to our species, wouldn't Francione's case for nonhuman animals having the right not to be treated as property or resources make sense? If your answer resides anywhere near "No," it's important for you to continue reading this book because I believe the concerns you are still holding on to will very likely be answered. For now, let's continue onto the next section, which will go into more detail about what many vegans, nonhuman animal ethicists, and social scientists believe is the overarching system, including individual beliefs and habits, that allows most humans to disregard the interests and lives of nonhuman animals: *speciesism*.

Further Reading:

- Taylor, Nik. 2013. *Humans, Animals, and Society: An Introduction to Human-Animal Studies*. New York: Lantern Books.
- Dunayer, Joan. 2001. *Animal Equality: Language and Liberation*. Ryce Pub.

5

Speciesism is Real

Why, in spite of all the facts, and in the face of strikingly better philosophical arguments, does the system of speciesism seem as entrenched as ever?

—John Sanbonmatsu (2014:29)

Facts do not cease to exist because they are ignored.

—Aldous Huxley

Many people to whom I've mentioned the concept of speciesism have simply laughed or scoffed at it. It is also often put in scare quotes as if it is a word that was randomly made up or plucked from nowhere. "Speciesism? Pfffft." But this type of reaction ignores the fact that all words and concepts are created by someone somewhere. It is true, however, that the idea is relatively new—British psychologist Richard Ryder coined it in 1970. In the original 1975 publication of the popular book *Animal Liberation*, Peter Singer, an influential Australian philosopher, spelled out his understanding of speciesism as "a prejudice or attitude of bias in favor of the interests of members of one's own species and against those of members of other species" (Singer [1975] 2015:35).[12] It is used like other *-isms* related to oppression in that it can be applied as an individual prejudice against species of animals that are not *Homo sapiens*. It can also be used to describe the systemic oppression of these animals (Wrenn 2018). For example, an individual can have a speciesist view towards rats and believe that rats are "inferior" to humans in particular moral and ethical ways. Systemically, a society can hold that humans have legal rights that rats do not, simply because rats are not humans. Anthropocentrism, a prominent form of speciesism, is also frequently dismissed as "ridiculous" or based on an argument that it is "normal" for a species to be more concerned with "their own." Anthropocentrism is 'a form of human centeredness that places humans not only at the center of everything but makes "us" the most important measure of all things' (Probyn-Rapsey 2018:47).

We also are often tempted to consider "too much" concern for non-human animals, or likening any human characteristics to other animals, as "anthropomorphism"—or "the attribution of human characteristics or behavior to non-human entities, including animals" (Psychology Today n.d.). There is a general fear that considering other animals as having human-like qualities overstates their abilities. This is a curious anxiety to put so much emphasis on. Frans B. W. de Waal (1999:256) eloquently replies to this apprehension:

> To say that an animal follows its [sic] "instincts" is as much a matter of interpretation as to say that it [sic] acts "intentionally," yet it is only the second kind of description that gets one into trouble. Given that the absence of intentionally is as hard to prove as its presence, and given the lack of evidence that animals differ from people [sic] in this regard, such caution would be acceptable if human behavior were held to the same standard. But, of course, it is not. Cries of anthropomorphism are heard particularly when a ray of light hits a species other than our own.

de Waal goes on to ask the obvious question if we are so concerned about anthropomorphism: shouldn't we also care about *under*estimating nonhuman animal cognitive abilities and *over*estimating human complexities? He terms this tendency as "anthropodenial," which is "the *a priori* rejection of shared characteristics between humans and animals when in fact they may exist" (258).

There are some notable examples of Leftist denial (and mockery) of speciesism[13][14][15], but it must be noted that speciesism is an observable social and psychological phenomenon that has decades of evidence to support its existence, which we will get into in a few paragraphs. It can be tempting to wave this idea away as something "natural" to almost every animal species. But, as we saw before, with the logical fallacy known as the "appeal to nature," something being "natural" does not necessarily give it ethical or moral weight. As François Jaquet (2021:6) explains, speciesism probably developed (at least in part) from tribalism, which is "the tendency to favor individuals who belong to one's social circles as compared to those who do not" (6). In other words, we tend to favor those in our own in-group over those of what we consider an "out-group." And while tribalism has evolved throughout history and could have led to speciesism, there is the possibility that "speciesist beliefs are shaped by evolution. If evolution is disconnected from ethical truth, this means that [these speciesist beliefs] are unjustified" (12). Suppose we see tribalism as influencing our sense of who is in our in-group and who is in the out-group, and evolution is one of the mechanisms by which these tribalisms form and evolve. In that case, we still cannot deem those tribalisms and those designations of "in-group" and "out-group" as holding any ethical weight. If we were to gauge these evolutionary social categorizations of others as "normal," "natural," or "good," we would also be forced to see evolutionary ethical truth in other forms of discrimination (12). This prospect is something I hope we all reject outright.

But, that way of looking at the origins of speciesism might be considered largely taking an ideological and symbolic view of it all.

Most Marxists and others that look at things from a historical materialist perspective would look at what economic forces or social and labor relations changes may have brought about the "material possibility" of such an ideology. Marco Maurizi (2021) makes the case that there must have been something materially that laid the foundations for an ideology like speciesism to be able to develop. Maurizi sees early human history—when humans were hunters and gatherers—as relatively egalitarian. As human groups began to be less nomadic and more sedentary, the domestication of nonhuman animals and plants began. Because of domestication, social hierarchies *between* and *within* human groups became more pronounced. Specifically, control over more nonhuman animals became a status signifier. And while human groups were being more clearly differentiated socially, the environment and nonhuman animals were beginning to become more heavily exploited and became "resources" for humans because doing so could elevate one's status. These two states of change—egalitarianism to social hierarchy and the domestication of nonhuman animals and nature into "resources"—created, as Maurizi describes it, a "feedback" loop. As nonhuman animals were devalued into "resources," those humans lower in the social hierarchy were devalued and viewed more "like" nonhuman animals. In contrast, those at or near the top of the social order were considered more distant from other animals. From this, the oppression of humans would affect nonhuman animals, and the oppression of nonhuman animals would affect humans (51-2). Maurizi formulates,

> [C]ivilisation is not only due to the exploitation of nature: without human exploitation it would be impossible. Yet, these two forms of exploitation go together and escalate exponentially once combined. The material domination over nature has serious repercussions on the symbolic level. The magic-animist culture of nomadic societies establishes a weak opposition between the human and the nonhuman. It is only in patriarchal

> and hierarchical societies that the phenomenon of *deification of the human being* arises. (P. 52) [Maurizi's emphasis]

Social hierarchies, which resulted from changes in labor relations, helped give rise to the (symbolic and ideological) distancing between humans and nonhuman animals. Add to this the shift from animist religions to anthropocentric religions, whereby deities are no longer other animals but rather those humans higher on the social hierarchy; nonhuman animals became something to disparage and equate to lower-status humans. This is how speciesism originated, according to Maurizi. Nonhuman animals and humans lower in the social hierarchy became materially exploitable; thus, the ideologies involved in speciesism and human oppressions became aids in this exploitation—albeit historically *later* than the material form. Nonhuman animal and human oppressions co-constitute one another, as *"without animal exploitation there is no class society, but without class society there is no speciesism"* [Maurizi's emphasis]. He continues,

> It is only when a hierarchy *inside* society is established that the relation between the human being and the animal becomes hierarchical: h*umans control humans who control animals*. It is a dialectical process. If it is true that the enslavement of the oxen made the enslavement of the human being possible, from the other side, human enslavement reinforced the distance between the top of the social pyramid and its basis. Individual peasants may have domesticated individual animals even at the end of the Palaeolithic. But it is only with the Neolithic class struggle that animal exploitation becomes systematic and totalitarian. (P. 53) [Maruizi's emphasis]

Casually dismissing speciesism, as many people do, according to Bruers (2021), can be considered a "moral illusion." Bruers likens moral illusions to optical illusions: "Just as one line appears to be longer than another in an optical illusion, we can have a spontaneous moral judgment that one individual is more important than another." Often, we make automatic "pseudo-ethical" judgements about individuals or groups of people, all without much evidence or reflection. And since speciesism is a form of arbitrary discrimination (and a discrimination that helps the ruling class!), we might try to remedy this moral illusion by adopting an "ethical principle to avoid unwanted arbitrariness" (957). However, as we shall see, speciesism is not easily remedied or even acknowledged. What follows are some of the most interesting and important findings in psychology, social psychology, and sociology regarding speciesism.

Psychology and speciesism

Psychology is "the study of the mind and behavior" (American Psychological Association 2014), and its aim as a discipline is to understand the behaviors of the individual and the influences of group processes. This is a perfect area to study how speciesism works within humans.

Literature and research regarding speciesism have often been confined to the discipline of philosophy. However, psychology has produced fascinating evidence of its existence. In 2019, Caviola, Everett, and Faber published findings from five of their studies on the question of speciesist attitudes. The results provided some of the best empirical data about speciesism as a psychological construct. The researchers not only found that speciesism is indeed a measurable and stable form of prejudice but also 'that speciesism predicts people's willingness to help humans and "superior" animals such as dogs (rather than "inferior" animals such as pigs), in terms of allocating donation money and investing time. We also found that speciesism predicts people's (meat vs. vegetarian) food choices" (1026). These results show how speciesism exists in many humans' attitudes towards nonhuman animals, but it also exists in how we view different nonhuman animals. So, not only do we see humans as an "in-group" and nonhuman animals as an "out-group," but we also see other animals like dogs as a type of "in-group" that is separate and "superior" to the other nonhuman animals like pigs that we consider "inferior."

Other findings within these authors' research are worth considerable attention. Remember that in 1975, Peter Singer defined speciesism as "a prejudice or attitude of bias in favor of the interests of members of one's own species and against those of members of other species" (Singer 2009:35). In addition to this, Singer also made an analogy that many people might feel was exaggerative or even completely false: he said that speciesism is analogous to racism and sexism. I will talk more about the issue of analogies in a future chapter; in this space, I want to focus specifically on whether this analogy has merit. In their research, Caviola, Everett, and Faber (2019:1026) found "that speciesism is psychologically related to human-human types of prejudice such as racism, sexism, and homophobia." But how could negative attitudes towards nonhuman animals correlate to negative attitudes towards certain marginalized groups of humans?

Pratto et al. (1994:742) explain that a person's **social dominance orientation** (SDO) is a measure of "the extent to which one desires that one's in-group dominate and be superior to out-groups." They explain further that

> We consider SDO to be a general attitudinal orientation toward intergroup relations, reflecting whether one generally prefers such relations to be equal, versus hierarchical, that is, ordered along a superior-inferior dimension. The theory postulates that people who are more social-dominance oriented will tend to favor hierarchy-enhancing ideologies and policies, whereas those lower on SDO will tend to favor hierarchy-attenuating ideologies and policies.

In other words, the higher a person's SDO score, the more likely they will support unequal hierarchical social relations. The SDO model was also used as a basis for the **Social Dominance Human-Animal Relations Model** (SD-HARM), which

> proposes that human outgroup prejudices (such as racial and ethnic prejudice) and speciesism share common ideological motives, including the desire for group-based dominance and inequality, indicated by SDO. Put differently, this model proposes that SDO represents a key ingredient underpinning prejudicial and exploitative tendencies towards both human and animal outgroups. (Dhont, Hodson, and Leite 2016:508)

Further research has provided more confirmation for SD-HARM's validity and that "[t]he more people accept SDO beliefs, the less they morally condemn harm done to animals by humans" (Jarmakowski-Kostrzanowski and Radkiewicz 2021:229). SD-HARM has also been shown to connect speciesism and sexism. Five studies published in a report by Graça et al. (2018) showed that higher speciesist attitudes correlated to being more likely to dehumanize women and consider them as "more closely related to nature," a form of benevolent sexism[16]. The empirical evidence supporting the philosophical notion that speciesism is like (but not identical to) other human prejudices is impossible to ignore. SD-HARM and its use of SDO have contributed significantly to our understanding of speciesism from an individual psychological vantage point.

Many psychological processes underpin how one views nonhuman animals, which may reinforce preconceived "justifications" for consuming and using them. As was mentioned in the previous paragraph, sexism is closely linked with speciesism in many ways. Ideas of masculinity and femininity and the degree to which one holds human supremacist values can affect the probability that someone will consume nonhuman animals (Weber and Kollmayer 2022). These are important factors to remember as we continue examining the phenomenon of speciesism. Next, we turn to research from social psychology and its contributions to empirical evidence for speciesism.

Further Reading:

- Tomaž, Grušovnik, Reingard Spannring, and Karen Lykke Syse, eds. 2022. *Environmental and Animal Abuse Denial: Averting Our Gaze*. Lanham, Maryland: Lexington Books.

Social psychology and speciesism

As a subdiscipline of psychology, social psychology is defined as "the scientific study of the way in which people's thoughts, feelings, and behaviors are influenced by the real or imagined presence of other people (Allport 1985, as cited by Aronson et al. 2021:25). Social psychology is emerging as one of the most critical areas for studying speciesism. Many researched areas of human interaction can, and have been, extended to how humans view themselves in relation to nonhuman animals (Amiot and Bastian 2015).

Loughnan, Haslam, and Bastian (2010:158) put forth evidence that the practice of eating nonhuman animals "leads people to withdraw moral concern from both animals in general and the animal they ate." Additionally, the researchers found that eating nonhuman animals' bodies "indirectly leads people to deny the animal they ate the mental states closely linked to the capacity to suffer." It's a given that many, if not most, people care about nonhuman animals, yet most people harm nonhuman animals by eating them and using them as resources. Consider this fact with how the researchers summed up their findings: "It appears that people may resolve the conflict between liking meat and caring about animals by withdrawing moral concern from animals and derogating the moral status and minds of the animals they eat" (158).

This phenomenon cannot simply be used to demonize folks who are not vegan, of course. It's an effect that every single one of us, vegans included, has engaged in and felt psychological pressure from people around us to engage in. It is crucial, however, that we all become aware of these phenomena and do our best to counteract them. They are not unchangeable or necessary. And as we've seen already, some may argue that these are "natural" effects of being human, but that gives no justification for their continuation. Next, we turn to what has been called the "meat paradox," which is a term coined by two of the authors of the previous journal article.

The **meat paradox** is described by Bastian and Loughnan (2016:278) as the conflict that is created by the fact that

> [m]ost people the world over eat meat, yet a vast majority of meat-eaters also find animal suffering offensive, emotionally disturbing, and potentially disruptive to their dietary habits. We term the apparent psychological conflict between people's dietary preference for meat and their moral response to animal suffering "the meat-paradox."

This psychological conflict creates **cognitive dissonance** within people. Cognitive dissonance, as described by the social psychologist Leon Festinger, who coined the term, is when "a person knows various things that are not psychologically consistent with one another, he *[sic]* will, in a variety of ways, try to make them more consistent" (Festinger 1962).[17] The specific form of cognitive dissonance around the meat paradox has been termed **"meat-related cognitive dissonance"** or **"MRCD"** (Rothgerber 2019). Rothgerber explains that people employ five main tactics to prevent the psychological discomfort that MRCD creates: avoidance, willful ignorance, dissociation, perceived behavioral change, and do-gooder derogation. By *refusing to acknowledge* the issue of non-human animal harm caused by their exploitation and consumption by humans or by *avoiding* thinking about this problem, MRCD is often prevented. Through *willful ignorance*, MRCD is avoided by *self-deception*; choosing not to seek out information allows one not to dwell on the harsh realities imposed on nonhuman animals. *Dissociation* is also a way to avoid MRCD by those that consume nonhuman animals, whereby the nonhuman animal is completely dissociated from what, or *who*, someone is consuming. One very effective strategy to accomplish this has been to use terms like "beef, "poultry," and "veal," which allows individuals (and society, in general) to not think about the individual nonhuman animal being consumed. Another common method to quell MRCD is to *perceive a behavioral change* in oneself when there hasn't been a change. Rotherberger explains this tactic as "pretending that the troubling behavior does not apply to them" (4). In other words, the person experiencing MRCD *convinces themselves* that they "don't eat much meat." Hence, they are, in essence, not the "typical" nonhuman animal consumer that should be under scrutiny. Finally, reducing MRCD can take form via *do-gooder derogation*, which is a fancy way to say that people often condemn vegans and vegetarians when MRCD is activated. Think of the times you have heard vegans and vegetarians called "pretentious," "preachy," "weak," and as thinking they are "morally superior" to non-vegans (5). Doing this may allow the person to avoid the discomfort of having conflicting views about other animals by insulting those that advocate for them.

Consider also the paradoxical process known as the "boomerang effect," (sometimes called "reactance") "which occurs when a strategic message generates the opposite attitude or behavior than was originally intended" (Byrne and Hart 2009:4). Changing peoples' opinions, beliefs, and behaviors can be extremely difficult. Attempts at interventions designed to alter peoples' harmful behaviors suggest that simple "debunkings" of original views can result in a boomerang effect:

> It is possible that an attempt to change peoples' biased behavior in a manner that threatens their self-image, or challenges their world view will result in a negative boomerang effect. This

> boomerang effect may also result in entrenchment, that is, not only that they will not change their judgments or behavior, but they will even fortify their existing opinions. Think, for example, of moderate conservatives during the 2016 presidential elections campaign who are considering to vote for Trump. Once they are exposed to information regarding racist and misogynistic biases that may be affecting Trump supporters, are they likely to accept the fact that they too might be affected by those biases, and reconsider their political behavior, or are they more likely to backlash after being implicitly (or explicitly) accused of being misogynistic racists? If the latter option takes place, it is also likely to assume that this backlash will cause them to be more inclined to justify their actions using other explanations, and in turn reinforce their original judgment and behavior. (Levy and Maaravi 2017:40)

It's even the case that educating non-vegan environmentalists does not often change their minds. They can dig further into their original opinions when they feel they are being guilted (Scott, Kallis, and Zografos 2019).

Unsurprisingly, when people feel that others judge them morally about their behaviors and actions, they feel resentment. In their research, Minson and Monin (2011) showed that when people who consume nonhuman animals feel morally judged by vegetarians and vegans (or *assume* that they are being judged), they think more negatively about vegetarians and vegans. Piazza et al. (2015:115) explain that non-vegans feel this way because "sometimes [they] find themselves in social situations where they must defend their commitments to eating meat." Additionally, non-vegans frequently only follow other non-vegans' recommendations to cut back on or to stop consuming nonhuman animals because they dislike vegans and vegetarians. This has been explained as an intergroup sensitivity effect, whereby those identifying as "meat-eaters" trust more in those identifying the same way (Thürmer,

Stadler, and McCrea 2022). Confirmation bias has been researched heavily in psychology. It is generally defined as "the seeking or interpreting of evidence in ways that are partial to existing beliefs, expectations, or a hypothesis in hand" (Nickerson 1998:175). Feeling judged can be valid, but we must remember that feelings of judgment can also be the work of our confirmation biases against vegans and vegetarians.

Research has shown interesting yet perplexing findings when people are asked about their justifications for consuming or using nonhuman animals. The social psychologist Melanie Joy (2011:96-7) refers to the three most common explanations people use to defend their nonhuman animal consumption as the "Three Ns of Justification": that it is believed to be *normal*, *natural*, and *necessary*. Joy explains further:

> [T]hese justifications do more than just direct our actions. They alleviate the moral discomfort we might otherwise feel when eating meat; if we have a good excuse for our behaviors, we feel less guilty about them. The Three Ns essentially act as mental and emotional blinders, masking the discrepancies in our beliefs and behavior toward animals and explaining them away if we do happen to catch on. (P. 97)

Piazza et al. (2015) provide some of the earliest systematic evidence for this phenomenon in six studies, and they increase the Three Ns to include a fourth N: *nice*. They explain that the inclusion of "nice" into this list of common justifications involves the "[a]ppeals to the tastiness of meat, or that it is fulfilling or satisfying" (116). This phenomenon has also been studied successfully with those that consume dairy with similar effects (Collier et al. 2023). It is essential, however, to remember that even though these four justifications are used very often, it does not mean that they are accurate or ethically sound arguments. We saw earlier that appealing to the "naturalness" of something is a logical fallacy. What is deemed "natural" is not intrinsically "correct" or "good." And when people attempt to justify something because it is "normal," they are engaging in another fallacy called the "appeal to tradition." This fallacy points to the so-called normalness of something in the past or present. Finally, considering the use and consumption of nonhuman animals as "necessary" is a little trickier and more complex a question to answer. We will examine the subject of necessity in the chapters on veganism and plant-based diets.

Caviola et al. (2022) provide fascinating research regarding what likely underpins our anthropocentric beliefs that humans are more important than nonhuman animals. They found that several different logics sustain these beliefs—primarily speciesism and attributed mental capacities to nonhuman animals. Valuing humans over nonhuman animals, or even some nonhuman animals over other nonhuman animals, is mainly due to determining someone's moral status based on their cognitive abilities; in other words, anthropocentrism and speciesism are strongly connected to ableism.[18] Additionally, the authors of this research argue that mental capacities are not the only determinants of anthropocentric thinking—nonhuman animals simply being categorized as different species than humans is also a decisive factor.

When does speciesism drastically start to shape our beliefs and values about nonhuman animals? According to recent research, children exhibit less speciesism than young adults and older adults (McGuire, Palmer, and Faber 2022; Neldner and Wilks 2022). With age, people "were more likely to categorize a farm animal as food rather than a companion animal." Moreover,

> children did not perceive pigs ought to be treated any differently than humans or dogs, whereas young adults and adults reported that dogs and humans ought to be treated better than pigs. Relatedly, older participants evaluated both eating animals and eating animal products as more morally acceptable than children did. (Neldner and Wilks 2022:8)

This evidence adds to earlier data suggesting that speciesism is socially learned and increases as we age (Wilks et al. 2021). It is often assumed that speciesism is built into us, like an evolutionary trait or instinct. But this view does not exactly align with what has been shown through research. And when a set of views and practices like speciesism is so ubiquitous in society, it can seem almost impossible to unlearn. Take, for instance, how early childhood media shapes the way we relate to nonhuman animals:

> [T]he combination of childhood literary and film traditions relating to animals and associated promotional food tie-ins aimed at children contribute to a food socialization process whereby children learn to conceptually distance the animals they eat from those with whom they have an emotional bond or for whom they feel ethically responsible. (Stewart and Cole 2009:458)

Attempting to deal with one's speciesist prejudices comes with its own cost. The results of three studies published in 2015 by MacInnis and Hodson found that vegetarians and vegans are on the receiving end of bias by non-veg*ans (I'm shortening the combination of vegetarians and vegans here). They found that "[o]verall, attitudes toward vegetarians and vegans are equivalent to, or more negative than, attitudes toward common prejudice target groups, and bias toward vegetarians and vegans is associated with these other biases" (6). In one of their studies, among other interesting findings, the researchers found right-wing ideology was related to more of a willingness to discriminate against vegetarians and vegans. The authors explain that intergroup threat can explain why those with right-wing ideologies exhibit intergroup threat towards marginalized human "outgroups." And because veg*ans are seen as going against societal norms, they become a human outgroup (16-19). One notable sentence stood out to me: "Although our findings suggest that vegetarians and vegans face less severe and less frequent discrimination than that experienced by other minority groups, they nonetheless are targets of (and experience) meaningful bias" (19). This is evidence that a bias against veg*ans exists, but *why*? The researchers suggest one answer might be that veg*ns go against accepted social norms and traditions in a society where nonhuman animal use and consumption are almost everywhere. This could also explain why the researchers also found that veg*ans who became veg*an because of concern for nonhuman animals are viewed more negatively than those who became veg*an for environmental or personal health reasons. Veg*ans are seen as "moralizing" and, therefore, viewed negatively. Earle and Hodson (2017) also found that veg*ans are especially targets of bias from people with more "pro-beef" attitudes—mainly liking, desiring, and consuming cows' flesh.

Sexism and toxic masculinity are also highly entangled in perceptions of veg*ans. Ruby and Heine (2011) found that people generally view veg*ans as both "virtuous" and "less masculine." Regarding sexism and careers, evidence suggests that veg*an men are seen as less competent in typically men-dominated jobs; women are not seen in this manner (Adamczyk and Maison 2022). Men have been found to feel more defensiveness toward plant-based diets, especially showing more negative affect (anger, disgust, fear, etc.). This negative affect has been linked to feelings of the fear of freedom loss and the triggering of feeling the need to rationalize and justify nonhuman animal consumption (Hinrichs et al. 2022).

Additional evidence suggests that vegans are considered both more "moral" and less "socially attractive" (De Groeve et al. 2022; De Groeve, Hudders, and Bleys 2021).[19] Cole and Morgan (2011) label the negative portrayals of vegans and veganism as "vegaphobia." Research looking at depictions of vegans and veganism in national UK newspapers (albeit from 2007) found that derogatory discourse was the norm. They listed the top ways in which vegans and veganism were portrayed negatively, ordered by most common first:

- Ridiculing veganism
- Characterizing veganism as asceticism
- Describing veganism as difficult or impossible to sustain
- Describing veganism as a fad
- Characterizing vegans as oversensitive
- Characterizing vegans as hostile (P. 139)

Cole (2013:706) found that veganism was often portrayed as asceticism within the social sciences. Cole explained that '[t]ypical descriptive terms of a veg*an diet include "strict," "restrictive," or "avoidance." This ascetic discourse reproduces the hierarchical ordering of Western diets such that veg*anism is denigrated and made to seem "difficult" and "abnormal."' So, despite veganism being fundamentally about nonhuman animal liberation (which I will show in the section on veganism), the predominant portrayal by both the media and the social sciences paints veganism as something inherently negative.

Social psychology has also uncovered evidence that the binary nature in which humans and nonhuman animals are categorized (i.e., the "human-animal divide") influences how society might believe in solving social issues of dehumanization and prejudice. Costello and Hodson (2014) suggest that laypeople (non-experts) either ignore or do not understand how human in-groups have a bias towards and dehumanize human out-groups through mechanisms that present the out-groups as "animal-like" and "less human" (284-5). In essence, even though substantial evidence shows how the belief in a strict human-animal divide harms humans and nonhuman animals, most people do not believe this or do not know about it. This evidence, though, is often confined to the margins of the social sciences, so it is unsurprising that many have never heard or learned about it.

So far, we have seen evidence from psychology and social psychology about human prejudices against nonhuman animals. Psychological research has shown that speciesism exists on an individual level, and social psychological research has provided substantial evidence that speciesism also exists and affects us by way of our social interactions with other people. The next section will show through a sociological lens how speciesism exists on a structural level.

Further Reading

- Dhont, Kristof, and Gordon Hodson. 2020. *Why We Love and Exploit Animals: Bridging Insights from Academia and Advocacy.* London: Routledge.

Sociology and speciesism

Sociology is described as the "scientific study of social structures and human relationships and behaviors" (Mirfakhraie 2019). The confining of sociology to strictly *human* social structures, *human* relationships, and *human* behaviors has its history in the foundations of the discipline. However, there has been a slow but growing acknowledgment that nonhuman animals are indeed a part of society (Peggs 2012:6). Think about how most of us share our homes and lives with our fellow dog and cat companions and how the capitalist economic system is built on and continues to rely heavily on nonhuman animal labor and exploitation. Human lives are intertwined with nonhuman animal lives. As a result, sociology can be of great value in looking at speciesism within human societies, and sociology can benefit greatly from opening up to a much more comprehensive understanding of what a "society" includes.

Many societies, especially in the West, have built up the notion of clear and significant differences between humans and all other animals—the "human/animal divide," as it is sometimes called. Sociologist Kay Peggs (2009) used the work on ideas of "hierarchy" of the French philosopher Jacques Derrida in which he explained that "[t]here is no animal in the general singular, separated from man [sic] by a single indivisible limit" (cited from Derrida 2004:125). Peggs elaborated that, despite this premise by Derrida,

> in scientific and public discourses such identification is typically based in assumptions of natural differences that focus on the shared characteristics of designated groups. These discourses take for granted the view that the essentialist premise of the fundamental categorization of human/animal is universal and natural, and in so doing obscure the social construction of the categorization and the attendant power relations. (P. 88)

In other words, the assumed fundamental differences between humans and all other animals are socially constructed and based on ideas of what different groups share. The socially constructed view that there are innate differences is so great that it also pervades the sciences and general "knowledge." These socially constructed categorizations hide and reinforce the power imbalances created through the human domination of all other animals. Peggs also asserts that this creates essentialized categories of humans as the superior "Us" and all other animals are grouped into a singular group as the inferior "Other" (extremely relevant to the research on tribalism that we looked at earlier). By exploring an example of nonhuman animal experimentation by humans, Peggs explains that experimenting on other animals is often claimed to be "justified" because of these supposed categorical differences between humans and other animals. But, in reality, the differences in power dynamics are the root mechanisms at hand. We, humans, have socially constructed categorical differences between us and other animals, which are then used to exploit nonhuman animals without much restraint. Peggs summarized the example of nonhuman animal experimentation: "Scientific progress is synonymous with human progress but…this conceptualization is forged within the virtual region of human superiority and within the actual region of human power" (98). Again, these social constructs by humans lead us to believe in and assume a "natural" or "inevitable" human superiority over all life. As we examined in the earlier chapter on nonhuman animal capabilities, scientific investigation of the lives and minds of nonhuman animals has led to a path marked by human exceptionalism being dismantled over and over again. It is crucial to understand how we have socially constructed artificial differences between ourselves and other animals through what we have decided to be our particular intrinsic differences—differences that we believe make us so unlike other animals that these "differences" automatically and legitimately give us justified dominance.

Even though nonhuman animals have been shown to have subjective minds (as seen in the earlier section of nonhuman animal sentience)—capabilities that were once thought of as uniquely human qualities—and live within, interact with, and help shape human lives and societies, ascribing them as being "oppressed" by humans is often considered to be as ridiculous as a car being "oppressed." From what we've examined so far in this book, speciesism and anthropocentrism ground how we view nonhuman animals as *separate* from humans and *resources* for humans. So why would we also consider nonhuman animals as being unable to be oppressed by humans? What would make nonhuman animals so dramatically different from humans that would prevent them from being considered *vulnerable* and *marginalized* people? We saw how conceptualizing speciesism as "natural" or "normal" is a fallacious argument. We even looked at evidence showing how speciesism is not really present when we are young, but it becomes a stronger set of beliefs and behaviors when we get older as we are socialized into a social structure where human domination and supremacism are pervasive. This attitude means that nonhuman animals are tortured, violated, devalued, and killed generally out of a socially-learned assumption that humans are "superior" to all other animals. This arrangement is not unlike the forms of oppression that affect humans. Vulnerable and marginalized human groups are often harmed in various ways, devalued, and assumed to be "inferior" to the humans of the dominant culture. These are formulas, road maps, and recipes for oppression.

And it would be a mistake to view all forms of oppression—human and nonhuman animal alike—as compartmentalized from one another. That is to say, oppressions are not walled off from other forms. A person who is oppressed in some way, such as by racism, is not always *only* oppressed by racism. David Nibert, a vegan sociologist, highlights sociologists Margaret Andersen and Patricia Hill Collins as spearheading the move within sociology to view oppressed identities, such as race, gender, and class, as "interlocking" systems. He explains, "Many sociologists now accept the idea that the oppression of various devalued groups in human societies is not independent and unrelated; rather, the arrangements that lead to various forms of oppression are intricately woven together in such a way that the exploitation of one group frequently augments and compounds the mistreatment of others" (Nibert 2003:6). Kimberlé Crenshaw (1991:1244) developed the concept of **intersectionality** to describe:

> the various ways in which race and gender interact to shape the multiple dimensions of Black women's employment experiences. My objective there was to illustrate that many of the experiences Black women face are subsumed within the traditional boundaries of race or gender discrimination as these boundaries are currently understood, and that the intersection of racism and sexism factors into Black women's lives in ways that cannot be captured wholly by looking at the race or gender dimensions of those experiences separately…Nor do I mean to suggest that violence against women of color can be explained only through the frameworks of race and gender considered here. Indeed, factors I address only in part or not at all, such as class or sexuality, are often as critical in shaping the experiences of women of color. My focus on the intersections of race and gender only highlights the need to account for multiple grounds of identity when considering how the social world is constructed.

Ahir Gopaldas (2013) makes the case that intersectionality has since expanded and that newer definitions of intersectionality do not mention any particular group or social identity structures:

> By not specifying particular social identity structures, these newer definitions expand the concept of intersectionality beyond race, class, and gender to include age, attractiveness, body type, caste, citizenship, education, ethnicity, height and weight assessments, immigration status, income, marital status, mental health status, nationality, occupation, physical ability, religion, sex, sexual orientation, socioeconomic status, and other naturalized—though not necessarily natural—ways of categorizing human populations. (P.90)

The concept of speciesism is often used to describe how individuals perpetuate human domination and exceptionalism against all other animals at the micro-level. For instance, when a human kills a deer for "sport," or when we care more about "cute" nonhuman animals than those we consider "ugly," we are engaging in speciesism at the level of the individual. But sociologists also use speciesism to describe the social structures that sustain speciesism throughout society as a whole; *ideology* is one example of this. "[A]n ideology," as Nibert (2003:8) explains, "is a set of socially shared beliefs that legitimates an existing or desired social order." Speciesism, in other words, is not just what one person engages in but also what *society* engages in through its beliefs and practices of human exceptionalism. Humans desire to be the dominant species on the planet and have subsequently created various overarching beliefs that we believe legitimize our dominance. And this ideology of speciesism has commonalities with the other ideologies that sustain human oppression, like racism, sexism, and classism, which we will take a look at in later chapters on human oppressions.

Through a sociological lens, nonhuman animals have been subjected to many differing forms of violence by humans that have traditionally been thought of as violence only subjected to oppressed groups of humans. Erika Cudworth (2015:14) examines how the study of the sociology of violence can also be applied to the violence inflicted on nonhuman animals. Speciesism can be viewed "as constituted through *groups of social relations.*" All industries that involve the exploitation of nonhuman animals "are *institutional systems* and *sets of production relations.*" Physical and psychological harm of nonhuman animals "reflects the complex *intersections of relations of social power.*" Violence against nonhuman animals "is *institutionalized* and constitutive of the *social relations of species* which *privilege* the human." This violence also involves "complex inequality," and is intertwined with "capitalism, colonialism [and] the systematic deployment of what is not simply 'intra-personal' violence." Generally speaking, "violence towards domesticated animals is routinized, systemic and legitimated. It is embedded in structures of authority, such as the nation state, and in formations of social domination." Twine (2020) makes the case that sociology's lack of engagement in the last few decades with nonhuman animals and our interactions and oppression of them does not allow for research in the field to fully account for the global climate emergency's impacts and potential mitigation strategies. It's not just a consequence for academia; it's a consequence for all life on the planet.

As we saw with Marco Maurizi, David Nibert (2002) also contends that using the methodological approach to studying history developed by Karl Marx, historical materialism, has great promise to illustrate the situation of nonhuman animals. In addition, Nibert sees all oppressions as interlocking systems:

> The exploitation of other animals and the justification of their mistreatment not only closely resemble human oppression but are inextricably tied to it...[O]ppression is motivated primarily by economic interests and, what is more, that it is profoundly and permanently entwined with human oppression of other humans. (P. 3)

He goes on to explain what sociology shows about the origins and maintenance of oppression:

> The oppressive treatment of different devalued groups—including exploiting a being's labor, raising others for food and resources, and physically displacing or exterminating other groups—is entwined not only materially but also with the systems of beliefs and values that guide human society. Oppression has to be rationalized and justified. It relies heavily on hierarchical views in which certain groups are believed to be undeserving of consideration and fair treatment, promoting a ranking based on purported virtue or worth.

Nibert has written extensively on how the State, with its laws and protection of private property and a relatively few elites, must be confronted with a broad, cross-movement counterbalance of liberationists if we are to have any hope in dismantling all forms of oppression. He says, "those involved in any one liberation movement should realize their entanglement with all other oppressed groups and their common purpose" (5). And in another brilliant piece of work of his, *Animal Oppression and Human Violence: Domesecration, Capitalism, and Global Conflict*, Nibert (2013) uses again a historical materialist approach to show the history of how the domestication of nonhuman animals (which he renames "**domesecration**,"[20] a combination of the words "domestication" and "desecration") went hand-in-hand with colonialism, the expansion of global capitalism, and the oppression of both humans and other animals.

French philosopher Pierre Bourdieu (1930-2002) developed two concepts that help explain nonhuman animal exploitation from a sociological perspective. Though originally an ancient Greek term, Bourdieu's concept of *doxa* is described as "what is essential goes without saying because it comes without saying: the tradition is silent, not least about itself as a tradition" (Bourdieu 1977:167). Headache-inducing, right? Let's seek someone else to translate this concept. Rodolfo Maggio (2018:40-41) interprets *doxa* as societal ideas and truths that are "undiscussable; that is, there is no room for dissidence. [They are] unanimous, and taken for granted. [They go] unnoticed and there is no questioning of legitimacy and power." Furthermore, Maggio explains that "[s]ymbolic power uses *doxa* to replace visible and explicit forms of violence with invisible and implicit ones. In this way, symbolic power enables the establishment of categories that prevent actors from thinking in ways that could liberate them from their condition of subjugation." *Doxa* is an important concept because of its potential for understanding and engaging in social change. As Maggio illustrates,

> Although *doxa* remains undiscussed most of the time, its arbitrariness becomes evident when conflicts arise between dominant and dominated classes. When that happens, it slips into a space where agents are able to discuss and even question it. When *doxa* is questioned, a fracture in social order occurs that can potentially translate into social change. (41)

It's clear that *doxa* can be useful when thinking about how speciesism and nonhuman animal exploitation are so embedded in society, so entrenched that we often grow up taking part in it without much thought given—nonhuman animals equal food for us. When we eat nonhuman animals for breakfast, lunch, and dinner, their being on our plates is simply assumed when planning meals. And it's taken a step further when those nonhuman animals' bodies and fluids are processed into "products" that most often have no resemblance to the original person that existed.

The second concept theorized by Pierre Bourdieu that is important to our discussion is **habitus**. Maggio describes this as "the attitudes that [people within society] internalize while being conditioned by past experiences, and re-enact in present everyday practices, though with a certain degree of freedom," or, in the concise laymen's terms that

Bourdieu is so known for, "orchestrated improvisation of common dispositions" (11, 28). If speciesism and anthropocentrism are considered a part of the *doxa* of society, by which I mean that they are unquestioned "truths" that most people take for granted, *habitus* "conveys not only the singular instances of social action, but also the very history that each individual carries, which structures his or her [sic] behavior. It is not the mere product of structures, for it also depends on practices and strategies" (33). As Ragnhild Aslaug Sollund (2016:96) explains Bourdieu's conception of *doxa* and *habitus* as they relate to nonhuman animal exploitation, "The practices of animal (ab)use are so extensive – so culturally diverse and widespread – that they are part of *doxa*," which means that they are "unspoken of, as there is no reflection connected to [them]." As such, "using animals, especially eating their 'meat', is consequently part of *habitus* for the majority of people on earth." The *habitus* of using and consuming nonhuman animals is not only reproduced by each of us and brought to us in the form of traditions and habits, but the practices themselves involved in the use and consumption of nonhuman animals also create and order the paths in our lives that we are likely to follow. For instance, a consumer of nonhuman animals would probably not have a *habitus* that involves or leads to demonstrating against slaughterhouses. These concepts seem to fit nicely and are closely tied with social psychological concepts like cognitive dissonance and the meat paradox.

Despite current and historical sociology being heavily anthropocentric, this section has shown a small slice of the burgeoning subject of nonhuman animals in society. With a growing list of magnificent works in this area, it would be worth anyone's time and effort to dive into the sociology of human-nonhuman animal relations. Sociology is my area of education, so hopefully, some of this will tempt you to brave its magical waters of researching and attempting to identify and explain the patterns of relations within society.

Further reading:

- Nibert, David. 2013. *Animal Oppression and Human Violence: Domesecration, Capitalism, and Global Conflict*. New York: Columbia University Press.
- Nibert, David. 2002. *Animal Rights/Human Rights: Entanglements of Oppression and Liberation*. Lanham, Md.: Rowman & Littlefield.
- Nibert, David, ed. 2017. *Animal Oppression and Capitalism*. Santa Barbara, California: Praeger.
- Taylor, Nik, and Richard Twine. 2015. *The Rise of Critical Animal Studies: From the Margins to the Centre*. London; New York: Routledge, Taylor & Francis Group.
- Taylor, Nik, and Tania Signal. 2011. *Theorizing Animals: Re-Thinking Humanimal Relations*. Leiden; Boston: Brill.
- Grušovnik, Tomaž, Reingard Spannring, and Karen Lykke Syse. 2022. *Environmental and Animal Abuse Denial: Averting Our Gaze*. Lanham, Maryland: Lexington Books.
- Peggs, Kay. 2012. *Animals and Sociology*. Houndmills, Basingstoke, Hampshire; New York: Palgrave Macmillan.
- Pellow, David Naguib. 2014. *Total Liberation: The Power and Promise of Animal Rights and the Radical Earth Movement*. University of Minnesota Press.

6

Nonhuman Animal Exploitation

Think for a moment about what kind of effects might come from oppression where individuals, groups, and entire social structures devalue, exploit, and kill members of a particular group of people in a continuous cycle. Add to this the evidence that, as people living within these structures, our brains have paradoxical psychological processes that try to shield us from the discomfort of having harmed these people. These processes encourage us to lash out at others who advocate for us to adopt a different way of looking at and relating to this group of marginalized people. We view those advocates as "pretentious," "zealots," and maybe even "cult members." I don't know about you, but to me, this is a recipe for absolute death and destruction of unimaginable depths. The breadth of this death and destruction that we inflict on this marginalized group can be seen in the nonhuman animals that directly receive this oppression, but it doesn't end there. Because this planet is a system that is made up of infinite other systems, filled with life and landscapes and elements, forever interacting with one another, widespread harm to trillions of nonhuman animals inevitably spills over to have negative consequences on humans and the ecosystems that sustain all life. It is not something we often think about in our daily lives because we have other things going on—things that are either dazzling or annoying us.

In the film series, *The Matrix* (1999), the main character, Neo, chooses to take the red pill, which forces him to wake from the matrix—a virtual and interactive world created by artificially-intelligent robots that keep humans in a constant dream state. At the same time, humans in this world are unknowingly exploited by the robots for their bodily processes. Our world, which we have all helped to build, concurrently hides the truth and allows us to hide from the truth. If our personal and collective values involve a sense of justice, compassion, autonomy, fairness, or respect, we must choose, as Neo does, to immerse ourselves in this truth. Let us push past the fear and discomfort of what we think we know and dive deep with bravery and humility into the ocean of visible and invisiblized horrors of our own making.

The effects of nonhuman animal exploitation on nonhuman animals

The most apparent effect of speciesism is the exploitation of nonhuman animals. In 2020 alone, around **80 billion** nonhuman animals living on land were killed worldwide for food, which only includes the numbers reported. *Around 80 billion people. Around 80 billion people. Around 80 billion people. Around 80 billion people. Around 80 billion people in a single year.* And chickens were by far the most killed. Here's a graph that shows the number of each species of nonhuman animal who live on land that has been killed each year since 1961:

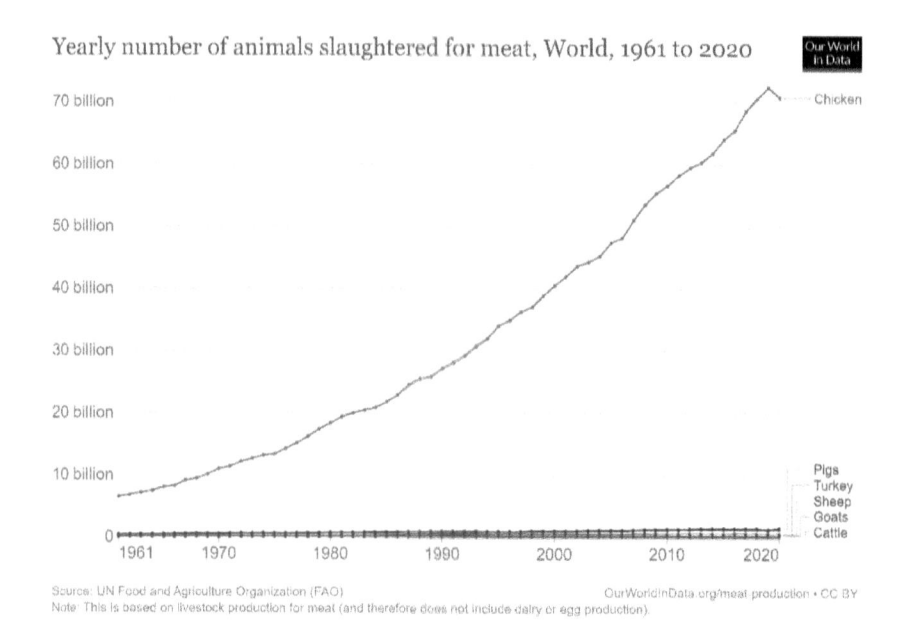

Yearly number of nonhuman animals slaughtered for meat worldwide, from 1961 to 2020 (Our World in Data 2020). Republished under the original Creative Commons BY license. https://creativecommons.org/licenses/by/4.0/.

But that's not even half the story. Those numbers don't include aquatic nonhuman animals or nonhuman animals killed in scientific experiments, for clothing, during crop cultivation, or for many other purposes. Consider these available numbers of non-human animals killed per year:

- Farmed fishes, crustaceans, mollusks: tens of millions per year (Our World in Data 2018)

- Fishes killed from aquaculture and wild-caught: 0.79-2.3 ***trillion*** per year (fishcount.co.uk 2019)

- Nonhuman animals used and killed in experiments: 192.1 million in 2015 alone (Taylor and Alvarez 2020)

- Nonhuman animals killed on fur farms: around 100 million per year (Humane Society International 2019)

- Nonhuman animals killed in North America by trapping for pelts: 3 million in 2017 alone (Humane Society International 2019)

Death is not the only harm to nonhuman animals that we inflict on them. There is also what they go through *before* they are killed. And you know what? I don't even want to talk about this part. I don't even want to *know* this part. Almost every single way that nonhuman animals are exploited and killed, we are told that it isn't as bad of a process as we imagine. But, then again, those voices telling us that the industry isn't that bad are often from those who profit from it. Please think of how oil companies lie to all of us when they also tell us that everything is fine and dandy and that they have everything under control. They say that not because it is the truth but simply because the alternative would put them all out of business and in prison.[21] And I'm not saying that your Uncle Bob, the local farmer, is just like the oil companies. Obviously, he's not. But he has the same *motive* they do: to keep his job. Does Uncle Bob know a lot about keeping and raising nonhuman animals? Yes, but that still doesn't give credibility to his understanding and truthfulness of the *ethics* of it all.

I used to oversee the bulk foods department at Whole Foods Market in my town a few years back. I did it for eight years. I knew that department like the back of my hand. I learned how much product to order daily to have enough to last until the next order arrived two days later. I knew the official "organic" standards. I often read as much as I could about how each type of product was produced so that I could answer customer questions about them. I washed and maintained all the equipment used for the hundreds of items I sold. I knew my top-selling products for the year, including the increased sales during the holidays. If I sold fewer products from my department or customers decided to stop buying bulk products, my work hours could be reduced or eliminated altogether. It was my livelihood at that time. But you could not rely on me to know the ethics involved in selling all those products. I didn't truly know how the farm workers in other countries felt about their work or how much they were exploited. I didn't know how Whole Foods Market (later bought by Amazon) was doing with any certainty about its overall environmental impact. Do you think the overwhelming majority of farmers who raise and slaughter nonhuman animals for a living have read the literature on nonhuman animal rights or ethics in general? They know the business aspect of it. They know how to maximize profit. That does not mean they know what "humane" should entail or what justice for nonhuman animals looks like. So, let's take the red pill and dive deep into what is often hidden or hidden by us.

Beekeeping and honey production
Beekeeping and honey production are often considered "harmless" and even "beneficial." However, many studies show adverse effects on wild bee populations by so-called "managed" bees, often used to pollinate crops. Increased resource competition and pathogen transmission are some of the most impactful effects (Fürst et al. 2014; Mallinger, Gaines-Day, and Gratton 2017; Russo et al. 2021; Thomson 2016; Weekers et al. 2022). Introducing honeybees can negatively impact wild bee populations (Iwasaki and Hogendoorn 2022; Su et al. 2022; Weaver, Ascher, and Mallinger 2022). Some evidence shows that wild pollinators are more effective at pollination than "managed" honeybees. The authors of the study concluded that, while both "managed" and wild insects promote pollination, wild insects do more of the work, while "managed" honeybees are more "supplemental" to the area (Garibaldi et al. 2013). Geldmann and González-Varo (2018) concluded that the solution to global pollinator declines[22] is not the conservation of "managed" honeybees, as they can negatively affect wild pollinator populations. Experts have made the case that beekeeping for honey or conservation does not help the environment or local wild populations of insects; in fact,

they have the opposite effects (Angelella, McCullough, and O'Rourke 2021; Charles 2018; Valido, Rodríguez-Rodríguez, and Jordano 2019). Additionally, "domesticated honeybees contribute to wild bee declines through resource competition and spread of disease, with so-called environmental initiatives promoting honeybee-keeping in cities or, worse, protected areas far from agriculture, only likely to exacerbate the loss of wild pollinators" (University of Cambridge 2018). When we think of beekeeping with honeybees, it is often described as being the epitome of "local" and "pro-environment." There is also a widespread belief among the general population that the decline in insects and bees worldwide is helped by beekeeping and honey production, despite the evidence to the contrary (Nicholls, Epstein, and Colla 2020). However, beekeeping is more like industrial agriculture: "Honeybees are artificially-bred agricultural animals similar to livestock such as pigs and cows" (Ward 2018).

Those adverse effects don't even consider the ethical issues involved in buying, selling, using, exploiting, harming, and killing bees. Remember that there is good evidence that bees are sentient and feel pain (Gibbons et al. 2022). And there is sound reasoning for why personhood should rely solely on whether sentience exists within a given living being (Francione 2012a). So, why do we commodify these animals and treat them like resources? Queen bees are confined to their colony before being "artificially inseminated." Then,

> [o]n the day of insemination, typically when the queen is 7 days old, she is taken to the laboratory. There she is restrained in a specialised instrument, narcotised with carbon dioxide (CO_2), and a syringe containing drone semen introduced into the vagina via the sting chamber...Semen is injected, typically 8μL, collected from 8 to 10 drones. After the operation the queen is returned to her colony. To induce [egg laying], a second CO_2 narcosis is administered the day before or the day after the insemination itself. (Gillard and Oldroyd 2020:7-8)

Many beekeepers will also trim the wings (called "wing clipping") of queen bees because there is a common belief that doing so may prevent the hive from swarming. Swarming involves beehives splitting into two hives by way of a part of the original hive flying somewhere else. When the queen bee's wings are clipped, she is unable to fly to a different place from the swarm (Katy 2019). It is also not uncommon for beekeepers to kill entire hives during each winter and purchase new "batches" in the spring. This can be more cost-efficient because beekeepers sometimes must buy sugar water for the hive to survive during the cold months, which can be more expensive than a new "batch" of bees.

A forager honeybee can reach an area of 100 square miles each day and visit between 50 and 1,000 flowers during that time (McKay 2011). And according to the National Honey Board (2022), honeybees must visit 2 million flowers to create a single pound of honey; that same pound of honey requires a hive of bees to travel approximately 55,000 miles. A single honeybee will only make about 1/12 of a teaspoon (0.41ml) in their lifespan. Non-consenting honeybees will be "artificially inseminated" or have sperm removed from their bodies. Some bees will be crushed during the honey removal process. It is often said that this all is a "symbiotic relationship" between humans and honeybees because the bees are given a place to stay and are "safer." However, from the information in this section, we can gather that the use of honeybees and the consumption of honey are anything but "natural" or "symbiotic." When we are honest with ourselves, there are significant parallels between the exploitation of the use and labor of honeybees to the exploitation of labor by human workers by capitalists. Is it the same situation? Of course not. But the common link is the extraction of surplus value by a relative few in the pursuit of profit. The exploitation of honeybees' behaviors and labor is not agreed upon by the bees themselves. They are bred, bought, sold, and discarded as commodities and free laborers. It is an entirely different process than wild bees and other wild insects pollinating crops without being "managed" in any way—

that type of situation is more "symbiotic" than how honeybees are currently used.

If we are concerned with the decline of insects and wild bees, and we should be, a better approach to dealing with it would be having more gardens, fewer neonicotinoid insecticides and other pesticides, fewer lawns, the end of honey production and consumption by humans, and doing the hard work of decreasing our speciesist and anthropocentric worldviews. Attempts at "bee-washing" by honey industries and policymakers only worsen things (Colla 2022). Media and policies that do not make it clear that "managed" honeybees are not in decline contribute to the conservation and protection of bee species that are already abundant (Iwasaki and Hogendoorn 2021). Bees are individuals, and we should treat them as such. Exploiting them harms them, but it also harms everyone in the process.

Zoos and aquariums

Nonhuman animals kept in zoos and aquariums are instrumentalized by a focus on physical welfare at the expense of their emotional and mental welfare as well as their inherent rights to bodily autonomy. Standard problematic zoo practices involve the captivity of sentient persons, breeding and forced impregnation, and culling. Despite the intended goal of conserving a collective species, zoos exploit the bodies and behaviors of these persons. This is done assuming and hoping that patrons will be educated about conservation and the environment; often, however, the only thing that patrons will ultimately receive is a day of "entertainment" (Clay and Visseren-Hamakers 2022). Unsurprisingly, zoos and aquariums never give patrons the space to question the legitimacy of these institutions or the overarching belief of human domination over other animals (Ergin Zengin 2019). And rarely discussed, zoos and aquariums exemplify the contradictory nature of capitalist profit and expansion. Consider the critique from Emmerman (2019:384):

> [Z]oos are problematic manifestations of capitalism and rampant consumerism. Consider the dissonance between zoos' mission to inspire care about the devastating loss of natural habitat and species worldwide and the zoo gift shop where you can purchase a stuffed animal or mug manufactured thousands of miles away. Or consider the hot dog from factory-farmed cows that zoo-goers munch on as they shake their heads in dismay while reading the zoos' placards about the destruction of the Amazon. Since [nonhuman animal] agriculture is a leading contributor to habitat destruction worldwide, this underscores a disturbing disconnect between zoos' purported mission and the consumption-driven behaviors they encourage among zoo-goers.

A study by Clifford-Clarke, Whitehouse-Tedd, and Ellis (2021) found no evidence that patrons of a particular zoo gained conservation knowledge from seeing the nonhuman animals on display. In fact, when patrons did gain conservation knowledge, it was from other education methods on display, such as signs and exhibits showing facts. Evidence claiming otherwise has been met with strong criticism of methodological invalidity (Malamud et al. 2010). Status (2019:371) found that "[d]espite many zoos' claims regarding their success as conservation education providers, the research to date reveals mixed and sometimes contradictory results." But conservation and education are just one side of the debates surrounding zoos and aquariums. What about the captive nonhuman animals themselves?

An excellent concept to understand this exploitation is "**slow violence**," coined by Rob Nixon (2011:2) to describe the often unseen and slow-growing environmental effects that affect predominantly marginalized humans; mostly, it is "not viewed as violence at all." Mollie

Holmberg (2021:865) adapts slow violence to apply to the situations of nonhuman animals kept captive in zoos and aquariums as "conditions that gradually attenuate health and well-being (in contrast to more rapid, dramatic forms of violence). For example, much of the harm during captive care operates through routine care activities and gradually degrades animals' health." Zoo and aquarium staff remove nonhuman animals from their original homes and habitats and attempt to recreate those areas through an anthropocentric lens. These reconstructed spaces can, at most, only be imperfect replicas of the nonhuman animals' native homes. The effects of slow violence, such as in the form of psychological and emotional harm, are ubiquitously hidden from patrons. This type of harm is also not often a top priority of the institutions, so the staff interacting with the nonhuman animals must be more attentive to physical harms like sickness and injury. The de-prioritization of addressing psychological and emotional stress inevitably makes "enrichment" programs and practices inadequate to the captive people's needs (Tuite et al. 2022).

Since captive individuals' mental health is not typically a priority within zoos and aquariums, it is often not discussed enough. Reading through some of the literature on this aspect of captive life is exactly what you may think it would be like: *fucking heartbreaking*. For instance, one study examined 40 chimpanzees across separate groups held captive in various US and UK zoos. The researchers of the study found that all 40 chimpanzees exhibited "abnormal" behaviors (abnormal behaviors being behaviors that either are not found in free-living chimpanzees or were found to be exhibited at a higher rate than free-living chimpanzees) because of being held captive. Those behaviors included eating feces, rocking, hitting and biting themselves, plucking their hair, and more. These are classic signs in humans of unresolved mental health issues. The researchers describe these abnormal behaviors as "endemic" in these institutions. Additionally, they note that these behaviors either "dominate" each individual's life or are especially "persistent" in their daily lives (Birkett and Newton-Fisher 2011). And this is just one study.

I encourage you to read more studies about the mental effects of captive life on nonhuman animals—it's a nightmare.

Clay and Visseren-Hamakers (2022) found that zoos tend to attempt to justify their dismissal of concern for individual nonhuman animals and the ethics of their captivity on the zoo's beliefs in the material value of the educational and conservation efforts by zoos. In other words, zoos are inclined to reject the idea that "individuals matter" in favor of rationales that frame nonhuman animals in captivity as "reproductive components" and "species ambassadors" (9). They elaborate further, saying, "[b]y focusing…on current efforts to save collective species, zoos tend to center on what animals represent, erasing the captive individuals themselves" (Clay and Visseren-Hamakers 2022:3). Wallach et al. (2018:1262) also explain that

> conservation efforts have focused on the preservation of collectives, with wildlife individuals viewed and valued as instances of their type, rather than unique and distinct organisms. Conservation practice does not completely exclude concern for individuals, who are protected to the extent enforced by animal welfare standards and ethical codes of conduct.

Another study revealed the common speciesist language used at the expense of captive nonhuman animals. Some of the language reproduces the objectification and anthropocentrism involved in how we often view nonhuman animals, such as "specimens," "surplus animal stock," and "seafood." When nonhuman animals are no longer "needed" or "usable" in these spaces, their killing is often masked with terms such as "euthanasia" and "culling," and it is couched within the context of "management" of the nonhuman animals (Mitra 2018:48). Mitra explains further about how language often masks reality:

> Focusing the discourse on species instead of individuals, as well as the use of hedging and euphemisms, are discursive

> strategies meant to create emotional detachment and soften the discourse on captivity. The enclosures and cages are referred to as "housing" or "accommodation", while the captive animals are "resident animals" or animals "in human care". Euphemisms are also employed in order to introduce ambiguity in sentences describing the treatment of the captive individuals, who are "managed", "handled" or "cared for" by the zoos and aquaria. Hedging further obscures the authorship of statements regarding conservation or animal welfare. In other occasions it is used to introduce statements which could be considered controversial, such as the importance of funding and the economic value of conservation for humans. Hence, these linguistic strategies result in a softening of the discourse with regards to ethically questionable practice or, for example, economic interest. (P. 49)

Zoos and aquariums often tout "benefits" to their captive breeding programs, conservation, and education, but these are both ethically and practically dubious claims (Tyson 2018). These institutions appear as self-evident saviors of endangered species and beacons of environmental education, but behind their glimmering façades, couched in altruistic language, there exists a gloomier reality. Rather than beneficial, zoos and aquariums act as nothing more than capitalist prisons for nonhuman animals to be gawked at by patrons. They also facilitate the further establishment of anthropocentric and speciesist beliefs.

Human prisons are sites of oppression and domination, replete with racism, queer antagonism, slave labor, sexual violence, and with a capitalist profit motive (Stanley and Smith 2015). Nonhuman animal zoos (prisons) are touted as spaces of support, education, and safety for endangered nonhuman animals. But, in reality, they act as sites of speciesism, objectification, and, in captive breeding programs, sexual violence. Human prisons are created as devices for "punishment" and "rehabilitation," yet they mostly facilitate a cycle of racism, poverty, and violence. Nonhuman animal prisons are the supposed saviors of vulnerable nonhuman animals, but they punish individual nonhuman animals for the misdeeds of humans. If you are in disbelief that I am comparing human prisons to zoos and aquariums, I understand the urge to resist. However, there are two points I want to raise here. First, I am not saying that human prisons are *just like* zoos and aquariums —that would be entirely incorrect, as human prisons have an entire history, past and present, based on racism and punitive "justice." I aim to highlight here that they have similar effects and *foundations* rooted in oppression and domination. Second, *humans have been subjected to being "exhibits" in "human zoos."* To say that zoos and prisons are not comparable is not supported by historical evidence. Humans, primarily Indigenous, Black, Brown, and Asian people of color, were enslaved by colonialist powers, confined by fences and gates and shackles of all types, and considered chattel for "human zoos"—property to be exploited, bought, and sold at their legal owners' discretion (Abbatista 2015; Putnam 2012; Sánchez-Gómez 2013; Trupp 2015). Both human zoos and human prisons have served as sources of the *animalization* of marginalized human groups, a concept that we will take a more extended look at later (Montford 2016).

To say all this is not to demonize the staff of zoos and aquariums— most of them are not intentionally harming these captive nonhuman animals or with any malice. They are simply doing their job and believe in the institutions' conservation and educational missions. Most have not examined the nature of zoos and aquariums *outside* of an anthropocentric lens. But, it's time for them and us to remove the rose-colored glasses, which show us examples of species population rehabilitation and zookeepers having close relationships with the other animals they care for. It's time to acknowledge the intrinsically destructive nature of keeping sentient beings captive. The harm done has been documented time[23] and time[24] and time[25] and time[26] and time[27] and time[28] again (to infinity). We must recognize the root issue here: human exploitation of other animals. If we are concerned about species extinctions, we must understand that the most significant driver of this is killing nonhuman animals for food (Ripple et al. 2019). That means that the best way to help other species of animals is not to put them on display as "specimens" and "entertainment" but instead to work to end our consumption and use of other animals and to take collective action against the structural mechanisms that help to sustain it (Morell 2015). Emmerman's (2019:391) pointed critique of zoos and human procrastination is especially appropriate:

> The central question of zoos is not whether individual animals should be sacrificed to ensure future members of their own species. The central question of zoos is whether individual animals should be sacrificed to ensure humans can delay facing profound regret caused by the knowledge that we have wreaked irrevocable devastation on the natural world. For many of us, the answer is a resounding "no."

Further Reading:

- Rothfels, Nigel. 2002. *Savages and Beasts: The Birth of the Modern Zoo*. Baltimore, MD: Johns Hopkins University Press.

Conservation ethics / compassionate conservation / "invasive" species

It may be that many species will not survive without human intervention. But this does not mean that they will survive with human intervention. Indeed, our track record as planetary managers is deplorable: we generally make things worse when we try to make them better.

—Dale Jamieson (1995 [cited by Emmerman 2019])

JOHN TALLENT

If the task of conservation is to actualize a human relationship with non-human nature that is not only sustainable but also ethically appropriate...it is important that morally relevant individuals not be excluded from the scope of conservation concern.

—Wallach et al. (2018:4)

Mainstream conservation practices to control or eliminate so-called "invasive" or "overpopulated" species often involve the act of killing. This go-to practice is notorious for having tremendous unintended consequences, such as the torturous deaths of the intended species, the inadvertent killing of a different species, and the psychological effects on human children and others resulting from the normalization of violence as a first step to complex issues (Bègue 2020; McGuire, Palmer, and Faber 2022; Stewart and Cole 2009; Wallach et al. 2015). Fortunately, there are growing perspectives not borne out of speciesism and anthropocentrism but rather on all-inclusive justice for all peoples, which aim to overturn the dominant conservation discourses.

"Compassionate conservation" (CC) is a perspective aimed at minimizing harm and suffering of all nonhuman animals, rejecting the widespread ideas that human supremacy and human exceptionalism are more important than individual nonhuman animal lives and autonomy, and seeking alternatives to killing as much as possible (Ramp and Bekoff 2015; Wallach et al. 2018). A similar perspective, "multispecies justice" (MJ), is also gaining support within the area of conservation. Based upon the ethic of justice, it sees specific duties toward nonhuman animals. The obligatory nature of these duties is founded in the science of nonhuman animal cognition and sentience, where consciousness necessitates specific duties to safeguard a being's life and prevent undue pain and suffering when possible. Like CC, MJ rejects speciesist and anthropocentric reasoning when considering conservation data and strategies (A. Treves, Santiago-Ávila, and Lynn 2019).

"Nativism" in conservation describes the prevailing view that life native to a given area should be valued morally. In contrast, non-native life is valued less or not valued at all, morally speaking (Wallach et al. 2018). This is ethically dubious because it overlooks the lives of individual nonhuman animals and disregards the complexities between so-called "native" species and "invasive" species. For instance, there are cases where "invasive" species (or a less-derogatory name, like "non-native") have increased species diversity and had the effect of preserving vulnerable species (Wallach et al. 2020).

It's not clear that free-living nonhuman animal conservation practices consider all relevant information before deciding which approach to take. A review of 190 papers on "wildlife conservation and management" practices revealed that nonhuman animals are not typically acknowledged as complex individuals with agency (Edelblutte, Krithivasan, and Hayek 2022). While much of the debate and language surrounding free-living nonhuman animals in conservation and hunting is focused on environmental aspects, this belies one of the most important problems: the harm done to individual nonhuman *persons*. The culling (killing) of non-native nonhuman animals for the assumed preservation of "native" species has been called "environmental fascism" by some (Regan 2004:361). Using the language of "invasive" has also been criticized as "demeaning," which contributes to the wrongful discrimination of nonhuman animal species that do not conform to human desires.[29] There is a tendency to speak of issues of biodiversity of species, property damage, and aesthetics, which ignores any admission of fundamental rights violations *by* humans *upon* nonhuman animals (Prisner-Levyne 2020). In effect, humans and human lifestyles are rarely seen as something to change for the benefit of ecosystems and conservation, but nonhuman animal lives are up for debate:

> The environmental movement defends the needs to kill individuals belonging to certain non-native animal species...It is alleged that these individuals should be sacrificed because

> preserving native species and maintaining the balance of habitats constitutes a greater good than individual lives. However, these species have appeared in an exotic habitat either because humans have transported them for business purpose…or because global transportation of people and goods unwittingly displaced them. Yet we conceal our responsibility and blame these animals by calling them "invasive" and condemning them to death. Although it may be true that non-native species can damage native ones in some cases, it is striking that the environmental movement invests so much effort culling these animals compared with the much lesser effort invested in promoting changes in human lifestyles and consumption patterns, like the use of private cars, the number of flights or, particularly, the animal-based diet. It seems easier to demand that animals sacrifice their entire lives than to renounce human caprices. Furthermore, since the human being is the type of individual that produces a greater imbalance in the ecosystems, this biotic precept, to be consistently applied, should request for the culling of the over populous Homo sapiens for the greater biotic good. This would be immoral of course, which shows that the ideology is flawed in its attempts not to be human-centred and ethical, for it allows for first- and second-class sentient beings towards whom compassion and cruelty are applied differently. (Almiron and Tafalla 2019:261-2)

Remember these perspectives the next time you hear anyone talking about "invasive" or "overpopulated" species of nonhuman animals. We habitually put fault and consequences on others rather than ourselves as a species.

Further Reading:

- Heister, Anja. 2022. *Beyond the North American Model of Wildlife Conservation: From Lethal to Compassionate Conservation.* Springer Nature.
- Stanescu, James, and Kevin Cummings, eds. 2017. *The Ethics and Rhetoric of Invasion Ecology.* Lanham: Lexington Books.

"Meat"

"Meat," or more accurately called "flesh," inherently involves the consumption of someone. There are many ways in which nonhuman animals are reduced to a "meat" product—so many, and each gruesome in its own right—that I am not going to go into it at all. I will link to resources for you, and I hope you will consider looking at them. Personally, seeing the documentary *Earthlings* (linked below) was what shocked me into first going vegetarian. It is not an easy watch, but it's not supposed to be. It is the grim truth. I still have triggering flashbacks even today of some of the scenes from this film, and I also don't regret watching it.

Further Reading:

- Eisnitz, Gail A. 2009. *Slaughterhouse: The Shocking Story of Greed, Neglect, and Inhumane Treatment Inside the U.S. Meat Industry.* Prometheus Books.
- Pachirat, Timothy. 2013. *Every Twelve Seconds: Industrialized Slaughter and the Politics of Sight.* New Haven, CT: Yale University Press.
- Kim, Hemi. 2022. "Slaughterhouses: The Harsh Reality of How Meat Is Made." *Sentient Media.* Retrieved January 14, 2023 (https://sentientmedia.org/slaughterhouses/).

- Nationearth.com. n.d. "Earthlings—the documentary." *Nationearth.com*. Retrieved January 14, 2023 (https://www.nationearth.com/).
- Geyrhalter, Nikolaus. 2005. *Our Daily Bread*. USA: Icarus Films. [can usually be found for free on sites like YouTube.]

Hunting

Despite the relatively robust literature[30] that says hunting, specifically "trophy hunting," is "beneficial," one must understand that most of the research in this area only uses an anthropocentric lens to weigh the pros and cons. Without considering the rights, lives, autonomy, and well-being of all the nonhuman animals affected by such a "hobby," the "benefits" of hunting will no doubt be biased in favor of human interests only. When the only considerations evaluated are monetary and business related, of course hunting will seem "beneficial." But that only shows one possible way of prioritizing interests (Latombe et al. 2022). Moreover, though hunters' language has evolved over the last few decades about an assumed "stewardship" of the environment and "care" of nonhuman animal suffering, it should not be surprising that unnecessarily killing nonhuman animals for recreation is a moral paradox.[31] Brian Luke (1998:634) explains the strange situation of hunting:

> North American white men do not hunt out of necessity; they typically do not hunt to protect people or animals, nor to keep themselves or their families from going hungry. Rather, they pursue hunting for its own sake, as a sport. This point is obscured by the fact that many hunters consume the flesh of their kills with their families, thus giving the appearance that hunting is a subsistence tactic. A close reading of the hunting literature, however, reveals that hunters eat the flesh of their kills as an *ex post facto* attempt at morally legitimating an activity they pursue for its own sake. The hunter often portrays himself as providing for his family through a successful kill and

> "harvest." This posture seeks to ritually reestablish a stereotypical masculine provider role less available now than it may once have been. In reality hunting today is typically not a source of provision but actually drains family resources. Deer hunters, for example, spend on average twenty dollars per pound of venison acquired, once all the costs of equipment, licenses, transportation, unsuccessful hunts, and so forth, are calculated.

The fact at hand here is that because nonhuman animals are sentient, conscious persons, killing or exploiting them for "conservation," "biodiversity," economics, or any other reason is not morally justifiable.[32] The case has been made that any "trophy" hunter that considers themselves "ethical" in how they hunt has an obligation *not to hunt at all*. Brian Luke (1997:39) explains,

> [H]unters' ethics are paradoxical: hunters become more ethical by hunting in a way that is sensitive to the animal's interests in avoiding pain and in continuing to live; nevertheless, this very sensitivity and respect for animals entails that hunting is not justifiable, that even true sportsmen are not acting ethically.

Fishing

So much literature concerned with aquatic life discusses the consequences of "overfishing." This type of focus commonly raises concerns about how the industrialization of fishing severely decreases biodiversity and biomass in bodies of water (Myers and Worm 2003; McKeever and National Geographic Staff 2022). The solutions suggested to these problems are usually something along the lines of "changing fishing practices," "ending illegal fishing," or "eating sustainably caught fishes." But this emphasis on "overfishing" reminds me of how liberals in the US approach the intrinsic issues within capitalism: by calling for reform and "better" capitalism. What these two issues have in common is that they attack the leaves and not the roots of the problems. Like capitalism, the killing and exploitation of sentient aquatic life is a fundamental issue that requires dismantling. Almost every behavior can be made "sustainable" if it isn't scaled up to the entire world's population of humans. A single human, or a single village of people, fishing on the banks of a river can potentially continue doing so without a significant decline or collapse in the population of fishes; likewise, a single human in a Midwestern US town is not going to significantly alter the Earth's climate systems by driving a Hummer.

But for whom is small-scale fishing "sustainable"? If we were in the fishes' position, killing us wouldn't be "sustainable" *for us*. From this perspective, one fish killed is "overfishing" and "unsustainable." As we examined in a previous section, and despite the common assumption that fishes do not have emotions, the evidence clearly shows that fishes are highly likely sentient and conscious. To act in a way that assumes otherwise would be extremely disingenuous. Still, trillions of fishes and aquatic nonhuman animals are killed and exploited every single year.

Some people believe that "catch-and-release" fishing is ethical because the fishes are assumed to continue living their lives after being thrown back into the water. But this rosy picture hides the harm done throughout the process. Because fishes are (more than likely) sentient beings with the capacity for pain and suffering, a hook going through their mouths will be painful. They are also plucked out of their aquatic environment, where they freely breathe. They are brought into an environment where they are quite literally suffocated until they are thrown back into the water or until they die a slow death. There is also the fact that some fishes thrown back into the water die afterward because of the incident. Estimates for this mortality rate are not easy to ascertain, and the percentages vary wildly. Estimates available to me ranged from 18% to 43%. There is also evidence that, even if the fishes do not die from the incident, they have a significantly decreased ability to feed (Drews 2016). But it's important to understand that the variations were all influenced by the species of fishes, location, and other factors

(Bartholomew and Bohnsack 2005; Gilliland 1997). The bottom line is that fishing harms fishes, which makes it unethical.

Further reading:

- Ritchie, Hannah, and Max Roser. 2021. "Fish and Overfishing." *Our World in Data*. Retrieved November 2, 2022 (https://ourworldindata.org/fish-and-overfishing#what-does-sustainable-fishing-mean).

"Humane" animal use

Of the currently living nonhuman animals confined for agricultural use and sold within the US, 99% are kept in so-called "factory farms" (Anthis 2019). Globally, 90% of nonhuman animals confined for agricultural use are kept within these types of farms (Anthis and Anthis 2019). One study reported that 62% of its respondents believed that nonhuman animals are treated "well" on farms. The study also found that the average respondent believed that about 68% of nonhuman animals come from "factory farms" and that 80% of respondents believed that they usually purchase "humanely-treated" nonhuman animal "products" (Anthis and Ladak 2021). Nonhuman animal flesh that is considered to be from beings that were treated "well" or "humanely" on farms is often called "happy meat" (Francione 2009). Not only is this an entirely subjective concept and based completely on assumptions (how do you know that they were happy?), but from the terminology, the nonhuman animal *person* is removed and reduced to "meat"—a thing, an object, a commodity. Eco-feminist scholar Carol J. Adams (2017:66-7) describes the dismissal of a person involved in using and consuming nonhuman animals as an **absent referent**. In place of the nonhuman animal person, excised by killing, is a piece of "meat." The person no longer exists, or, to the humans consuming the "meat," the person *never* existed. Carol explains that there are three ways in which nonhuman animals become absent referents: in a literal sense, "through meat eating they are literally absent because they are dead"; in a definitional sense, by changing our language to refer to objects, like "beef" and "poultry"; and in a metaphorical sense, as seen in the way we talk about human women being seen as "a piece of meat." The absent referent, in Carol's words, "is both there and not there. It is there through inference, but its meaningfulness reflects only upon what it refers to because the originating, literal, experience that contributes the meaning is not there."

Kathryn Gillespie (2011) relates so-called "humane" nonhuman animal exploitation to the concept of "doublethink" from George Orwell's novel *1984*. For Gillespie, the act of exploiting and consuming nonhuman animals is in direct contradiction to how we personally connect with them through shared experiences. We know that nonhuman animals are persons, yet we deny that understanding when we exploit them. We are fully aware of our disconnection in this process but also somehow unconscious. The idea that there can be "happy meat" assuages the cognitive dissonance that we get when we understand that nonhuman animals are persons. At the same time, we ignore that understanding in favor of their continued consumption. In this way, the labeling and marketing of "happy meat" and "humane" nonhuman animal production "work[s] to appease and deflect ethical concerns while facilitating the continued exploitation of 'farmed animals'" (Cole 2011:83). Purchasing and consuming this "happy meat" can have the effect of making us feel content with ceaseless exploitation (Francione 2012b).

The concept of "humane-washing" has been developed in response to the exploitation of nonhuman animals, which is ignored and Disneyfied as "harmless." Stucki (2020) describes it as "a type of whitewashing, which is a metaphor for communications that gloss over or obscure unpleasant, negatively connoted facts" and as similar to "green-washing."[33] Euphemisms like "happy meat" and marketing tactics such as certifying certain nonhuman animal "products" as "Humanely-raised," "Animal Welfare Approved," and "Free-range" come down to this fact: "[W]hat is presented by humane labels as humane is in fact not humane." Furthermore, Stucki explains that "[t]he issue is not just that what is presented as humane is not humane, but that it cannot be. Put differently, it is not just that humane labels promise something which they factually do not deliver—it is that they envisage something that is actually impossible" (124). As nonhuman animal ethicist Gary L. Francione (2007b) is fond of saying, "Because animals are property, we consider as 'humane treatment' that we would regard as torture if it were inflicted on humans." Killing someone unnecessarily cannot be made "humane."

What exactly would make any amount of exploitation, harm, suffering, or death "humane" when done in a manner wholly removed from any genuine notions of necessity? We don't mean "humane" when referencing these actions against nonhuman animals. We don't seriously mean that nonhuman animals were confined "humanely" and disallowed from living their best lives. We don't seriously mean that they were forcefully impregnated by a farmer's arm "humanely." And we don't seriously mean that a cow living their "best" life, albeit confined on a farm of rolling hills and relative tranquility, is killed "humanely" when the practical alternative was to purchase tofu, seitan, or chickpeas from the grocery store. We really mean that these nonhuman animals are confined, tortured, forcefully impregnated, castrated, separated from their kin, mutilated, had their throats slit, or have been shot through their brains with a bolt gun "less severely" than the most common means. We mean that some farmers relieved some of the horrors of the nonhuman animals' lives, whether for most of their lives or for that brief moment before they are reduced to a lifeless "commodity" on the killing floor. Just as the white-collar criminal launders his embezzled money through an offshore bank account so that he may use it freely, we process the objective horrors of nonhuman animal exploitation through the mental gymnastics and capitalist alienation that is "humane" nonhuman animal use and killing—and out comes "happy meat," the paradoxical, oxymoronic, horseshit bullshit human-shit that we are all-too-willing to be spoon-fed.

We often believe that a "painless" death (killing) of nonhuman animals for human consumption does not carry much moral weight.

But how is that so? Not being tortured before being killed is better than being tortured before being killed. But how can being killed, albeit "painlessly," not harm someone? This type of logic is not applied to humans because we assume that killing a human, without necessity or cause, harms that person. Killing a human ends their autonomy; it violates their bodily integrity; it violates their legal rights; and it prevents them from their desires, present and future. From what we have examined so far in this book about nonhuman animal sentience, it is highly probable too that they will be harmed by at least some of those things that make it wrong to kill a human unnecessarily (Kaldewaij 2006). As a result, it is fair to say that "happy meat" is a myth.[34] Death undoubtedly harms nonhuman animals, just as it does with humans.[35] This does not deter nonhuman animal farmers and corporations from presenting nonhuman animal farms as places of happiness.[36]

Beyond the issue of whether physical harm is commonplace or a rarity in nonhuman animal agriculture (it's commonplace), Matthew C. Halteman (2011) argues that nonhuman animals are still harmed in other ways that make their exploitation morally wrong. Halteman states that one way nonhuman animals are still harmed is by "procedural harm"—the harm nonhuman animals endure during their confinement and from the profits gained by the exploiters from their production. These types of harm include traumas, dehorning, de-beaking, transport handling, etc. Another harm that nonhuman animals will inevitably experience is "institutional harm"—described as the "deprivation of goods required for realizing well-being." This type of harm would be how nonhuman animals in agriculture are systematically denied the autonomy to live their lives as they wish.

Further Reading:

- Deininger, K. 2022. "32. The Problem of Justifying Animal-Friendly Animal Husbandry." Pp. 217–22 in *Transforming Food Systems: Ethics, Innovation and Responsibility*, edited by D. Bruce

- Krásná, Denisa. 2022. "Towards Horizontal Relationships: Anarcha Indigenism, Decolonial Animal Ethic, and Indigenous Veganism." *Canada and Beyond: A Journal of Canadian Literary and Cultural Studies* 11:31–51. doi: 10.14201/candb.v11i31-51.
- Stanescu, Vasile. 2014. "Crocodile Tears, Compassionate Carnivores, and the Marketing of 'Happy Meat.'" Pp. 216–33 in *Critical Animal Studies: Thinking the Unthinkable*, edited by J. Sorenson. Toronto: Canadian Scholar's Press.
- Bekoff, Marc. 2010. "Going to Slaughter: Should Animals Hope to Meet Temple Grandin." *Psychology Today*. Retrieved December 5, 2022 (https://www.psychologytoday.com/us/blog/animal-emotions/201002/going-slaughter-should-animals-hope-meet-temple-grand).

Dairy

A common misconception, especially in vegetarian social spheres and beliefs, is that the dairy industry is entirely separate from the "beef" industry. More to the point, it is assumed that consuming cows' milk does not contribute to the "beef" industry or the deaths of cows. However, dairy goes hand-in-hand with the "beef" industry. From the Beef Board (2021) itself, they say that "dairy represents approximately 20 percent of the total [beef] supply...Dairy beef production has become an important pillar of the beef industry and plays a key role in contributing to U.S. beef demand."

Beyond the economic aspects of the dairy industry, supporting the consumption of nonhuman animals' milk leads to many negative aspects of the industry. Familial bonds are either broken or completely prevented, emotional/mental/physical torture are commonplace, and sexual violence is inherent (April 2019; Ventura et al. 2013). "Artificial insemination" is used to bring more and more unwitting cows into existence and is done with what is sometimes called in the industry "rape racks."[37] The dairy industry is full of horrors that most of us can never imagine—but most people still inevitably ask vegans the same question: "Won't the cows explode (or otherwise experience pain) if we don't milk them?" Cows are forced and bred to produce more and more milk by constantly being impregnated. No, cows won't explode if they aren't milked. Still, cows might live better lives if they weren't "artificially inseminated" by a human's arm into their rectum and a semen-depositing instrument pressed into their uterus. The dairy industry is an industry of *total reproductive domination* and the *total denial of bodily autonomy*. In a human context, this would be called something else.

Veal

Like the dairy industry, the "veal" industry is closely integrated into the "beef" industry. From the Beef Board (2021), "While dairy producers are contributing more cattle to the U.S. beef supply, the veal industry also plays an active role." "Veal" calves are the male offspring of dairy cows who cannot produce milk. Instead of being forced to produce milk or turned into "beef," they are often turned into "veal." If you want to learn more about "veal," please see this footnote.[38] But, beyond the awfulness of the treatment involved in the "veal" industry, cows and calves should not be used as resources or property, no matter if the *treatment* is seen as "harmless" or "horrific."

Further Reading:

- Elbein, Saul. 2018. "Gruesome Footage of Dairy Calves Exposes a Gaping Loophole in California's Landmark Animal Welfare Law." *The Intercept*. Retrieved January 14, 2023 (https://theintercept.com/2018/10/08/california-prop-12-animal-welfare-dairy-calves/).

Leather

The global leather trade in 2021 was valued between $271-$407 billion (Grand View Research 2021; Smith 2022). Leather made from the skins of nonhuman animals, especially those of cattle, is commonly thought to be "waste" or "by-products." However, this ignores the entire industry's enormous monetary value. Leather is considered a "co-product" alongside the dairy and flesh industries (Brugnoli 2012; Marmer 1996). But the difference between a co-product and a by-product means very little overall: purchasing leather goods puts money into not only an industry built on the commodification of nonhuman animal skins, but a portion of that money also goes into buying more skins from the flesh and dairy industries. Also, consider that the economics of it all isn't the only aspect that makes the leather industry a morally dreadful enterprise.

Leather has a tremendous negative effect from an environmental standpoint (Hansen, Monteiro de Aquim, and Gutterres 2021). Most pollution from leather production comes from the pre-tanning and tanning steps. In these stages, there is an increase in chemical oxygen demand, sulfates, chromium, chlorides, volatile organic compounds, total dissolved solids, and heavy metals in wastewater (Sivaram and Barik 2019). Tanning sludge diminishes local groundwater (Dixit et al. 2015). Air pollution can also be released through hydrogen sulfide, ammonia, and other chemicals (Tasca and Puccini 2019). This is an environmental and human health catastrophe.[39] Nonhuman animal-based leather is often compared to nonhuman animal-free leather, commonly criticized as "plastic leather." However, this disregards two points: 1) a wide variety of materials, which are constantly expanding, have been used to create nonhuman animal-free leather, and 2) polyurethane is used to produce nonhuman animal-based leather (Tian 2020).

The production of leather starts with viewing and treating nonhuman animals as property and resources for use. Regarding cattle exploitation for this product, forced impregnation begets a calf often separated from their mother. In this process, cows go through mutilations, stress and trauma, violations of bodily integrity, skinning, and killing. Then we must also account for the resultant deforestation, pollution, water scarcity, and greenhouse gas emissions from the "beef" and dairy industries that supply the skins (Gerber et al. 2015; Hussain 2022). These consequences negatively affect human workers and others that eat, drink, or breathe in the pollutants from these industries.

Experimentation and vivisection
Nonhuman animal experimentation is widespread for things like medicine, new surgical techniques, the study of diseases and their progression, new food ingredients, household cleaning products, hygiene products, environmental research, and others. This type of testing is commonly done on living nonhuman animals. The best estimates show that between 2005 and 2015, nonhuman animal experimentation increased globally from 115.2 million to 192.1 million *people*, while procedures increased from 53.3 million to 79.9 million during the same period. (Taylor and Alvarez 2020; Taylor et al. 2008).

Funk and Hefferon (2018) from the Pew Research Center found that, when it comes to citizens of the US, 47% support and 52% oppose nonhuman animal experimentation. This slight disparity was more pronounced in terms of gender, as the percentages of those that favor this experimentation in those who identify as "men" to "women" was 58% and 36%. Regarding mainstream political leanings and support, both identified Republicans and Democrats were very similar. There was nearly a 50/50 split between those who supported it and those who did not.

The justifications for nonhuman animal experimentation by its supporters are varied. The two main justifications, as explained by Aysha Akhtar (2018:475), are "that (1) animals make sufficient models of human biology and diseases, and (2) animals lack cognitive and emotional abilities that would require higher moral consideration." Despite these common justifications for nonhuman animal experimentation, Akhtar criticizes that both present an ironic truth: nonhuman animals are much like us, especially in their capacities to suffer, and these experiments are unreliable.

As we saw in an earlier section, *nonhuman animals are sentient, conscious, feeling, and thinking persons*. When we understand the harms that experimentation causes and empathize with the subjective individuals who are the victims of such harm, the ethics of experimentation become impossible to ignore. When a nonhuman animal is used in an experiment, such as when TV's "Dr. Oz" was the principal investigator of a study that opened up dogs' chests to install pacemakers and then induced heart failure (nonhuman animal experimentation that involves surgery is called "vivisection"), or when experiments have involved separating mother monkeys from their newborn babies to observe how each reacts, or the suffering and death of hundreds of nonhuman animals (including pigs, sheep, monkey, mice, and rats) for Elon Musk's brain implant technologies, *people* are confined, tortured, and killed in the name of "science" (Herbst 2022; Livingstone 2022). A *person* is deemed a piece of "scientific equipment," used and tortured as both a "subject" and a "thing," and often killed and discarded like one would a used syringe or piece of bloody gauze. A *person* has their neck purposefully broken while awake. A *person* is given electric shocks to "train" them. A *person* is shot with a gun. A *person* has harsh chemicals put in their eyes with no way to alleviate the pain. A *person* is forced to grow cancer within their body and to suffer until they are finally disposed of so unceremoniously and disrespectfully that only human tyrants and serial killers could rival in showing their human victims.

The efficacy and necessity of nonhuman animal experimentation are also major causes of concern (Van Norman 2019). Several studies show insufficient evidence of nonhuman animal experiments being efficacious (Knight 2008; Robinson et al. 2019). Robinson et al. (2019:11) conclude, "it has become increasingly clear that conclusions drawn from animal studies cannot be simply transferred to human studies." Evidence suggests that methodological quality can be low in many studies involving nonhuman animals (Mueller et al. 2014). Additionally, there are questions about the necessity of this type of experimentation. Alternatives to nonhuman animal experimentation exist for many studies (Doke and Dhawale 2015; Hutchinson, Owen, and Bailey 2022). Switching to these alternative methods even makes economic sense (Meigs 2018).

Defenders of nonhuman animal experimentation often point to its "necessity" for humans, and they also attempt to convince us that it is done "humanely":

> What some scientists call "good welfare" really isn't "good enough". "Good welfare" and allowable research according to existing regulations permit mice to be shocked and otherwise tortured, rats to be starved or forced-fed, pigs to be castrated without anesthetics, cats to be blinded, dogs to be shot with bullets, and primates to have their brains invaded with electrodes. Only about 1 percent of animals used in research in the United States are protected by this legislation, and the legislation is sometimes amended in nonsensical ways to accommodate the "needs" of researchers. The desperation of science to rob animals of their sentience produces distortions that open the door for egregious and reprehensible abuse. (Bekoff 2008:T6)

Putting aside the uselessness of considering exploitation "humane" in any logical sense, we must consider the fact that we do not permit, legally or morally, the experimentation of humans without proper consent. That doesn't mean it doesn't happen; it absolutely does, and we should be horrified and outraged (CDC n.d.; Miller 2013; Post 1991; plus, many more ad nauseam). However, strictly limiting those moral and legal reasons to humans doesn't stem from any rational basis. When we remember that nonhuman animals are sentient people, any experiment's potential for helping others does not justify the harm it does to that one person who cannot and would not consent. To argue otherwise requires an anthropocentric form of rationality and morality.

Further Reading:

- Demello, Margo. 2012. "Animals and Science." Pp. 170–93 in *Animals and Society: an Introduction to Human-Animal Studies*. New York: Columbia University Press.
- Knight, Andrew. 2013. *The Costs and Benefits of Animal Experiments*. Houndmills, Basingstoke; New York, N.Y.: Palgrave Macmillan.
- Twine, Richard. 2010. *Animals as Biotechnology: Ethics, Sustainability and Critical Animal Studies*. Routledge.

The effects of nonhuman animal exploitation on humans

For most human workers, work can be grueling, exhausting, debilitating, stressful, emotionally and psychologically damaging, tedious, demeaning, horrifying, and even deadly. This is especially true for the types of jobs of great interest to the topics of this book: human farm workers.

Human farm workers, who work within the produce and nonhuman animal agriculture industries, are typically a part of our society's super-exploited class (Holmes 2013). According to the American Farm Bureau Federation (2018), the US needs 1.5-2 million agricultural workers yearly. Immigrant farm workers make up approximately 73% of the industry workforce. Xenophobic immigration policies and dangerous workplace conditions exemplify some of the significant reasons why agricultural work is highly precarious, especially for immigrants (FWD.us 2021). The Food Empowerment Project (2022) states that,

> Most agricultural workers have an extremely poor quality of life. Although they work an average of 45 hours a week, farm

> workers in the U.S. earn an average of about $17,500 to $20,000 per year. One-third of farm workers' families have a combined income below the national poverty level. In addition, only 13% of workers are covered by employer-provided health insurance.

Agricultural work is quite literally essential work. The workers are also people, inherently deserving of compassion, legal rights, and a non-exploited life. They are often forgotten in social justice discussions, however.

Vegans are often faulted for focusing on nonhuman animal exploitation and ignoring human farm worker exploitation (AFROPUNK 2017; Amara 2018; Blake 2018; Winstead 2021). Anecdotally, I think this can be a relatively fair critique. I have talked to many vegans through the years that believe that human rights issues are separate from nonhuman animal liberation issues and vegans that have absolutely no compassion or interest in the rights of humans. This is disappointing, to say the least. We shall see in this book how human and nonhuman animal oppressions are inherently interconnected. Compartmentalizing oppressions ignores the reality of how they operate and compound one another. But while vegans are often critiqued about their too often lack of interest in farm worker issues, the criticism usually goes beyond this and into fallacious realms.

One common fallacy on this topic is to use the argument, "Yes, I know I eat meat, but vegans exploit farm workers for their produce." This is a *tu quoque* fallacy, which, as we saw earlier, attempts to derail the discussion with a "you also exploit!" argument. This argument essentially seeks to equalize and equate the exploitation involved by each side: non-vegans exploit nonhuman animals, and vegans exploit humans. Beyond the fallaciousness of this argument, it also suffers from a lack of accuracy and context. Plant-based foods indeed involve the exploitation of human workers within the capitalist system, and "foods" made from nonhuman animals certainly involve the exploitation of nonhuman animals. This comparison, however, overlooks the fact that vegans are not the only ones that consume plant-based foods; non-vegans do as well! So, while it's true that vegans consume foods within the capitalist system that relies on exploiting human workers, it is equally true that non-vegans consume "foods" within the capitalist system that exploit both human workers and nonhuman animals. This fact also obscures the critical aspect of non-vegans, most often exploiting nonhuman animals *unnecessarily*. At the same time, the exploitation of human farm workers is not something that we have much control over in this current economic arrangement.

One group of workers in the agricultural industry that often gets overlooked in these discussions is slaughterhouse workers. Winders and Abrell (2021:23) point out, "Slaughterhouses are incredibly dangerous places to work, populated by some of the most exploited and disempowered members of society." Evidence for this by the Center for Economic Policy Research shows the realities and demographics of slaughterhouse work:

> People of color, immigrants, and people in relatively low-income families are disproportionately employed in meatpacking plants. Almost one-half (44.4 percent) of meatpacking workers are Hispanic, and one-quarter (25.2 percent) are Black. Across all the occupations of people working in the Animal Slaughtering and Processing Industry, more than half of all workers are people of color (34.9 percent are Hispanic, and 22.5 percent are Black). In some occupations within the industry, more than two-thirds of workers are people of color, including: Hand Packers and Packagers (75.3 percent); Laborers and Freight, Stock, and Material Movers, Hand (68.6 percent); and Industrial Truck and Tractor Operators (67.3 percent). Immigrants are particularly overrepresented in frontline meatpacking occupations. About 17 percent of workers in the US workforce today are immigrants. But more than one-half (51.5 percent) of frontline meatpacking workers are immigrants. About one-quarter (25.1

percent) of these workers live in households in which all of the members (age 14 or older) have limited proficiency in English, over six times the rate for US workers overall. Other occupations within the Animal Slaughtering and Processing Industry also have a high share of immigrants: Hand Packers and Packagers (52.9 percent); Industrial Truck and Tractor Operators (38.8 percent); and Laborers and Freight, Stock, and Material Movers, Hand (38.2 percent). Nearly half of frontline meatpacking workers (45.1 percent) live in low-income families (below 200 percent of the federal poverty line, or less than $52,400 for a family of four in 2020) and about one-in-eight (12.4 percent) have income below the poverty line. This compares to 20.6 percent of all workers from low-income families and 6.7 percent of all workers with income below the poverty level. Meatpacking workers also disproportionately lack health insurance (15.5 percent), have one or more children to care for (44.3 percent), and are less educated (2.5 percent have a college degree or more). (Fremstad, Rho, and Brown 2020)

There is an abundance of research examining the horrors of slaughterhouse work (Baran, Rogelberg, and Clausen 2016; Dias et al. 2020; Jenkins 2018; Montford and Wotherspoon 2021; Picon 2020; Slade and Alleyne 2021; Ursachi, Munteanu, and Cioca 2021), though vegans are often pointed at exclusively for engaging in consumption practices that harm human workers.

Nonhuman animal exploitation also involves its considerable contributions to racism in many forms. Courtney G. Lee (2022) exposes how, particularly in the US, nonhuman animal agriculture is built upon and maintained by racism. In addition to the industry's preponderance of vulnerable and marginalized immigrants and people of color working in hazardous positions, the US government has a long history of passing laws specifically targeting Black farmers and ignoring and denying the environmental racism that results from these industries frequently being located close to communities of racialized minorities. (Núñez 2019). And, as we are about to learn, the environmental harms that come with nonhuman animal agriculture are detrimental to all life on this planet.

Further Reading:

- Nibert, David. 2014. "Animals, Immigrants, and Profits: Slaughterhouses and the Political Economy of Oppression." Pp. 3–17 in *Critical Animal Studies: Thinking the Unthinkable*, edited by J. Sorenson. Toronto: Canadian Scholar's Press.
- Krásná, Denisa. 2022. "Animal Colonialism in North America: Milk Colonialism, Environmental Racism, and Indigenous Veganism." *AUC STUDIA TERRITORIALIA* 22(1):61–90. doi: 10.14712/23363231.2022.9.
- Food Empowerment Project. 2022. "Environmental Racism." *FoodIsPower.org*. Retrieved January 15, 2023 (https://foodispower.org/environmental-and-global/environmental-racism/).

Environmental impact of nonhuman animal agriculture

A distinct picture is beginning to form around the consequences to the environment of human exploitation of nonhuman animals. Nonhuman animal consumption and exploitation are leading drivers of anthropogenic climate change (Gerber et al. 2013; IPCC 2022). As of this writing, a prevailing approximation of global greenhouse gas emissions, specifically from the nonhuman animal agricultural sector is around 14.5% of all emissions by humans (Gerber et al. 2013:15).[40] That means the global greenhouse gas emissions strictly from nonhuman animal agriculture are higher than the entire transportation sector (United States Environmental Protection Agency 2022).

One of the major environmental influences in the production and consumption of nonhuman animals is that crops must be grown and harvested to feed them; this is an extraordinarily inefficient and resource-intensive process. Bojana Bajzelj from the University of Cambridge's Department of Engineering explains,

> The average efficiency of livestock converting plant feed to meat is less than 3%, and as we eat more meat, more arable cultivation is turned over to producing feedstock for animals that provide meat for humans. The losses at each stage are large, and as humans globally eat more and more meat, conversion from plants to food becomes less and less efficient, driving agricultural expansion and land cover conversion and releasing more greenhouse gases. Agricultural practices are not necessarily at fault here — but our choice of food is. (University of Cambridge 2014)

Consider this inefficiency in its effects on calories: "For every 100 calories of grain we feed animals, we get only about 40 new calories of milk, 22 calories of eggs, 12 of chicken, 10 of pork, or 3 of beef" (Foley 2014). There is also a common assertion that nonhuman animals exploited in agriculture eat mostly by-products and inedible crops to humans, meaning that these beings don't require many crops to be grown for their consumption. This is incorrect, however. According to Cassidy et al. (2013), "36% of the calories produced by the world's crops are being used for animal feed, and only 12% of those feed calories ultimately contribute to the human diet (as meat and other animal products)" (3). Approximately one-quarter of the global feed intake of nonhuman animals in agriculture comprises crop residues or is inedible to humans (FAO n.d.).[41]

Diets lower in nonhuman animal consumption and higher in vegetable/fruit consumption tend to be better for the environment (Nelson et al. 2016). Consider the absurdity of the following statistics concerning some of nonhuman animal agriculture's costs and "benefits" versus those of plant-based foods:

> [T]he impacts of animal products can markedly exceed those of vegetable substitutes...to such a degree that meat, aquaculture, eggs, and dairy use ~83% of the world's farmland and contribute 56 to 58% of food's different emissions, despite providing only 37% of our protein and 18% of our calories. Can animal products be produced with sufficiently low impacts to redress this vast imbalance? Or will reducing animal product consumption deliver greater environmental benefits? We find that the impacts of the lowest-impact animal products exceed average impacts of substitute vegetable proteins across GHG emissions, eutrophication, acidification (excluding nuts), and frequently land use... (Poore and Nemecek 2018:990)

Takacs et al. (2022) found that fully plant-based meals were consistently better for the environment than nonhuman animal-based ones, as flesh-based meals, on average, had 14 times the environmental impact than fully plant-based meals. They also noted that buying "local" nonhuman animal "products" was not the best solution; the best solution was removing nonhuman animal "ingredients."

Soybeans are often thought of as providing food for vegans and vegetarians; however, soy is a crop used most often in nonhuman animal agriculture. Brazil, the USA, Argentina, India, and China are the largest soy producers, accounting for 90% of worldwide production (De Maria et al. 2020). Biofuels, cattle ranching, and the production of soybeans for consumption by nonhuman animals in agriculture are some of the biggest influences on the expansion of soybean production in the last several decades (Silvério et al. 2015). The World Wildlife Fund (WWF) explains how soy cultivation, in addition to nonhuman animal flesh and dairy production, contributes highly to worldwide deforestation:

> Animal products have dominated agricultural land-use change over the last half-century. Global per capita meat consumption has almost doubled since the 1960s and is for instance projected to increase by 4-6 times more in sub-Saharan Africa by 2050. Meat production requires about five times more land to produce the nutritional value of its plant-based equivalents. If livestock is kept indoors, relying on feed grown elsewhere, land requirements increase even more. Currently, 36% of calories from the world's crops are used for animal feed, with only 12% of those feed calories contributing to the human diet. Beef is by far the most inefficient form of livestock produce commonly available. When land used for grazing and feed crops is combined, livestock production accounts for around 70% of agricultural land. While aimed at supplying domestic markets, beef production in the Amazon continues to be the main driver of deforestation; which involving different types of farmers from large-scale cattle ranchers to diversified smallholders, it is often linked to low-production extensive systems. (Pacheco et al. 2021)

WWF also notes that soy cultivation in Brazil contributes highly to soil erosion, soil degradation, soil compaction, pollution of bodies of water, reduced access to freshwater, and greenhouse gas emissions from deforestation and land conversion. Social impacts are also a significant issue: "In Brazil, Argentina, and Paraguay, the concentration of farmland in the hands of a few has pushed small farmers and communities off the land and encouraged exploitation of [human] workers. Survival International notes that the expansion of agricultural and grazing land threatens 650,000 Brazilian Indians in more than 200 tribes" (WWF n.d.).

Deforestation in the Amazonian rainforests is primarily due to the nonhuman animal agricultural sector (Hecht 2011). And with deforestation, species extinction is also a typical result. Several studies have found that nonhuman animal consumption and exploitation are major factors in biodiversity losses, so much so that solutions must include reductions or eliminations in these areas (Machovina, Feeley, and Ripple 2015; Stoll-Kleemann and Schmidt 2016).

The US Bureau of Land Management (BLM), tasked with maintaining the country's public lands, has seen significant land degradation primarily due to grazing by nonhuman animals. A recent report noted that 54 million acres of its total 246 million acres of public land failed to meet "land-health standards," which "generally measure biological conditions, including soil health, water quality, plant species diversity and the quality of habitat for threatened and endangered species." Forty million acres of the 54 million that failed health standards are primarily due to grazing. It's also important to note that of the 246 million acres the BLM manages, only 109 million acres are assessed for land-health standards. That means that it is highly likely that if all 246 million acres were considered for land-health standards, the 54 million currently failing would rise (Mohr 2022; Ruch and Rosenthal 2022). And while we are examining the US now, note that 41 percent of its land in the lower 48 states is used for nonhuman animal agriculture (Merrill and Leatherby 2018).

JOHN TALLENT

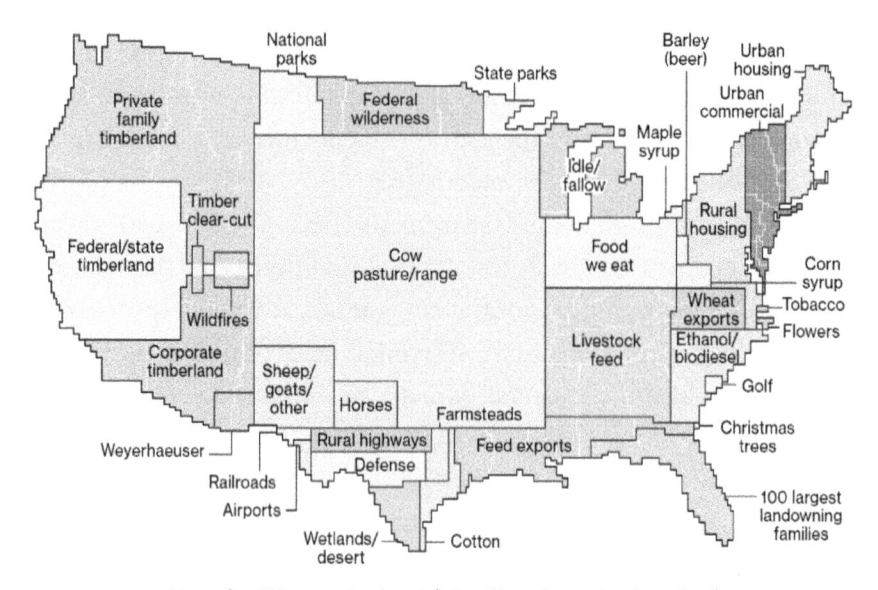

How the US uses its land (Merrill and Leatherby 2018)

Surprising to many, "grass-fed" and "pasture-raised" forms of non-human animal agriculture are sometimes *worse* for the environment (Hayek and Garrett 2018; Klopatek et al. 2021). Feeding grass to cows requires more land and creates more methane than feeding them grains (Clark and Tilman 2017; Nijdam, Rood, and Westhoek 2012). Hayek and Garrett (2018) conclude their analysis on converting the US cattle feedlot production system to "grass-fed" with this striking series of consequences:

> Future management shifts towards grass-finished beef cattle production would require a large increase in the US cattle population, both in finishing cattle and cow-calf herd populations, to accommodate slower fattening rates and lower slaughter weights. The required 30% increase in the overall cattle population must be accompanied by massive increases in the productivity of existing pastures to avoid native ecosystem encroachment or competition with the human food supply. Changes in cattle population and management would also create an even higher land and methane environmental footprint

for beef. Other impacts such as fresh water eutrophication, soil erosion and native vegetation suppression from overgrazing, and nitrous oxide emissions are likely to create additional environmental burdens, but must be more precisely quantified. Given the environmental tradeoffs associated with raising more cattle in exclusively grass-fed systems, only reductions in beef consumption can guarantee reductions in the environmental impact of US food systems. (P. 7)

Plant-based versus nonhuman animal-based diets: environmental comparisons

Looking into the environmental impacts of various diets is like swimming in the murkiest, muddiest water, except it's not mud and decaying organic matter but tons of fresh bullshit. Besides the ability of nefarious think tanks to provide misleading and cherry-picked data, differences in worldviews play a significant part in how this kind of research is carried out and presented.

For instance, one study by Allenden et al. (2022) sought to determine the most sustainable diet that both reduces the environmental footprint and is "realistic." Their data showed that a standard "omnivorous" diet was by far the lowest-scoring diet in terms of environmental effectiveness. In contrast, a vegetarian and a fully plant-based diet (they called it a "vegan diet") scored the highest. Other metrics were also evaluated, such as human health impact, land use, water use, and "animal welfare." The vegetarian and fully plant-based diets gained the highest scores for all these, minus a fully plant-based diet scoring low on water usage. Overall, a fully plant-based diet received the best score, followed by vegetarian, Mediterranean, pescatarian, flexitarian/semi-vegetarian, and the lowest score went to the standard omnivorous diet. The final step by the researchers was to evaluate via surveys the "probability" of respondents adopting a specific diet. In their results, they determined that you guessed it,

> Despite the Mediterranean diet being only moderately effective in reducing environmental/heath/animal-welfare impacts (relative to the standard omnivore diet), it had the highest overall weighted impact score, largely by virtue of its relatively high probability of adoption…Despite the sustainable diets with the greatest health, environmental, and animal welfare benefits (e.g., vegan and vegetarian) had the lowest probability of adoption. This result is not surprising, given that most participants identified as meat-eaters. (P. 545)

Though the data was interesting, the researchers' conclusions were highly disappointing. Obviously, they were taking into large consideration peoples' willingness and probability to adopt certain diets. Regardless, this shows a specific worldview and ideology invisibilized by the appearance of "objective" data and research. "Animal welfare" was considered, but the "adoptability" of each diet was prioritized over nonhuman animal lives, ecosystems, and human health. And because of this primacy of adoptability, the researchers insisted that further research and resources go into using the Mediterranean diet as an intervention strategy—not fighting the misinformation that most people have about plant-based diets or attempting to tackle unwillingness—but rather seeking the middle-of-the-road, "moderate" choice. Another study found that more protein and calories could be utilized if "beef" production was switched to plant-based food production; the authors, however, chose to portray "poultry" as the best alternative because it was "less radical" and "more practical" (Shepon et al. 2016). This framework of thinking, though largely unconscious, makes human palate pleasure and comfortability the overriding and central considerations. It is not easy to criticize from the outside because speciesism and anthropocentrism are major structural influences in our society. Unless a person has been exposed to anti-speciesist messaging, it's unlikely that they would break away from that framework. But you, the reader, now have that opportunity.

Poore and Nemecek (2018) published interesting research about the environmental impacts of various plant-based and nonhuman animal-based "products," including their contributions to GHG emissions, terrestrial acidification, water scarcity, and eutrophication.[42] Overwhelmingly, "products" from nonhuman animals increase these negative environmental consequences more than plant-based products. In an interview with *The Guardian* (Carrington 2018), the lead researcher of the study said that

> [a] vegan diet [sic] is probably the single biggest way to reduce your impact on planet Earth, not just greenhouse gases, but global acidification, eutrophication, land use and water use…It is far bigger than cutting down on your flights or buying an electric car…Agriculture is a sector that spans all the multitude of environmental problems…Really it is animal products that are responsible for so much of this. Avoiding consumption of animal products delivers far better environmental benefits than trying to purchase sustainable meat and dairy.

Marlow et al.'s (2009:1699S) research suggested that when they tested several different "food" items,

> the nonvegetarian diet required 2.9 times more water, 2.5 times more primary energy, 13 times more fertilizer, and 1.4 times more pesticides than did the vegetarian diet. The greatest contribution to the differences came from the consumption of beef in the diet. We found that a nonvegetarian diet exacts a higher cost on the environment relative to a vegetarian diet. From an environmental perspective, what a person chooses to eat makes a difference.

Considering the benefits to the environment and human health, another study looked at previous research and found that an entirely plant-based diet "consistently reported reductions in greenhouse gas emissions" and was also the best diet for reducing them. Additionally,

> [u]p to 19.3% reductions were reported for health outcomes such as diabetes...and large average reductions reported for food system greenhouse gas emissions and land use...and extreme greenhouse gas reductions of up to 80% associated with vegan diets [sic]. (Jarmul et al. 2020:11)

Strong evidence points to plant-based diets being more environmentally friendly than those based on nonhuman animal consumption (Bryant 2022; Clark and Tilman 2017; Coffey, Lillywhite, and Oyebode 2022; Sabaté and Soret 2014). On average, a fully plant-based diet is associated with the lowest freshwater footprint of all diets (Konar and Marston 2020; Vanham, Mekonnen, and Hoekstra 2013; Vettori et al. 2022). Global plant-based diets are considered essential for mitigating global climate catastrophe (Cardwell 2022; Mbow et al. 2019). Evidence has shown that instead of using land for nonhuman animal agriculture and using it for plant-based food production, "by 2050 [this] could lead to sequestration of 332–547 $GtCO_2$, equivalent to 99–163% of the CO_2 emissions budget consistent with a 66% chance of limiting warming to 1.5 °C" (Hayek et al. 2020:2).

Researchers and governments have long underestimated the carbon cost of using land for nonhuman animal use. Searchinger et al. (2018) assessed the greenhouse gas emissions of various "food" items, taking into account their uses of land, and found that "foods" made from nonhuman animals are wildly inefficient. They also found that a diet comprising only plant-based foods was the most efficient at land use and greenhouse gas emissions. George Manibot (2022) of *The Guardian* summed up another important aspect of this research: "while the global average cost of soybeans is 17kg of carbon dioxide for each kilogram of protein, the average carbon opportunity cost of a kilogram of beef protein is an astounding 1,250kg." Land is finite, and its use is not neutral on the environment or people.

It's indisputable that human exploitation of nonhuman animals is not the only manifestation of harm done to the planet's ecosystems. However, since it is a relatively large part of the problem, doing something about it cannot be deprioritized or postponed. And rather than being inconsequential beings with little individual agency to create change, it's essential to understand that we actually *can* do something to help mitigate this disastrous problem. But consumer awareness of the differences in environmental impacts of various products considered "food" is lacking, to say the least. For instance, Hartmann, Furtwaengler, and Siegrist (2022:5) found that consumers "generally seemed to underestimate the environmental impact of animal-based products and overestimate the environmental impact of meat substitutes."

Greenwashing
Clare, Maani, and Milner (2022:5-7) found that companies that are based on the commodification of nonhuman animal flesh, specifically "red" and "processed" forms, engage in propaganda-based marketing. This marketing frames the health and environmental harms of these forms of consumption as "still open for debate," "most people have no need to worry," "keep eating meat to be healthy," and "no need to cut down to be green." These companies can continue profiting from the pain and suffering by obscuring the data showing how nonhuman animal exploitation has many negative consequences for human health, the environment, and nonhuman animals (Taft 2022; Willett et al. 2019). The tactics of denial, funding, and lobbying that nonhuman animal agricultural industries engage in have been compared to those of the oil, gas, and tobacco industries.[43][44][45][46]

The various industries that make up nonhuman animal agriculture spend a lot of money to influence politicians, especially Republicans in the US. From 2020 data at *OpenSecrets.org*, a nonpartisan and nonprofit organization that tracks campaign contributions in the US, shows that the "livestock" industry, which is "largely composed of individual ranchers and the organizations that represent them," contributes to both Democrats and Republicans, but more so for the latter; 64% of donations went to Republicans (OpenSecrets 2020a). The dairy industry donated 63% to Republicans (OpenSecrets 2020b); 88% of the "meat" processing and products industry goes to Republicans (OpenSecrets 2020c); and the "poultry" and egg industries donate a whopping 91% to Republicans (OpenSecrets 2020d). Nonhuman animal agricultural industries also play heavily into trying to downplay or mischaracterize the science of the effects of the industries on the climate crisis: "The largest meat and dairy companies in the U.S. have spent a considerable amount of time, money, and effort into downplaying the link between animal agriculture and the global climate catastrophe, and into fighting climate policy more generally," states an author of a study about the industry's lobbying efforts and influence in politics (NYU News 2021). The study's authors also say, "US beef and dairy companies appear to act collectively in ways similar to the fossil fuel industry, which built an extensive climate change countermovement" (Samuel 2021). Speciesism and capitalism work in tandem to increase profits and human supremacy.

There has also been a propagandistic move by "beef" companies and lobbyists to portray the production of their "products" in the US as methane-neutral since 1986 and "may not be contributing much at all to global warming" (Stanescu 2019). They began using a highly criticized methane emissions metric called "GWP*" (Global Warming Potential) to do this. This metric is described as "focus[ing] on changes in methane emissions, penalizing new or growing sources and putting less blame on large, steady emitters, like cattle herds in well-to-do countries." They explain, "Under GWP*, the 80 million-cattle herd in the U.S. counts little toward increased warming because of its stable size. But a far smaller herd in a country like Ethiopia gets blamed for increasing atmospheric methane—and the accompanying warming—simply because its cattle population is growing" (Elgin 2021).

Further Reading:

- Boscardin, Livia. 2018. "Greenwashing the Animal-Industrial: Complex Sustainable Intensification and the Livestock Revolution." in *Contested Sustainability Discourses in the Agrifood System*, edited by D. H. Constance, J. T. Konefal, and M. Hatanaka. London: Routledge.
- Hannan, Jason. 2020. *Meatsplaining: The Animal Agriculture Industry and the Rhetoric of Denial*. NSW, Australia: Sydney University Press.

Regenerative grazing

The term "regenerative agriculture" (RA) has been around for several decades, but its popularity took off in the late-2010s (Giller et al. 2021). The concept does not have a universal definition, and answers will vary depending on who is responding. Schreefel et al. (2020) provide this provisional definition based on their review of RA literature:

> an approach to farming that uses soil conservation as the entry point to regenerate and contribute to multiple provisioning, regulating and supporting ecosystem services, with the objective that this will enhance not only the environmental, but also the social and economic dimensions of sustainable food production. (P. 5)

RA clearly has admirable goals in mind. Those goals, however, do not have standards or procedures that are set in stone; what "supporting ecosystem services" and "enhanc[ing]...the environment" means to someone depends on their own social and scientific views (5). Unfortunately, most RA advocates view it as allowing for or even necessitating nonhuman animal use in the processes.

So-called "regenerative grazing," "holistic management," and "intensive rotational grazing" are often lauded by the nonhuman animal agricultural industry as an environmentally-friendly approach to grazing. The theory behind this type of grazing, as Nobari (2021:386) describes, goes something like this:

> [H]ealthy grasslands are great at sequestering carbon, therefore we need more healthy grasslands. Large ruminants are a key component of healthy grasslands (by breaking up the soil with their hooves, for instance) and cattle are large ruminants, therefore we need to keep cattle in depleted grasslands. [Regenerative grazing advocates] argue that if we manage cattle correctly (i.e., so they mimic the grazing behavior of the wild grazing animal herds in nature), they will restore the grasslands that have been depleted by industrial agriculture and other harmful practices and the new, healthy grasslands will sequester carbon.

These hypotheses have been critically assessed and have not been found to be evidence-based (Briske et al. 2013; Briske et al. 2014; Carter and Mehta 2021; Carter et al. 2014; Dutkiewicz and Rosenberg 2021; Ranganathan et al. 2020). A report by the Food Climate Research Network (Garnett et al. 2017) came to a few conclusions regarding the evidence, or lack thereof, of grazing for regenerative purposes. They asked, "could grazing ruminants also help sequester carbon in soils, and if so, to what extent might this compensate?" To this, they answered, "not much" (118). Regarding GHG emissions, the authors explained that scaling up any grazing system to match the level of intensity of standard confined systems ("factory-farming") "would have very damaging consequences for land use change and associated CO2 release" (121). Though their final concluding remarks are incredibly generous and diplomatic (and through an anthropocentric lens), they should be read carefully:

> The inescapable conclusion of this report is that while grazing livestock have their place in a sustainable food system, that place is limited. Whichever way one looks at it, and whatever the system in question the anticipated continuing rise in production and consumption of animal products is cause for concern. With their growth, it becomes harder by the day to tackle our climatic and other environmental challenges. (P. 124)

A report (Eldridge et al. 2016:1273) regarding the effects of grazing on Australian rangelands drew a more negative outlook:

> Grazing reduced plant biomass (40%), animal richness (15%), and plant and animal abundance, and plant and litter cover (25%), but had no effect on plant richness nor soil function…Grazing effects were largely negative, even at very low levels of grazing. Overall, our results suggest that livestock grazing in Australia is unlikely to produce positive outcomes for ecosystem structure, function, and composition or even as a blanket conservation tool…

An evidence-based review of the available literature on grazing's impacts on free-roaming nonhuman animals (wildlife) showed mostly mixed or negative results (Schieltz and Rubenstein 2016). Another study found that grazing increases GHG emissions rather than acting solely as a carbon sink, negatively affects native plants through trampling and other means, and affects ecosystems by making them warmer and drier (Kauffman et al. 2022).

A common focus in the ideas of (nonhuman animal-based) RA and grazing revolves around using "marginal" land for grazing. It is said that this type of land is of "little" use and, therefore, would be "wasted" if not used for agricultural purposes. Dutkiewicz and Rosenberg (2021) describe this way of viewing and treating "marginal" lands as "capitalist assumptions" created by those ranchers that stand to profit from them:

> Conventionally defined, "marginal land" is land that has little current agricultural or industrial value, often because of poor soil, water resources, or climate conditions. What ranchers mean is that grazing cattle can extract value, in the form of commoditized beef, from dry, rocky, difficult to access lands. Of course, such lands are only "marginal" from an instrumental, Lockean view that all land must be worked to create value. But from a biodiversity and ecosystem health perspective, so-called marginal lands can be thriving, biodiverse habitats for myriad flora and fauna, which can be disrupted by the introduction of grazers.

They go on to explain how this way of thinking is rooted in American colonialism against Indigenous peoples, where colonists often used the pretext of "waste" and "emptiness" to violently uproot Indigenous lifeways and ecosystems and replace them with "productive" commercial ranching.' And consider one last point from these authors that really drives a stake through the heart of the capitalist vampirism involved in all of this:

> [The] mismatches between theory and empirics prompts an important question: Who *does* benefit from more demand for holistic-grazed beef? Ranchers and dairy farmers, of course. Regenerative ranching begins with the assumption that cattle must be commercially ranched and then backfills an ecological narrative to sustain that assumption. (Dutkiewicz and Rosenberg 2021)

A now-infamous study was published in 2020 that supposedly showed that a nonhuman animal farm, White Oak Pastures in Georgia, US, was capturing more carbon in the soil than it emitted in the lifetimes of all the nonhuman animals that they kept by using regenerative agricultural methods (Rowntree et al. 2020). This statement implies that the company is carbon-negative. However, the study also demonstrates significant conflicts of interest. Although these conflicts of interest do not debunk the study necessarily, as considering such would be committing an association fallacy; this type of fallacy happens when one seeks to disprove another's claim by associating them with something or someone considered negative, one must keep in mind that General Mills, Inc. funded the study, which purchases from White Oak Pastures. Additionally, the two research authors and the initial study that preceded it have career ties to General Mills, Inc. Carter and Mehta (2021) also thoroughly debunked the study.

Nobari (2021:385) criticizes the greenwashing involved in regenerative agriculture that uses nonhuman animals:

> With a sleight of hand, regenerative grazing proponents have transformed grazing from a destructive colonial practice to a necessity, critical for our survival. These vocal and influential advocates have leveraged the increased awareness of the central role of food in the current climate crisis to sell their message, contending that holistic and well-managed grazing is a key component to restoring ecosystems, fighting desertification and climate change, and building sustainable food systems.

Similarly, Cusworth et al. (2022) contend that the regenerative agriculture movement has "rebranded" itself from earlier modes of nonhuman animal use to harken back to what its advocates see as "earlier" methods that are more "natural." One of the ways that they do this is by framing nonhuman animal use as crucial and necessary in agriculture. There is also a large current within these industries and organizations that seems to grow animosity toward critics of nonhuman animal use, as exhibited by one author in *The American Journal of Economics and Sociology*:

> The role of animal agriculture in climate change has been highly politicized recently with many well-meaning people advocating meatless diets as a way to reduce or eliminate the contribution of livestock to greenhouse gas emissions. However, this viewpoint does not take into account the larger picture of how ecosystems function. *It is simply not possible to sequester the necessary amounts of carbon dioxide in the soil to slow global warming without utilizing grazing animals, particularly since grasslands are one of the largest terrestrial biomes on the planet.* Cattle are not the problem—our management of them is. (White 2020:808-9) [emphasis from original text]

The author goes on to quote Gabe Brown's (2018) pro-regenerative agriculture (nonhuman animal use-based) book:

> I thoroughly enjoy debating with vegetarians and vegans as to the importance of animals on the landscape. My contention is that if they are truly concerned about the health of ecosystems, they have to recognize the benefits that grazing ruminants provide, even if they choose not to partake of eating meat. (White 2020:809)

Removing nonhuman animals once grazing in a particular area has been shown to have significant positive effects (Kauffman et al. 2022). Filazzola et al.'s (2020) research has demonstrated that removal in these areas increases nonhuman animal abundance, biodiversity, and especially plants, pollinators, and herbivores. They found that grazing reduced the abundance and diversity of many types of native herbivores, which includes various small mammals. It also reduced the number of local predators. We must also remember that these environmental impacts, typically shown in numbers, charts, and graphs, do not even reflect the full implications of nonhuman animal agriculture. They rarely consider the torturous months and years, the emotional devastation, the heartache of losing one's loved ones, the fear and dread and trauma, or the deaths experienced by the nonhuman animals involved. These environmental assessments, at best, only capture some of the side effects of unnecessarily exploiting people.

It's also important to use every tool we can think of that allows us to avoid, as much as is possible and practicable, harms to all people, which includes humans and nonhuman animals. If regenerative agriculture is a framework that we should apply to food production, and I believe it probably is, we should look at what a vegan approach could and currently does look like.[47] [48] [49] Veganic agriculture is a great place to start (Biocyclic Vegan International 2022; Vegan Organic Network 2022; The Vegan Society 2017; Veganic Agriculture Network 2022). As we have seen, there is no reason that the grazing of nonhuman animals is necessary for carbon sequestration or in increasing biodiversity in a given area; in fact, grazing actively does not help in those areas. Agriculture does not necessitate nonhuman animal use (Mann 2020), but it often is a given in mainstream society that nonhuman animal use is inherent to any system. Nobari (2021:382) explains these assumptions further:

> When domesticated animals are depicted as helpful to the system—be it through manure, tilling, labor, or other—lack of knowledge around other ways of fulfilling the same functions makes it seem that the only alternative is an agriculture based on fossil fuels. Other ways of ecological farming have long been practiced but they are not readily acknowledged. It is somewhat ironic that the early study of agroecology largely focused on the milpa, a Mesoamerican farming system that is based on corn, beans, and squash and did not traditionally rely on farm animals for labor or inputs. In the milpa system, the beans complement the corn by fixing atmospheric nitrogen in the soil, which is then used by the corn and avoids depleting the soil. Agroecology scholarship has also touted the modern

use of green manures, which uses the same principle (soil fertility is increased by growing legumes that fix nitrogen in the soil). Despite this, many agroecology advocates present the integration of crops and farm animals as a default aspect of closed-looped systems.

7

Ethics—How Should We Respond to All This?

*Do not unjustly eat fish the water has given up, and do not desire as food the flesh of slaughtered animals,
Or the white milk of mothers who intended its pure draught for their young, not for noble ladies.
And do not grieve the unsuspecting birds by taking their eggs; for injustice is the worst of crimes.
And spare the honey which the bees get industriously from the flowers of fragrant plants;
For they did not store it that it might belong to others, nor did they gather it for bounty and gifts.
I washed my hands of all this; and wish that I had perceived my way before my hair went gray!*

—Abū al-ʿAlāʾ al-Maʿarrī (CE 973-1057), a blind Arab poet, philosopher, and one of the earliest known people that could be considered "vegan," wrote a poem titled "I No Longer Steal From Nature", which is partially quoted here

JOHN TALLENT

Touch me again, and I will fucking kill you!

—Petrol Girls, from their song "Touch Me Again"[50]

It might be helpful at this point to remember the path we've taken so far in this book. We examined how logical fallacies often alter our perceptions of truth and knowledge. Keeping those in mind, we then sought to exist within the same reality as one another by unlearning some of the things that we were taught to be true but are false. Doing this makes it apparent that nonhuman animals have been *under*estimated in their capacities, and plants are often *over*estimated in theirs. With nonhuman animals repeatedly being denied a full self because of human beliefs and assumptions, a type of individual discrimination and structural oppression has emerged called speciesism. We then found that speciesism, created within our psyches, perpetuated through our social interactions, and glued together in an overarching and patterned system of domination and oppression, has had devastating, torturous, and heartbreaking effects on all life on this planet. So now we have arrived at the point at which we must ask ourselves, how should we respond to all of this?

Since most, if not all, nonhuman animals are sentient and conscious, by which I mean they are self-aware and experience pain, it's strange that we all go through the psychological gymnastics of trying to pretend that 1) nonhuman animals don't suffer or they suffer less than us, 2) we as humans and as consumers are not directly and unnecessarily influencing this suffering, and 3) we don't have to change ourselves to address this human-caused suffering on other *people*. We looked at "meat-related" cognitive dissonance and its effects on our views and treatments of other animals. And we learned that it involves trying to alleviate the discomfort we feel when presented with the dissonance between how we believe we care about other animals and how we treat them badly. Another concept that can be applicable here relates to cognitive dissonance: bad faith.

French existentialist philosopher Jean-Paul Sartre (1905-1980) introduced the idea of *bad faith* in his 1943 book, *Being and Nothingness: An Essay on Phenomenological Ontology*. This idea is very similar to the concept mentioned a few sections ago, "doublethink," which came from the book *1984*. Due to its complex and abstract nature, I will risk reducing the concept of "bad faith" to an admittedly diluted but easier-to-manage and articulate definition of "self-deception." "Bad faith" commonly means attempting to deceive someone else. For instance, so-called "trolls" on the Internet often try to "debate" others, but their real purpose is to waste people's time and to make them angry; it can be said that the troll is engaging in the discussion "in bad faith." In contrast, Sartre's use of the concept means that a person is deceiving *themselves* rather than another person. As such, the person is both the "deceiver" and the "deceived." Since Sartre rejects Freudian psychology's notion of the compartmentalization of the mind into the realms of "conscious," "pre-conscious," and "unconscious," Sartre sees the mind as a single, conscious entity that is aware of itself. And since the conscious mind is aware of itself, according to him, it cannot "hide" anything in an unseen part of itself. Bad faith creates a paradox of someone lying to themselves and (seemingly) not knowing that they are lying to themselves (Kirby 2003; Sartre [1943] 2018). For Sartre, the essence of bad faith ultimately comes down to this fact: you cannot lie to yourself, so bad faith is an intentional act by one's consciousness:

> [T]he person to whom one is lying and the person who is lying are one and the same person, which means that I must know—insofar as I am the deceiver—the truth that is hidden from me insofar as I am deceived. Better still, I must know this truth very precisely in order to hide it all the more carefully from myself… (Sartre [1943] 2018:155)

For Sartre, cognitive dissonance always follows bad faith, but bad faith does not always follow cognitive dissonance. This is because bad faith creates the paradox of both knowing the lie and (again, seemingly) not knowing the lie (Bahnmiller 2015:7).

I mention the concept of bad faith because I (and many others before me[51][52][53][54]) think it is particularly relevant to how we currently relate with other animals. We know other animals used by humans are harmed in the process. We know that by eating them and buying things made from them, we are personally involved in harming them. And most of us understand that other animals have feelings and emotions. But, we push those facts down and reach and claw for comforting excuses for why we perpetuate all the harm even when we don't need to participate. We tell ourselves pacifying fictions about the naturalness of eating other animals, how all vegans are sick and dying from malnutrition, that soybean plants are conscious like cows, and that those that advocate for these animals have no moral right to do so. We all understand these things, yet so many of us continue with the views and habits of human supremacy. In this way, we are all acting in bad faith, in self-deception. We are our deceivers, and we are also deceived by ourselves. As this psychological process flows, cognitive dissonance sets in, and we use some of the methods we examined in the section on social psychology, like avoidance and denial, to be able to push the truth out of our minds. By doing this, we may assuage the discomfort and maintain our fantasies about a human-nonhuman animal symbiosis in what we are doing. And the illusion continues, as countless humans die from preventable diseases brought on by diet (Kim, Caulfield, and Rebholz 2018), the environment plunges deeper into the Anthropocene[55] extinction, and trillions upon trillions of sentient, conscious, thinking, and feeling nonhuman animals are tortured and killed in proportions never before seen in the history of our planet. So, how should we respond to this? Let's seek out the expertise of ethicists.

I believe we can start in the "modern" nonhuman animal movement to avoid tons of tedious and unnecessary history. The 1975 publication of ethicist Peter Singer's *Animal Liberation* proved pivotal in this movement. The book describes in often horrific detail how nonhuman animals are used for food and experimentation, why speciesism is wrong and why human ideas of equality should be extended to other animals and the importance of responding to nonhuman animal exploitation with vegetarianism and veganism. Singer uses a utilitarianist framework as a basis for his ethical views (Singer [1975] 2015), a consequentialist ethical framework that determines what is morally "good" as whatever produces the most good (Driver 2014). For instance, if experimenting on one nonhuman animal or one human would lead to "the greater good," then it would be ethically "good" to do so.

Another important text for the nonhuman animal movement was philosopher Tom Regan's book *The Case for Animal Rights*, published in 1983. In contrast with Peter Singer's utilitarianism, Regan steeped many of his views in Kantianism, a deontological[56] ethical philosophy that grounds the capacity for rationality as necessary for moral value. Regan rejected rationality as necessary for moral value and instead saw those that are "subjects-of-a-life," or those whose lives matter to them personally, as having an intrinsic moral value, moral rights, and a right not to be harmed or used as a resource by others, whether they are human or nonhuman (Regan 1983). A significant difference between Regan's view on nonhuman animals and Singer's is that Regan's approach concerns nonhuman animal *rights*, and Singer's approach concerns nonhuman animal *welfare*. Singer's views often revolve around the treatment of nonhuman animals, while Regan's centralizes intrinsic rights for humans and nonhuman animals with "subjects-of-a-life." Regan was known as an abolitionist vegan, meaning he believed in the abolition of nonhuman animal use in all forms. These differences with Singer are amplified and brought to the forefront by the following important figure in the nonhuman animal movement.

Gary L. Francione is a philosophy and law professor in the US who has written many books critiquing the nonhuman animal welfare movement, the organizations that support it, and the property status of other animals; he is also a major advocate of veganism. When I first got into nonhuman animal issues, I was reading a lot of Peter Singer and agreed with a lot of what he said—that all changed when I read Francione. In my early university days at East Carolina University in North Carolina, I read Francione's pointed criticisms of Singer in his books *Rain without Thunder: The Ideology of the Animal Rights Movement* and *Introduction to Animal Rights: Your Child or the Dog?* and was immediately captivated by his views. What drew me in so intensely was the fact that his main ideas, especially when he explained them, were clear, concise, and seemed to make sense instantly. Rather than determining moral worth by "subject-of-a-life" and the possibilities for future well-being, as Regan does, and rejecting Singer's utilitarian calculation and rejection of rights, Francione sees sentience as giving any person moral worth and, thus, the right not to be treated as property by another. Additionally, Francione theorizes that, unlike Regan, cognitive characteristics beyond sentience are not necessary to factor into a person's moral rights. Regarding welfare versus rights, Francione believes that mere nonhuman animal welfare "protections" do not safeguard their interests and rights adequately. As opposed to rights-based approaches, which would give persons inalienable rights from being used as resources by others, Francione believes that nonhuman animal welfarist approaches only seek to make usage and treatment of nonhuman animals "more humane" and to protect the economic interests of nonhuman animal agribusinesses; he argues that this inherently violates the moral value of any sentient being with rights. He also believes that veganism and an end to the status of nonhuman animals as property are the only solutions to nonhuman animal oppression. Like Regan, Francione is an abolitionist vegan; he developed what he calls the "abolitionist approach" to nonhuman animal rights. (Francione 1996; [2000] 2007; 2009; Steiner 2011).

Singer, Regan, and Francione are frequently called the "fathers" of the modern nonhuman animal movement. They are not, by far, the only voices in the movement, however. The nonhuman animal movement is large and diverse, and this trio could be said to represent the more liberal approaches. All three men range from relatively politically progressive to somewhat socialist. However, they all theorize within the confines of capitalism as a mechanism of significant change for other animals. Peter Singer, who considers himself part of "the Left," has said that he does not identify as an anti-capitalist and has talked about Marxism's positive and negative aspects (Lewis 2010). Tom Regan, who died in 2017, did not speak much on politics or economics. However, I found an interview with him from 2010 where he disagreed with the interviewer that nonhuman animal liberation could not happen until capitalism was dismantled. The interviewer said that Regan responded that "[h]e felt if enough consciousness was raised and laws were changed, animal rights could happen under any system" (Shields 2017). Finally, Gary Francione has been quite vocal about his political and economic views. On social media, he has advocated (sometimes, anyway) for progressive ideals (Francione 2014; Francione 2022).

Outside of the so-called "fathers" of the movement, it's important that I mention some of the other influential people and ideologies that may not get as much credit. Ecofeminism has had a tremendous impact on the nonhuman animal movement. Academics such as Carol J. Adams, who wrote *The Sexual Politics of Meat: A Feminist-Vegetarian Critical Theory* (1990) and *The Pornography of Meat* (2004); Josephine Donovan, Greta Gaard, and Marti Kheel have paved the path for vegan ecofeminism. This diverse set of theories often posits a connection between the exploitation of nonhuman animals and human women—speciesism and sexism. Black veganism has been a growing movement, often connecting the oppression of nonhuman animals and humans. It has been a philosophy that often critiques white normativity, an issue in mainstream nonhuman animal circles. Some of the most important figures within this movement have been Aph and Syl Ko (Ko and Ko 2018; Ko 2019), Christopher Sebastian, Dick Gregory, A. Breeze Harper (Harper 2010), Bryant Terry, and many others. Then there are the vegan anarchists (veganarchists), who frequently call for direct action against nonhuman animal exploitation, human oppression, and State violence; this book is heavily influenced by the movement within veganarchism known as total liberationism (more on that later).

|129|

Finally, it's crucial to briefly talk about the more mainstream and non-radical approaches in the movement for nonhuman animals. These would be the viewpoints and organizations that do not critique capitalism, have worked closely with the nonhuman animal agricultural industries, do not openly embrace or call for veganism, or can be considered nonhuman animal welfarist in ideology. People for the Ethical Treatment of Animals (PETA), Farm Sanctuary, Humane Society of the United States (HSUS), Vegan Outreach, Animal Legal Defense Fund (ALDF), and countless others across the world fit into this category. While some of the organizations may promote veganism to some extent or an end to the exploitation of nonhuman animals, they also may not enter into political discussions about capitalism or human oppression, the importance of veganism as critical, or rights over welfare measures. These types of organizations may promote "part-time veganism," vegetarianism, "flexitarianism," or simply reducing flesh consumption. Some even work hand-in-hand with companies that directly exploit nonhuman animals. This type of advocacy is almost wholly incompatible with the types of approaches mentioned in some of the previous paragraphs of this section.

The assumptions throughout this book will be that every sentient being deserves the intrinsic right not to be property or a resource for another. It also means that from how I define veganism's practices, every human on Earth with moral agency also has the duty, obligation, responsibility, and ethical requirement to live a vegan life. Furthermore, I believe that anarchist political, social, and economic praxes are also essential to fight against all oppression and create a better world for all of us. This leads us to be anti-authoritarian and to critique and dismantle all harmful forms of hierarchy, including capitalism.

Further Reading:

- Adams, Carol J., and Lori Gruen. 2022. *Ecofeminism: Feminist Intersections with Other Animals and Each Other.* 2nd ed. New York, NY: Bloomsbury Publishing USA.
- Jones, Robert. 2021. "Why Is Sentience Ethically Significant?" *Rcjones.me.* Retrieved December 9, 2022 (https://rcjones.me/why-is-sentience-ethically-significant/).
- Nobis, Nathan. 2016. *Animals & Ethics 101: Thinking Critically about Animal Rights.* S.L.: Open Philosophy Press.

8

We have All Been Misled about Veganism

Whether you are vegan or not or describe yourself as Leftist, no doubt you have been misled about what veganism is. The media has told you and even vegans themselves that veganism is a diet; that to be vegan, one must consume a plant-based diet, no matter what; that people can be vegan if their only focus is on better health or concerns about the environment; or that some people cannot go vegan due to specific disabilities, poverty, or a lack of access to healthy plant-based foods. Let me be clear: I believe these statements about veganism are wrong, but probably not for the reasons you might think. Let's investigate further.

Many of the debates surrounding nonhuman animals and veganism on the Left result from misunderstandings on both sides about veganism. In this chapter, I will attempt to clarify why both nonvegan Leftists and Leftist vegans miscommunicate the nuances of veganism and, therefore, cannot adequately delve into a fruitful discussion with one another. Without a clear understanding of veganism, advocating for it, critiquing it, and improving it is next to impossible. So, let's take a look at how both sides of these discussions *typically* conceptualize veganism:

Vegans:

The last thing I want to do is to give the impression that the vegan community is monolithic. The dominant view, however, is that veganism is the belief that killing and using other animals is wrong and that this belief logically entails certain personal practices that avoid purposeful nonhuman animal use and death. Such practices would include not viewing animals as a source of food, clothing, entertainment, or scientific experimentation. It is also a common understanding within the community that people that eat or use nonhuman animals **for any purpose** are, by definition, not vegan. It is also generally understood that people who do not particularly concern themselves with the oppression of other animals can be considered "vegan" if they eat a plant-based diet.

Non-vegan Leftists:

Views about, and understandings of, veganism and vegans can also be diverse when enunciated by non-vegan Leftists (and non-vegans, in general). It has been my experience that this group is split on whether veganism is defined by the abstention of all "foods" made from the bodies of nonhuman animals or only certain "foods." Surprisingly, it is often believed that vegans consume bees' honey[57], chickens' eggs[58], and even fishes[59] and mollusks[60] (clams, oysters, scallops, etc.). The most common criticisms I have experienced that non-vegan Leftists level against vegans is that veganism is "ableist" and "classist." This claim is a reaction to the mainstream vegan community's view that everyone can afford, thrive on, and have access to a fully plant-based diet devoid of all nonhuman animal products. Non-vegan Leftists assert that many people are poor, disabled, or lack access to many plant-based options due to systemic issues like **food deserts**[61]. I think the best way to begin attending to these differences in understanding regarding veganism is to first look at how it has been defined throughout its history and everyday interactions.

JOHN TALLENT

A history of ambiguity

A member of the very first vegan organization, Leslie J. Cross of The Vegan Society (n.d.a), suggested as far back as 1949 for the definition of veganism to be "[t]he principle of the emancipation of animals from exploitation by man." The Vegan Society's website goes on to say, "This [definition] is later clarified as 'to seek an end to the use of animals by man for food, commodities, work, hunting, vivisection, and by all other uses involving exploitation of animal life by man.'" The current "official" definition of veganism by the UK's Vegan Society is:

> Veganism is a philosophy and way of living which seeks to exclude—as far as is possible and practicable—all forms of exploitation of, and cruelty to, animals for food, clothing or any other purpose; and by extension, promotes the development and use of animal-free alternatives for the benefit of animals, humans and the environment. In dietary terms it denotes the practice of dispensing with all products derived wholly or partly from animals.

Although some of the first few iterations[62] of the definition focused almost exclusively on veganism in dietary terms, we can see that the later versions saw veganism as much more than mere abstention from non-human animal-based "food" consumption. With the current definition, veganism (from the UK's Vegan Society, at least) has become a *philosophy* and a *way of living* that strives to remove all manifestations of the use of nonhuman animals by humans. Despite the "official" definition evolving into a more holistic, nonhuman animal rights concept, veganism is still reduced to simple dietary terms in most conversations and debates today.

Dictionaries do not help this problem, either. At the time of writing, Merriam-Webster.com defines a vegan in this way:

HOW TO UNITE THE LEFT ON ANIMALS

> : a strict vegetarian who consumes no food (such as meat, eggs, or dairy products) that comes from animals
>
> also : one who abstains from using animal products (such as leather) (Merriam-Webster n.d.)

From this definition, we can gather that a vegan does not consume anything related to nonhuman animals as food, and (maybe "and"? Maybe "either/or"?) a vegan does not use nonhuman animal "products," like leather. So, no flesh, no eggs, no milk, no honey, no leather, no silk, no fur, no wool. OK, got it. But what about vivisection? Zoos? Aquariums? Rodeos? Dogfighting? "Trophy" hunting? Bullfighting? Dropkicking a giraffe for "fun?" There doesn't seem to be a coherence to how veganism is defined. Someone typing "what is veganism" into Google will inevitably be misinformed and probably confused.[63]

One major problem is that the "official" definition of veganism ends with this sentence: "In dietary terms it denotes the practice of dispensing with all products derived wholly or partly from animals." I think that sentence is extremely easy to misconstrue as presenting two "types" of veganism that people can choose from—the "ethical vegan" type[64] or the "dietary vegan" type (also sometimes referred to as a "health vegan" or "vegan for health"). I cannot tell you how often I've seen this differentiation presented. Hell, even the UK's Vegan Society mentions this separation (Casamitjana 2020). The strange thing is that if one were to take this categorical distinction at face value, someone considering themselves as just a "dietary vegan" would be making the first part of the definition irrelevant. How can veganism be "a philosophy and way of living which seeks to exclude...all forms of exploitation" of nonhuman animals, yet then be claimed by a person who only believes and practices the abstention of certain "food" items? This distinction is completely without necessity. It is clear to many vegans that the last sentence of the official definition is not some standalone form of veganism but rather a small explanation of what veganism's philosophy and way of living would demand regarding food practices. Maybe a more explicit, updated definition is in order.

But let's take a step back from here for a moment. I'm not advocating for definitional originalism with the Vegan Society's definition of veganism, where we argue forever about what the original members "meant" for veganism to entail. Even if they were decidedly creating a veganism where the "way of living" people and the "diet" people could both claim the "vegan" identity, a veganism that evolves philosophically based on social and cultural contexts is important. One of this book's main arguments is that whether veganism *is* or *was* in the past, it *should* be a movement based on *total liberation*. Whether we attempt to use the principles and definitional terms from its founders or we blaze a new trail into the future, any logical regard for nonhuman animals demands a comprehensive practice of ending harm to nonhuman animals, as well as a likewise regard for humans and ecosystems; this is the essence of total liberation.

The "desert island" scenario is not always only theoretical

A common counterargument to veganism is the "desert island" scenario. In this scenario, vegans are asked if they would continue consuming only plant-based foods if stranded on a desert island with little to no edible plants. Essentially, the questioned vegan is forced to admit that they would kill and eat nonhuman animals in a survival situation or else they would risk certain death from starvation. This line of questioning is designed to show that vegans are supposedly hypocritical in their beliefs. And this argumentation might seem to be the perfect way to debunk and corner vegans, but it is not. This "you are also a hypocrite" situation is itself logically fallacious.

The "desert island" fallacy falls within a few different types of logical fallacies, but the one most important to this issue and this discussion, which we examined earlier, is called a *tu quoque* fallacy (pronounced "too qwoe-qwee). Latin for "you also," this fallacy does not usually attempt to make any strong or valid argument, other than to paint those it's directed at in a hypocritical light. Vegans claim they do not eat or use other animals, but if forced into a survival scenario, they might have to go against their usual beliefs to survive. And if vegans say that they do not eat or use other animals and they are shown how they might be forced to in certain dire situations, that will make them hypocritical to some extent, right? Let's look at two reasons why this is not how veganism, or any other ethical commitment, operates:

1. The "official" definition of veganism includes the phrase, "seeks to exclude—as far as is possible and practicable..."
2. All ethical claims necessarily contain the ethical assumption that "ought implies can."

Regarding reason (1), veganism can be seen as the good faith endeavor of eliminating nonhuman animal use—as much as can be reasonably expected. Note that there is no demand in absolutist terms on any person. All that is being sought is ending one's own contributions to nonhuman animal use as much as is feasible. Other synonyms for the word "practicable" (from the "official" definition) are "workable," "viable," "achievable," "attainable," "doable," "realistic," and "accessible." Remember, "practicable" is not the same as "practical." "Practicable" means that something is capable of being put into practice; "practical," on the other hand, means that something is sensible. And it is also essential to remember that this way of looking closer at the definition of veganism is not common in the vegan community, as personal experience leads me to understand. Viewing veganism as what is "viable" and "accessible" means accepting that the social practices involved in veganism will not necessarily look the same for every individual because every human on the planet has a different life and cannot possibly have the same circumstances. This is where the mainstream vegan movement and the "typical" vegan explanation of veganism fall short. For the record, I am not a medical, diet, nutrition, poverty, or food accessibility expert. Because of this, I have never felt comfortable with the common assumption within the vegan community that every human on Earth can afford, thrive, and access a completely plant-based diet. I do not find it helpful to make such broad assumptions that, at least at this point, are almost impossible to prove empirically. What can be said with some certainty is that most folks in "Western" societies will have little difficulty thriving, affording, and accessing a completely plant-based diet. To drive home this point, consider one of the earliest definitions of veganism by Leslie Cross (1951) of The Vegan Society:

> The Society pledges itself "in pursuance of its object" to seek to end the use of animals by man [sic] for food, commodities, work, hunting, vivisection and all other uses involving exploitation of animal life by man [sic]. Membership in the Society is available to all who wish to see the object achieved and who undertake to live *as closely to the ideal as personal circumstances permit.* [emphasis added]

The second reason (2) why the "desert island scenario" does not inherently "debunk" a commitment to veganism is due to the ethical standard known as "ought implies can." This concept was first stated by the German philosopher Immanuel Kant (1724-1804) (Stern 2004). In essence, it can be assumed that a person only has ethical obligations to do the things that they have the capacity to do. With this understanding in mind, a person has ethical obligations to nonhuman animals only as far as they have the capacity for them. If a person can reasonably eat a completely plant-based diet without putting themselves in danger, then they have an ethical obligation to do so. Logically, this would mean that if a person cannot eat a completely plant-based diet, then they should do so as much as they possibly and practicably can. This concept does not otherwise give carte blanche to consume and exploit nonhuman animals simply because a person has some limitations to their abilities.

As vegan philosopher and author Benny Malone puts it, "The existence of 'grey areas' in no way justifies not avoiding the 'black and white areas' (Malone 2022a).

However, the non-vegan Left routinely criticizes veganism and vegans as "classist" and "ableist" because they believe that some disabled and poor people are excluded from veganism. The mainstream vegan movement has not made eradicating this belief any easier. It is all too common to portray an unnuanced view of veganism as being *only* and *always* a diet free of other animals. This view *is* ableist and classist, and it should be criticized outright because it *does* exclude some poor and disabled people. This is not to say that there are no disabled people and no houseless or poor people that are vegan; this is wholly untrue. It contributes to a very problematic and incorrect view that erases the incredible diversity within the vegan community. The vegan community is not solely made up of wealthy, non-disabled, white people. For example, at this very moment in history, the fastest-growing demographic within veganism is Black folks (Reiley 2020).

Given this interpretation of veganism that I have laid out, does it really make sense to generalize veganism as "classist" and "ableist?" Wouldn't it make more sense to consider *certain vegans* and *particular views on veganism* ableist and classist? Admittedly, I began as one of those problematic and shitty vegans who never considered every person's circumstances when I first went vegan. I assumed everyone could eat, thrive, and access a completely plant-based diet, and I determined that anyone who couldn't was simply making a selfish excuse. It took learning more about the complexities of capitalism and ableism before I could comprehend these barriers. I was not intentionally seeking to be exclusionary in my beliefs, but the outcome made that exclusion inevitable. It was a mistake that I had made, and I'm sure it had negative effects on the disabled and poor folks that had the unfortunate luck to attempt to educate me on social media. Who knows precisely how opinions ultimately change psychologically, but I'm grateful for finally having a better understanding of veganism. Not seeking out more information and sticking to our beliefs no matter the new information we receive makes us no more informed than Flat Earthers, queer antagonists, and Christian fascists, right?

Gruen and Jones (2015:156) take issue with veganism being used as an identity and lifestyle, specifically in a way that "ascribe[s] moral purity and clean hands to veganism." The authors suggest that rather than using veganism as an identity and lifestyle that would falsely claim that vegans' lives are entirely "cruelty-free," a better way to conceptualize veganism is to think of it as something *aspirational*. If the vegan ideal is to end harm to nonhuman animals, including in our personal lives, then every vegan is doing their best to move toward that ideal.

Certain factions and individuals within the vegan movement do not accept these nuances, though. Often from the "Animals First" camps (Ko 2013), many of these vegans believe that the liberation of nonhuman animals should be prioritized "above" human liberation. They typically do not believe in structural barriers to eliminating nonhuman animal exploitation from individuals' lives, even poverty, access, and disability. To them, people should accept sickness and death if someone's circumstances would require nonhuman animal consumption or use. This thinking is steeped in extreme privilege and a lack of understanding of the nuances that exist in the definition of veganism and how every life has differing circumstances. Interestingly, not all these folks have had to make those personal commitments in their lives, but they insist on it for others. And not only do these "Animals First" vegans not believe in structural barriers to individuals' abilities, but they also do not believe that anyone should be considered "vegan" that consumes nonhuman animals, even if the person has no other choice. And this position does not only come from this "Animals First" camp, but I have found this worldview unnervingly common in many vegan communities.

HOW TO UNITE THE LEFT ON ANIMALS

If we were to interpret veganism and its practices like these "Animals First" vegans, the common saying that "not everyone can go vegan" would be correct. The typical way vegans answer this counterargument to veganism is to claim that plant-based foods are cheaper than non-human animal-based ones. This can be true[65][66], though it is not always the case. But this approach leads to making assumptions about other people's lives, including their monetary and medical situations. To be clear: poverty, ability, and class can affect people's consumption habits and choices, but there are many folks throughout the world who overcome those difficulties and succeed and thrive on a completely plant-based diet. Does this mean that is the case for every human in the world? Can we say empirically that no individual's ability to consume no nonhuman animal foods is hampered by access, poverty, or ability? If we are honest, we must admit that this question is almost impossible to answer. And since this is the case, it doesn't always make sense to convince others that strangers can generalize, diagnose, or treat their personal situations.

For many Leftist and intersectionality-aware[67] vegans, there are no accommodations for those with specific disabilities or who live in severe poverty. They believe that anyone identifying as "vegan" inherently does not consume or exploit nonhuman animals in any way. To avoid charges of "ableism" and "classism" to this specific interpretation of veganism, they often make the argument that "not everyone can be vegan, and that's OK." This argument makes sense, at first, because it does not place impossible ethical obligations on certain marginalized folks. It simply asks people to do as much as they can; however, those marginalized folks cannot claim the "vegan" identity. I think this is both unnecessary and makes veganism exclusionary. If some of the most marginalized people cannot consider themselves a part of the vegan movement through no fault of their own, it makes veganism an exercise of privilege.

Imagine a person that hates zoos, aquariums, and rodeos and refuses to support them. They think fur, leather, wool, and silk are "products" of violence and refuse to buy and wear them. They want nonhuman animal testing eliminated in favor of alternatives and refuse to purchase products that use nonhuman animals for testing. They rescue and adopt other animals when they can, and they would forever refuse to buy them from "pet" shops and breeders. They believe that humans are not the center of the universe and that speciesism is oppression. They seek a world in which nonhuman animals are no longer resources and commodities for humans. But, due to some disability, poverty, or access issues, this person could not survive or afford to eat a completely plant-based diet. Not because of a lack of trying or attempting to receive medical advice and nutritional information from a doctor—they exhausted those options. They eat plant-based as much as they possibly and practicably can to reduce their harm to nonhuman animals. This person is genuine in their belief and pursuit of liberation for everyone. This person does not seek exemptions for unethical behaviors and desires. If this person only ate plant-based foods, their survival would be jeopardized; this person's situation is not simply anecdotal evidence but is backed up by doctors and evidence-based science. Is this person not vegan?

The only things separating this person from an entirely plant-based diet and a diet based on other animals' bodies are certain illness or death. For them, "as far as is possible and practicable," from the "official" definition of veganism, is exactly what they are doing. This person understands that this part of the definition can't be misconstrued as "to the extent that you are willing or have the desire to go." It means to the extent that you can plausibly go. So, what is the point in excluding certain marginalized and vulnerable people from identifying in this community, not for lack of desire, willingness, or passion for nonhuman animal liberation, but simply based on their unwillingness to harm themselves or worse? Do we demand that every other vegan that can eat completely plant-based engage in such life-threatening tolls? What is "possible" and "practicable" varies from person to person and society to society, based on local and individual material conditions. If some people are required by veganism to risk their health and lives, then that means that all vegans are required to risk their health and lives, or else it is not a movement based on justice and equity.

Whether you believe it is what the current definition of veganism *intends* or what it *should be,* a clear but controversial statement can be made: *every single human on the planet, given that they have moral agency, can become a vegan.* (Side note: I know that morality is often considered a dirty word in some spheres on the Left, but I will talk more about morality later in the section on multiculturalism). My use of moral agency means that the person can understand "right" and "wrong" and act on that ability. For example, most humans can distinguish between "right" and "wrong" and choose whether to cause direct harm to others. Some humans, however, may be able to distinguish between "right" and "wrong" but may not have a complete choice.

Additionally, some people may be unable to distinguish between "right" and "wrong," and therefore, they cannot choose much of their behavior. Suppose you have the ability to distinguish between "right" and "wrong," "good" and "bad," and you likewise have the freedom and ability to make choices about your behaviors and beliefs. In that case, it means that you can augment your views about nonhuman animals (if needed) and make moral and ethical choices to whatever extent your life's circumstances allow. With this view of moral agency in mind, anyone who has it (can distinguish and can act accordingly) can choose to believe in and practice—as far as is possible and practicable—veganism.

JOHN TALLENT

The glaring potential for dishonesty

The possibility of some people being dishonest about their extenuating circumstances is not something to ignore. A common question raised by this view of veganism that I have attempted to lay out because it concedes that individual practice of veganism might look different based on each person's circumstances is that people can easily misrepresent their circumstances and continue to live a life of harming nonhuman animals unnecessarily. I think this will happen and already does happen. However, this certainty does not necessitate a universal practice of veganism that does not acknowledge conditions that can make it more difficult or impossible to reduce or eliminate the use and exploitation of nonhuman animals. The matter of dishonesty is not limited to the vegan movement. We can see dishonesty in beliefs and practices in every social movement. From my experience, the best way to determine whether people are genuine in their beliefs in nonhuman animal liberation is not by looking only at their practices but also at their beliefs. Having frank conversations with people gives fantastic opportunities to understand people's beliefs, hear other people's stories, and hopefully educate everyone involved. And with mutual, respectful communication like this, paternalistic approaches to seeking information about people's personal lives, which can be both ableist and classist, can be avoided. For example, some good questions to ask can be, "Do you believe nonhuman animals should be considered resources for humans?" "Realistically, what would it take for you to stop using other animals completely?" "Have you had any conversations with other folks with similar poverty/disability issues who succeeded in eating a completely plant-based diet (or whatever the nonhuman animal usage might be)?" "Is there anything practically that I can help you with?"

    I contend that a holistic understanding of nonhuman animal exploitation, which is interconnected with the oppressions of marginalized humans and the destruction of ecosystems, must take into account the structural barriers and individual circumstances that might prevent some people from consuming a completely plant-based diet (or may force them into using nonhuman animals in some way). A veganism with a comprehensive aim to dismantle the many forms of human and nonhuman animal oppression worldwide, must look to, and be guided by, a total liberationist framework. In the final chapter, I will sketch out what a total liberationist veganism could look like.

9

Plant-Based Diets

The mainstream vegan movement too often portrays a completely plant-based diet as a panacea. Numerous "vegan" documentaries, books, and quack doctors engage in terrible medical advice and dabble heavily in pseudoscience. So many people I've talked with over the years view an entirely plant-based diet as "unhealthy" or even "deadly."[68] A more nuanced, evidence-based approach to understanding plant-based diets requires us to acknowledge that there is empirical evidence to show that they can indeed be healthful and supplementation for one or more essential nutrients can be critical (and that's OK!).

There is strong evidence that a completely plant-based diet can be good or even great for most people's health (Bryant 2022; Coffey, Lillywhite, and Oyebode 2022; Herpich, Müller-Werdan, and Norman 2022; Lederer and Huber 2022; Marrone et al. 2021; Norman and Klaus 2020; Selinger et al. 2022). It can be beneficial for gut health (Glick-Bauer and Ming-Chin 2014); it has been shown to significantly reduce the risk of incidence of cancer by 15% (Dinu et al. 2016), and specifically colorectal cancer in people assigned "male" at birth (Kim et al. 2022); it "tend[s] to contain less saturated fat and cholesterol and more dietary fiber," and "[v]egans tend to…have lower serum cholesterol, and lower blood pressure, reducing their risk of heart disease" (Craig 2009); it "generally reduces the risk of developing chronic non-communicable degenerative diseases, such as metabolic syndrome (MetS)" (Marrone et al. 2021); it can be appropriate for athletes (Rogerson 2017; Wirnitzer 2020); it is appropriate for all stages of life (Craig 2021; Melina, Craig, and Levin 2016), including people who are pregnant (Sebastiani et al. 2019), babies (Salinas 2019; Sebastiani et al. 2019) and for breastfeeding (Karcz and Królak-Olejnik 2020), children (Sutter and Bender 2021), adults (Mariotti and Gardner 2019), and older adults (Mariotti and Gardner 2019); can be beneficial against the effects of Type 2 diabetes (Pollakova et al. 2021); and, if weight is a concern for you, it can also be helpful in that respect (Medawar et al. 2019).

Two things should always be stressed when it comes to plant-based diets, however: you should supplement vitamin B12 (Bakaloudi et al. 2021; Koeder and Perez-Cueto 2022; Niklewicz et al. 2022), and you may want to consult with your doctor. Some people consuming a completely plant-based diet may not eat a sufficiently well-rounded assortment of foods, so they can have deficiencies, such as "proteins, [Omega]-3 fatty acids, iron, vitamin D and calcium, zinc, [and] iodine" (Marrone et al. 2021:1). Deficiencies can happen in all types of diets, though, including diets based in the consumption of nonhuman animals. As Neufingerl and Eilander (2021:1) stress, "Meat-eaters [are] at risk of inadequate intakes of fiber, PUFA, α-linolenic acid (ALA), folate, vitamin D, E, calcium and magnesium." Marrone et al. (2021:1) state, "Oral food supplements especially fortified foods are recommended in these cases to restore the nutritional deficiencies." It is also essential to understand that certain deficiencies do not always lead to health issues (Bakaloudi et al. 2020).

Though I mentioned that your doctor should be consulted when necessary regarding diet, it is sad that nutrition education is not unanimous or expert-level with all doctors.[69] In a systemic review of nutrition education in medical schools, Crowley, Ball, and Hiddink (2019:e385) conclude that "nutrition is insufficiently incorporated into medical education, regardless of country, setting, or year of medical education." Pediatricians tend to have less education and knowledge of nutrition and plant-based diets (Anishchenko et al. 2022). Astonishingly, even cardiologists were found to be mostly deficient in nutrition knowledge in one study (Devries et al. 2017:1298):

> A total of 930 surveys were completed. Among cardiologists, 90% reported receiving no or minimal nutrition education during fellowship training, 59% reported no nutrition education during internal medicine training, and 31% reported receiving no nutrition education in medical school. Among cardiologists, 8% described themselves as having "expert" nutrition knowledge. Nevertheless, fully 95% of cardiologists believe that their role includes personally providing patients with at least basic nutrition information. The percentage of respondents who ate ≥5 servings of vegetables and fruits per day was: 20% (cardiologists), 21% (fellows-in-training), and 26% (cardiovascular team members).

A common argument many people have against veganism is that vegans should supplement vitamin B12. There is a notion that because of this, a plant-based diet is neither "natural" nor "sufficient." Firstly, as we've already examined, the idea of supposed naturalness is a logical fallacy—an appeal to nature. This fallacy assumes that because something is "natural," it is good or beneficial, which is both irrelevant and untrue. For example, anthrax is "natural," cyanide is "natural, and cannibalism is "natural." Vitamin B12 comes from bacteria inside the gut of some nonhuman animals; they get it from eating plants grown in soil rich in cobalt. When nonhuman animals in agriculture are raised in areas deficient in cobalt, they are often injected with a vitamin B12 supplement, or cobalt is supplemented into the surrounding soil (González-Montaña et al. 2020). In other words, nutrient supplementation is not limited to a completely plant-based diet. Vitamin B12 is also found in some non-animal sources, such as fortified foods, nutritional yeast, seaweed/nori, shiitake mushrooms, fermented soybean products like tempeh, and algae (Watanabe et al. 2014). There is also the possibility that duckweed/"water lentils" contain vitamin B12 (Xu et al. 2021). It's also important to genuinely ask ourselves: which is a more important issue—taking a supplement or the unnecessary deaths of trillions of nonhuman animals? Picture one multivitamin in the palm of your hand and a living cow in front of you.

Nonhuman animal field deaths associated with plant-based agriculture

A viral article appeared online in 2014 that made the bold claim that vegetarians "have more blood on [their] hands" than those that consume nonhuman animals (Archer 2014). To back this claim, the author suggested that vegetarians (and vegans) required more nonhuman animal deaths for their plant-based foods than nonhuman animal agriculture, such as "pasture-raised beef." This type of analysis isn't inherently problematic because one of the basic understandings of veganism (and sometimes vegetarianism) is that fewer deaths, fewer rights violations, and less suffering will result from a plant-based diet; so, if that premise would turn out to not be true, veganism/vegetarianism might actually make nonhuman animals "worse" off. As we shall see, though, the author's claims are nearly impossible to substantiate, and there are also philosophical flaws in the arguments themselves.

First, there is a good breakdown of the problems associated with the claims in articles like Archer's in a journal article by Bob Fischer and Andy Lamey (2018). Averaging the calculated field deaths per year in the US between two researchers' data (Mike Archer and Steven Davis), Fischer and Lamey estimate that there are over 7.3 billion nonhuman deaths per year in the US. The authors explain the potential problem for vegans/vegetarians with such an account: "That's remarkably more than the number of cattle or pigs slaughtered every year in the U.S. (roughly 40 and 120 million, respectively) and not too far from the number of broiler chickens killed there also (roughly 9 billion)." But that number has several problems. The first problem is that "the estimates...rest on a dubious assumption: namely, that we're in a position to generalize from the mortality rate of one field animal or crop to other animals or crops" (6). This type of calculation cannot be taken as a given for *all* crops and *all* nonhuman animals because too many variables exist between crops, nonhuman animals, climate, area, predators, food access, etc. Along with this issue, nonhuman field animals vary in how they react to crop harvesting. Some don't live within the cropland but rather live outside of it and only travel into the cropland *after* the crops have been harvested. Some run away and hide before they are harmed. Some remain safe underground. Another issue with the existing data is that the sample sizes are usually very small, which does not allow for generalizations. Overall, Fischer and Lamey make the case that there is an extreme lack of empirical data that would prove Davis or Archer's case. Fischer and Lamey also stress that the issues of field deaths are not something that must always occur. Better technology and practices can curb and prevent deaths and harm. They end their article with this insightful idea: "Agriculture has taken a wide variety of forms throughout history, and current trends would seem to raise the serious possibility that plant agriculture might someday kill very few animals—perhaps even none" (17).

Perhaps the most crucial aspect of the field death issue is remembering what we learned in the previous section about plant-based agriculture versus nonhuman animal-based agriculture: feeding nonhuman animals requires many times the number of crops to be grown than feeding crops directly to humans. In effect, field deaths increase with nonhuman animal agriculture because so many more crops must be cultivated. When we really think of this, and if we are genuinely concerned about field deaths, it is but one more reason to eat a plant-based diet.

Further Reading:

- Moriarty, Patrick. 2012. "Vegetarians Cause Environmental Damage, but Meat Eaters Aren't Off the Hook." *The Conversation*. Retrieved December 3, 2022 (https://theconversation.com/vegetarians-cause-environmental-damage-but-meat-eaters-arent-off-the-hook-6090).
- Keim, Brandon. 2018. "The Surprisingly Complicated Math of How Many Wild Animals Are Killed in Agriculture." *Anthropocene | Innovation in the Human Age*. Retrieved December 3, 2022 (https://www.anthropocenemagazine.org/2018/07/how-many-animals-killed-in-agriculture/).
- 2021. "Debunking Mike Archer's Ethical Case (and Bad Statistics) for Eating Grass-Fed Meat." *Substack.com*. Retrieved December 3, 2022 (https://vstats.substack.com/p/does-ordering-the-vegetarian-or-vegan).

What about when some people quit their plant-based diets?

Unfortunately, there are indeed people that quit their plant-based diet. There are many reasons that this can happen. Sometimes people say they "didn't feel quite right" during. It's important to try not to judge or assume people lie when making these kinds of statements. Some people are telling the truth. These situations should motivate vegans to educate others about healthy plant-based diets. However, anecdotally, the number of people who have told me that they know someone that "almost died" from a plant-based diet makes me wonder where this epidemic of vegans is, lying in hospital beds, regretting that last glass of oat milk.

One interesting reason some people quit a plant-based diet is due to their beliefs in social justice. Hodson and Earle (2018) published their findings from a study of current and past vegans and vegetarians, which showed that people who hold a more conservative ideology tend to be in the "former" category rather than "current." The research also showed that this group tended to try a plant-based diet for reasons outside social justice concerns (i.e., for health). Another study explored the differences between people that hold fast to a plant-based diet and those that eventually stop it. The study found that people who succeed at sustaining a plant-based diet typically have ethical views about the diet; those who do not succeed more often attempt a plant-based diet for personal health reasons (Ruehlman and Karoly 2022).

But let's face it: people end their plant-based diets for many reasons. Some do it because they aren't really committed to social justice; some do it because they "miss" the taste of what (and whom) they used to eat. Some do it because they may feel like their health has decreased since. And with how our brains work, these become even more complicated than a simple change of mind. However, none of these reasons are adequate to justify someone not being vegan. And since my interpretation of veganism, as stated above, doesn't preclude any single human on Earth with moral agency from becoming vegan, we must investigate and be active about what might keep us from a fully plant-based diet—as much as we can. Besides, did the person also return to buying and wearing leather, wool, and silk? Did they go back to attending zoos, aquariums, rodeos, and circuses? Do they now believe that nonhuman animals are resources for humans?

Are eating disorders, like orthorexia, associated with veganism and plant-based diets?

Emphatically, no. Recent research found that orthorexia is not related to veganism (Çiçekoğlu and Tunçay 2018). The authors state, "The results reveal that orthorexic eating behavior is associated with the importance of the underlying motives health, esthetics and healing, whereas animal welfare, politics and ecology are not linked to orthorexia" (Barthels et al. 2020). In another study, people who followed a completely plant-based diet did not "differ much from omnivores in their eating attitudes and behaviors, and when they do, differences indicate slightly healthier attitudes and behaviors towards food" (Heiss, Coffino, and Hormes 2017). Hanras et al. (2022) found that non-vegans and non-vegetarians have an increased risk for various types of disordered eating. Some research has claimed otherwise, but most of these studies do not distinguish between ethical and health-related eating behaviors (for example, here[70] and here[71]). Other data points out that there's not enough evidence to conclude that plant-based diets are correlated with eating disorders (McLean, Kulkarni, and Sharp 2022).

Where do vegans get their protein? And what about complete protein?

Langyan et al. (2022) wrote an excellent article about plant-based protein nutrition, and the following image is one of their helpful illustrations:

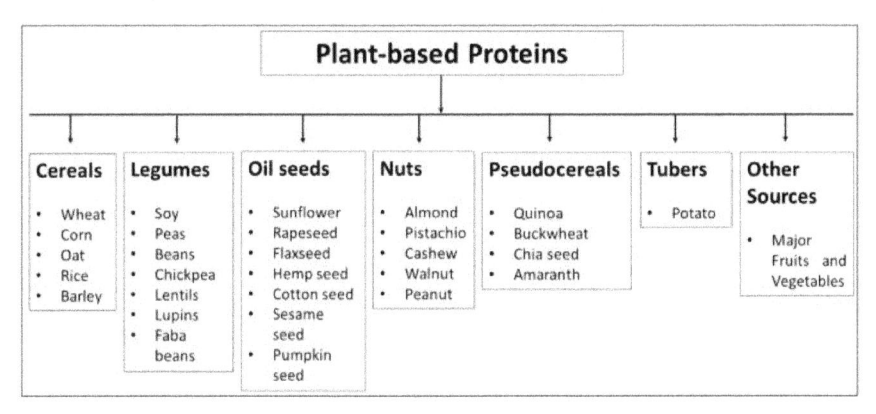

Cereals	Legumes	Oil seeds	Nuts	Pseudocereals	Tubers	Other Sources
Wheat	Soy	Sunflower	Almond	Quinoa	Potato	Major Fruits and Vegetables
Corn	Peas	Rapeseed	Pistachio	Buckwheat		
Oat	Beans	Flaxseed	Cashew	Chia seed		
Rice	Chickpea	Hemp seed	Walnut	Amaranth		
Barley	Lentils	Cotton seed	Peanut			
	Lupins	Sesame seed				
	Faba beans	Pumpkin seed				

All under heading: **Plant-based Proteins**

This image is Copyright © 2022 Langyan, Yadava, Khan, Dar, Singh, and Kumar. I am reproducing it under the authors' terms as permitted by the Creative Commons Attribution License (CC BY).

| 153 |

As you can see from this image, edible plants provide abundant quality protein for a plant-based diet. As for meeting the required amounts of amino acids in a plant-based diet, it's not that difficult. You must eat enough daily protein and a variety of foods—if you only eat crackers, cookies, and peanut butter & jelly daily, you will have a bad time.[72] For more in-depth information on plant-based protein, amino acid profiles, and the myth of complete protein, have a look at these three excellent sources.[73] [74] [75]

What about soy?

"Man boobs?" "Lower sperm count?" "Increased breast cancer risk?" These are all common myths about plant-based diets and soy consumption but are factually incorrect. And beyond the misinformation, there is deep misogyny and fear of feminization behind many soy myths. But, for emphasis, let's look at a tiny snippet of some of the most recent empirical evidence:

- Soy does not affect testosterone, estrogen, or sperm (Messina 2010).

- Those assigned "female" at birth (AFAB) are less likely to get breast cancer if they consume soy; soy may reduce other types of cancers; soy does not affect hormones or reproductive health; soy can reduce the risk of prostate cancer and fibroids (Physicians Committee for Responsible Medicine 2013)

- "Generally, soy and isoflavone consumption is more beneficial than harmful" (Li et al. 2019).

- "Soy and its isoflavones may favorably influence risk of mortality. In addition, soy protein intake was associated with a decreased risk in the mortality of breast cancer. Our findings may support the current recommendations to increase intake of soy for greater longevity" (Nachvak et al. 2019).

- Consuming soy over time can help reduce cholesterol (Jenkins et al. 2019).

- Again, soy does not affect the hormones of those assigned "male" at birth (AMAB) (Reed et al. 2021).

- Soy reduces the risk of prostate cancer (Applegate et al. 2018).

- "Soy supplementation has no effect on the thyroid hormones" (Otun et al. 2019).

- "The results showed that soy isoflavones may improve cognitive function in adults" (Cui et al. 2019).

- "Higher amount of soy intake might provide reasonable benefits for the prevention of breast cancer" (Wei et al. 2019).

- Soy-based nonhuman animal-alternative products are more sustainable and can be as healthful as their nonhuman animal-based counterparts that are "unprocessed" or "minimally processed" (Messina et al. 2021).

- Soy isoflavones are "effective in slowing down bone loss after menopause" (Barańska et al. 2022).

In other words, **soy is safe and beneficial.**

JOHN TALLENT

Health effects of a diet based on nonhuman animal consumption

I won't sit here and tell you that consuming nonhuman animals will have any specific and definite negative or positive effects on your body. Is the evidence persuasive that a plant-based diet tends to be better for most people's health than a diet based on nonhuman animal consumption? Yes, we already saw that. I tend not to discuss the health aspect of nonhuman animal use because I think the rights and, to a lesser extent, the environmental arguments hold more weight and are more persuasive. Like the literature on plant-based diets, the literature on nonhuman animal consumption can be murky and inconclusive, not to mention that the nonhuman animal industries often fund and influence research (Lazarus, McDermid, and Jacquet 2021). And let's be honest: humans' consumption of nonhuman animals necessarily leads to adverse health outcomes for nonhuman animals in agricultural industries. Most importantly is that they have a real tendency to *die* early. This health effect is often ignored, but it cannot be disentangled from a holistic look at health without a serious omission of facts.

Plant-based diets are not inherently more expensive

There is a persistent view that plant-based diets are less cost-effective than diets based on the consumption of nonhuman animals. This belief, however, has been called into question by recent research. Some data from Europe has suggested that fully plant-based diets are less costly than nonhuman animal-based diets (Berners-Lee et al. 2012; Pais, Marques, and Fuinhas 2022). At least one study also examined how low-income households in the US receiving governmental SNAP benefits could obtain a healthful diet of fruits and vegetables. They concluded that prioritizing approximately 40% of SNAP benefits in a given household may allow for more purchasing and consumption of these two food categories (Stewart et al. 2020). Additionally, one study concluded that vegans and "true vegetarians" (those that claim vegetarianism and do not purchase flesh products) save more than "partial vegetarians" (those that claim vegetarianism but also do purchase flesh products) and flesh-consuming non-vegans (Lusk and Norwood 2016). Of course, these studies do not necessarily take into account the entirety of each individual's experiential and financial circumstances, but they do cast reasonable doubt on a widely held belief that a plant-based diet is only available to the economically privileged. The cost of food wouldn't be complete without a look at government subsidies, especially here in the US. Subsidies that benefit the nonhuman animal agricultural sector have been tremendously harmful to all life on the planet (Winebarger 2012). In the US specifically, a cheap supply of "products" made from nonhuman animals comes from government (taxpayer) financial support. Smith (2019) notes that approximately 60% of these farm subsidies fund three crops that ensure artificially low prices: soybeans, corn, and wheat. These crops have many uses, but soybeans and corn are overwhelmingly used for feed for nonhuman animal agriculture. Dorning (2019) of *Bloomberg* reported that, during former US President Donald "The Johnald" Trump's[76] trade war with China, he made sure to bail out the US soybean industry about double what they had lost during his Sinophobic battle with the country. Cheap feed equals cheap "products" and more profits (Smith 2019). It must also be understood that the negative effects of nonhuman animal agriculture on humans, the environment, and other animals are partially due to these subsidies, which often make "animal products" "significantly underpriced" (Funke et al. 2022).

Dogs, cats, and plant-based diets

The subject of feeding dogs and cats a plant-based diet is extremely contentious (Bennett 2021). Many people even think that nonhuman animal welfare laws should prevent guardians of companion animals from feeding dogs and cats this type of diet (Loeb 2020).

Unfortunately, few studies look at the healthfulness of plant-based diets for companion animals, such as cats and dogs. However, some research says evidence of harm to companion nonhuman animals from a plant-based diet is lacking (Domínguez-Oliva et al. 2023). A recent study concluded that guardians of dogs self-reported fewer health issues compared to the reports of guardians that feed their companion dogs a flesh-based diet. It was also reported that the guardians who fed their companion dogs a plant-based diet noticed greater longevity (Dodd et al. 2022). It's necessary, though, to consider that self-reported studies can have validity problems. This study relied on companion animal guardians' *perceptions* of how they felt about their dog's health. It is highly possible that people can lie or exaggerate (or be completely wrong) on this type of questionnaire, and the guardians' perceptions do not equate to the accuracy of veterinary examinations. And since there are no similar studies to this one to compare results with, concurrent validity is not possible. Overall, this study is interesting but cannot provide concrete evidence because of its unreliable methods. Other studies have concluded that dogs can thrive on a plant-based diet, but their guardians should ensure that they receive proper nutrition and see a veterinarian (Knight and Leitsberger 2016; Wehrmaker et al. 2022). Dogs are not carnivores like their ancestors, wolves. Adaptations have led to modern dogs having the ability to thrive on starch-rich diets (Axelsson et al. 2013).

Feeding cats an entirely plant-based diet is not implausible. All the requirements for proper cat nutrition are available in non-animal forms (Knight and Leitsberger 2016), including taurine (European Food Safety Authority 2012), arachidonic acid, and vitamin A. It's also interesting to note that synthetic taurine is used by many of the significant companion animal food brands, including Purina (Purina Institute n.d.).

It is important to check the nutrition labels on plant-based dog and cat food because some brands can be deficient or contain excess macronutrient profiles (Zafalon et al. 2020); a well-balanced diet is also not guaranteed for homemade recipes found online (Pedrinelli et al. 2021).

Part II

CONSIDERING ARGUMENTS FROM THE LEFT

In this passivity of ordinary people before normalized violence lies the origins of both genocide and speciesism. Indifference toward the cruel fate of the others...pervades our relations with other animals, whose lives or deaths, rendered invisible by society, become to us as insubstantial as air.

—John Sanbonmatsu, (2014:41)

The discriminatory, hierarchical, and domineering ideology of speciesism infects social and environmental movements as much as it poisons mass consciousness. This atavistic ignorance necessarily calls into question the "radical," "enlightened," or "progressive" nature of left politics. While championing democracy, equality, justice, rights, respect, and peace for all, the Left/progressive traditions have ignored—often defended—the most severe forms of exploitation and violence on the planet today, as they remain oblivious to the catastrophic consequences of speciesism. Although priding themselves on being critical, rational, moral, just, egalitarian, and defenders of the weak, leftists impale themselves on the hypocrisy of speciesism and dramatize the shallowness of humanist values. Champions of "dialectics," holistic theorizing, and systemic analysis, they completely miss the most portentous connections of our time—the hideous chains linking animal exploitation to human exploitation and environmental catastrophe. They excoriate exploitation, denounce domination, preach peace, and vie for the vulnerable, while consuming the diseased and dismembered bodies of the most oppressed beings on the planet. They rail against profit fetishism, growth imperatives, total commodification, exploitation, slavery, and corporate domination, yet the animal products they consume daily are mass-produced for the enrichment and expansion of transnational market systems that further cannibalize the earth's resources. Those with an ecological sensibility prattle on about the "unsustainable" nature of capitalism and decry its ruinous effects on environments and peoples, while remaining oblivious to the fact that agribusiness is the leading cause of environmental destruction today.

—Steven Best (2016:91-2)

10

"There's No Ethical Consumption under Capitalism"

I am unsure if this counterargument is used as often in the "real world," but it has become almost ubiquitous in Leftist online spaces that are more hostile to veganism. Typically, if a vegan advocates in any way for veganism or nonhuman animal liberation, it's almost guaranteed that they will be met with "No thanks—there's no ethical consumption under capitalism." This counterargument claims that capitalism is inherently exploitative, so any vegan claiming that consumption practices are non-exploitative is shifting the exploitation from nonhuman animals to plant-based food workers. After all, there is a lot of exploitation in food production. But now, let's talk more about this counterargument (from now on referred to as "TNECUC").

Interestingly, the phrase "TNECUC" never appears in any real anti-capitalist literature other than more recent usage of it on social media, blogs, and opinion pieces. Malone (2022b) locates the origins of this phrase to a meme circulating via the social media platform Tumblr from 2014. The meme is an image of the video game character Sonic the Hedgehog, with text around him that reads "TNECUC." Since then, the phrase has been used against the ideas of products being "cruelty-free," "fair-trade," and "sustainable" (Pape 2018). Capitalism is exploitative because of the problematic dynamics of the employer-employee

| 163 |

and capitalist-proletariat relationship, which necessarily involves power and coercion from the employers/capitalists. Human workers are forced to work, accept the capitalists' rules and demands, are alienated from their labor, and live at the risk of unemployment and starvation. (Jaeggi 2016; Tucker 1978). Subsequently, it is necessarily the case that exploitation exists under capitalism, whether one is consuming as a vegan or not. But this fact lacks necessary contextualization.

For example, an article on a more popular Marxist website talks against the idea of "ethical consumption under capitalism." The article is by Pape (2018), from the Canadian website *Fightback: The Marxist Voice for Labour and Youth*, entitled 'Why there is no "ethical consumption" under capitalism.' In short, the article argues that despite corporations' use of terms like "eco-friendly" and "sustainable," human workers are often coerced into working long hours under harmful conditions simply for "the West" to have cheap products. The main problem with the article is that the author sees the solution to issues like this wholly in abolishing capitalism. But is the abolition of capitalism the only thing that we can do?

The first issue with the logic of focusing strictly on abolishing capitalism to end exploitation is that it puts all exploitation on the same level of *impact*. In this view, an individual purchasing a pound of tofu has the same exploitative impact as an individual purchasing a pound of cow's flesh, or a glass of cow's milk has the same impact as a glass of soymilk. These comparisons, though, severely misconstrue the actual impacts involved in each item's production. Take tofu versus cows' flesh, for example. To analyze these two things accurately, we must account for how they affect human workers, the environment, *and* nonhuman animals. Regarding the environmental effects, tofu (made from soy) and other plant-based foods drastically reduce the carbon footprint within production. Ritchie (2020a) explains,

> Plant-based protein sources – tofu, beans, peas and nuts – have the lowest carbon footprint. This is certainly true when

> you compare average emissions. But it's still true when you compare the extremes: there's not much overlap in emissions between the worst producers of plant proteins, and the best producers of meat and dairy...[P]lant-based foods tend to have a lower carbon footprint than meat and dairy. In many cases a much smaller footprint.

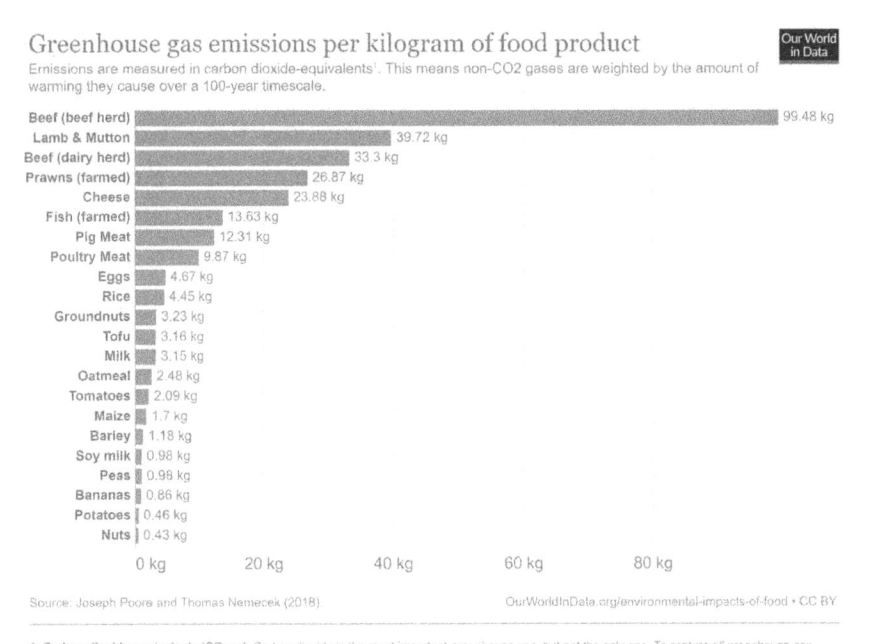

Greenhouse gas emissions per kilogram of food product

Emissions are measured in carbon dioxide-equivalents¹. This means non-CO2 gases are weighted by the amount of warming they cause over a 100-year timescale.

Food	kg
Beef (beef herd)	99.48 kg
Lamb & Mutton	39.72 kg
Beef (dairy herd)	33.3 kg
Prawns (farmed)	26.87 kg
Cheese	23.88 kg
Fish (farmed)	13.63 kg
Pig Meat	12.31 kg
Poultry Meat	9.87 kg
Eggs	4.67 kg
Rice	4.45 kg
Groundnuts	3.23 kg
Tofu	3.16 kg
Milk	3.15 kg
Oatmeal	2.48 kg
Tomatoes	2.09 kg
Maize	1.7 kg
Barley	1.18 kg
Soy milk	0.98 kg
Peas	0.98 kg
Bananas	0.86 kg
Potatoes	0.46 kg
Nuts	0.43 kg

Source: Joseph Poore and Thomas Nemecek (2018). OurWorldInData.org/environmental-impacts-of-food • CC BY

1. Carbon dioxide-equivalents (CO_2eq): Carbon dioxide is the most important greenhouse gas, but not the only one. To capture all greenhouse gas emissions, researchers express them in carbon dioxide-equivalents' (CO_2eq). This takes all greenhouse gases into account, not just CO_2. To express all greenhouse gases in carbon dioxide-equivalents (CO_2eq), each one is weighted by its global warming potential (GWP) value. GWP measures the amount of warming a gas creates compared to CO_2. CO_2 is given a GWP value of one. If a gas had a GWP of 10 then one kilogram of that gas would generate ten times the warming effect as one kilogram of CO_2. Carbon dioxide-equivalents are calculated for each gas by multiplying the mass of emissions of a specific greenhouse gas by its GWP factor. This warming can be stated over different timescales. To calculate CO_2eq over 100 years, we'd multiply each gas by its GWP over a 100-year timescale (GWP100). Total greenhouse gas emissions – measured in CO_2eq – are then calculated by summing each gas CO_2eq value.

As we can see in the above chart, all "foods" made from the bodies of nonhuman animals tend to be higher in their carbon footprints than plant-based foods, and they also tend to include high methane emissions (Ritchie 2020b). Ritchie goes on to answer a common talking point in favor of "low-impact" forms of nonhuman animal production,

> Many argue that this overlooks the large variation in the footprints of foods across the world. Using global averages might

| 165 |

> give us a misleading picture for some parts of the world or some producers. If I source my beef or lamb from low-impact producers, could they have a lower footprint than plant-based alternatives? The evidence suggests, no: plant-based foods emit fewer greenhouse gases than meat and dairy, regardless of how they are produced.

There is also a common belief that eating "local" nonhuman animal "products" is a better option than plant-based products that are not local. Ritchie (2020c) debunks this notion: transport often only accounts for a small amount of a product's carbon footprint. Ritchie goes on to say,

> Eating local beef or lamb has many times the carbon footprint of most other foods. Whether they are grown locally or shipped from the other side of the world matters very little for total emissions. Transport typically accounts for less than 1% of beef's GHG emissions: choosing to eat local has very minimal effects on its total footprint...Whether you buy it from the farmer next door or from far away, it is not the location that makes the carbon footprint of your dinner large, but the fact that it is beef.

Additionally, there is a myth that vegans' soy consumption causes massive amounts of deforestation, especially in the Amazonian rainforests. In reality, most soy is grown and produced as feed for consumption by nonhuman animals used in agriculture; only a tiny amount of soy grown and produced directly reaches consumers as food (Ritchie and Roser 2021).

We also must look at the human worker and nonhuman animal impacts related to "beef" and tofu production. Since around 75% of soy production goes to produce nonhuman animals for consumption (Ritchie and Roser 2021), most soy-related crop deaths are due to nonhuman animal consumption and production. And the entire nonhuman animal use and consumption system relies explicitly on directly exploiting and killing nonhuman animals. So, no direct nonhuman animals are used to produce tofu; at least one nonhuman animal is directly and purposefully exploited and killed to produce a pound of "beef." Regarding human worker exploitation, tofu production requires less soy than "beef" because of the **feed conversion ratio**, or "feed-to-meat ratio." As *A Well-Fed World* (2021) explains, "Feed Conversion Ratios (FCRs) measure the amount of feed/crops needed to produce a unit of meat." They also state that the FCR of cows is 6x-25x; pigs, 4x-9x; and chickens, 2x-5x. Slaughterhouse work is also one of the most dangerous work areas currently. The choice is between feeding humans directly with that soy or feeding nonhuman animals many times the number of crops and then feeding them to humans, which is "inefficient" and harmful to humans, the environment, and nonhuman animals. Here in the South of the US, we like to say, "That is like going around your ass to get to your elbow."

Capitalism, a system built upon exploitation and extractivism, can never be truly ethical. This is not unlike the system of nonhuman animal use. However "ethical" each system is reformed to be, their foundations and continued existence require harm to others. With this idea in mind, it is also important to understand that this does not mean that each commodity created under each system contains the same "amount" of harm. It might be impossible to live an entire cruelty-free life, but choosing commodities that rely on less harm is not impossible. Even though there may not be "ethical consumption under capitalism," there seems to be a *spectrum of unethical consumption*. With the example of "beef" versus tofu, under capitalism, you can choose either having someone killed (a cow) and exacting a massive cost on the environment and other humans, or you can choose the *less unethical* option that does not involve direct killing and has a much less toll on the environment and other humans. And I do not mean here that capitalism can be abolished through this method of consuming less unethically. I am saying that when a less unethical product exists, and we are forced to live under capitalism, social justice demands that we seek that product if we have the ability.

Nonhuman animal use and consumption pose a unique issue for TNECUC. Given what has been said previously in this book, nonhuman animal exploitation is inherently wrong because it harms sentient people. And in a socialist, communist, or anarchist society, people should not be considered "products" or exploited. For this reason, we should go beyond the saying that "there's no ethical consumption under capitalism" and instead think of the idea that there's no ethical consumption or exploitation of sentient people under *any* system. The fall of capitalism does not necessarily entail a utopia, and it absolutely does not mean that nonhuman animal exploitation automatically becomes "humane" and "ethical." In a discussion regarding Upton Sinclair's pro-socialist book about the exploitation of immigrants in slaughterhouses in the US, *The Jungle*, Natalie Woodward (2019:163) explains how a socialist system would not necessarily end tyranny,

> [T]ransferring power over to the masses under a socialist regime may mean that more people [humans] are treated justly, but it will not mean that the tyrannical force has disappeared, it merely will have shifted. Ostensibly, without a system in place that gestures toward the sacred ideals of justice for all creatures, there is still the possibility of atrocity.

An anarchist collective running a slaughterhouse or a dairy exploits nonhuman animals as "products." Only when nonhuman animals (and all people!) are viewed, treated, and respected as individuals with an inherent right not to be commodities and resources will production be able to be considered "ethical." There are even vegan Marxists that agree.[77]

Nonhuman animals exploited in agriculture inhabit the strange region between "objects" and "workers." Their bodies are commodified, their lives and emotions minimized and ignored, and their labor goes unacknowledged and unappreciated. These living, thinking, feeling, suffering, and emotional beings are both "things" to be bought, sold, and invested in, and they are also forced and relied upon to exert bodily movement for the profits of their legal owners. As unpaid, coerced, and tortured commodities and workforce members, they are denied the profits of their labor and fundamental legal rights to personal freedoms and autonomy. Unlike chairs, soybean plants, treasury bonds, and iPhones, nonhuman animals do not belong in the same category as commodities. They are indeed bought and sold as commodities, but that does not tell us anything about the ethics of such a predicament. Though the phrase "TNECUC" makes sense when we are talking about so-called "eco-friendly" commodities versus their "conventional" counterparts, bringing nonhuman animals into this formulation makes little sense. As we've seen, switching from "beef" exploited in and shipped from South America to the United States to tofu does not have the same environmental impacts and ethical implications. This kind of imprudent thinking is a false equivalence fallacy. Tofu is not sentient and has a much lower environmental impact than the "beef" that necessitated an egregious number of resources, worker physical/emotional/psychological exploitation and harm, and of course, the torture/exploitation/murder of a sentient being. Equating the harms in this scenario is disingenuous and factually incorrect.

At its core, capitalism requires the exploitation of workers. Capitalist wealth accumulation cannot happen without appropriating the surplus value created by workers. Workers work for a wage or a salary. Workers produce the goods and services of a business. The profit created by workers, minus their wage or salary, is taken by the capitalist(s) of the business and used how they see fit. Capitalism also utilizes coercion through its hierarchical system, which includes owners, boards of directors, managers, supervisors, administrators, salaried and wage laborers, etc. Every step up in the hierarchy usually provides for more power and/or privileges over the lower levels within the structure. With this power, those at higher levels in the hierarchy can put forth demands, more responsibilities for others, threats of discipline and firing, not to mention the myriad ways in which power is utilized outside of "official" policies, effectively in secret, to gain personal, professional, and sexual benefits.

Here's some more meaningful context, though. How do we end the exploitation of human workers? Whatever methods we take to get us there, the answer is that we must dismantle and replace capitalism. Workplaces have to be run democratically by the workers; communities and local councils have to be led by direct democracy of all constituents; the few can no longer accumulate capital but instead spread it around so that everyone has what they need. By doing this, societies can be altered and organized around their needs. Automation can be used to lighten the burden of arduous labor. What I'm getting at here is that the exploitation of humans can be achieved by eliminating capitalism. But what about the exploitation of nonhuman animals?

Abolishing capitalism does not end the exploitation of nonhuman animals. It may decrease the harm done to nonhuman animals, but it does not *end* exploitation. No matter the extent that a post-capitalist enterprise could reduce the harms of "factory farms" or any damage done in the name of profit, if nonhuman animals are being used, killed, confined, experimented on, "culled," sexually violated, having their bodies altered, or any other form of harm, they are being exploited. "Enhancing" a nonhuman animal's welfare while they are being exploited does not negate the wrongness of the exploitation itself. The exploitation of nonhuman animals does not disappear because of an economic system's replacement. The only way for the exploitation of nonhuman animals to be remedied and abolished is to ultimately end their use and property status. This is the case for domesticated nonhuman animals and those that are free-roaming.

"TNECUC," when used as either a "gotcha" towards vegans or a way to skirt individual responsibility in consumption practices, is not a helpful way to think about ethics and capitalism. It does not accurately show the genuine differences in ethics between various commodities. It is often mistaken to mean that every consumer living under capitalism is equally unethical in their purchases. The phrase also tends to make people feel they have little to no agency to affect change. Social structures are powerful forces in developing and perpetuating social relations within a given society. But that does not mean that individuals within a social structure have no agency to dismantle and change these social structures. "TNECUC" puts primacy on structures and gives little or no power to individual choice and behavior. But, also, the speciesist and anthropocentric structures within society leave most people in false consciousness about nonhuman animal exploitation. It has convinced us that nonhuman animal exploitation is good, humane, natural, environmentally friendly and helps in class solidarity with marginalized humans worldwide. But wait—a system that exploits trillions of nonhuman people in every way possible and completely dominates them—being promoted as a global mechanism that solidifies class solidarity against capitalists? It's incredible what capitalism, tribalism, speciesism, anthropocentrism, human supremacism, and our psychologies will cook up to keep us and the world in a status quo of total global strife (Pickett 2021).

"We must dismantle capitalism first"

Viewing the negative consequences of nonhuman animal agriculture as solely a problem of capitalism and, therefore, dismantling capitalism will solve these negative consequences ignores a fundamental aspect of it all. Most folks, at least in wealthier countries, freely choose to use and consume nonhuman animals even when alternatives exist and are not vastly different in price. If capitalism were abolished tomorrow and an anarcho-communist world emerged soon after, nonhuman animals would still be exploited and killed for most humans' unnecessary desires, and their environmental footprint would not disappear or decrease dramatically. If most people create demand for this exploitation, the negative consequences will continue. Change cannot only come from a revolution of the economic system and the producers, but it must also involve a revolution in the desires and ethics of consumers (Poore and Nemecek 2018). With rising demands for the consumption of nonhuman animals expected in Southeast Asia and sub-Saharan Africa between 2020 and 2050 (Komarek et al. 2021), focusing on the abolition of capitalism will not end the dire predicament of the global climate emergency that we are all in. Dietary and other consumption changes must also be a part of the changes that we seek because scientific reality demands it:

> Although it is theoretically possible to decarbonize energy supply, complete reductions are not feasible in the livestock part of the agricultural sector because of the biological realities of ruminant digestion—farm animals release excessive amounts of methane. (Smith 2019:30)

To illustrate the impact of nonhuman animal agriculture further, consider the following:

> The EPA estimates that emissions from agriculture account for nearly 8% of annual U.S. greenhouse gas emissions...[T]his may appear rather insignificant, particularly when juxtaposed with energy-related activities, including electricity generation and transportation. Indeed, the energy and transportation sectors are the primary sources of the [US's] anthropogenic greenhouse gases, accounting for over 84% of total emissions. But upon closer inspection, agriculture is the primary climate-impacting culprit because of the outsized radiative effects of methane and nitrous oxide as compared to carbon dioxide...The average global warming potential of nitrous oxide and methane is, respectively, 265-298 times and 28-36 times that of carbon dioxide over 100 years...[W]hile the energy and transportation

> sectors combined emit 97% of the nation's carbon dioxide, their climate change impacts are outweighed by the agriculture sector's contribution of 35% of the nation's methane emissions and 80% of its nitrous oxide emissions...[A]gricultural emissions of methane and nitrous oxide were the equivalent of 520 million metric tons of carbon dioxide—or the carbon emissions from 111 million automobiles in an average year. (P. 33)

But also understand that Leftist vegans are often highly critical of capitalism and work actively to dismantle it. Leftist veganism cannot be conflated with the mainstream vegan movement, which tends to be heavily influenced by capitalist logic. Anti-capitalist (and pro-human liberation) veganism is well-documented and rich in content. One qualitative content analysis of "radical animal liberation movement" (RALM) activists' online content revealed

> the ways in which activists understand anguish, captivity and injustice as entrenched in the ubiquitous inequalities that beget other social harms such as colonialism, classism, criminalization, imprisonment, police violence, racism and sexism...RALM activists reject the mainstream animal rights framework, and instead understand consumer boycotts and legislative reforms as techniques of cooptation that perpetuate capitalism and lend legitimacy to unjust power structures. While some RALM activists use the phrase 'animal rights', it is understood to refer to inherent moral rights to autonomy and freedom from harm, rather than legal rights, since most RALM activists are critical of state power...They emphasize the alliances they have formed with other social movements such as anarchistic, anti-capitalist, Indigenous, immigrant rights, prison abolition, prisoner support and radical feminist groups...The conflation of mainstream and radical discourses is extremely problematic because it obscures significant differences in the ideological

JOHN TALLENT

> and strategic approaches of both movements, and ignores the similarities between the RALM and other progressive social justice struggles…Radical animal liberationists…press for drastic changes to current political, economic and social structures that oppress animals, and view grassroots social movements, rather than state institutions, as the most important actors in creating more equitable relationships with animals…For liberationists, no amount of 'cruelty free' consumerism or animal welfare reform will ever emancipate animals from human exploitation, and therefore direct action must be taken to free animals and damage animal industries. Many animal liberationists construct the mainstream animal rights movement as a moral crusade that defends consumerism…Despite RALM activists focusing much of their attention on animal issues, they do not view the suffering of animals as isolated or distinct from the oppression of marginalized humans. Ideological and strategic comparisons have been made between the RALM and other liberation struggles… (Johnston and Johnston 2017:2-3)

It's also interesting to think about what the world would look like if nonhuman animal exploitation had never been created. Imagine this speculative history: Other forms of oppression may have developed over time, but nonhuman animals would have been left alone, aside from genuine survival situations. With nonhuman animal exploitation, a nonhuman *person* is taken out of their desired setting, forced or coerced into performing some behavior, and often killed directly. A *person* is reduced to an object, a tool, and/or a resource for someone else who has complete control. The nonhuman animal had no choice; the human did. This is the epitome of capitalist ideology: dismiss bodily autonomy, personal desires, collective solidarity, and environmental connectedness, all for the profit and desires of the few. But how could capitalism against humans have developed without this capitalist ideology created against nonhuman animals? How could any human or small group invite global environmental catastrophe on all life on Earth without first believing that nonhuman animals do not matter as much as humans? Taking land, resources, and labor from others necessitates the violation of others' autonomy. If humans did not view themselves as intrinsically more worthy of life than nonhuman animals, humans would have never developed any system or ideology that dismissed other animals' equal life claims and resource needs. When you don't feel morally superior or biologically "better" than another, there's no purpose in developing a mentality that would put your desires over their requirements for life (without some survival scenario, of course). Speciesism and anthropocentrism—the foundations of human exceptionalism and discrimination against nonhuman animals—contributed to and allowed capitalism to be created. The same applies to all other forms of human oppression before capitalism. Nonhuman animal exploitation and capitalism go hand-in-hand, as do nonhuman animal exploitation and feudalism, etc. As long as we believe in and tolerate nonhuman animal exploitation, capitalism thrives in our minds and practices.

Despite the capitalist logic built into nonhuman animal exploitation, vegans are often blamed for capitalism's devastation of the environment and the lives of marginalized humans and other animals. A few specific food commodities have production issues that are often blamed on vegans and veganism, especially in social media spaces. Let's take a look at a few of them.

Quinoa production issues

Popular myth #1: Veganism has increased demand for quinoa / Vegans consume most quinoa.

Around 2013, Joanna Blythman wrote a piece in *The Guardian* claiming, or implying, that veganism and vegans were responsible for the increased demand for quinoa. By extension, vegans consume most of the quinoa globally (Blythman 2013). This piece has often been cited on social media, especially by nonvegan Leftists attempting to "gotcha" vegans. Despite the finger-pointing in the headline and the article, there is no data on what agents increased the demand for quinoa. Going by one estimate (Williams 2020), vegans account for about 3% of the population worldwide. That's a meager percentage of the population. And it's vital to understand that vegans are not the only ones consuming quinoa. So, it's incorrect even to suggest that vegans or veganism led to an increase in demand for quinoa; it's also wrong to suggest that vegans are consuming most of the quinoa in the world.

Popular myth #2: Increased demand for quinoa has led to local farmers being unable to afford to buy & consume quinoa themselves.

An article from *The New York Times* in 2013 (Romero and Shahriari 2011) stated that global quinoa consumption and demand were rising, enriching local quinoa farmers and making quinoa less affordable for poorer Bolivians. *NPR* (Aubrey 2013) soon brought more context to the situation. The article points to upsides, like some small Indigenous farmers increasing wages and personal consumption of quinoa, and some downsides, like price increases.

Fast forward a few years, and *Smithsonian Magazine* (Blakemore 2016) reported on a working paper by Towson University in Maryland (Bellemare, Fajardo-Gonzalez, and Gitter 2018) about this issue. *Smithsonian Magazine* summarizes the findings: "Using a database of Peruvian household information that includes crop and consumption information, the economists were able to look at the relationship between rising quinoa prices and what Peruvian families ate and grew. They compared three groups: people who don't grow or eat it, people who eat it but don't grow it, and people who do both. They found that as the purchase price of quinoa rose, so did household welfare in all three groups. The welfare of those who produced and consumed quinoa rose more quickly than the other two groups, but even families who didn't produce quinoa saw an effect." The *Smithsonian Magazine* article also mentions another study in the journal *Food Policy* (Stevens 2017) showing, despite initial reports, "quinoa farmers did not cut back their own consumption of quinoa, even when prices rose four times." An article by *BBC* from 2018 (Livingstone 2018) shows how competition from outside Peru and Bolivia by the United States, Canada, and others has led to a "bust" in prices of quinoa, affecting local farmers. All of this is not to say that the quinoa boom of the 2010s had no adverse effects; it did (Bonifacio et al. 2022).

Popular myth #3: Quinoa production involves slavery.

There is no evidence of slavery in quinoa production. This myth is likely due to confusion about the slavery in producing cacao (Food Empowerment Project 2013) and avocados (Dehghan 2019).

Despite the misleading claims by popular media outlets about quinoa and vegans, there is still much to be done to help support local farmers in Peru, Bolivia, and Ecuador regarding sustainability and the effects that the markets in the Global North have on the Global South (Alandia et al. 2020; Angeli et al. 2020; Gamboa et al. 2020).[78]

Agave production issues

"vegans won't eat figs because a bee died in it but will use flown in brown child labour agave"

"Agave harvesting is extremely harmful to the bat population"

'Vegans will be like "I excuse the use of slave labor to make my agave but I draw the line at indigenous people practicing their culture"'

"vegans will come for me eating honey made ethically by my friend's parents' beekeeping and then eat child slave labour agave and argue that they have the moral high ground"

"honestly so many strict vegans are absolutely insane and literally do Not care about the environment lmaooo and there's proof by how many of

them consume agave because it's not honey, save the bees while agave is farmed with slave labor"

'Vegans be like "I sure do love encouraging slave labour and abusive work conditions for agave and plant based honey substitutes instead of from consenting bees who benefit from human [p]rotection."'

"vegans love 2 say they live an ethical lifestyle and then pay $12 for agave syrup collected with slave labor lol"

—Various Twitter posts

Agave is a plant genus that humans have used in many forms for at least 9,000 years. Approximately 75% of *agave* species can be found in Mexico. *Agave*s have been used to make many different products, such as fibers, food, biofuel, and, most important to this discussion, tequila and agave nectar (Trejo-Salazar et al. 2016).

The environmental and nonhuman animal impacts of agave production have been criticized relatively recently. In particular, a few species of endangered and threatened bats are currently experiencing a loss of food sources and habitat due to industrial agave production. These agave plants and bats have co-evolved together—so close, in fact, that the agave plants pollinate overnight when bats are awake. The sweet nectar is found inside the plant's flowers, which the bats seek out using their very long tongues. When the bats reach for the nectar, they are covered in the plant's pollen (which they also eat and eventually poop out). The bats then fly to another agave plant and consequently help the plants successfully pollinate (and the bats' poop, which contains pollen, also helps pollinate). Unfortunately for bats and agaves, the plants' tall stalks are cut by human workers before they are ready for reproduction. This prevents the plants from developing pollen, which decreases the amount of available food for the bats and decreases the chance for future pollination by the bats. These plants take many years to fully mature (some between 5-30 years!), so it's impossible to simply plant more for the next season (Trejo-Salazar et al. 2016; Ulaby 2017).

These negative impacts of industrial agave production have often been placed at the feet of vegans. Agave nectar/syrup is a plant-based alternative to bees' honey, so it can be an excellent sweetener that avoids the direct exploitation of nonhuman animals. Additionally, agave nectar contains several B vitamins and vitamin C (United States Department of Agriculture 2019). However, the main product of industrial agave production is not this nectar. As González-Montemayor et al. (2020) note, "The primary use of *Agave* species is for producing alcoholic beverages"—mainly tequila and mezcal. So, why are vegans often blamed for the impact of agave production? A few opinion articles online do just that [79] [80] [81], and one of them was shared almost 35,000 times on Facebook alone (ShareScore.com 2022). However, most of the criticism leveled at vegans comes directly from social media. Fake news and misinformation are not only aspects of the Right.

This section of the book on agave production began with several quotes about agave and vegans from Twitter. To gather these criticisms, I did a basic search on Twitter with the terms "vegans + bats + agave" and "vegans + slavery"—I knew from experience that the non-vegan Leftist Twittersphere confuses the production issues of agave with those of cocoa production.[82] Scrolling through the results for just a minute or so garnered these criticisms about vegans over and over. The criticisms were all very similar to one another, and they could be seen from at least a few years back. Tumblr was another social media platform where these kinds of baseless claims proliferated. One extremely popular post was either "liked" or shared almost 200,000 times.[83] Ignoring the biggest issue with these arguments, that agave syrup is only a small portion of agave production, and tequila and mezcal are the primary culprits, we must remember that 1) vegans account for such a small fraction of the general population, and 2) there's no evidence that most vegans even consume agave nectar. I have a sneaking suspicion that maybe most of these folks saw some critical articles or social media posts that used the word "agave" and didn't know that the term often refers to the nectar *and* the plant. Or they didn't realize that alcohol production is the primary commodity of agave production. Either way, disparaging veganism and vegans for this issue makes little sense.

Oh, yeah, and there is absolutely no evidence to support the notion that there is an epidemic of slavery or child labor involved in agave production. Even the website for the US Department of Labor's "List of Goods Produced by Child Labor or Forced Labor," which was updated in 2022, includes zero entries for "agave," "tequila," or "mezcal." Let's put these completely false myths to rest.

11

Indigenous Rights & Traditions

I...believe, if my Indian ancestors could comment on our present "right to hunt" in a world with so many people and so few nonhuman animals, that they, who listened to the land and killed only as was necessary, would not be wasteful. I think my ancestors would tell us that it is time to stop the suffering and the killing.

—Linda Fisher, Indigenous author[84]

There is no view on animals that is shared by all Aboriginal people. Aboriginal is an umbrella term combining three distinct groups of people —First Nations, Inuit, and Metis—each with different histories shaping their worldview, their food practices, and their relationship with animals. Even among the First Nations in Canada there are over 600 governments or bands with unique histories and geographic locations. For this reason I will focus on my own Mi'kmaq tradition, although our nation is not homogenous either. I approach this work as a Mi'kmaq woman who grew up in the woods of Nova Scotia and now lives in Toronto, an urban city with a population over two million. As a vegan who sees my food practices as deeply rooted in my Mi'kmaq heritage, our relationships with animals are a key concern for me.

—Margaret Robinson, Indigenous academic[85]

There was nothing good or clean about the last shot I fired at a doe...My friend, who had the buck knife in his jacket pocket, cut her throat and ended it. I have some rituals, personal ones, and I did them after he'd walked out of sight to the car to get something. I don't know what I was thinking then, probably not much of anything as far as suffering goes, but I know what I think now, years later. If somebody shoots me with a high-powered rifle, I'm not going to like it no matter how many prayers and ceremonies the guy does before he pulls the trigger. For me there is no longer any respectful way to kill an animal. (Although I'm not an absolutist, and I believe in advocating for the most painless deaths possible for animals if they must be killed, my point is that it will never be a matter of respect—it will be a matter of moderating disrespect.) The prayers and ceremonies do something for us, not the deer, at the very least not the same thing for the deer, and there is no way to escape the fundamental inequity of the relationship. I would go as far as to say the lack of relationship: she's dead, we're not. If, as some would suggest, a relationship between hunter and prey is realized through respectful rituals, it is hard to get around the fact that one of the most significant aspects of that relationship—its symmetry and equity and power balance—is ended when one party is dead. This is not to say that prayers and ceremonies are of no value for the person who has no choice but to kill. It is to say the deer will always get the worst part of the bargain no matter how carefully it is done, and any hunter who is experienced, and honest, knows that in spite of the most thoughtful efforts to minimize suffering it doesn't always go well. Even with the ceremonies and prayers it's an ugly business. Some hunters can live with this injustice. I can't.

—Craig Womack, Indigenous scholar[86]

HOW TO UNITE THE LEFT ON ANIMALS

Before we delve into this section, I want first to make some acknowledgments. I was born and live in the southeast region of the US in the state of North Carolina. The city and county where I live were inhabited by the Occaneechi, Haw, and Eno Native American tribes. Archaeological evidence shows humans settling in this area around 10,000 years ago. Though Native Americans still live in this area, most were killed by war or disease during European colonialism in the region. This is not an uncommon history. Before European colonization of the Americas beginning in 1492, approximately 60-64 million Indigenous people lived in the Americas. Throughout the history of settler colonialism in this part of the world, it is estimated that 55-56 million Indigenous people died; most of these people died of diseases introduced by Europeans and, to a lesser extent, war and slavery. Koch et al. (2019:21) describe their study on the genocide of Indigenous peoples by European colonizers:

> [E]pidemics were introduced by European settlers and African slaves and were passed on to an indigenous population that had not been previously exposed to these pathogens and therefore did not initially possess suitable antibodies [...] Such diseases included smallpox, measles, influenza, the bubonic plague, and later malaria, diphtheria, typhus and cholera. Most of these diseases originated from domesticated farm animals from Europe to which Native Americans had no prior exposure [...] The relative absence of American diseases arriving in Europe can therefore be explained by the low number of domesticated animals in the pre-contact Americas [...] Thus, influenza, smallpox, bubonic plague and other diseases ravaged the Americas, and not vice versa. Such diseases typically individually killed ~30% or more of the initial population. Hence a series of epidemics in rapid succession could have led to the loss of whole societies. Overall, hemisphere wide post-epidemics population estimates range between 4.5 million and 14.4 million for 1600—1700CE.

Using various sources of data, the authors of the study concluded that the pre-colonial Indigenous population of the Americas of 60-64 million was reduced to approximately 6 million people; this is a 90% decrease. The genocide of Indigenous peoples was so severe that the authors concluded with this chilling and sobering sentence: "[T]he Great Dying of the Indigenous Peoples of the Americas led to the abandonment of enough cleared land in the Americas that the resulting terrestrial carbon uptake had a detectable impact on both atmospheric CO2 and global surface air temperatures in the two centuries before the Industrial Revolution" (30). So many people were killed that it noticeably affected the level of carbon dioxide in the atmosphere.

The history of the US and of European colonialism is built upon the exploitation, death, and slavery of millions of Indigenous peoples, Africans, and all other human groups that have been devalued, marginalized, and oppressed alongside countless nonhuman animals. As a white person, this is the history of my ancestors. While it is not my fault as an individual that these things happened, I and all other white people in this society must acknowledge that these events privilege us in innumerable ways, and we must work for justice.

I debated internally whether it is even my place, as a person who has benefited from the settler colonialism of the US, to write this section. I am not a Native American Studies scholar, nor have any firsthand experience with any Native American tribes. What I can offer is my perspective as a vegan and nonhuman animal liberationist for over a decade who has seen Indigenous peoples around the world used as nothing more than rhetorical devices and shields for non-Indigenous peoples to deflect from their own unethical behaviors and beliefs. People in various social circles and on the Internet, especially those non-Indigenous peoples with Leftist tendencies, commonly feign solidarity with Indigenous peoples and denounce colonialism by countering any advocacy of veganism with phrases like, "What about Indigenous people, though?", "Veganism is anti-Indigenous," "Vegans are colonizers," and "Indigenous people kill animals respectfully and sustainably." These phrases have the veneer of coming to the "aid" of Indigenous peoples in need of support from "colonizer vegans," However, as I will argue, they misrepresent vegan advocacy and harm Indigenous humans and non-human animals.

The logic and dangers of essentialist thinking

The phrase "all my relations" summarizes a view rooted in Mi'kmaw culture that humans aren't a separate, special being, or superior to others. We're part of a network of related creatures. It's a focus on the communal rather than the individual. To have integrity we need to honor those relationships. For me, that means not killing other animals, and avoiding practices that make me complicit in their death. It's not always easy. I don't always know enough to make a good decision. But the effort is always worth making.

—Margaret Robinson, Indigenous vegan academic, when asked by an interviewer about the Mi'kmaq phrase "M'sit No'maq" and how it could relate to veganism[87]

In Baja, I met what I was fighting for, face to face. A mother whale rose up out of those warm waters right under my hand. She looked me straight in the eye, mother to mother. Then I saw a harpoon scar on her side, probably from up north in Siberia where the native people still hunt the whales for sustenance. The mother brought her baby over to our little boat. I talked to them and I petted them. I felt their spirit of trust was somehow being conveyed to me. I laughed and I cried all the way back to shore, and all that night. I've never been the same since. When times get hard, I think of those great big wonderful beings.

—Alberta Thompson, Makah tribal elder[88]

| 185 |

JOHN TALLENT

In modern Western culture, most of us, including the American Indian, no longer need to hunt to survive. However, we almost always associate the Indian—even today's Indian—with wearing and using nonhuman animals' hides, furs, and feathers. I assure you, even though I avoid hides and furs and choose a vegan diet [sic], my Indianness is critical to who I am. The same is true of my mother, who is both an elder of our Ojibway tribe and a vegetarian. It is not our dark hair, dark eyes, or Indian facial features that speak for who we are, but something much deeper, something not visually apparent: our commitment to the teachings of our ancient Ojibway ancestors...[W]hen I hear that some of today's Indians are slaughtering whales in the name of tradition, killing eagles for the sake of ceremony, or destroying any nonhuman animal for the sake of vanity and "tradition," I wonder what has happened, what has changed.

In a world where most people have traded in guns for cameras, has Indian philosophy become unfashionable and politically incorrect among my own people? Can we maintain such traditions and consider ourselves to be ecologically minded?

—Linda Fisher, Indigenous author[89]

> *Framing veganism as a uniformly White colonial practice requires depicting Indigenous people who refrain from eating animal products as cultural inauthentic. This presents a challenge for people like me, who view our veganism as an expression of our Indigenous identity, rather than a source of identity conflict. I vigorously object to the idea of being told what is and is not appropriately Indigenous by White settlers, however well intentioned they might be...I take comfort in the fact that adaptation to new cultural circumstances has been one of the strengths that have carried the Mi'kmaq through to the present day.*
>
> —Margaret Robinson[90]

> *Each concrete, personal stand-in for the oppressed group can only speak as a group member, whose "experiences, outlooks, and ideas" are his or her [sic] own, refracted through his or her [sic] irreducible individuality, and are at most, and only by serendipity, representative of the plurality opinion of the group.*
>
> ——Norman Finkelstein, Jewish scholar[91]

Just as with most things in life, there is not a universal story to be told about Indigenous peoples. Agency, variability, and cultural shifts are often denied from them in favor of stereotyped, romanticized, monolithic, and culturally static versions of reality. We often speak of them as "Indigenous People," a singular account of a collection of different cultures worldwide, unbound from a particular place or point in history or clear-cut belief system, forever changing, and wholly composed of agentic individuals. As Margaret Robinson says, "Indigenous cultures are alive, and they grow and change over time" (Forest 2020). Sebastian

F. Braun (2007:192) notes that this generalizing is an **essentialization** of Indigenous peoples, which is "[a] definition of others [that] in general either paints a positive or a negative picture; but in either case, the picture painted is only a mirror reflection of the painter." One form that this essentialization takes is describing all Indigenous cultures, peoples, and traditional practices as "noble," "sustainable," and "ecological." This has been termed the "ecological noble savage" trope, which is an extension of the "noble savage" trope (Ellingson 2001).[92] Indigenous vegan scholar Margaret Robinson also states that Indigenous peoples in the Americas are often essentialized with "a cultural purity" that supposedly existed before European colonialism (Robinson 2014:673).

Since colonialist societies have marginalized many Indigenous peoples worldwide, there is a growing movement to include, enhance, and center Indigenous voices. Lindroth and Sinevaara-Niskanen (2013) make the case that because many Indigenous peoples have been made vulnerable and marginalized, the essentializing of Indigeneity has had positive and negative consequences; nonetheless, essentialism is usually problematic. One positive result of this essentialization has been the establishment of conceptions of Indigenous peoples as intrinsic "custodians of nature" (285). This categorization has allowed more Indigenous voices to be "heard and recognized" (276). On the other hand, the essentialization of Indigeneity has come at the cost of reducing Indigenous differences, downplaying or ignoring change in individuals and groups, and moderating each Indigenous person's agency. This essentializing has been embraced by many settler colonialists and Indigenous peoples alike. Lindroth and Sinevaara-Niskanen warn that '[i]n the context of environmental issues and despite the heterogeneity among indigenous peoples, indigenousness becomes fixed—even by the indigenous peoples themselves—"as one thing" that is shared by all indigenous peoples' (286). As Singleton et al. (2021:5) explain, "Essentialism is not only a practice that an outsider does to another group. Groups essentialise themselves and such essentialising has been part of many emancipatory calls for action."

Essentialist ideas about objects and people have a long history that goes back at least as far as Plato. Essentialism can be defined in many ways, but more important to this discussion, I will use the following definition that is most useful in the social sciences: theories are considered essentialist "when they claim...social distinctions have deeply rooted biological underpinnings, that they are historically invariant and culturally universal, or that their boundaries are sharp and not susceptible to sociocultural shaping" (Haslam, Rothschild, and Ernst 2000:114). Additionally,

> [i]n relation to culture, essentialism often means that certain characteristics of a given culture are deemed definitive and indicative of any given instance of it. These characteristics can be almost anything...Often essentialism draws on narratives of the past, present, and future, for example in relation to particular practices...Within anthropology, critiques of essentialism often relate to the political (power-related) implications of specific essentialisms (such as representations of "indigenous groups") as well as the tendency of essentialism to homogenise and disguise diversity within groups. (Singleton et al. 2021:5)

Even in research regarding "traditional ecological knowledge" (TEK), there is a "tendency toward essentialism." The effect of this is that TEK is often generalized across all Indigenous peoples and within groups, disregards dynamism and adaptivity, ignores the specificity of TEK, omits power dynamics within groups, "disguises individual creativity," and can also "overplay the sustainability of TEK" (Singleton et al. 2021:6-7).[93]

Further Reading:

- Davis, Anthony, and Kenneth Ruddle. 2010. "Constructing Confidence: Rational Skepticism and Systematic Enquiry in

Local Ecological Knowledge Research." *Ecological Applications* 20(3):880–94. doi: 10.1890/09-0422.1.

The "noble savage" and "ecological noble savage" tropes

Despite the vast differences between Indigenous cultures and individuals, the "ecological noble savage," sometimes also called the "ecological Indian," is assumed to be universally and without exception a noble, sustainability- and ecologically-minded people and persons. Even though these racist tropes are familiar and often taken for granted, logic and the evidence itself show that Indigenous cultures and individuals have the obvious capabilities to believe and act in all the various ways that most non-Indigenous peoples would label "good" and "bad" (Rowland 2004). Unlike hostile forms of prejudice, **benevolent prejudice** takes a seemingly positive stereotype of a people and applies it in a completely general way that ignores individual differences. The harm in this form of prejudice comes from generalizing Indigenous peoples, effectively rejecting the complexities that other privileged groups enjoy. Disparate cultures, groups, and unique individuals with complicated thoughts and experiences are reduced to easily definable and Disney-fied caricatures of simplicity.

Like mentioned above, there is a common understanding of Indigenous peoples, and here I'm mainly speaking about North American Indigenous folks, living in near-utopian societies before Christopher Columbus "discovering" the Americas. Of this view, Tawinikay (2018) presents a more nuanced case,

> Indigenous communities used to meet each spring to negotiate territories, form new agreements, and redistribute resources. Not all, of course, sometimes they just burned down their neighbors houses when they wanted them to move out. I am

not here tonight to romanticize some pre-contact utopia free from oppression and conflict.

The creation of these tropes was not just an instance of simple ignorance; instead, they were developed to convince white societies to either revere or look down on Indigenous cultures. Gregory D. Smithers (2015:85) explains,

> The modern ecological Indian idea has its antecedents in the imaginations of Europeans and Euroamericans from the late fifteenth century. It was a product of a relational history in which Europeans and Euroamerican traders, missionaries, and settlers believed their civilization was socially and culturally more advanced than the civilizations nurtured by North America's Native peoples. By the eighteenth and nineteenth centuries, Europeans and Euroamericans focused their mythologizing on "noble" ecological Indians living in harmony with nature as a way to highlight how Western civilizations had produced spiritually broken people—societies of isolated individuals who had become overly materialistic. In contrast, Europeans and Euroamericans imagined Native Americans as transhistorical figures possessing nurturing feminine qualities that allowed them to remain connected to the rhythms of the natural environment, thereby anchoring an emotive spirituality thought to be long extinguished in the white man's soul.

Take, for example, Indigenous Australians, historically called "Aboriginal people," who are often lumped all together as one people. Waldron and Newton (2012:66) explain, "With several hundred pre-contact languages, marked regional cultural differences and radical variation in the effects of the European colonial encounter, the idea of one monolithic Australian Aboriginal culture is unsustainable." As for Native Americans, "[they] remain locked in the confines and time warps of American iconography so that, even in this time of multicultural America, we are typically accepted and recognized only in our crudest forms—as generic, buckskin clad warriors and exotic maidens" (Grande 1999:308). Other racial stereotypes show Native Americans as "soft-spoken" and beholden to "traditional" ways of life (TallBear 2001, as cited in Smithers 2015:84). Analyzing Robert F. Berkhofer Jr.'s 1979 book, *The White Man's Indian*, Grande explains Berkhofer's central thesis as critiquing how white America fluctuates between images of Native Americans as "noble" and "ignoble," based on the current conditions of Native American and white relations. Essentially, Grande (1999) describes Berkhofer's book as illustrating how, "when white civilization is in favor, Indians are deemed ignoble, and when white civilization is in disfavor, "Indian-ness" becomes the elixir"; which version of Native Americans becomes more prominent in society is based on the "polemical and creative needs of whites" (309). Grande explains that, as opposed to non-Indigenous societies, Indigenous ones like those of Native Americans are reduced to "uncomplicated primitive utopias" (309). Ultimately, to maintain the current "domination, resistance, and subjugation" of Indigenous peoples like the Native Americans by whites, white society must continue "the image of Indians as 'primitive' peoples living at one with nature. This allows white society to distance themselves from Native Americans by categorizing them as part of "nature"—both an act of **dehumanization** and **animalization** (312).

But the "ecological Indian" trope can be malleable, depending on which agenda is being pushed. The earliest views of Native Americans by European settlers saw them "as a constituent part of nature and apart from civilization" (Kim 2020:51). When the "ecological Indian" trope was developed, it saw "the Native American" as "a natural conservationist, lives simply and virtuously, maintains a spiritual balance with nature, and thus serves as the perfect foil for the Western capitalist." And then, late in the 20th century, Native Americans who wished to take up some of their ancestors' traditional hunting practices were often met with non-Indigenous outrage, such as the case of

> the Makah for acting non-ecologically, or betraying their Indian-ness. That is, the "ecological Indian" trope functioned as a disciplinary tool, essentializing Native Americans (in the guise of lauding them) and erecting a behavioral ideal that was both restrictive and unattainable. (P. 51)

Charges of "colonialism," "imperialism," and "racism" are commonly lobbed at those critical of hunting nonhuman animals because of the long history of these forms of oppression against Indigenous peoples. For many Makah tribespeople, "To resume whaling meant honoring and connecting with those ancestors, recovering a suppressed tradition, restoring a severed bond between the Makah and the whale, making real a treaty right, and reinvigorating tribal culture and identity...[and] resisting colonial domination and asserting sovereignty" (74).

Claire Jean Kim insists that pro-Indigenous hunting advocates and pro-nonhuman animal advocates should avoid a politics of disavowal, whereby both groups ignore or denounce the other side as "wrong." Instead, both sides should consider that the other side may be correct in their understanding of reality. She also ultimately makes the case that everyone should "err on the side of caution and act as though [other animals] wish to live" (86).

It should go without saying that the larger nonhuman animal liberation movement should not single out Indigenous nonhuman animal practices over more common non-Indigenous nonhuman animal practices. Doing so would prioritize criticizing Indigenous practices over practices that take place on a much greater scale. In my view, non-Indigenous people who are for nonhuman animal liberation can be against these practices, especially those not done out of survival, and also not prioritize criticism toward them.

JOHN TALLENT

Just "normal" people

I think anyone who attempts to make such wide-ranging generalizations about so many groups and individuals across many different localities, and spanning different times in human history, will ultimately have their work cut out about scientific evidence. In my view, one of the most reasonable ways to think about this situation is from the following two quotes. The first is by anthropologist Ernest S. Burch Jr (2007:147), who concluded his article about the academic debates over the romanticization and denigration of Indigenous peoples concerning environmentalism and sustainability:

> I recommend that the polarizing debate over whether Native Americans were either rational conservationists or rapacious overkillers be dropped; it has become an ultimately arational debate rather than a scientific one. The evidence…shows early contact Native American hunters to have been ordinary human beings who engaged in behavior that involved cognitive orientations manifesting a complex mixture of rational and nonrational elements under a specific set of conditions. A nuanced understanding of the particular mix of cognitive orientations that guided specific peoples operating under specified conditions, without the wholesale categorization of the people involved as being either conservationists or savages, would make for better science. It would also help us achieve a greater understanding of social and ecological change and, in the contemporary world, might lead to more effective resource management.

Another interesting perspective stems from Graeber and Wengrow's discussion on past Indigenous peoples (2021)[94]:

> One of the most pernicious aspects of standard world-historical narratives is precisely that they dry everything up, reduce

people to cardboard stereotypes, simplify the issues (are we inherently selfish and violent, or innately kind and co-operative?) in ways that themselves undermine, possibly even destroy, our sense of human possibility. 'Noble' savages are, ultimately, just as boring as savage ones; more to the point, neither actually exist. Helena Valero was herself adamant on this point. The Yanomami were not devils, she insisted, neither were they angels. They were human, like the rest of us.

Appealing to tradition but not to personhood

Like Indigenous peoples, "traditions" are almost ubiquitously thought of as static, universalized, etched-in-stone behaviors. But that's not how traditions work, given that nonhuman animal populations, technology, material conditions, and beliefs change. Considering the "hunting, fishing, gathering, and trapping" by Indigenous peoples, especially in North America, as "traditional" in the modern era would be inaccurate, according to scholar Lisa Kimmerer. For her, these 'are best viewed as new practices, or as potential "new traditions,"' given the differences between how these were once practiced versus today concerning their "methods, means, and desired ends" (Kimmerer 2004a:no pagination). Kimmerer (2004b) further points out that many Indigenous peoples' current and past ethics are not the same, especially considering that killing in the past was a necessity for survival and today it might not typically be.

We must be extremely reticent to make claims that allow for nonhuman animal exploitation or death for any reason, including claims of "tradition." Traditions develop under specific conditions and are not necessarily continuously appropriate or morally relevant. As Linda Fisher (2011:114) quips,

> At one time Mayans sacrificed young maidens each season, throwing them into deep pits to appease the gods. Tribes in the jungles of New Guinea and New Zealand have recently practiced cannibalism for spiritual and religious purposes. When Europeans invaded those territories, such religious practices were outlawed. So what about those tribes' right to retain tradition?

Even the decolonization movement has largely left nonhuman animal subjectivity and autonomy out of most discussions. Billy-Ray Belcourt (2014) critiques more mainstream decolonization theories that allow for nonhuman animal exploitation and killing in the name of "tradition" and "ceremony." Instead, Belcourt reconceptualizes decolonization as necessarily including an Indigenous veganism and nonhuman animal ethic. And despite the insistence by many Indigenous peoples that killing and exploiting nonhuman animals is by no means "respectful" or "humane," as some of the quotes in this chapter show, nonhuman animal advocates are still critiqued for "colonizing" by much of society. However, I believe it is important to remember that most nonhuman animal advocates simply ask for the same right to different cosmologies for nonhuman animals as any human.

Multiculturalism and universal morals

Proponents of "traditional" and "cultural" nonhuman animal practices often use "multiculturalism" as the basis for why nonhuman animal advocates should not criticize these practices. As Claire Jean Kim (2007) aptly explains when discussing the practices of some US immigrants, multiculturalism fails to address these issues for several reasons:

> Like all interpretive frameworks, the multiculturalist framework slides easily into reductionism, involving the following problem-

> atic moves. First, the multiculturalist framework essentializes the activity of animal advocates as a form of *cultural imperialism*. Second, it essentializes cultures (both majority and minority) as coherent, unitary wholes. Third, it elides ideological, rhetorical, and strategic differences among animal advocates, the mainstream media, politicians, and others, by lumping these distinct entities together as "the dominant group(s)!" Finally the multiculturalist framework denies that animal advocates are in fact as critical (if not more so) of the animal practices of the majority as they are of the animal practices of immigrant minorities. (P. 239)

Contrary to multiculturalism is the idea of universal morals—morals shared by all humans or that proponents think *should* be shared. Is it "ethnocentric" to believe in universal morals? Claire Jean Kim (2007) doesn't necessarily think so. It's more important to look at *what* those morals might be. She explains that, in the case of nonhuman animal advocates that criticize "traditional" or "cultural" nonhuman animal practices, the nonhuman animal advocates could engage in ethnocentrism if they also believe that their own culture's exploitation of other animals is not morally wrong. So many nonhuman animal advocates also criticize their culture's exploitation of other animals, though. It isn't advocacy directed *only* at these marginalized cultures; it's advocacy that *includes* these cultures and the greater advocacy against *all* cruelty and exploitation of other animals.

We, as people within society, do not believe that universal morals exist, and we are also convinced that they do. For instance, many people will self-assuredly deny that they believe in morality. They insist that morality is similar to religion in that it is up to each individual to decide their own morality. In this sense, these folks believe in **moral relativism**, which "is the view that right and wrong, good and bad are relative to and vary with individual or cultural perspectives and frameworks" (Wright 2015:236). It's important to understand that there are a few subdivisions of moral relativism, but I will only focus on two here: *descriptive* and *ethical*. *Descriptive moral relativism* simply suggests that different people and cultures believe in different morals. *Ethical moral relativism* says that it is *wrong* to impose your morals on others; in other words, ethical moral relativism sees all morals as subjective and, therefore, true or false relative to each person or culture (Wright 2015:236).

I argue that some morals may be subjective, especially those that do not negatively affect others, but some morals are objectively and universally true. For example, every human on Earth might not believe that genocide is morally wrong, but genocide is objectively wrong, and its wrongness universally applies to all people and cultures. The same prescription can also be applied to other issues, such as slavery, sexual violence, child abuse, nonhuman animal abuse, sexism, racism, cissexism and heterosexism[95], and the general idea that it is morally wrong to harm people unnecessarily.

There is a glaring problem with denying that there are universal moral truths. If they do not exist, why would anyone believe that it is worthwhile or even their right to impose on others the beliefs in anti-slavery, anti-genocide, anti-sexual violence, etc.? Dismissing the idea that there are inherent, universal morals that are "true," when brought to its logical conclusion, is an assertion that "anything goes" and that all beliefs and actions can be "good." But even that kind of understanding of morality is underpinned by the fact that to believe no one should impose their morality on others, one must observe that it is universally "wrong" to impose morality on others. It is an inescapable paradox.

Going back to the issue of "traditional" and "cultural" nonhuman animal practices, it is indeed common, however, and mostly even "expected," for nonhuman animal liberationists to share the view that denouncing or intervening in "traditional" forms of nonhuman animal exploitation is "colonialism" and "cultural imperialism." For instance, Legge and Taha (2017) of the group Hamilton Animal Liberation Team (HALT) in Canada write that it is "intersectionality" that demands that they do not take a strict stance on either side of the debate. Yet, they absolutely do take a strict stance *against* other animals' intrinsic rights to self-autonomy:

> HALT is a grassroots collective of individuals fighting to end human and OTH [Other-Than-Human] animal oppression in their communities and across Southern Ontario. Even though the membership is in constant flux, the collective's core values remain grounded; HALT operates from an intersectional anti-oppressive lens and is anti-capitalist, with an emphasis on its firm stance in support of Indigenous self-determination, sovereignty, and land defense. HALT is comprised of both settler and Indigenous activists...There is a clear tension that was experienced by the authors of this paper during their involvement in the demonstrations at Short Hills. It was challenging for us to reconcile our dedication to animal liberation with supporting Indigenous hunting; this tension is representative of the very nature of intersectionality itself, where two salient identities clash: identifying as vegan and animal liberation activists, and recognizing the privilege of being settlers. Intersectionality rejects the notion of separating identity categories but instead focuses on their intertwining and inextricable natures...When AR activists protest Indigenous peoples' right to hunt, HALT's stance is that AR activists are not adequately acknowledging or addressing their role in the perpetuation of colonization and oppression of Indigenous peoples as settlers. HALT does not endorse the hunting of animals; however, HALT cannot and will not intervene in the traditional practices of Indigenous peoples, in order to avoid replicating colonial patterns of oppression, and the demonstration of white saviourism...(P. 67-9)

In this context, if the group were to take a firm stance against this type of hunting and trapping, it would be "replicating colonial patters of oppression, and the demonstration of white saviourism"; on the other hand, what do they consider themselves *when they deem nonhuman animals as harmable and exploitable in certain instances where survival is not the case?* Wrapped in this language and interpretation of "intersectionality," nonhuman animals are further marginalized, and stripped of agency and self-determination. The authors go on, with open questions and mixed messaging,

> Taking into account population growth alone, it becomes clear that Indigenous rights movements will not be easily overpowered in the future. This will have deleterious effects for AR activists who refuse an intersectional lens. That said, not all AR activists will be comfortable with all forms of solidarity with Indigenous activists. In her analysis of the Makah whale hunt in Dangerous Crossings, Kim (2015) eventually comes to the conclusion that "it may be prudent to err on the side of caution and act as though gray whales wish to live. Otherwise, we humans, Native and non-Native, run the risk of imposing our own systems of meaning on those who lack the power to contradict us" (p. 245). While there is value in considering what Kim (2015) makes clear here–that we cannot fully know the perspectives of the OTH animals who are the third party in AR activism–the authors of this article were unable to reconcile whether this perspectival anthropocentrism was enough to justify potential neocolonialism. On the other hand, will hunting more animals truly heal past pain and suffering faced by the Indigenous people of this land? Or must we do as [Margaret] Robinson...suggests, and look at how we can adapt ethical models of eating and living in nature to fit an Indigenous way of living and knowing? (P. 76)

I hope I've convinced you enough to believe that morals are not all subjective and that we all believe in some universal morals. With this understanding, we can move away from the typical disservice we do to nonhuman animals by denying them the same right to life that we humans all believe we have. It is from the human vantage point—a vantage point too often of supremacism of other animals—that would entertain any suggestion that an act of unnecessary harm to other animals without their consent could be morally just. Additionally, it is unreasonable to consider the argument that criticizing traditions that cause unjustified harm to others is *necessarily* "imperialist," "colonialist," or "racist."

I also hope to discourage non-Indigenous Leftists who bring up Indigenous peoples in veganism discussions and debates from continuing to tokenize and deflect from their own behaviors. Indigenous peoples are not a monolith. And it should also be clear that the exploitation of the history of genocide against Indigenous peoples all around the world should not be used as a shield to defend one's exploitation of other animals. Using this history is not the solidarity you may think it is. Especially given that the exploitation of other animals has commonly been used as a tactic of worldwide colonialism *against* Indigenous peoples and others (Alvarez n.d.; Deckha 2020; Ficek 2019; Krásná 2022).

Further Reading:

- Krásná, Denisa. 2022b. "Towards Horizontal Relationships: Anarcha Indigenism, Decolonial Animal Ethic, and Indigenous Veganism." *Canada and Beyond: A Journal of Canadian Literary and Cultural Studies* 11:31–51. doi: https://doi.org/10.14201/candb.v11i31-51.
- Parekh, Bhikhu C. 2006. *A New Politics of Identity: Political Principles for an Interdependent World*. Basingstoke: Palgrave.
- Twine, Richard. 2022. "Ecofeminism and Veganism: Revisiting the Question of Universalism." Pp. 229–46 in *Ecofeminism: Feminist Intersections with Other Animals and the Earth*, edited by C. J. Adams and L. Gruen. New York, NY: Bloomsbury Academic.

12

Entanglements and Analogies

I have learned that oppression and the intolerance of difference come in all shapes and sexes and colors and sexualities; and that among those of us who share the goals of liberation and a workable future for our children, there can be no hierarchies of oppression. I have learned that sexism and heterosexism both arise from the same source as racism.

—Audrey Lorde (1983)

If animal and disability oppression are entangled, might not that mean their paths of liberation are entangled as well?

—Sunaura Taylor (2017:xv)

This chapter, as well as the previous chapter regarding Indigenous traditions, is difficult to write. These issues are complex, provoke deep emotions, and opinions about them in the vegan community vary *wildly*. These issues are also where I'm putting myself out there in an extremely vulnerable way that could attract criticism. As a person with life-long social phobia and agoraphobia, this is not a typical corner to put myself into. While I do my best to present all these issues fairly and with appropriate nuance, I am also not traveling in the same direction as many other Leftist vegans who more often don't enter into these discussions. We often get caught up in these discussions, partly due to some formulations of identity politics, standpoint theories, and intersectionality, where progress can sometimes be stagnated or delayed. Discussions meant to move things forward devolve into Oppression Olympics, where the only valuable insights can come from those with the "most" forms of oppression against them. This is essentialism dressed as "progress." Instead of bringing marginalized people together and creating a united front against capitalism and all forms of social hierarchy, preference is given to more compartmentalization, separatism, and the narrowing of "acceptable" ideas.

I do not present a case to completely upend "identity politics," standpoint theories, or intersectionality. I'm not presenting myself as an expert here. Direct experience is a great educator but does not guarantee a sense of truth *or* objective reality. However, I think there are crucial insights from others that criticize these theories in legitimate ways. So, suppose we abandon the bandwagon fallacy in favor of logical yet nuanced critiques and alternatives. In that case, we can progress without giving in to the consequences of some popular ideas' constraints. Volcano (2012:34) explains this perfectly concerning how anarchists should engage:

> Think of how many times you've sat around with a group of well-meaning folks and the conversation has gone something like this: "As a working-class person, I have to say..." (a few nods of agreement) "As a poor woman, it seems to me..." (even more nods) "As a poor lesbian of color, I think..." (even more furious nodding, making sure everyone registers each other's frenetic agreement) And so on. These kinds of displays are often referred to as "the Oppression Olympics." People in these situations seem like they're playing a game together—a grand

contest to assert who is more authentic, more oppressed, and thus more correct. It's at this point where identity becomes fetishized; where essentialist understandings of people trump good sense; and where a patronizing belief in the superiority of the wise, noble savage often overrides any sense at all. Often this tactic of agreeing with "the most marginalized in the room" will be used as a substitute for developing critical analyses around race, gender, sexuality, etc. This tactic is intellectually lazy, lacks political depth, and leads toward tokenization. There is a point to allowing our experiences of various forcefully-assigned identities to be at the forefront of conversations. People do have different experiences based on these social constructions and we should take these differences into account. But when they become markers of authenticity and "correctness," it poses a problem for anarchists. After all, we seek to dissolve hierarchical relations, not create new ones formed from the margins.

Another point I want to make clear before going further in this section is how analogies, metaphors, comparisons, parallels, and similarities are not always synonymous with *equating* things. When we compare, for example, an apple and an orange, we are not saying that apples and oranges are the same. We are noting similarities and differences between the two—they are both fruits, round-ish, originate from trees, etc. Comparisons can be made in highly problematic ways, such as if someone says, "Speciesism is morally worse than racism." Such a comparison is subjective and creates a hierarchy of oppressions where racism is viewed as "not as bad as" speciesism. This pits two forms of oppression against one another in competition for an assumed scarcity of resources (such as the general public's attention, funding, etc.). Analogies, metaphors, parallels, comparisons, and similarities have many likenesses in that they are not necessarily viewing two or more things as "the same." Critiques of drawing parallels between various forms of oppression frequently confuse this as having a lack of nuance or an unwillingness to acknowledge important distinctions. To clarify my view here, especially in this section, I am *never* equating oppressions. All oppressions are different in that they have unique histories and effects, and they all intertwine in ways that we may not even be able to fathom. To equate oppressions would necessitate diluting the qualities of each and disrespecting real dissimilarities. But for something to be different also does not demand *complete* difference. There are fundamental similarities between all oppressions. For example, oppressions affect people, human and nonhuman animals alike. Speciesism and ableism often involve problematic beliefs about perceived intelligence and capabilities. Racism and speciesism (and many others) often involve placing a targeted group *outside* of what is considered the "human" category. Speciesism and sexism (and many others) often involve the exploitation of bodily autonomy and violating peoples' reproductive systems. Notice how none of these comparisons pit any oppressions against one another; none create a hierarchy where one is "worse" than another; none deny differences; none equate one another as "the same." They simply note how each intertwines with one another and how they can have similar effects on people. When we say that oppressions can never be compared, we create infinite uniqueness and obscure or prevent evidence of commonality and mutual struggle.

Who said we must engage in theories and ideas that we don't really agree with? And who's to say that a majority's opinion or belief in a particular idea or theory means that it is "good" or "true?" When did the bandwagon fallacy become an acceptable way of discussing serious issues? This does not mean that every widely held belief needs to be abandoned. Suppose there are logical arguments against a theory or idea that make sense. In that case, it is not "wrong" or "problematic" to accept criticisms or seek a better alternative that explains a social phenomenon better.

One theory that I believe can help us better understand the entanglements of human and nonhuman animal oppressions is **multidirectional**

memory theory. In this next section, I will explain what this theory is, its benefits, and (with my own adjustments) how it can lead us to a path forward that does not lead to some of the issues involved with some of our current Leftist paradigms.

Multidirectional memory theory

[C]omparisons, analogies, and other multidirectional invocations are an inevitable part of the struggle for justice. Against the alternatives to comparison—an intense investment in the particularity of every case...—I offer the multidirectional option: an ethical vision based on commitment to uncovering historical relatedness and working through the partial overlaps and conflicting claims that constitute the archives of memory and the terrain of politics.

—Michael Rothberg, Jewish academic[96]

Michael Rothberg, a professor of English and Comparative Literature and a scholar in memory studies, Holocaust studies, postcolonial studies, and others, developed what is called "multidirectional memory theory." In his words, this theory is

> a way of conceptualizing what happens when different histories of extreme violence confront each other in the public sphere. While acknowledging the struggles and contestations that accompany public articulations of memory, the theory of multidirectional memory seeks an explanation of the dynamics of remembrance that does not simply reproduce the terms of partisan groups involved in those struggles. (Rothberg 2014:176)

His conceptualization of this theory was articulated at length in his book *Multidirectional Memory: Remembering the Holocaust in the Age of Decolonization*. It posits, essentially, that memories of oppressions, such as the Holocaust, US slavery, and colonialism, should not be considered "worse" or "more important" to talk about than others. Instead, a comparison can be drawn between them that "memorializes them simultaneously" (Woodward 2019:158). There is too often a logic of scarcity at play, whereby memories compete with one another for limited space and resources. The book opens with the following questions that it seeks to answer:

> What happens when different histories confront each other in the public sphere? Does the remembrance of one history erase others from view? When memories of slavery and colonialism bump up against memories of the Holocaust in contemporary multicultural societies, must a competition of victims ensue? (Rothberg 2009:2)

He explains his thesis:

> I argue that the conceptual framework through which commentators and ordinary citizens have addressed the relationship between memory, identity, and violence is flawed. Against the framework that understands collective memory as competitive memory—as a zero-sum struggle over scarce resources—I suggest that we consider memory as *multidirectional*: as subject to ongoing negotiation, cross-referencing, and borrowing; as productive and not privative. (P. 3)

There are a few fundamental arguments within this work. The first is to dispel what he calls "competitive memory," which is the nearly ubiquitous way horrific events and the subsequent memory of such events, such as the Holocaust, US race-based slavery, and the colonization and genocide of Native Americans by European settlers, "compete" in a zero-sum game against one another. By doing this, any comparisons between these events or emphasis on any individual event marginalizes, trivializes, lessens their "uniqueness," or otherwise pushes the others to the side. Rothberg (2014:176) gives an example,

> According to this understanding, memories crowd each other out of the public sphere—for example, too much emphasis on the Holocaust is said to marginalize other traumas or, inversely, adoption of Holocaust rhetoric to speak of those other traumas is said to relativize or even deny the Holocaust's uniqueness.

Second, instead of marginalizing and trivializing each of these traumas, Rothberg suggests that it is beneficial to borrow and "cross-reference" events like these because they will inevitably *add* memory to them on the basis that they are being brought up and referenced *because* they live so atrociously in the public's mind. He also argues that traumas like these are not entirely distinct entities; they "emerge dialogically." In this way,

> not only has memory of the Holocaust served as a vehicle through which other histories of suffering have been articulated, but the emergence of Holocaust memory itself was from the start inflected by histories of slavery, colonialism, and decolonization that at first glance might seem to have little to do with it. (P. 176)

As a result, memory of the Holocaust has borrowed from the language and images of prior human atrocities. But, because memory and identity are not static things, memory of the Holocaust allowed for previous human atrocities to be re-remembered with the newer contexts of the Holocaust itself; this is multdirectionality in practice.

In this theory, "'multidirectionality' names a type of logic and serves as a theory of memory and political violence, both distorted by a linear view of time and unidirectional thinking" (Skitolsky 2013:no pagination). In other words, too often, eras of violence such as these are thought of as completely disparate and disconnected, with definite beginnings and endings whereby they could never interact with or influence one another. Take, for instance, this following quote in a *Salon Magazine* interview (Palumbo-Liu 2015) by the philosopher and political activist Cornel West:

> [T]here is no doubt that Gaza is not just a "kind of" concentration camp, it is the hood on steroids. Now in the black community, located within the American empire, you do have forms of domination and subordination, forms of police surveillance and so forth, so that we are not making claims of identity, we are making claims of forms of domination that must be connected. And those are not the only two — we could talk about the Dalit people in India and the ways that their humanity is being lost and there are parallels there; we could talk about peasants in Mexico. So all of these are going to have similarities and dissimilarities. But there is no doubt that for the Ferguson moment in America and the anti-occupation moment in the Israel-Palestinian struggle there is a very important connection to make and I think we should continue to make it.

To demonstrate the potential for cross-movement solidarities and solidarities based on comparisons between oppressions, West draws attention to the parallels he sees between the oppression Black people in the US experience and the Israeli apartheid against Palestinians.

We often see various oppressions compartmentalized as neatly wrapped experiences and only by a particular group of people that have been particularly affected by these oppressions. There is a common belief that comparisons and analogies of violent histories "dilute" and "relativize" the history being referenced. In multidirectional memory theory, this is not how history and ideas function. Multidirectional memory theory

> is not simply a one-way street; its exploration necessitates [a] comparative approach...My argument is not only that the Holocaust has enabled the articulation of other histories of victimization at the same time that it has been declared "unique" among human-perpetrated horrors...I also demonstrate the more surprising and seldom acknowledged fact that public memory of the Holocaust emerged in relation to postwar events that seem at first to have little to do with it...[E]arly Holocaust memory emerged in dialogue with the dynamic transformations and multifaceted struggles that define the era of decolonization. The period between 1945 and 1962 contains both the rise of consciousness of the Holocaust as an unprecedented form of modern genocide and the coming to national consciousness and political independence of many of the subjects of European colonialism...[T]he early postwar period contains an important insight into the dynamics of collective memory and the struggles over recognition and collective identity that continue to haunt contemporary, pluralistic societies. The fact that today the Holocaust is frequently set against global histories of racism, slavery, and colonialism in an ugly contest of comparative victimization...is part of a refusal to recognize the earlier conjunction of these histories...But the ordinarily unacknowledged history of cross-referencing that characterizes the period of decolonization continues to this day and constitutes a precondition of contemporary discourse. (Rothberg 2009:7)

With the example of the Holocaust here, it is easy to consider the Holocaust as a history "unlike" any other violence. However, this obscures the history of the Holocaust, where the ideas that enabled it were created and evolved over time. Rothberg explains that focusing on "uniqueness" is faulty and risky because "it potentially establishes a hierarchy of suffering" (9). For instance, while each atrocity and oppression *is* unique in its own way, focusing on how each is "unlike" any other can consciously or unconsciously pacify the general public in such a way that they don't feel like new or current atrocities "measure up" to an atrocity such as the Holocaust (10).

Multidirectional memory could be considered closely linked with the conceptualization of all oppressions interlocking, interacting, and ultimately being connected. Atalia Omer, in her book *Days of Awe: Reimagining Jewishness and Solidarity with Palestinians*, notes how the theory of intersectionality allows for cross-movement and cross-trauma solidarity based on relating various movements, such as US anti-Blackness and the oppression of Palestinians by Israeli occupying forces, to their historical and ideological foundations; this is especially important in how "the security machinery of Israel and the militarization of US police" mirror one another. She also gives an example, "Angela Davis, the African American feminist scholar and activist, was an early voice in exposing the interconnections between Israel and the prison-industrial complex in the US" (Omer 2019:179-80).

While the examples I've given are just a few compared to the myriad literature on these subjects, I think it's important to keep in mind the messy, subjective, diverse, and jagged nature of identities and oppressions. While correlations and tendencies can be found, there is not one "gay and disabled view," "Black and lesbian view," or "trans Palestinian view." We already saw the problematic nature of essentialism in how Indigenous peoples worldwide are singularized and assumed to have monolithic views and traditions. The subjectivity of sentient experience does not work like that. Thus, differences in experience and identity may contribute to attributing commonalities between traumatic histories. As we will see, some Jewish people see similarities, whatever they may be, between the Holocaust and nonhuman animal oppression. Some people see parallels between human sexism and the exploitation of nonhuman animal bodies. Comparisons are often seen as "equating" two histories, and thereby comparisons are misjudged as not just *politically* wrong but also *morally* wrong. But, these comparisons, commonalities, similarities, parallels, analogies, resemblances, juxtapositions—whatever words one uses—do not trivialize, minimize, dismiss, erase, belittle, disparage, or diminish the uniqueness of any trauma or oppression *intrinsically*. Changes in understanding can happen through comparisons. Linkages between ideas and emotions can be grounded in the empathy one might eventually find in comparisons, which can blossom into grand epiphanies of collective struggle and solidarity.

Memory and history can also be more interesting and complex than simple. Rothberg explains how accepting this can benefit our current understanding,

> [T]he borders of memory and identity are jagged; what looks at first like my own property often turns out to be a borrowing or adaptation from a history that initially might seem foreign or distant. Memory's anachronistic quality—its bringing together of now and then, here and there—is actually the source of its powerful creativity, its ability to build new worlds out of the materials of older ones. (Rothberg 2009:5)

We too often see our own oppression, or our ancestors' oppression, as developing and working in total uniqueness. What do others know about our oppression if they haven't experienced it directly? Well, a sense of collective struggle affords us not direct experience but the capacity for genuine empathy. Learning about our direct experiences is crucial and essential, but even in the absence of such direct experience, one can still know and understand that our shared struggle in a world of domination is against purposeless and unwelcome suffering. I don't know your exact struggle, and you don't know mine, but struggle do we both.

Ableism and disability were rarely in my mind before I read Sunaura Taylor's *Beasts of Burden: Animal and Disability Liberation* (2017). After reading, sometimes immediately and other times a while after, connections began to be made not only about how humans experience disability but also about how those experiences have apparent similarities to the speciesism and ableism experienced by nonhuman animals. And even after those similarities were realized, a moment of reflexivity ultimately happened. The ableism I saw against nonhuman animals allowed me to see even more ways in which disabled humans experience the animalization of their bodies and minds by a society that often conflates differences in ability and differences in species.

Capitalism only values profit and profit-making, and I was made further aware of these facts when my disabilities became unavoidably clear during the early parts of the COVID-19 pandemic. I was working at Whole Foods Market at the time when the outbreak first began. Just a few months prior, I started feeling strange: I was constantly dizzy and constantly had a migraine. My balance was off; I was often nauseous; one of my ears always felt "full" and was painful; I had brain fog; my short-term memory was not the same, and I was sometimes confused; I began having muscle spasms all over one side of my face and neck that felt like a slow-moving spark of electricity; my facial muscles and jaw would tremble; the muscles under my eyebrow felt tense and, when I looked in the mirror, it looked as though I was raising just that one eyebrow; and the scariest part for me was when that "spark of electricity" feeling moved towards and over my ear, I felt as though I was going to lose consciousness. I feared I would not wake up. At this point, I thought I might have multiple sclerosis (MS) or myasthenia gravis (MG), which both run in my family.

I saw many types of doctors, but eventually, I saw an oral surgeon who told me that I most likely had severe symptoms from a temporomandibular disorder (TMD), which means that I have something going on where the jawbone meets the cheek bone. These disorders/dysfunctions can create havoc on the bones, inflame the area, and affect the surrounding nerves. After various X-rays, we found out this was all likely caused by wisdom teeth, a lack of space for all my teeth along the jawbone, and a misaligned bite (my teeth don't fit together correctly in a relaxed fashion). This was both good news and bad news for me: the good news was that it probably wasn't MS or MG, but the bad news was that the doctor told me that the only way to fix the problem was to get a $2,000 mouth appliance that helps my jaw relax and also to get extensive jaw surgery eventually. This fucking jerk had me sit down with him in his office to explain that he offered a "package deal" surgery, where I'd go to a private out-patient surgery center, and he would do the procedure—all for the low, low price of $30,000. What a steal!

Anyway, the main point of this story is that while the doctor diagnosed me with the disorder, knew all of my severe symptoms, and knew my monetary situation (working in retail doesn't usually make you rich), he still refused to sign paperwork that would allow me to take short-term disability leave from my job. Eventually, I found a primary care doctor who signed the paperwork, but it wasn't easy. My symptoms and disorder were not "typical" of the disabilities people receive disability leave for. Asking these doctors about disability leave would often illicit a kind of smug smirk, a sort of look that said crudely but subtly, "You can still work, you lazy fuck." Even with knowing my history with the illness, the constant fears of dying from these spasmatic "zaps" in and around my brain and nerves, feeling like I was losing my mind and would eventually deteriorate in health, thereby my wife would be forced to "deal with" and take care of this newly helpless spouse, I was still expected to go to work and even during the pandemic.

From July 2020, when I was first diagnosed, to December of the same year, I had to deal with my insurance company, my employers, and doctors—all while being sick and terrified of being fired from being unable to work. Against all the doctors' advice, I stayed out of work that entire time. I had to. There was no way that I could function at a job, especially safely. Luckily my short-term disability pay was approved by the insurance company, but only after a remarkably caring nurse practitioner explained the entire situation to them and how my condition was much worse than one might think. And when that limited time of paid leave ended, I was essentially out of options and had to quit my job. And in this way, my illness (illnesses, really) was considered "profit-losing" for capitalism. I was expected to use my body to labor and produce goods and services, but I couldn't. So I then became disposable to the system. I wasn't "sick enough" to "deserve" more paid time off, so capitalism had to remove my parasitic lazy ass from its capital-seeking body. But, for me, this seemed familiar to some of the circumstances of others that I had heard about. Not just of other disabled humans, who are so often considered "useless" to the system, but from the things I had read about and learned from Sunaura Taylor's book—how disability is also used to oppress nonhuman animals, and especially in capitalism.

Nonhuman animals, especially ones exploited in industry, are often forced to be disabled. As Taylor notes, "What does it mean to speak of a 'healthy' or 'normal' chicken, pig, or cow when they all live in environments that are profoundly disabling? Indeed, when they are all bred to be disabled?" (38). And not only are other animals made disabled in certain contexts, but they also are killed or discarded when they are no longer "productive." They also aren't given the same fundamental rights as humans because they are considered "less intelligent" and "less capable." I will let Taylor's words speak for themselves at length, as they explain much better than I could paraphrase or sum up in one sentence:

> Justifications for human domination over animals almost always rely on comparing human and animal abilities and traits...But isn't it ableist to devalue animals because of what abilities they do or do not have?...The fact that one of the most ubiquitous arguments people use in support of our continued exploitation of nonhumans is that animals are incapable of a myriad of cognitive processes that human beings engage in shows the extent to which speciesism uses ableist logics to function. Presumed to be deficient in human markers of

intelligence, animals are understood, to put it bluntly, as stupid. Their lack of various capabilities is often cited as proof of our superiority as human beings and as justification for our continued use of them for our own benefit...Ableism allows us to view human abilities as unquestionably superior to animal abilities; it propels our assumptions that our own human movements, thought processes, and ways of being are always not only more sophisticated than animals' but in fact give us value. Animals, in their inferior bestial state, can be used by us without moral concern, and those humans who have been associated with animals (people of color, women, queer people, poor people, and disabled people, among others) are also seen as less sophisticated, as having less value, and sometimes even as being less or non-human. In fact, certain abilities and capacities are central to definitions of the human; they are thought to mark the boundaries between humanity and the rest of the animal world. In this way ableism gives shape to what and who we think of as human versus animal. Ableism also fosters values and institutions that perpetuate animal suffering. The various animal industries that exist in this country (from factory farms to animal research) rely on the public belief that using animals is okay because they lack the capacities that would make their use wrong. These industries also rely on ideologies of nature to justify what they do (perpetuating the idea that it is simply natural to use animals for our benefit, for instance). But even ideas of nature and naturalness are bound up with ableism, because constructions of nature often conflate such things as health, normalcy, and independence with evolutionary fitness or ecological compatibility. Ableist values are central to animal industries, where the dependency, vulnerability, and presumed lack of emotional awareness or intellectual capacity of animals creates the groundwork for a system that makes billions of dollars in profit off of animal lives. The very norms and

JOHN TALLENT

> institutions that perpetuate animal suffering and exploitation are supported by ableism. (Pp. 36-7)

I use my own experiences with oppression to try my best to understand what others might be going through in their forms of oppression. And even though the forms of oppression that I experience (ableism, plus others) are just one of the ways in which I attempt to empathize with other animals' experiences with ableism and speciesism, I can still begin to understand and empathize with them through different forms of oppression that I might experience. I don't have to have lived as a nonhuman animal to see the pain on their faces and in their screams; I don't have to have lived as a nonhuman animal to see their forms of familial love and friendships with one another. Their fear, suffering, frustration, mental illness, excitement, shame, grief, and confusion can be seen, understood, and empathized with because we all know these experiences. Completely? No. Every single nuance? Of course not. But, especially those of us that understand the effects of oppression, we can feel pain, suffering, confusion, mental illness, and all other emotions that many humans and nonhuman animals have in common. We do not live on different planets; we are not made of different elements. If we have similar ways of feeling, we can also begin to understand some of what others feel because it is similar to how we feel. Donald Trump doesn't know what it's like to be a transgender person living in a profoundly transphobic society. But, even though he doesn't have direct experience, his lack of trying to learn and empathize with transgender folks (among many other things) is why he both fears and hates them. He has thus far refused to apply his personal experiences with physical pains and emotional heartaches to begin the lifelong project of relating to others. We aren't all Donald Trump.

As Rothberg (2009:313) ends the epilogue of his book, he gives a simple yet important fact regarding how we can begin to dismantle these forms of oppression and to understand these eras of violence more clearly: "The only way forward is through their entanglement."

Singh (2018) does a wonderful job of this by including the exploitation of nonhuman animals in multidirectional memory theory. Singh preemptively answers an essential and genuine question that others may have against including nonhuman animal exploitation into this type of framework: how can multidirectional memory theory be used for a group of beings who may or may not have traumatic memories of their exploitation? She surmises,

> While the animal may not remember its [sic] traumatic past in a conscious way (or does it?) [sic], it [sic] certainly continues to experience and be molded by its [sic] trauma. The absence of evidential animal memory in no way exonerates human populations from linking the modern violence done to the animal with other acts of violence enacted by and on humans (some remarkably similar in nature when we consider the striking resemblance between the extermination camp and the slaughterhouse). Rothberg argues that "a certain bracketing of empirical history and an openness to the possibility of strange political bedfellows are necessary in order for the imaginative links between different historical groups to come into view; these imaginative links are the substance of multidirectional memory. Comparison, like memory, should be thought as productive—as producing new objects and new lines of sight—and not simply as reproducing already given entities that either are or are not 'like' other already given entities" (Singh 2018:145-6, citing Rothberg 2009:18–19)

Holocaust analogies

The holocausts—burnt offerings—of the ancient Hebrews consisted of countless nonhuman animals, as did the religious animal sacrifices conducted throughout the ancient world by the Greeks, Hindus, Muslims,

JOHN TALLENT

Native Americans, and other cultures...Yet we are not supposed to regard those animals or their counterparts in today's world, where the consumption of animals for food rises to ever-greater levels. We are not supposed to contemplate the experience of animals in being turned into "burnt offerings," meat, metaphors, and other forms that obliterate their lives, personalities, feelings, and identities that we choose to confer.

—Karen Davis[97]

*Blood spilled for lust
In these temples of terror.
Factory farms, vivisection laboratories
Fur ranches, slaughterhouses
All replace concentration camps.
Still injustice remains
End this evil empire built upon the graves
Of the murdered
And devoured creatures.
Salvation I whisper thy name
And scream for liberation.
Consumption
Of lifeless bodies is a vote for
Genocide.*

—Arkangel, from the song "Built Upon The Graves"

I'm neither Jewish nor know for sure of any family members, present or past, that are either. I grew up in a town, a state, a country, and a world that is largely antisemitic. Even now, as I'm writing this in 2022 and 2023, antisemitism has increased in the US, especially since the election of Donald Trump (Contreras 2022). This section is written from my perspective, based on two things: 1) what I know from people with direct experience and 2) my own sense of justice.

There are several interesting aspects of the comparisons between the Holocaust and nonhuman animal exploitation. I will start with this one:

> It is not often known that the very term, "Holocaust," intrinsically involves a comparison to animal exploitation. Boria Sax points out that the term, "Holocaust," originally denoted "a Hebrew sacrifice in which the entire animal was given to Yahweh [God] to be consumed with fire"...In a twist of history, then, a form of animal exploitation became a metaphor for what happened to the Jews at the hands of the Nazis. It is asked if the Holocaust can be compared with animal exploitation, even though the very term involves such a comparison, albeit metaphorically. (Sztybel 2006:98)

Yes, we commonly use the term for the Nazi genocide of Jewish people (and Roma, disabled, queer folks, and others); however, as we've learned, atrocities throughout history are *multidirectional* in memory. So, as it turns out, it wasn't nonhuman animal advocates that were initially using comparisons. Comparing, borrowing, and relating to other atrocities is common, and this atrocity indeed confirms Rothberg's theory. Just as slavery and colonialism were referenced through the memories of the Holocaust, so too was nonhuman animal oppression. These human atrocities are now being borrowed from, compared to, and related to in the context of nonhuman animal advocacy. And, as Rothberg has also mentioned, memories like these are subject to perpetual "dialogical" and historical changes. As atrocities happen or are re-remembered, the memories of them are in constant flux, re-shaping and re-interpreting—i.e. memories of atrocities are not static.

Consider the fact that many Jewish people who advocate for the liberation of nonhuman animals do not sugarcoat their opinions on the matter; they refer to the treatment of nonhuman animals as a "holocaust" (Alloun 2020:4). For them, comparing nonhuman animal oppression to the oppression of Jewish people throughout history is necessary because both forms of oppression disregard and devalue a group of people. As a prisoner of the Dachau concentration camp in Nazi Germany, Edgar Kupfer-Koberwitz wrote to a friend about his experiences and how he saw the connections to other animals:

> My dear Friend!
> How shall I begin to tell you what I want to say? It is hard, and I hardly know how to begin.
> And yet I will try my best; at first, I want you to know my fundamental thoughts, before come to the details:
> I believe that, as long as man tortures and kills animals, he will torture and kill humans as well — and wars will be waged — for killing must be practiced and learned in a small scale, inwardly and outwardly. As long as animals are confined in cages, there will be prisons as well — for incarceration must be practiced and learned, in a small scale, inwardly and outwardly. As long as there are animal slaves, there will be human slaves as well, — for slavery must be learned and practiced, on a small scale — inwardly and outwardly.
> I don't think it necessary to be shocked at the little or big atrocities and cruelties others are committing, but I do not think it very necessary that we begin to be shocked where we are acting cruelly ourselves, in a large or small scale. As it is more easy to accomplish small things than great ones, I think we should try to overcome our own small thoughtless cruelty, to avoid it, to abolish it. Then one day it won't be so hard to fight and overcome our great heartlessness.
> But all of us are still asleep in our traditions. Traditions are like a greasy, tasteful gravy, which lets us swallow our own selfish heartlessness without noticing how bitter it is.

> But I don't want to point at him or her— no, I want to wake up myself and begin to be more understanding, more helpful, and kinder, on a small scale. Why shouldn't I succeed on a large scale later on? (Akers n.d.)

He was also said to have been so

> moved, after his liberation, to "furtively scrawl" the following message on the wall of a hospital barrack: I refuse to eat animals because I cannot nourish myself by the sufferings and by the death of other creatures. I refuse to do so, because I suffered so painfully myself that I can feel the pains of others by recalling my own sufferings. (Gold 1995:25, as cited by Sztybel 2006:99)

In his book, *Eternal Treblinka: Our Treatment of Animals and the Holocaust*, Charles Patterson (2002:169, 181, 186-7)) argues that industrial killing of nonhuman animals and antisemitism co-constituted the path to the Holocaust. Patterson also quotes many people affected by the Holocaust that have since compared it to the situation of nonhuman animals. For example, someone directly affected by the Holocaust, Isaac Bashevis Singer, a Yiddish writer and Nobel Prize in Literature winner in 1978, fled from Poland to the United States just years before many of his family members were killed in the Holocaust. Singer often invoked comparisons in his works between humans in the Holocaust and nonhuman animal exploitation. For instance, one of his more famous instances of this is found in his novel, *Enemies, A Love Story*. In this story, Singer declares that "'every man is a Nazi' when it comes to animals." He even used concentration camp descriptions to detail nonhuman animal zoos. Singer also saw the massive number of nonhuman animals killed for food "as an eternal Treblinka."

Jewish vegan and founder of the organization United Poultry Concerns, Karen Davis (2004) explains how her use of Holocaust analogies is beneficial when they are used non-competitively:

> When the oppression of one group is used metaphorically to illuminate the oppression of another group, justice requires that the oppression that forms the basis of the comparison be comprehended in its own right. The originating oppression that generates the metaphor must not be treated as a mere figure of speech, a mere point of reference. It must not be treated illogically as a lesser matter than that which it is being used to draw attention to. (P. 1)

Comparisons are not simple or easy. But comparisons are almost ubiquitous. She goes on:

> A problem that remains to be solved, notwithstanding, is how to win attention to sufferers and suffering that most people do not want to hear about, or have trouble imagining, or would just as soon forget. One way is to use an analogy (a logical parallel), or a metaphor (a suggested likeness) that already has meaning and resonance in the public mind. For example, oppressed people, such as slaughterhouse workers, say of themselves, "We are treated like animals," and people who raise chickens for the poultry industry likewise compare themselves in the situation they are in to "animals." (P. 3)

Nonhuman animal suffering and exploitation are often appropriated to draw parallels to human suffering; it is also often dismissed and trivialized as "not as harmful" or "important" as human suffering. This allowance for analogizing is not echoed back to nonhuman animals, though. As we've seen, when human atrocities and suffering are analogized in nonhuman animal contexts, most people react extremely negatively.

Davis recounts an angry response in the form of a letter to the editor to an article she wrote in 1999, where she compared the Holocaust and nonhuman animal exploitation. The indignant responder justified the use of nonhuman animal exploitation to describe Holocaust victims as being treated "like animals, maybe worse than animals" (4). Davis goes on to suggest an important question that is never asked:

> It is acceptable…to appropriate the treatment of nonhuman animals to characterize one's own mistreatment, but not the other way around. Advocates of this position believe that they can legitimately use the experience of nonhuman animals to characterize their own experience, even when the animals' experience has not been duly acknowledged or imaginatively conceived of to any degree, and perhaps has been dismissed without further inquiry. If so, it may be asked why anyone would compromise the case for the incomparability of one's own suffering by comparing it to the suffering of animals, given that nonhuman animals and their suffering are regarded as vastly inferior. (P. 8)

Some folks might think these comparisons are "wrong" because they don't believe that the Holocaust against Jewish peoples and others had the same fundamental bases as nonhuman animal exploitation. For them, it was hatred of Jewish, queer, disabled, and Roma peoples that formed the premise and that hatred is not why we exploit and kill other animals. But that is not accurate. For one thing, we do kill certain nonhuman animals because we hate them; think of nonhuman animals that we consider "pests" or "dangerous." However, there are other ways that these two forms of oppression are grounded in hatred. Consider this view by John Sanbonmatsu (2014:32):

> While *Anti-Semite and Jew* is today a largely forgotten work, with Sartre himself reduced to a historical footnote in contemporary social theory and philosophy, Sartre's existentialist critique of

> anti-Semitism as a form of bad faith can provide us with key insights into the nature of speciesism as a way of life. In anti-Semitism, it is negation of "the Jew" that serves as the basis of the anti-Semite's positive self-valuation, while in speciesism, it is hatred and negation of "the animal" as such. Simply by virtue of my belonging to a particular category of beings—Homo sapiens—an inherent value is bestowed upon me, one that, because it always precedes me, I need have done nothing to earn. ("There is nothing I have to do to merit my superiority," Sartre observes of anti-Semitism, "and neither can I lose it. It is given once and for all. It is a thing"...like anti-Semitism, speciesism too is less an assemblage of particular "opinions" about non-human beings than it is a "comprehensive attitude" to the world, one arising from a "free and total choice of oneself." As free beings, we could choose a way of life that does not require us to dominate and exterminate the other beings. The fact that we do not, however—that, instead, we continue affirming a way of life that is not only immoral but inimical to our own long-term survival and well-being—suggests that, like anti-Semitism, speciesism is as much an existential as a political question.

I think these issues are important to discuss, even though they might be challenging to discuss. Is there good reasoning as to why comparing the Holocaust to nonhuman animal exploitation is considered either "wrong" or "apples and oranges?" Speaking openly, honestly, and with mutual respect is how we should discuss issues like this, rather than resulting to petty character attacks or reductionist and essentialist forms of identity politics, which are most common and certainly the least helpful. When we begin to understand that comparisons are not inherently problematic, all oppressions are entangled, and nonhuman animals are oppressed peoples, we can truly begin to create a just world where no one is considered "more important" than any other and where domination is being pulled up firmly by its roots.

Further Reading:

- Rothberg, Michael. 2011. "From Gaza to Warsaw: Mapping Multidirectional Memory." *Criticism* 53(4):523–48. doi: https://doi.org/10.1353/crt.2011.0032.
- Woodward, Natalie. 2019. "Eternal Mirroring: Charles Patterson's Treatment of Animals and the Holocaust." *Journal of Animal Ethics* 9(2):158–69. doi: 10/gps8qw.

Slavery analogies

Like Holocaust analogies, analogizing nonhuman animal exploitation with human slavery has been an extremely contentious issue, to say the least. Comparing nonhuman animal oppression to human slavery, particularly anti-Black slavery, is said to contribute to the animalization of Black peoples. A lot of literature argues against the analogies, though the arguments are often diverse and can be nuanced. Another particular type of argument against these analogies is a disagreement about whether nonhuman animal exploitation is similar enough to human slavery to be a helpful analysis. In one article that seeks to determine if the analogy can be used for companion nonhuman animals, the author ultimately claims that it is not sufficiently similar enough because companion nonhuman animals' capacity for rationality 'falls well short of the idea of autonomy as requiring "reflection, foresight, self-assessment, sensitivity to values that might structure a life, knowledge of the kinds of life one [might] pursue,"' (Kendrick 2018:250). In my view, this is a tall order for a being to be considered to have the capacity for rationality. Does the label "slavery" really require these kinds of abilities? For instance, going by sentience alone, would a sentient person not meet these prerequisites to be considered a "slave" simply because they lack some or all forms of rationality? If that is the case, even some humans could never be regarded as enslaved people because these capacities are viewed as "lacking" in them. In other words, I think it should be rejected outright that certain types of intelligence determine the ability to be subjugated under slavery. It seems like good old-fashioned ableism intertwined with speciesism.

Nonhuman animal advocates in the 1800s in the US often compared the exploitation of nonhuman animals to human slavery at the time. As Claire Jean Kim explained, this was not controversial then for two main reasons. The first reason is that the methods and tools of nonhuman animal exploitation directly inspired many of how enslaved Black Africans were treated (Kim 2011). Marjorie Spiegel rigorously documents documented examples of comparisons of this relationship in her book, *The Dreaded Comparison: Human and Animal Slavery*.[98] Kim also stated that another main reason 19th-century nonhuman animal advocates used an analogy of slavery was that enslaved Black peoples were viewed the same as other animals: "dumb beasts fit only for servitude" (Kim 2011:314).

At least in her earlier writings, Kim sometimes defended the moral correctness of using analogies like slavery and the Holocaust. According to her, since nonhuman animals have long been considered categorically "different" from humans—the so-called "human-animal divide"—many times, the comparisons to forms of human oppression are meant to jolt people into a deeper understanding and can be made without devaluing the human oppression referenced. Cognitive dissonance may be created and can begin a journey of exploration and reconciliation within individuals. If nonhuman animals are not so different from humans and are more often falsely denied similarities with humans, the resemblances between humans and other animals sometimes obligate comparisons. And as we examined earlier, comparisons do not intrinsically equate two forms of oppression; instead, they can bring to light underlying mechanisms that can influence one another. Maneesha Deckha (2021) explains further, invoking a vital point by Lynn Worsham (2013) at the end:

> Yet the contextual unpalatability of the association should not erase the legitimacy of careful comparisons and multifocal analyses that affirm the ongoing and systemic nature of racism while trying to highlight animals' plight as they endure unrelentingly atrocious conditions of living and dying that most humans ignore or deny, and expose the shared animalizing narratives that sustain violence across species lines…We should be mindful that this resistance to comparisons with animals is the symptom that anti-exploitative animal theories and activism are trying to address. We should also consider that controversies over comparisons "may be yet another instance of deflection, another instance of the refusal to see or care about…the animals [that] continue to suffer the cruelty and indifference of the vast majority of their human animal kin." (Pp. 29-30)

Those final ellipses of that quote left out a commanding point by Worsham (2013:63-4) that I think should be read, and which I will denote using italics: "…may be yet another instance of deflection, another instance of the refusal to see or care about *the suffering of those for whom the subjection of animals is an atrocity of genocidal proportions. Of course, while we debate the accuracy or appropriateness of the analogy,* individual animals continue to suffer the cruelty and indifference of the vast majority of their human animal kin."

When we endeavor to genuinely look at the similarities, though, of human slavery and nonhuman animal exploitation, I think it becomes almost impossible to deny the similarities. Pleasants (2010:160) has written about the striking similarities of how both forms of exploitation have been viewed structurally as "a natural, necessary, and inevitable feature of the social world" beyond the similar material mechanisms (restraints, tools of "discipline," cages, etc.) that have had a direct back-and-forth influence on one another and that exemplify both nonhuman animal exploitation and the history of human slavery. Moreover,

JOHN TALLENT

> Defenders of slavery and animal exploitation were and are able to invoke a variety of warnings issued by expert authorities on the dire consequences of doing away with the functions that these practices serve, such as, for example, economic collapse, social disorder and disintegration, financial hardship, mortal damage to medical research, starvation, and ill health. For most people today, the idea that meat production and scientific research on animals might be prohibited is likely to elicit premonitions of a dull, impoverished, unhealthy, and uncaring world (a world in which the interests of rats, mice, cows, and pigs are protected at the cost of suffering and early death for human beings). It surely does not stretch the imagination to hypothesize that most people in slave trading and owning societies would have had an attitude to the necessity and dispensability of slavery that is similar to most people's today in relation to animal exploitation. If that hypothesis is well founded, then in order to gain some speculative insight into how it was that people living in slave owning and trading societies could have thought slavery indispensable and therefore not unjust, most people need only contemplate their own attitude toward animal exploitation. (P. 172)

So, we can see a great similarity between the two of how both groups have been seen as property and that using this "property" hasn't been considered "unjust." Also, the exploitation and ownership of nonhuman animals and humans have historically been defended as foundational to society. Removing either of them, it is believed, would mean the end of society, or at least the end of the "natural" way society "should" function.

Consider also how the general public has negatively represented abolitionists of both types of oppression. Before the antislavery movement became a critical force in the discussions over slavery (particularly in the US), abolitionists against slavery were deemed as engaging in "empty moralising" that was "sentimental, disconnected, and inconsequential" (173). Add to this the widespread criticisms of nonhuman animal liberationists today that can also be found as being used against the antislavery movement. Brown (2006, as cited in and paraphrased by Pleasants 2010) explained that the pro-slavery movement criticized those against slavery as "often motivated by an indulgent quest for purity of conscience rather than radical social change, and found immediate satisfaction in the 'delectable tear' of sentimentality" (173).

Human slavery is not the same as nonhuman animal exploitation for a variety of reasons; however, they can be compared—compared without creating a hierarchy of suffering or undermining the ethical justification for seeking the abolition of both. It's important to think about these similarities and comparisons not as "equations" of one another but rather as showing how these oppressions are often entangled in the logics, beliefs, materialities, and structures of one another. As Michael Rothberg (2009:19) explains regarding multidirectional memory, these comparisons and remembrances can create "unexpected acts of empathy and solidarity," and "they can often be the very grounds on which people construct and act upon visions of justice."

One final note about this because I know this is an emotionally charged subject. I am not saying that we should give carte blanche permission to anyone to use these analogies in any way they wish. There are practical reasons (does it help or make things wildly worse?) and moral reasons (am I simply seeking to hurt someone's feelings?) why these analogies should not be thrown around haphazardly. Let us be mindful agitators for a better world.

Further Reading:

- Robinson, Nathan J. 2018. "Meat and the H-Word." *Currentaffairs.org*. Retrieved August 3, 2023 (https://www.currentaffairs.org/2018/01/meat-and-the-h-word/).

JOHN TALLENT

Animalization / dehumanization

A major issue that is typically invoked to argue against comparisons of nonhuman animal exploitation to that of the Holocaust, human slavery, human genocide, and human rape is that of the potential for perpetuating the dehumanization of these devalued human groups *through* animalization. **Animalization** is the process of portraying particular human out-groups as having "negative" nonhuman animal characteristics, which thereby demeans the human groups and treats them as "inferior" to the human in-groups. **Dehumanization** refers to the "denial of humanness" to humans. This is often seen when certain human groups are depicted as "like" cockroaches, snakes, rats, etc. Animalization doesn't always lead to dehumanization, but it is more likely when used to "morally disengage" human in-groups into devaluing the out-group (Solomon 2017:44).

Unfortunately, I have seen the concepts of animalization and dehumanization frequently become vehicles that, purposefully or accidentally, reify nonhuman animals as both the "other" and the "lesser." As a prime example, much of the outrage that tends to occur around comparing nonhuman animal oppression with human oppression can stem from the fear of contributing to the continued animalization and dehumanization of marginalized human groups. If nonhuman animals are compared to humans, it is said there is the possibility that the marginalized humans could be "brought down" to the "level" of nonhuman animals rather than the nonhuman animals being "brought up" to a "level" on par with humans. But this concern rarely acknowledges that nonhuman animals should not be considered "inferior" to humans in the first place. If nonhuman animals were not seen as unequal to, morally speaking, humans, animalization and dehumanization could not take place. There is nowhere to be "lowered" if all sentient beings are viewed as morally equal. To put it another way, the fact that there are different sentient beings classified into hierarchical "levels" makes it possible for anyone to move up and down a ladder of moral worth.

Another argument that I have against the notion that we should avoid comparing nonhuman animals and humans due to its potential contribution to the animalization and dehumanization of marginalized human groups is that it seems to fight animalization *with* animalization. Nonhuman animals are arbitrarily excluded from the moral framework that acknowledges and respects sentience as the foundation for subjective experience and personhood. This erasure is done by being denied equal access to the rhetoric of human oppression, effectively disavowing the multidirectionality of the histories of human and nonhuman animal oppressions. For instance, by denying comparisons between nonhuman animals and human oppressions, nonhuman animals are kept animalized as not like humans or as beings that would somehow tarnish the worth of humans compared to them. If we wish to avoid the animalization and devaluing of humans, we should also avoid the animalization and devaluing of other animals.

Singh (2018:146) provides us with a different path than the widespread one of disowning or distancing ourselves from our animal-ness: "We might begin to assemble a politics that enables us—from within and beyond language—to be always both different from and proximate to those others to whom we are bound." Just as we aren't equating oppressions by comparing them and finding their similarities, it is not equating humans with nonhuman animals to embrace the facts that we *are* animals, we *are like* other animals, and, like all species, humans *have differences* from all other species.

JOHN TALLENT

Issues of race

Because I am a civil rights activist, I am also an animal rights activist. Animals and humans suffer and die alike. Violence causes the same pain, the same spilling of blood, the same stench of death, the same arrogant, cruel and brutal taking of life. We don't have to be a part of it.

—Dick Gregory

US football superstar, Michael Vick, was arrested in 2007 when he was found to be overseeing a dogfighting ring in Virginia. It was found later that the property on which he and others operated the dogfighting ring provided clues to what kinds of horrors occurred there. I will spare you the details, but Claire Jean Kim (2022) listed a few ways dogs were killed because they were not aggressive enough; these ways were shocking, brutal, horrendous, and cannot be described as anything less than "absolute torture." Vick was sent to prison, booted from his football team, lost his sponsors, and many people in the public viciously attacked him in the media at every turn. Some of the attacks were righteous in nature, criticizing Vick's torture of dogs; other attacks, however, were full of racist rhetoric.

While we *shouldn't* be mad when likened to other animals, these analogies aren't made in a vacuum. As we saw earlier, many groups of marginalized humans are not seen as "human." They are considered as more closely connected to or the actual embodiment of what we consider the "animal," which violence and discrimination often flow from. If some people aren't considered fully human, it's easier for a society built around anthropocentrism and speciesism to dismiss their suffering. Some vegan scholars have written on Vick's complex case (Francione 2007a; Kim 2022). One critical point often brought up about this case is that while what Michael Vick did was horrendous and morally wrong, the torture and killing of the dogs was similar to the torture and killing of nonhuman animals in the meals most humans eat several times a day. So, if Michael Vick is not doing anything morally different from what most other humans are doing, why did he receive so much hate? The answer is that because of the animalization of Blackness, his harm to other animals is seen by society as "worse" than the type of harm that most other people (often white people) engage in. And what adds to this case's complexity is that there was so much outrage over one nonhuman animal species (dogs). In contrast, most other species of nonhuman animals are devalued and reduced to "killable" and "exploitable" *things*.

Often, people ask, "Why are we talking about race when we are talking about animals?" Since oppressions are always, and I mean *always*, intertwined with other forms of oppression, solving one form of oppression will also require dismantling the structures of oppression with which it happens to be intertwined. In this particular case, we are looking at both speciesism (the torture of dogs) and racism (the dehumanization and animalization of Michael Vick). It just so happens that there is a lot of scholarship on the ways in which speciesism and racism affix to one another. For example, Claire Jean Kim (2017) explains how anti-Black racism and speciesism are cocreated:

> Blackness and animalness...form poles in a closed loop of meaning. Blackness is a species construct (meaning 'in proximity to the animal') and animalness is a racial construct (meaning 'in proximity to the black'), and the two are dynamically interconstituted *all the way down*. In this sense, the anti-Black social order that props up the 'human' is also a zoological order, or what we might call a *zoologo-racial order*. [author's emphases] (P. 10, as cited by Ko 2019)

Aph Ko (2019) explains this further:

> [W]hat Black folks are experiencing is a type of animality and what animals are experiencing is a type of racialization. This means that the current ways in which we've been discussing racism and animal oppression do not accommodate a more complex understanding of what's really happening. We cannot possibly create effective liberation movements if we don't understand how these phenomena are intrinsically entangled and how they constitute one another. The zoologo-racial order is the true foundation of white supremacy. (Chapter 1, section titled "White Supremacy as a Zoological Machine," para. 12)

It would also be egregious if I did not plead for you to watch the TEDx talk by Christopher Sebastian titled "3 ways going vegan helped my anti-racism advocacy."[99] From these theories of the connections between speciesism and (anti-Black) racism, we can see how white supremacy is based on and is a fusion of both to compound the oppression and add to its complexity. White supremacy uses categories of "race" and an arbitrary divide between "humans" and all other nonhuman "animals" to racialize nonhuman animals and animalize all non-white humans. Attempting to dismantle only one aspect of this dual mode of oppression will not sever the root; it will simply result in counter-movements and counter-ideologies that can exploit the roots in different ways which we didn't attend to in the first place.

And while the anti-speciesist movement has been reluctant (in large part) or unwilling to take on the co-problem of racism, the anti-racist movement has (in large part), according to Syl Ko, been reluctant or unwilling to address anti-speciesism:

> [M]ost of the analysis in anti-racist discourse concerning animality stops…[at] protestation about the animalization of groups of color. People of color are humans, too; so, we should treat them as humans, not animals. Notice that there is an open acceptance of the negative status of "the animal" here

> which, as I see it, is a tacit acceptance of the hierarchical racial system and white supremacy in general. The human–animal divide is the ideological bedrock underlying the framework of white supremacy. The negative notion of "the animal" is the anchor of this system. (P. 45)

Both the anti-racist and anti-speciesist movements have not historically, in any widespread way, been willing to effectively join forces to take down the twin forces that make up the White Supremacy chimera. Ko goes on to argue, 'Since racism requires this notion of animality, since racism and race-thinking would fail to make sense without animality, those of us interested in resisting or combatting racism need to take seriously why the status of "the animal" is what it is' (46). She continues:

> When we excuse a harm committed against a being saying, "It's just an animal," we need to interrogate the "just" in use here. The human–animal divide (binary), where "the human" and "the animal" form oppositional poles and, thus, oppositional status-markers on a "chain of being," is not an objective model handed to us from the heavens. "The human" and "the animal" were placed through the positing of a racial system. In the same vein, racial categories tracking modes of "being" and degrees of superiority/inferiority are not part of an objective framework that must be in place for us to think about or conceptually arrange members of the world. Both of these frameworks, which are deeply intertwined, and cannot be made sense of independent of one another, were creations invented by a small percentage of people who took themselves to be the singular point of knowledge and, through centuries of violence, genocide, and control made their view of the world, themselves, and others universal. (Pp. 46-7)

Further Reading:

- Roothaan, Angela. 2017. "Aren't We Animals? Deconstructing or Decolonizing the Human – Animal Divide." Pp. 209–20 in *Issues in Science and Theology: Are We Special? Human Uniqueness in Science and Theology*, edited by Michael Fuller, Dirk Evers, Anne Runehov, Knut-Willy Sæther. Cham: Springer International Publishing.

Issues of disability and ableism

We looked at ableism a bit in a prior section, but I believe it deserves a little more space here. As vegan disability scholar Sunaura Taylor (2014:14-5) explains, ableism is

> prejudice against disabled people that can lead to countless forms of discrimination, from lack of access to jobs, education, and housing to oppressive stereotypes and systemic inequalities that leave disabled individuals marginalized. Ableism breeds discrimination and oppression, but it also informs how we define which embodiments are normal, which are valuable, and which are "inherently negative."

And concerning nonhuman animals, it is commonplace for society, including vegans and non-vegans, to engage in problematic and hierarchical thinking regarding perceived differences in the "intelligence" of humans and other animals. Humans are regularly believed to be "more intelligent" than *all* other animals. For example, any and all groups of humans are commonly understood to be "more intelligent" or have "complex" emotions and states of mind than, for example, all chimpanzees, dolphins, pigs, elephants, and birds. As discussed in the earlier chapter on nonhuman animal sentience and consciousness, nonhuman animals have "complex" emotional lives and cognition. Research has suggested that human perceptions of nonhuman animal minds strongly influence how they view and treat nonhuman animals. The research of Bilewicz, Imhoff, and Drogosz (2011) showed how a belief in a supposed "uniqueness" of human emotions is a way in which "omnivores" (the category labeled by the authors of the article) disengage from the morality of their consumption of nonhuman animals. They also found that "vegetarians" (the other category in the paper) are more likely to ascribe certain emotions to nonhuman animals commonly considered wholly unique in humans.

Additional research from Maust-Mohl, Fraser, and Morrison (2012), and earlier research, such as Driscoll (1995), reveals that cognitive abilities are less attributed to the nonhuman animals typically seen on farms. This is not entirely surprising, given the evidence that "in-groups" often discount the emotional lives of "out-groups" (Leyens et al. 2001). Many people also create a hierarchy of emotional abilities. Based on their taxonomic classification, non-human animals are ranked lower than humans. At the top of the list is humanity, followed by other mammals and then other non-human animals. So, it certainly seems like humans typically decide on what cognitive abilities they will attribute to different nonhuman animals based on how similar they view the nonhuman animal to humans. Since humans are mammals, humans will often attribute more cognitive abilities to mammals over, for instance, amphibians and reptiles (Wilkins, McCrae, and McBride 2015). Knight et al. (2004) found that a higher Belief in Animal Mind (BAM) correlates to lower levels of support for using nonhuman animals. Humans very often use the perceived intelligence of nonhuman animals to determine the attributed cognitive abilities of differing species of nonhuman animals (Piazza and Loughnan 2016). Denying a mind is also a common way that people assuage their cognitive dissonance about exploiting nonhuman animals (Bastian et al. 2011a). It appears making comparisons between humans and nonhuman animals can make a positive difference in expanding one's sphere of concern.

Bastian et al. (2011b) found that comparing nonhuman animals to humans benefits both nonhuman animals and marginalized human groups; no significant effect was found when humans were compared to nonhuman animals. The abilities of humans are consistently held up as the pinnacle and minimum for moral concern of others. In other words, ableist thinking runs deep in speciesist and non-vegan reasonings.

Further Reading:

- Nocella II, Anthony J., Amber E. George, and J. L. Schatz. 2017. *The Intersectionality of Critical Animal, Disability, and Environmental Studies.* Lexington Books.
- Muller, S. Marek, and Z. Zane McNeill. 2021. "Toppling the Temple of Grandin: Autistic-Animal Analogies and the Ableist-Speciesist Nexus." *Rhetoric, Politics & Culture* 1(2):195–225.

Part III

> UNITING THE LEFT UNDER
> TOTAL LIBERATIONIST VEGANISM

Make no mistake, it's impossible to do nothing: you're always either going with a flow or against it, and neither option is free of risk. What of the possibility that, beyond failing to fight for the things in life that really matter, we'll even end up complicit in annihilating them?

—Anonymous, from the book *Total Liberation* (2019)

We won't fight for bigger cages; we will smash them all!
... We're here to end every form of oppression.
We call for an end to all domination.
We won't degrade sentient beings into products.
We call for an end to every form of degradation.
... We are the keys to the cages.

—CLEARxCUT, from the song "The Keys to the Cages"

13

A Proposal

If you're sincerely interested in ending racism, you must recognize racism's roots in our relationships with, and constructions of, "the place of the animal." And if you're sincerely interested in ending nonhuman animal exploitation, you must educate yourself on the connections between the social constructions of whiteness, racialization, and racisms (as well as sexisms, nationalisms, etc.), and animal abuse. It's simple: it's all connected.

—A. Breeze Harper[100]

I've been thinking a lot about some of the distressing issues that we are facing collectively. I think at times we feel, or we're made to feel, that we champion different causes. But for me, I see commonality. I think, whether we're talking about gender inequality or racism or queer rights or indigenous rights or animal rights, we're talking about the fight against injustice. We're talking about the fight against the belief that one nation, one people, one race, one gender or one species has the right to dominate, control and use and exploit another with impunity. I think that we've become very disconnected from the natural world, and many of us, what we're guilty of is an egocentric world view—the belief that we're the center of the universe. We go into the natural world, and we

HOW TO UNITE THE LEFT ON ANIMALS

plunder it for its resources. We feel entitled to artificially inseminate a cow, and when she gives birth, we steal her baby, even though her cries of anguish are unmistakable. Then we take her milk that's intended for her calf, and we put it in our coffee and our cereal. And I think we fear the idea of personal change because we think that we have to sacrifice something, to give something up, but human beings, at our best, are so inventive and creative and ingenious. And I think that when we use love and compassion as our guiding principles, we can create, develop, and implement systems of change that are beneficial to all sentient beings and to the environment. Now, I have been, I have been a scoundrel in my life. I've been selfish. I've been cruel at times, hard to work with, and I'm grateful that so many of you in this room have given me a second chance. And I think that's when we're at our best, when we support each other, not when we cancel each other out for past mistakes, but when we help each other to grow, when we educate each other, when we guide each other toward redemption. That is the best of humanity.

—Joaquin Phoenix, from his 2020 Oscar acceptance speech for the "Best Actor" award

This book, how I've thought about and formulated ideas and connections, and my purposefully chosen words have all been, hopefully, through a total liberationist lens. David Pellow (2014), who wrote the compelling book *Total Liberation: The Power and Promise of Animals Rights and the Radical Earth Movement*, described his conceptualization of total liberation as "stem[ming] from a determination to understand and combat all forms of inequality and oppression." Pellow goes on to describe its essentials: "I propose that it comprises four pillars: (1) an ethic of justice and anti-oppression inclusive of humans, nonhuman animals, and ecosystems; (2) anarchism; (3) anti-capitalism; and (4) an embrace of direct action tactics" (5-6).[101] Pellow's book is a culmination of his research into the nonhuman animal and Earth liberation movements:

> [I]t is clear from my research that the activists featured in this book believe there are multiple, interlocking, and reinforcing systems of inequality and domination that give rise to our socioecological crises, including statecraft, capitalism, speciesism, dominionism, patriarchy, heterosexism, racism, and classism. These activists maintain that ecological crises cannot be reduced to any one (or two) of these systems of domination; rather, they work together to contribute to the problem. I draw this conclusion based on my interviews with activists, my observations of movement gatherings, and analyses of thousands of pages of documents produced by radical earth and animal liberation activists. Total liberation sees inequality as a threat to life itself—for oppressed peoples, species, and ecosystems—and is organized around the struggle for life. These movements organize and mobilize in favor of symbols, metaphors, language, signs, representations, practices, and structures of equality and justice to do what social movements have always done: to imagine and create a better world. Only this world would be based on the idea that inequality and unfreedom in all their known manifestations should be eradicated. (Pp. 10-11)

It has not been a perfect movement, Pellow admits. The nonhuman animal and Earth liberation movements have indeed shown visible inequalities and possible ways to dismantle them. Still, many elements within these movements have also failed to be critical of hierarchy and other forms of oppression within and outside the movement itself.

Steven Best (2016:xii), one of the earliest developers of the concept of total liberation, detailed his views on the importance and nuances of this idea:

> By "total liberation" I do not mean a metaphysical utopia to be realized in perfect form. I refer, instead, to the process of understanding human, animal, and earth liberation movements in relation to one another and building bridges around interrelated issues such as democracy and ecology, sustainability and veganism, and social justice and animal rights. To be sure, total liberation is an ideal, a vision, and a goal to strive for, one that invokes visions of freedom, community, and harmony. But the struggle ahead is permanent and formidable, one to be conducted within the constraints of human nature and the limits imposed by ecology. Human, animal, and earth liberation movements are different components of one inseparable struggle—against hierarchy, domination, and unsustainable social forms—none of which is possible without the others.

As you can see, total liberation is not an endpoint. It's not a state of complacency. It doesn't see any struggle as "worse" or "more important" than any other. It is anti-compartmentalization of oppressions. It is holistic in understanding the commonalities between all forms of oppression. It understands that no form of oppression can be ignored unless the desire is to stifle *all* struggles against domination. If humans oppress one another, nonhuman animals and ecosystems will all suffer; if humans oppress nonhuman animals, marginalized humans and ecosystems will suffer; if humans devastate, degrade, and ruin ecosystems, all life on the planet becomes imperiled. This gives a more holistic interpretation to the words of Dr. Martin Luther King, Jr. in 1963: "Injustice anywhere is a threat to justice everywhere. We are caught in an inescapable network of mutuality, tied in a single garment of destiny. Whatever affects one directly affects all indirectly."

All life on this planet, sentient and non-sentient, is connected through an incomprehensible web of interdependency. The old, fallacious assumptions of human supremacy, dominionism, and human exceptionalism have begun to hasten and seal our seemingly cosmic fate as just one more extinct species. Armed with nothing but flimsy "claws," pathetic "canine" and wisdom teeth, and a dangerously egocentric perspective of our own intelligence, the human superiority complex that forever seeks to be on "top" of the natural world gives us the false and temporary belief that we are invincible. The universe does not abide by human vanity or desires. Confirmation bias convinces us that humans are "essential" to the world. Humanity as "special" is nothing more than a children's story that we refuse to accept as make-believe.

We as a species imprison ourselves and all life on this planet, constantly inching forward to the cliff of global climate disaster. So far, most of us have refused to accept that this fate has been brought on by the interconnected nature of the oppression of humans, nonhuman animals, and the environment. Neo-fascism isn't creeping into our lives but barreling toward our collective brain at an incomprehensible speed, like a bullet from a high-powered rifle in the hands of a Proud Boy. The genocide, the slavery, the holocaust, the rape that is nonhuman animal exploitation—intensified by the extortion and bloodlust of capitalism—objectifies, commodifies, and extinguishes the lives and autonomy of trillions of nonhuman animal *people* every single year. This is what we are up against. This is why solidarity has to take a front seat in all struggles for liberation. Thus, total liberation, in my view, is the best chance we collectively have to reduce suffering in the world, provide real justice to the chronically denied, and align our shared values with the realities of the natural world.

And that's why mainstream veganism cannot and will not save us. It has been compartmentalized, depoliticized, individualized, capitalized, and tempered from its radical possibilities. From problematic campaigns and embracing pseudoscience to nonhuman animals-only advocacy and "vegan" capitalism, the mainstream vegan movement hinders itself by embracing anti-science and anti-Leftist behaviors. In other words, the mainstream vegan movement *fucking sucks*. If vegans wish to see the end of speciesism and nonhuman animal use and exploitation, there are a number of problems that need to be addressed if veganism is going to gain widespread popularity. And while I don't believe that these issues within the vegan movement are the only reasons why most people choose not to become vegan, they unquestionably make it more difficult for veganism to be perceived as the liberatory movement that vegans believe it to be.

This book's main title, "How to Unite the Left on Animals," was purposefully specific in the area where I think Leftists can, right now, and in this very moment, unite: nonhuman animal liberation. Because of (currently unresolved) differences in methodology and praxis, writing a book that purported to unite Leftists, particularly Marxists and anarchists, would be much more challenging. Especially regarding praxis, the issue of the Marxist "dictatorship of the proletariat"[102] is a non-starter with anarchists (Neal et al. 2020; Tabor 2013). No, I make no such sweeping case here, unfortunately. Instead, I hope to contribute to closing the enormous gap between non-vegan Leftists and vegan Leftists. This gap separates those who believe in or engage in practices and actions that exploit nonhuman animals from those who believe in, practice, and engage in actions that support nonhuman animal liberation from human domination—a prerequisite for curbing the global climate crisis.

To address this, I propose refocusing, resharpening, readjusting, and reifying what it means to be vegan. The history of veganism has its roots in viewing the interconnectedness of humans, other animals, and the environment. Still, that history has been defanged by how veganism is widely viewed now: a plant-based diet. But because all currently-living life hangs in the balance, veganism must become something more. It must become one of the most important vehicles to carry us to a more liberated world. It must become an intrinsic part of Leftist praxis and theory.

I propose what I've termed *Total Liberationist Veganism*—a veganism founded in and that which demands a total liberation perspective—as a matter of justice and as a matter of survival. I do not know if mainstream veganism is able to be saved from itself, and I also don't know if creating a subcategory of veganism called "total liberationist veganism" is the best thing to do, either. All I aim to do here is to present what veganism *should* look like and also a way for people to distance themselves from the mainstream vegan movement, if they wish, without abandoning the important aspects of what it should mean to be vegan. It's time to demand that total liberation be an intrinsic part of veganism (and Leftism). As for concrete examples of what this entails, I hope my barebones and rough framework can provide some substance.

One note before I get into this further. I don't give a shit whether folks wish to take on the personal label of a "total liberationist vegan" or whether they choose to identify as a "vegan who believes in total liberation." It doesn't matter. Those who agree with me about the content of this "proposal" should feel free to start a new path in veganism called "total liberationist veganism," and they should also feel free to add total liberationist principles and practices to what it means to be a "vegan." Fighting for worldwide, universal liberation for all necessitates veganism; veganism necessitates a likewise fighting for worldwide, universal liberation for all. In this sense, veganism and total liberation are one and the same. Neither makes sense without the other. I hope the following helps the liberatory fire in your heart burn a little brighter, no matter what you decide to do.

Explicitly universally practicable

It has been argued previously in this book that the idea of veganism has been open to various interpretations. However, there are two arguments in favor of veganism being a universally practicable praxis for every single human with moral agency. First, the phrase "as far as is possible and practicable," is included in the current definition of veganism (The Vegan Society n.d.b.). Previous definitions had similar nuances, allowing for some necessary flexibility in adhering to vegan ideals depending on personal circumstances. This expression of veganism calls on everyone to do everything in their power to avoid harming non-human animals as much as they can. The second argument we saw for a universally practicable veganism was that ethical claims *always* entail the understanding of "ought implies can"—or, in other words, people have an ethical obligation to do something *only if they have the capacity and ability to do so*. From these two arguments, it should be abundantly clear that the commitments that veganism demands do not require anyone to do anything that they would not be able to do in a practicable and safe way. **Veganism requires nothing less than what one should do and nothing more than one can do.**

Others have spoken about this before me. Though he doesn't go as far as I do in calling for worldwide veganism, Robert C. Jones (2016) makes the case that those of us living in "Western" and affluent societies have a "moral obligation to adopt vegan practice"—specifically, what he calls "political veganism" (15-6). I believe his main point, "political veganism" is a respectable alternative to total liberationist veganism for some people, especially those married to such ideologies as Marxist-Leninism, which is firmly against anarchism. Along with Lori Gruen, his prior work also spoke of veganism as "aspirational," which I think is a great way to think of it (Gruen and Jones 2015). Veganism can be considered "aspirational" because no person in the world lives without harming others; we can only reduce our harm *as far as is possible and practicable*. So, all anyone can do is *aspire* to live up to the vegan ideal. This universal practicability should be the standard interpretation and praxis for all vegans because I believe it is perfectly inclusive and completely logical.

Further Reading:

- Twine, Richard. 2022. "Ecofeminism and Veganism: Revisiting the Question of Universalism." Pp. 229–46 in *Ecofeminism: Feminist Intersections with Other Animals and the Earth*, edited by C. J. Adams and L. Gruen. New York, NY: Bloomsbury Academic.

Explicitly not a diet

Veganism is nearly universally considered a "diet," but that way of thinking certainly ignores the other parts of the "official" definition that we looked at earlier regarding clothing, entertainment, nonhuman animal experimentation, etc. The "official" definition of veganism explains several aspects and practices that make up veganism:

- it's "a philosophy and a way of living";
- "seeks to exclude...all forms of exploitation, and cruelty to [nonhuman animals]"
- these exclusions include the practices of "food, clothing, and any other purpose"
- this also includes the "[promotion of] the development and use of animal-free alternatives for the benefit of animals, humans and the environment"
- with regards to diet, veganism is the avoidance of all nonhuman animal "products"
- and all of these aspects and practices are couched within the understanding that differing circumstances may change the ways in which some people are able to practice veganism. (The Vegan Society n.d.b.)

As we read through this summary of the definition, nowhere does it say that veganism is a diet. It explains that there are *dietary aspects* of veganism but not that these dietary aspects *make up* veganism. So, if we take the example of a human that eats a completely plant-based diet but does not necessarily exclude all other forms of exploitation and cruelty to nonhuman animals, *as far as is possible and practicable for them*, this person should not be considered "vegan." Since veganism entails more than diet, and nonhuman animal exploitation and cruelty involve more practices than just diet, a human that engages in other forms of exploitation and cruelty beyond diet would not be following a vegan "philosophy and way of living." For example, focusing on the diet aspects of veganism would allow any "vegan" to torture dogs for fun, engage in the vivisection of monkeys, purchase and wear fox fur as a luxury, and go "trophy" hunting for lions. Why should we be complacent with veganism being associated with those behaviors? We already have a name for people who eat a plant-based diet but might also engage in some of those nonhuman animal forms of exploitation—vegetarians. Plus, from a practical standpoint, there is strong evidence to suggest that going "vegan for health" (aka focusing on diet) has less of an impact on the consistency of diet than going vegan out of concern for nonhuman animals (Hoffman et al. 2013; Markowski 2022). **Total Liberationist Veganism sees veganism as more than, and impossible to be reduced to, diet alone.**

Explicitly requires anti-speciesism

A position such as veganism cannot adequately and effectively function in direct opposition to nonhuman exploitation without also being anti-speciesist (and anti-anthropocentric). This is directly related to mainstream veganism's (and mainstream, non-vegan society's) de-radicalization of veganism from a revolutionary stance against nonhuman animal exploitation into a fad diet to promote individual health. When we think about how exploitation and cruelty toward nonhuman animals exist and are perpetuated, they function through an assumed dissimilarity between them and humans, especially regarding moral worth. Speciesism and anthropocentrism support discrimination against nonhuman animals and are based in incorrect assumptions and faulty logics that encourage the idealization of "the human" as the "default" and the "superior" over all nonhuman animals. We have seen how the differences between humans and all other animals have been unjustly exaggerated to prop up an imagined human exceptionalism. Exploitation and cruelty thrive on these types of domination-inspired hierarchies of capacity, ability, cognition, moral value, and other forms of arbitrary categorization and separation.

It's possible for some people to become anti-speciesist by first being introduced to the health and environmental aspects of plant-based diets and then learning along the way; I don't mean to discount those journeys in the slightest. Everyone's path toward veganism is different, and many people, including myself, cannot really pinpoint the exact moment when everything "clicked" in our minds. But, as the previous section mentioned, the "vegan for health" method is the *least likely* to make long-term vegans, according to current evidence (Braunsberger and Flamm 2019). One study noted that "vegans' lower endorsements of speciesism may explain why they are more ethically motivated to follow their diets than vegetarians are" (Rosenfeld 2019:792) Therefore, it appears that not only does the trendy diet approach to producing vegans not work well, but it also does not produce a social practice that is politically coherent and opposed to exploitation.

I think it's great when folks advocate for plant-based diets for any reason, be it anti-speciesism, environmentalism, and/or health. However, there is little evidence that appealing to people's health concerns significantly increases the likelihood of most people being in favor of nonhuman animal liberation. If we want nonhuman animal liberation, part of the solution is to educate people about it.

Understands the importance of the (nonhuman) animal standpoint

According to Donovan (2006:319), standpoint theory was originally developed within a Marxist perspective

> in which [it was] posited that the proletariat evinces a particular and privileged epistemology because of its commodification or reification in the capitalist production process. When a subject is treated as an object,...the experience necessarily evokes a critical consciousness born of the subject's ironic knowledge that he or she is not a thing.

In other words, workers often obtain a better knowledge of their conditions than those who are not workers because of their continuous objectification and exploitation by the capitalist class. Capitalists cannot fully understand the experiences and hardships of workers because they don't live as workers. Feminist standpoint theory was then developed to explain oppressed people's "awakening" based on "bodily experience" rather than objectification. Donovan extends feminist standpoint theory to nonhuman animals and effectively defends this use of standpoint theory to apply to those whose worldviews we do not yet understand. She acknowledges this added uniqueness to the situation of nonhuman animals but ultimately rejects objections to using standpoint theory for nonhuman animals because there is such abundant evidence already (and much more since the article was published) about how similar nonhuman animal and human mental and emotional lives can be (321-22).[103] Horsthemke (2018) also attends to the problem of successfully obtaining a single "animal standpoint" without the possibility of direct discussions with other animals. Like other groups of people, the author explains, nonhuman animals are diverse, but it's not impossible to determine the basics of what nonhuman animals' standpoints would contain. Horsthemke explains:

> The morally significant aspects of the animal standpoint are not inaccessible. They concern the need and ability to live in peace, without being subjected to physical and psychological discomfort, stress, distress and trauma, and without their lives being prematurely terminated. These needs and preferences

> are essential features of the animal standpoint that are easily determinable… (P. 211)

I think this explanation can also be used for human groups that do not happen to be a part of the marginalized human groups that they may be speaking of and about. For example, as I mentioned earlier, a cisgender person does not have to be a transgender person to understand the pain and suffering of oppression. Does a cisgender person have the experience of a transgender person? No. However, the cisgender person may, in fact, know what heartache feels like; what being banished from your family is like; what losing your friends is like; what being stereotyped is like; what being intimidated and harassed in public is like. So, it is not impossible to understand *some of what it is like* to be oppressed in a particular way. Again, we are not all Donald Trump.

(Nonhuman) animal standpoint theory views nonhuman animals and their (largely non-consenting) relationships with humans as heavily shaping human history and life. As Steven Best (2016:1) explains:

> Animal standpoint theory, as I use it, looks at the fundamental role animals play in sustaining the natural world and shaping the human world in co-evolutionary relations. While animals have constituted human existence in beneficial ways, they have seldom been willing partners. The main thesis of animal standpoint theory is that animals have been key determining forces of human psychology, social life, and history overall, and that the domination of human over nonhuman animals underpins the domination of humans over one another and over the natural world.

Furthermore,

> this approach stresses the systemic consequences of human exploitation of nonhuman animals, the interrelatedness of our

> fates, and the profound need for revolutionary changes in the way human beings both define themselves and relate to other species and to the earth as a whole. (Pp. 1-2)

Best makes the case that human history has been dominated by oppressors' biases, such as racial biases, patriarchal biases, and, of course, species biases. He also critiques the dominant understanding of Marx's historical materialist approach. Marx was a radical humanist and, as such, viewed history through a speciesist and anthropocentric lens. Historical materialism sees human history through the "material forces of history in economics, production, and class struggle" (4). But that's not a complete understanding of human history. A speciesist rendering of a historical materialist approach does not include an analysis by which nonhuman animals impact human relations and economics. Nonhuman animals, "as an exploited labor power and productive force," as well as ecosystems, cannot simply be removed and ignored from a proper formulation of historical events. By presenting this speciesist and incomplete version as a "scientific" and "demystifying" view of history:

> the mystification is only relocated, not removed, when historians see social relations as the primary causal forces in history, isolated from the significant roles played by animals and the environment. Just as the story of ruling classes cannot be understood apart from their relations to oppressed classes, so too human history cannot be grasped outside the context of the powerful determining effects of animals and nature on human society. (P. 4)

A non-anthropocentric/non-speciesist historical materialist approach to history can help us understand the origins of human oppressions. Best goes on to explain how the end of hunter-gatherer societies and the creation of plant and nonhuman animal domestication ("domesecration,"[104] to use David Nibert's terminology) led to social stratification within and between societies via food surpluses, territorial expansion, and human population increases. The domesecration of nonhuman animals was one of the defining epochs in human history that allowed for a widespread increase in human-human oppression, but it also led to viewing nonhuman animals as intrinsically "less than" humans. In other words, domination began to thrive (8). Best shows us the importance of a (nonhuman) animal standpoint:

> Through the animal standpoint we acquire profound ethical insight made possible by a gestalt shift in evaluation, such that a crucial touchstone for gauging the moral character of a society, a culture, or an individual is how people view and treat other animals. One cannot adequately assess the moral worth, philosophical depth, and humanity of either cultures or individuals until one examines their views and relations toward animals and the natural world. (P. 13)

Further Reading:

- Kahn, Richard. 2011. "(PDF) Towards an Animal Standpoint: Vegan Education and the Epistemology of Ignorance." *ResearchGate*. Retrieved December 17, 2022 (https://www.researchgate.net/publication/240595554_Towards_an_animal_standpoint_Vegan_education_and_the_epistemology_of_ignorance).

Centers the nonhuman animal—human—ecosystems connection

The last thing that most folks want to admit is that they cause suffering to humans, nonhuman animals, or both, and have for their entire life. This realization can be traumatizing. But the potential for trauma is even greater if those of us in the animal rights movement don't explore these issues carefully, critically—if we are afraid to challenge other, linked zones of power, privilege, and comfort.

—A. Breeze Harper[105]

PETA (People for the Ethical Treatment of Animals) is a large stumbling block for veganism. First used in 2008 and re-launched in 2014 for a while, PETA developed a "Got Autism?" campaign that mimicked the cow's milk industry's "Got Milk?" campaign. PETA's campaign attempted to link milk consumption with an increased risk of developing autism (Jackson 2021). This type of campaigning is heavily constructed of ableism and pseudoscience. The organization also has a history of being absurdly white-centered. For example, in 2013, PETA wrote a letter to Arizona's Department of Corrections director to encourage the prisons to take "meat" off the menu within the prisons, following the lead of notorious Maricopa County, AZ, Sheriff Joe Arpaio. Arpaio did so because of the supposed taxpayer cost savings. In the letter, PETA's founder, Ingrid Newkirk, boasted about taxpayer savings and ethics while ignoring the racist prison system and Joe Arpaio's history of white supremacy (Newkirk 2013).[106] The organization also often treads heavily into healthism and extremely shameful fatphobia (Layne 2015). Unfortunately, these types of oppressive campaigning further marginalize vulnerable human groups.

Working for the liberation of nonhuman animals while simultaneously creating obstacles for oppressed humans simply creates a conduit for oppression to flow from one group to another. But even that analogy blurs the negative consequences for nonhuman animals in further harming other humans. I can't tell you how many fellow comrades of mine through the years have scoffed at veganism and nonhuman animal advocacy on the basis that they have "more important issues to fight for first" or how they don't want to join the nonhuman animal liberation movement because there are so many "problematic vegans." Problematic nonhuman animal advocacy can harm humans, but it can also compound the oppression of nonhuman animals. We also must think about how nonhuman animal exploitation has negatively affected marginalized humans through environmental racism[107], has added to the global climate emergency, and has led to overall declines in human and nonhuman animal health. A devastated environment harms human and nonhuman animal health; oppressing nonhuman animals leads to animalization, and poor health and horrid working conditions for marginalized humans. The oppression of humans destroys the environment and increases nonhuman animal vulnerability and exploitation (Nibert 2002).

Thinking and acting in this holistic manner is *critical*. While many of us accept and understand that multiple forms of human oppression can act on human groups simultaneously and that these intersecting oppressions can have back-and-forth relationships that mutually affect one another, we must think beyond how human oppressions can be co-constituted and interact with one another. Human oppression affects and is affected by nonhuman animal oppression, too. Nonhuman animal oppression affects and is affected by human oppression. Devastating ecosystems harms human and nonhuman animal oppressions also harm humans and nonhuman animals and ecosystems. Oppressions do not exist in a vacuum, where they are compartmentalized from the rest of the world. They are all connected and cannot be remedied by single-issue action. If we care about other animals, we necessarily must care about humans and the environment. If we care about humans, we necessarily must care about other animals and the environment. And if we consider ourselves environmentalists, we have to care about both human and nonhuman animal oppressions, as well. Nonhuman animal liberation is a fight against human oppression and the planet's devastation. Human liberation is a fight against nonhuman animal oppression and the exploitation of the Earth. Earth liberation is a fight against nonhuman animal and human oppressions.

Acknowledges the reflexive nature of individual agency and social structure

It seems strange to think of humans (and other animals) as entirely or mainly beholden to large social structures like capitalism, Christianity, or white supremacy. For sure, these things have tremendous effects on all of us. We are born into a capitalist system. Our parents usually dictate what religion (or non-religion) we will be. And our opportunities and daily lives are positively or negatively affected by white supremacy (depending on our own "race"[108]). But can we break free and choose our own path from these influences? Do we have any real agency at all? The answer is an absolute "yes." Many of us are staunchly anti-capitalist and attempt to do our best to reject capitalist logics. Many of us reject the dominant religions (or all religions). And many of us wish for and seek a society where whiteness is not the "default." To be completely unable to fight against these structures would mean we would not be able to resist them. The real question is, how much influence can individuals have on these intangible and entrenched structures while living within and under them?

Karl Marx (1852) said, "[Humans] make their own history, but they do not make it as they please; they do not make it under self-selected circumstances, but under circumstances existing already, given and transmitted from the past." In other words, we have free will, but our societal characteristics limit it. And in another critical interpretation, *we are not completely helpless and ineffective on a personal level*. We can affect others, and we can affect "the system." I've known too many Marxists (and anarchists!) that tend to believe that individual change is not important, or is not *as* important, as changing "the system." This kind of thinking is commonly thrown at those advocates seeking nonhuman animal liberation through, among other things, veganism. It is said that "personal change" and "lifestylism" are nothing but "purity" and "moralizing"; to actually change things, it is assumed, we have to dismantle capitalism *first*, and *then* we can work on other "less important" things. But this strikes me as an odd and even hypocritical understanding of how everyone lives and behaves in society. Anecdotally, most (non-vegan) Leftists I know do not *only* work to end capitalism. If that were the case, they would not attend political events like Pride or pro-choice rallies. Nor would they participate in boycotts or advocate their political perspectives to others. They wouldn't cheer as neo-Nazis like Richard Spencer get punched in the face.[109] They wouldn't think racist, sexist, transphobic, homophobic, or ableist slurs are essential enough to avoid saying. They wouldn't believe in giving money to houseless people. They wouldn't believe in stopping domestic violence or assaults that they witness. If we are politically or socially active, we participate in individual change, action, and "moralizing." Wouldn't it also be accurate to consider criticisms against individual change as "seeking personal change?" Many people and groups understand change in a binary fashion, *solely* or *largely* coming from individual change *or* social structures. But picking a "side" in this matter isn't really necessary. We can choose to understand social change through a dualistic manner in which individuals change or maintain social structures, and social structures affect and shape individuals. In fact, many theories posit just that, and I think some of them can help us avoid unnecessary infighting and tension on the "best" way to create social change.

Structuration theory, as articulated by the sociologist Anthony Giddens, attempts to reconcile the contention between the two seemingly separate entities of individual agency and social structures. The issue at the heart of this contention is whether one dominates the other in developing and continuing social systems. This issue is central to many discussions and disagreements of tactics regarding the "best" way to end white supremacy, abolish capitalism, and, the focus of this section, how to end nonhuman animal exploitation while living under the constraints and pressures of capitalism. In creating structuration theory, Giddens set it apart from other forms of social theory, which often attempt to explain society by choosing agency *or* structure as the primary culprit or mechanism of change. Against this, Giddens explains his view, "The basic domain of study of the social sciences, according to the theory of structuration, is neither the experience of the individual actor, nor the existence of any form of societal totality, but social practices ordered across space and time" (Giddens 1984:2). Giddens's way of looking at the agent/structure paradox is to focus more on social practices. Social practices to Giddens, as described by Ian Craib (2011:Action and the Actor section, para. 2), are actions that we produce or reproduce; these actions are "performed" by us and make up society. For example, think of everything involved in the actions of eating, voting, driving, protesting, playing sports, typing an email, etc. Structures, on the other hand, are more abstract entities. Giddens uses a linguistic analogy to describe what structures are like: actions and structures are related like speech and language. To butcher this theory by diluting it to a single, paraphrased idea, this view of agency and structure can be thought of like this: individuals and groups perform these actions (social practices), and these actions make up social structures; to change the large structures, one important thing we must do is to affect the practices that make up these structures and personal actions. Furthermore, "structuration theory acknowledges the interaction of meaning, standards and values, and power and posits a dynamic relationship between [agency and structure]" (Gibbs 2017). (Note: Structuration theory is tediously more complex than my extremely brief and unnuanced explanation here, so if this interests you, please check out my references.)

Speaking of social practices, (social) practice theories[110] are approaches found mainly in sociology and anthropology that I have found to be useful in conceptualizing how society may work, change, and be intervened in. Practice theories stem from and have been advanced from the works of Pierre Bourdieu (1977), Anthony Giddens, Theodore Schatzki (2012; 2016), Shove, Pantzar, and Watson (2012), and many others. Practice theories have also been used by academics like Judith Butler (1990) and Richard Twine (2017), among others. My main goal in explaining these theories is to demonstrate that there are perspectives and ideas beyond the binary thinking of "Should I improve myself and others, or should I seek to bring down the system?"

The fact is that we all probably do both every single day of our lives. Engaging on social media is seeking individual changes in others, but we also hope that our engagements on these platforms may increase the likelihood of society changing. Many of us enjoy reading and educating ourselves, talking to others about politics, and simply being nice to others. These are individual choices and changes seeking to change society. No matter how against or critical of personal change we might think we are, we are unconscious of the many ways we behave in ways that understand it as valuable and useful. When we think about it, isn't the individual essentially a tiny fraction of what makes up larger systems, and aren't larger systems simply macro reflections of the sum of all individual social behaviors and interactions? It would seem as though affecting ourselves, others, and institutions are all important and necessary features of liberation for all. As Steven Best (2014:44) says,

> Certainly, individuals need to take responsibility for their choices and the consequences of their actions, such as by engaging the ecological and ethical imperative to become vegan. However, it is also crucial to recognize the formidable power of corporations, the state, mass media, schools, and other institutions in peoples' lives, and to appreciate the constraints imposed by poverty, class, and social conditioning. Of course individuals must change, but so, too, must institutions...

Explicitly embraces radical approaches and rejects apolitization and reactionary beliefs

I don't care if he is a soldier with [a] vegan hat or vegan sweater, or non-vegan sweater, I don't care if his shoes [are] made with vegan leather or animal leather, this shoe is in my neck! [tilts his head, points to his

HOW TO UNITE THE LEFT ON ANIMALS

neck] So why would I? Yes, it is more soft if it is vegan, do you think? Really?? [raises his voice] Or when he shoots me, the bullet will be more soft to kill me?

—Ahmad Safi, cofounder and director of the Palestinian Animal League (Alloun 2020:11)

I was eating animals for 19 years, that's also a big mistake!

—Hannah, who was interviewed by a researcher who asked whether she had conflicting feelings about being vegan and joining the Israel Defense Forces (Alloun 2020:9)

Veganism and nonhuman animal liberation are not status quo ideas, so why do advocates in these areas too often embrace the status quo in other areas?

Why would vegans ever support the police or prison-industrial complex? The criminalization of sex work? **Prison abolition and transformative justice are the ways forward.**[111][112][113][114][115]

Why would vegans ever support top-down, hierarchical decision-making, the State, or the domination of some by others? **Anarchism is the way forward—returning power back to individuals and communities.**[116][117][118][119]

Why would vegans ever be against direct action? **Direct action is and has always been a valuable and necessary part of social change.**[120]

Why wouldn't vegans be against capitalism—a top-down, hierarchical system of those with and those without, premised on the idea

| 263 |

of perpetual exploitation, consumption, and infinite growth? **Anticapitalism is the only way forward.**[121][122][123][124]

Veganism cannot be compartmentalized away from politics. Rights are political. Liberation is political. Habitat destruction is political. The interconnections between speciesism, sexism, cissexism, colonialism, queer antagonism, racism, imperialism, classism, ageism, ableism, and all other oppressions are political.

Take, for instance, that some in the settler State of Israel, formerly known as "Palestine," have attempted to portray the country as the "Most Vegan Country in the World" (Ahronheim 2018; Staff 2014). A survey in 2015 stated that approximately 5% of Israelis claim to be vegan (Raz-Chaimovich 2019). Israeli writer Ori Shavit credits Israel's recent rise in interest in veganism to a popular online presentation given by infamous former vegan activist Gary Yourofsky, which was given Hebrew subtitles around 2011 (Kessler 2012). Yourofsky is noted for saying nonsense, such as, "Every woman ensconced in fur should endure a rape so vicious that it scars them forever. While every man entrenched in fur should suffer an anal raping so horrific that they become disemboweled" (Johnston and Johnston 2017). On Facebook and other social media, he would comment that nonvegans should "Go fuck yoursel[ves] you herpes-infested physcho[s]," and he called Palestinians and their supporters "the most psychotic group on the planet." He even had a video titled "Palestinians, Blacks and Other Hypocrites" on YouTube (it's since been taken down).

> **The Real Gary Yourofsky** ⊛ As Israelis are in the process of destroying the meat, dairy and egg industries - which will lead to the eradication of animal concentration camps - Palestinians and their psychotic human rights sympathizers are BUILDING more animal camps! While Israelis have made their land a haven for homosexuals, Palestinians ostracize, harm and even murder gay people as they consider homosexuality to be sinful. While Israelis (sans the ultra ultra Orthodox ones who comprise 1-2% of Israel and are as crazy as The Palestinians) allow women an equal say in society, Palestinians continue to oppress women in the same way all Arab nations do. While Israelis would LOVE to live amongst the Palestinians and ALL other people, The Palestinians are hell bent on destroying Jews, literally teaching HATRED towards them in their schools, and REFUSE to live peacefully amongst the Jewish people. The Palestinians ARE the problem. They are the most psychotic group on this planet. Even the Arab nations who sympathize with them (Egypt, Jordan, etc.) send those psychotic lunatics BACK after they catch them hiding out in THEIR country. So, don't be another mindless, bleeding-heart liberal who BLINDLY takes the side of Palestinians because they're the "cause du jour". Furthermore, even though I am sympathetic towards human rights issues (gay rights, women rights, etc.), I will NO longer fight for humans to be treated fairly/equally until those who are oppressed STOP oppressing the animals. Until animals are included in the discussion, I say TO HELL with any oppressed 2-legged creature who cant even realize the oppression they are actively supporting every time they eat a meal or buy a new pair of shoes. The animals got it the worst of all. Palestinians are living like KINGS & QUEENS compared to the cows, chickens, turkeys, pigs, sheep of the world. So focus on the ISSUE AT HAND: Animal Liberation. And forget about those Palestinian maniacs. And technically, even under the loosest definition, Palestinians are not living in concentration camps. Go visit a cow slaughterhouse where these innocent beings are beheaded one after the other, or a dairy facility where cows are raped to impregnate them and machines are hooked up to their breasts several times a day, or watch a slaughterhouse truck drive down the road with 1,000 chickens on board headed to a building to be murdered ... and then ask yourself: "How in the hell did I get duped into believing that Palestinians are oppressed and living in concentration camps?" Please wake up and focus on the ONLY critical and important issue of our time.
>
> Like 👍 6   March 19 at 6:04am

A post from Facebook

JOHN TALLENT

> Gary Yourofsky 1 month ago
>
> +bugyesz Have you been online? Humans have shit-eating fetishes, getting-pissed on fetishes, getting-vomited on fetishes, and love fucking 5 year old boys and girls. We sever each other's heads off and kill each other for being black, Jewish, Muslim, Christian. We have countless Holocausts against humans and animals. The air and water are polluted everywhere. The Hudson river is a toilet. STDs are rampant. People cough and sneeze INTO the open air in a crowded rooms. People don't wash after shitting. But animals are dirty? HAHAHAHA! thanks for the laugh, douchebag. As for isntincts, you haven't ONE original thought in your brain. You reiterate EVERYTHING your mommy & daddy, government, religion and schools told you to say/think.
>
> BTW, your comments are trite and lame. I addressed most of your insanity in a facebook post already: "Many people believe that animals are inferior because they don't wipe their asses, or play instruments and write symphonies. Well, I'm quite impressed that most of us have learned to wipe, and
> that some of us can create beautiful, melodic sequences using 'fake' instruments. But why would wiping, or creating and playing music, give us the right to enslave and kill? By the way, I say 'fake' when referring to the music we make because birds, cats, whales, crickets and many other creatures don't need artificial instruments made of wood, brass, steel, copper, etc. - along with years of lessons, practice and inspiration - to WRITE, CREATE and PERFORM symphonies."
>
> Go fuck yourself you herpes-infested psycho. And may all the violence you inflict on animals return to you & your family tenfold. And in your time of need, when you are screaming out for help, I hope some PRICK JUST LIKE YOU comes along and says, "He's an idiot. He isn't even able to think on his own. He is only writhing around and screaming because of instincts. Let's go smoke some Northern Lights instead."
> Show less
>
> Reply

Another post from Facebook

An analysis by Alloun (2020:2) describes how Israel's supposed "pro-animal" society is used as "a distinct and additional means by which Jewish Israeli identity is sedimented, and by corollary Palestinian un-belonging and exclusion enacted." Moreover, Alloun says that "animal welfare and veganism have been enrolled as another device to narrate the Israeli nation within terms of Jewish Israeli sovereignty amid intense settler colonial oppression and violence" (2). In other words, the Israeli State has taken to self-proclamations as a nation that is extraordinarily "animal-friendly" and "vegan" in an attempt to further the illusion that Israel is "good" and the Palestinians are "backward." This façade of Israel being more vegan and "moral" has been termed "vegan-washing" (Gross 2013). Alloun goes on to say that Israel appropriates veganism for its own purposes of claiming a nationalist exceptionalism—all the while ignoring settler colonial violence against the Indigenous Palestinians and claiming "[i]nnocence and victimhood" (5). Veganwashing by Israel illuminates "how animals, race and coloniality intersect" (Alloun 2017:2). The term "greenwashing" has also been applied to the Israeli State's appropriation of Palestinian land and using it for so-called "green technology" (Hughes, Velednitsky, and Green 2022).

With the headline "IDF most vegan army in world," media outlets like Israel National News play into highlighting the existence of vegans in their military, the Israel Defense Forces (IDF) (Sones 2018). Alloun (2020) has asserted that the IDF has claimed veganism in the same way that they have advertised themselves as women- and queer-friendly. The military has emphasized vegan-friendly boots, berets, and food to show that it is now "vegan-friendly." Veganwashing has become another way the Israeli State presents itself as "ethical" and "moral." Some vegan media outlets and organizations have even lent a hand to help with veganwashing Israel (LIVEKINDLY 2018; Starostinetskaya 2017; Sullivan 2021). There has been a "de-coupling" of an earlier understanding within Israeli nonhuman animal advocacy of the connectedness of human and nonhuman animal oppression. This de-coupling, exemplified in the State's highlighting of vegan-ness within the country, has been another way in which the oppression of Palestinians by settler colonialism can be hidden away behind the veil of a "progressive" and "ethical" Israel—which, like the US, the UK, Brazil, the Philippines, and many other areas of the world, have been marred by rising right-wing nationalist suppressions of rights (Weiss 2016).

From this examination of the complexity of Israeli nationalist "veganism," it should be clear that "veganism" by itself, removed from any sense of justice outside of nonhuman animals, is not intrinsically anti-oppression or "cruelty-free." And since all oppressions are linked, comparable, and affect one another, single-issue veganism simply attempts to remove one type of oppression from many. But, can we truly believe and act as though an entire form of oppression, especially as complex and entrenched and systemic as speciesism, can be dismantled without also affecting how it manifests within forms of human oppression?

None of this is to say that people can't put more of their focus on particular causes. Changing the world doesn't necessitate working on all forms of oppression with equal time and resources from each of us. Some of us primarily work against speciesism, and others mostly work against racism. Problems start when we turn our prioritized causes into competitive social movements or when we only value our "favorite" movement.

JOHN TALLENT

Affirms that veganism is beliefs + practices + action

Many people believe that a person that refuses to consume or use non-human animals in their personal life is a vegan. And that very well may be how we typically gauge someone's veganism. But what if someone doesn't care about other animals while still holding that it is wrong to harm them unnecessarily? What if someone only "performs" veganism through themselves but never advocates to others, never desires to work within the vegan community, and generally keeps their veganism as a "personal choice?" But, can deciding only to live vegan through your own personal consumption choice, or without advocating to others or participating in whatever forms of activism you can participate in helping bring about a vegan world? Sure, each person who decides to reject consuming and using other animals is a great thing, but does it really contribute to more change outside of that person? Maybe some people influence others by "walking the walk" and "leading by example," but those are based mostly on hope, right? Hope that non-action will lead to either similar non-action or action itself. It seems to me to be based almost exclusively on personal "purity." "I'm not taking part in harming animals, so that is the extent of my own responsibilities."

For veganism to have full coherence and sharp enough fangs to damage systemic speciesism, I believe it should entail three equally important aspects: beliefs, practices, and action. Since veganism is a philosophy, it should contain certain ideas about nonhuman animals not being resources or property for humans. As for practices, I think most vegans understand this aspect. These practices involve not consuming nonhuman animals, not wearing them, not using them as entertainment, not testing on them, and taking the active steps of seeking out and using alternatives to these actions. The third aspect, action, might be more contentious for some.

Action can mean many things, and it doesn't necessitate showing up at demonstrations or liberating fur farms (though it could for many folks!). Action simply means doing something, anything, in the service of other animals. And just as the definition of veganism goes, action does not insist on doing what is impossible for you to do. For example, in my own life, I choose to write, advocate on social media, work and volunteer at an animal sanctuary, and generally annoy the shit out of my family and friends about veganism. What else can people do?

> Rescue nonhuman animals from shelters.
> Help hurt/injured nonhuman animals.
> Write essays and articles in local newspapers.
> Liberate nonhuman animals from pet stores.
> Bring up nonhuman animal issues at conferences, talks, speeches, book clubs, reading groups, class discussions, community organizations, and in everyday conversations.
> Clean up areas where nonhuman animals may live or travel, such as forests, your backyard, beaches, streams, and lakes.
> Donate and volunteer at nonhuman animal sanctuaries and other vegan organizations.
> Engage in direct action on behalf of nonhuman animals.
> Organize a completely plant-based potluck and invite other folks to increase solidarity.
> Disrupt speciesism in any way that you can.
> Increase joy, pleasure, and solidarity in the world.
> Put some type of water container outside for free-roaming nonhuman animals.
> Move or arrange vegan literature in bookstores to more prominent areas.
> Sabotage traps, hunts, and fishing.
> Educate yourself and others, and present the situation of nonhuman animals, humans, and ecosystems as an ***emergency***, not as something that we can afford not to be militant about.
> Help nonhuman animals considered "pests" out of your home instead of killing them.

> Keep companion nonhuman animals safe, healthy, and also give them the best lives that you can.
> Demonstrate against nonhuman animal exploitation, environmental destruction, and human oppressions.
> For nutritionists/dietitians/doctors specifically: offer free or low-cost advice on a plant-based diet.
> Start a Food Not Bombs chapter in your local area, or help out at one.

And maybe we should at least consider revising the definition of veganism to reflect this. Something along the lines of:

> "Veganism is the belief that sentient nonhuman animals are not inferior to humans and should not be considered commodities, resources, foods, objects, clothing, test subjects, entertainment, or any other form of human consumption or use. With this belief comes the obligation to engage in social practices consistent with this view and that aid in the liberation of all sentient nonhuman animals from human subjugation—to the extent that each individual human's circumstances allow. Furthermore, according to the vegan viewpoint, the oppression of sentient nonhuman animals is inextricably linked to the oppression of humans and the degradation of the environment; thus, true and lasting liberation requires simultaneous commitments and actions toward the liberation of nonhuman animals, humans, and ecosystems. In other words, veganism is a set of beliefs, practices, and actions that seek the *Total Liberation* of the world."

Conclusion

We have no more time. The time is now. Do not follow. Do not command. Embrace one another. Increase joy. Increase pleasure. Don't be afraid to make mistakes. Allow for mistakes in others. Be skeptical of the past. Be idealistic of the future. And be radical in the moment. The planet is under attack. Nonhuman animals are under attack. Marginalized humans are under attack. Waiting for the system to change is complacency. Waiting for others to start a revolution is worthless. You cannot wait. We cannot wait. Non-militancy is unrealistic. It starts with anyone and everyone. We have no more time. The time is now. Walk out of your front door right now and be the revolution.

Total fucking liberation is upon us.

Notes

1. ^ From this point forward in this book, I will use the term "nonhuman animals" rather than the more common terminology of "animals." I do this because, scientifically speaking, humans are animals, so why would it make sense to label all other animals outside of humans as "animals" but call us "humans?" A more precise terminology would not conceal human animal-ness and would not single one species of animal out and group all others together unnecessarily. Politically speaking, I feel that reminding people that humans are animals is important, especially when it is so often forgotten or denied. Keep in mind the killing and exploitation of trillions of nonhuman animals is typically justifiable by many folks because humans are "humans" and all other animals are "just animals."
2. ^ Recently, my wife said they were supposed to have a virtual meeting with a bunch of Internet friends, but the meeting was almost rescheduled for a later date because there were some people expressing discomfort with having the meeting "during Mercury Retrograde."
3. ^ This book is a trove of information on logic, fallacies, and debunkings of common anti-vegan arguments.
4. ^ The correct opinion on this is Jupiter.
5. ^ For more on the dangers of social media and other tech companies capturing as much personal data from us as possible to make as much profit as possible, see: Zuboff, Shoshana. 2019. *The Age of Surveillance Capitalism: The Fight for the Future at the New Frontier of Power*. London: Profile Books.
6. ^ See: Paxton, Robert O. 2021. "I've Hesitated to Call Donald Trump a Fascist. Until Now | Opinion." *Newsweek*. Retrieved July 18, 2023 (https://www.newsweek.com/robert-paxton-trump-fascist-1560652).
7. ^ See: Logical Fallacies. 2022. "Logical Fallacies - List of Logical Fallacies with Examples." *Logicalfallacies.org*. Retrieved September 9, 2022 (https://www.logicalfallacies.org/).
8. ^ Read and see the rest of the speech here: https://www.all-creatures.org/articles/ar-wollen.html.

9. ^ I use the plural form of "fish" here which better acknowledges that fishes are individuals rather than simply a group of nonhuman animals as diverse as this and that is monolithicized and depersonified.
10. ^ When I started writing this book, I was almost embarrassed to include some of my favorite lyrics from hardcore and punk bands. I thought, "Will people take me less seriously?" Then I remembered that people who are taken way more seriously than me often include quotes from Winston Churchill and Ronald Reagan. My thinking now is, "Yeah, I quoted from some of the bands I like, but at least I didn't quote fucking Winston Churchill or fucking Ronald Reagan."
11. ^ Cisnormativity (sometimes also referred to as "cissexism") is "a systemic bias in favor of cisgender people that may ignore or exclude transgender people" (Erickson-Schroth 2014:18). For instance, people engage in cisnormativity when they assume everyone is either "male" or "female," or a "man" or "woman." This actively ignores the problematic ways in which sex and gender are reduced to certain formations of body parts—a social construction of both sex and gender.
12. ^ There are also interesting discussions about what speciesism should be defined as. Check out the following article: Horta, Oscar, and Frauke Albersmeier. 2020. "Defining Speciesism." *Philosophy Compass* 15(11):e12708. doi: 10/gj5rxf.
13. ^ Garbage article: Rose, Steven. 1992. "Do Animals Have Rights?" *Marxists.org*. Retrieved May 16, 2022 (https://www.marxists.org/history/etol/newspape/isj2/1992/isj2-054/rose-s.html).
14. ^ Lots of great points in this article, but the authors ultimately do a great disservice to nonhuman animals: Grey, Sarah, and Joe Cleffie. 2015. "Peter Singer's Race Problem." *JacobinMag.com*. Retrieved May 16, 2022 (https://www.jacobinmag.com/2015/08/animal-rights-cecil-the-lion-peter-singer-speciesism/).
15. ^ Another garbage article: D'Amato, Paul. 2009. "Socialism and 'Animal Rights.'" *SocialistWorker.org*. Retrieved May 16, 2022 (https://socialistworker.org/2009/10/26/socialism-and-animal-rights).
16. ^ Differentiated from hostile sexism, benevolent sexism involves seemingly positive attributes about women but are also stereotypes and generalizations. For more information, see: Glick, Peter, and Susan T. Fiske. 1996. "The Ambivalent Sexism Inventory: Differentiating Hostile and Benevolent Sexism." *Journal of Personality and Social Psychology* 70(3):491–512. doi: 10.1037/0022-3514.70.3.491.
17. ^ For a more detailed look at the meat paradox, check out the following structured literature review of the phenomenon: Gradidge, Sarah, Magdalena Zawisza, Annelie J. Harvey, and Daragh T. McDermott. 2021. "A Structured

Literature Review of the Meat Paradox." *Social Psychological Bulletin* 16(3). doi: 10.32872/spb.5953.
18. ^ Ableism is defined as "prejudice and discrimination toward individuals simply because they are classified as disabled – regardless of whether their impairments are physical or mental, visible or invisible" (Nario-Redmond 2020:6).
19. ^ Ouch!
20. ^ Defined by Nibert as 'is the systemic practice of violence in which social animals are enslaved and biologically manipulated, resulting in their objectification, subordination, and oppression. Through domesecration, many species of animals that lived on the earth for millions of years, including several species of large, sociable Eurasian mammals, came to be regarded as mere objects, their very existence recognized only in relation to their exploitation as "food animals" or similar socially constructed positions reflecting various forms of exploitation' (Nibert 2013:12).
21. ^ Remember this? Borunda, Alejandra. 2020. *Science*. Retrieved July 24, 2023 (https://www.nationalgeographic.com/science/article/bp-oil-spill-still-dont-know-effects-decade-later).
22. ^ For more information on global pollinator declines, check out Dicks et al. (2021) and Potts et al. (2010).
23. ^ Pynn, Larry. 2016. "Vancouver Aquarium's Belugas Showing Key Signs of Stress, Boredom, Experts Say." *Vancouversun*. Retrieved September 23, 2022 (https://vancouversun.com/news/local-news/repetitive-behaviour-of-vancouver-aquarium-beluga-evidence-of-madness-behaviour-specialist).
24. ^ Blackfish. 2022. "Blackfish." *Blackfish*. Retrieved September 23, 2022 (https://www.blackfishmovie.com/).
25. ^ Bekoff, Marc. 2020. "Research Shows Big Mammals Suffer Brain Damage in Captivity." *Psychology Today*. Retrieved September 23, 2022 (https://www.psychologytoday.com/us/blog/animal-emotions/202011/research-shows-big-mammals-suffer-brain-damage-in-captivity).
26. ^ Smith, Laura. 2014. "Zoos Are Fun for People but Awful for Animals." *Slate Magazine*. Retrieved September 23, 2022 (https://slate.com/technology/2014/06/animal-madness-zoochosis-stereotypic-behavior-and-problems-with-zoos.html).
27. ^ White, Robyn. 2022. "The Story of the Great White Shark Discovered at an Abandoned Zoo." *Msn.com*. Retrieved September 23, 2022 (https://www.msn.com/en-us/travel/news/the-story-of-the-great-white-shark-discovered-at-an-abandoned-zoo/ar-AA103Q2k).
28. ^ Lamont, Di. 2020. "Beyond the Zoo: How Captivity Affects the Mental Well-Being of All Animals." *One Green Planet*. Retrieved September 23, 2022 (https://www.onegreenplanet.org/animalsandnature/how-captivity-effects-the-mental-well-being-of-all-animals/).

29. ^ Abbate, C. E., and Bob Fischer. 2019. "Don't Demean 'Invasives': Conservation and Wrongful Species Discrimination." *Animals* 9(11):871. doi: 10.3390/ani9110871.
30. ^ For one instance, see: Enrico Di Minin, Nigel Leader-Williams, and Corey. 2016. "Banning Trophy Hunting Will Exacerbate Biodiversity Loss." 31(2):99–102. doi: https://doi.org/10.1016/j.tree.2015.12.006.
31. ^ von Essen, Erica, and Michael Allen. 2021. "Killing with Kindness: When Hunters Want to Let You Know They Care." *Human Dimensions of Wildlife* 26(2):179–95. doi: 10/gjzxpk.
32. ^ Prisner-Levyne, Yann. 2020. "Trophy Hunting, Canned Hunting, Tiger Farming, and the Questionable Relevance of the Conservation Narrative Grounding International Wildlife Law." *Journal of International Wildlife Law & Policy* 23(4):239–85. doi: 10/gqhnkm.
33. ^ See: Gibbens, Sarah. 2022. "Is Your Favorite 'Green' Product as Eco-Friendly as It Claims to Be?" *Environment*. Retrieved July 24, 2023 (https://www.nationalgeographic.com/environment/article/what-is-greenwashing-how-to-spot).
34. ^ Haynes, Richard P. 2012. "The Myth of Happy Meat." Pp. 161–68 in *The Philosophy of Food*, edited by D. M. Kaplan. University of California Press.
35. ^ Wrenn, Corey. 2016. "Human Supremacy, Post-Speciesist Ideology, and the Case for Anti-Colonialist Veganism." Pp. 55–70 in *Animals in Human Society: Amazing Creatures Who Share Our Planet*, edited by D. Moorehead. Lanham: University Press of America, Inc.
36. ^ Buddle, Emily. 2022. "Meet Your Meat! How Australian Livestock Producers Are Using Instagram to Promote 'Happy Meat.'" *Adelaide Research & Scholarship*. Retrieved November 2, 2022 (https://hdl.handle.net/2440/136239).
37. ^ For an excellent article on sexualized violence in the dairy industry, see: Gillespie, Kathryn. 2014. "Sexualized Violence and the Gendered Commodification of the Animal Body in Pacific Northwest US Dairy Production." *Gender, Place and Culture: A Journal of Feminist Geography* 21(10):1321–37. doi: 10.1080/0966369x.2013.832665.
38. ^ Kim, Hemi. 2022. "Where Does Veal Come From?" *Sentient Media*. Retrieved July 27, 2023 (https://sentientmedia.org/what-is-veal/).
39. ^ LaBarbera, Natalie. 2022. "How does leather production harm people?" *Collective Fashion Justice*. Retrieved July 27, 2023 (https://www.collectivefashionjustice.org/articles/how-leather-production-harms-people).
40. ^ This number has been criticized as being probably too low and outdated (it used data that is at least 16 years old). Because of this, at the time of this writing, an author of some of the criticism deemed the current calculation of total nonhuman animal agriculture's impact on GHG emissions as effectively impossible to calculate accurately until the FAO and/or IPCC update their data: Twine, Richard. 2021. "Emissions from Animal Agriculture—16.5% Is the

New Minimum Figure." *Sustainability* 13(11):6276. doi: 10/gpkvfb. Also look at the subsequent blog info by the author: Twine, Richard. 2021. "Emissions from Animal Agriculture: Not 18%, Not 14.5%, Not 16.5%, Not 15.6% but Presently Incalculable." *Centre for Human Animal Studies Blog*. Retrieved June 9, 2022 (https://sites.edgehill.ac.uk/cfhas/blog-post-july-2021/).

41. ^ A great article on the "feed-to-food" ratio: Roberts, Spencer. 2022. "Feed vs. Food: How Farming Animals Fuels Hunger." *A Well-Fed World*. Retrieved October 29, 2022 (https://awellfedworld.org/issues/hunger/feed-vs-food/).

42. ^ Eutrophication, as described by the United States Geological Survey website (n.d.), "occurs when a body of water receives an excessive nutrient load, particularly phosphorus and nitrogen. This often results in an overgrowth of algae. As the algae die and decompose, oxygen is depleted from the water, and this lack of oxygen in the water causes the death of aquatic animals."

43. ^ Jacquet, Jennifer. 2021. "The Meat Industry Is Doing Exactly What Big Oil Does to Fight Climate Action." *Washington Post*. Retrieved November 5, 2022 (https://www.washingtonpost.com/outlook/the-meat-industry-is-doing-exactly-what-big-oil-does-to-fight-climate-action/2021/05/14/831e14be-b3fe-11eb-ab43-bebddc5a0f65_story.html).

44. ^ Boren, Zach. 2021. "Meat Industry Pushes Factory Farming at UN Food Systems Summit." *Unearthed*. Retrieved November 5, 2022 (https://unearthed.greenpeace.org/2021/09/21/un-food-systems-summit-meat-climate/).

45. ^ Boren, Zach. 2022. "Revealed: How the Meat Industry Funds the 'Greenhouse Gas Guru.'" *Unearthed*. Retrieved November 5, 2022 (https://unearthed.greenpeace.org/2022/10/31/frank-mitloehner-uc-davis-climate-funding/).

46. ^ Lazarus, Oliver, Sonali McDermid, and Jennifer Jacquet. 2021. "The Climate Responsibilities of Industrial Meat and Dairy Producers." *Climatic Change* 165(1-2). doi: 10.1007/s10584-021-03047-7.

47. ^ Check out: Kassam, Amir, and Laila Kassam. 2021. *Rethinking Food and Agriculture: New Ways Forward*. Oxford Wp, Woodhead Publishing.

48. ^ Also check out: Tague, Gregory. 2022. *The Vegan Evolution: Transforming Diets and Agriculture*. Abingdon, Oxon; New York, NY: Routledge.

49. ^ And: Weis, Tony, and Rebecca A. Ellis. 2021. "Animal Functionality and Interspecies Relations in Regenerative Agriculture: Considering Necessity and the Possibilities of Non-Violence." Pp. 141–53 in *Routledge Handbook of Sustainable and Regenerative Food Systems*, edited by J. Duncan, M. Carolan, and J. S. C. Wiskerke. New York, NY: Routledge.

50. ^ I'm using this line out of context; this is a song about humans' rights to agency, reproductive healthcare, and in general, not to be touched without consent. I've listened to this song a million times, but today it spoke to me as the perfect disconnect most people have about nonhuman animals and social

justice. As Leftists, we demand agency, reproductive healthcare, and a consent-based society—we even threaten, as in this song, those who would attempt to limit our personal rights to our bodies. However, this is mostly not extended to other animals—one of our biggest disconnects from reality.

51. ^ See: Sanbonmatsu, John. 2014. "The Animal of Bad Faith: Speciesism as an Existential Project." Pp. 29–45 in *Critical Animal Studies: Thinking the Unthinkable*, edited by J. Sorenson. Toronto: Canadian Scholars' Press Inc.

52. ^ Also: Trapara, Katarina. 2022. "An Ecofeminist Critique of In/Humane Biopower: Bad Faith, Speciesism and Carnism in 'Happy Meat' Marketing." *Library.ubc.ca*. doi: 10.14288/1.0357025.

53. ^ And: Jones, Robert C. 2020. "Speciesism and Human Supremacy in Animal Neuroscience." *Neuroethics and Nonhuman Animals* 99–115. doi: 10.1007/978-3-030-31011-0_6.

54. ^ Another one: Risley, Suzanne Hamilton. 2016. "If We Were Really Being Deceived: The Spaces of Animal Oppression in the US, Bad Faith, and the Engaged Exposé." *Radical Philosophy Review* 19(2):381–407. doi: 10.5840/radphilrev201641962.

55. ^ Alves, Abel A. 2021. "The Animal Question: The Anthropocene's Hidden Foundational Debate." *História, Ciências, Saúde-Manguinhos* 28(suppl 1):123–40. doi: 10/gqmw24.

56. ^ Deontology is an ethical theory based on duties and obligations—things that we "ought" to do. See: Alexander, Larry, and Michael Moore. 2020. "Deontological Ethics (Stanford Encyclopedia of Philosophy)." *Stanford.edu*. Retrieved September 7, 2022 (https://plato.stanford.edu/entries/ethics-deontological/).

57. ^ Engber, Daniel. 2008. "Why Vegans Can't Decide Whether They're Allowed to Eat Honey." *Slate Magazine*. Retrieved May 27, 2022 (https://slate.com/human-interest/2008/07/why-vegans-can-t-decide-whether-they-re-allowed-to-eat-honey.html).

58. ^ Yu, Christine, and Life by Daily Burn. 2016. "Vegganism: Why Some Vegans Eat Eggs." *CNN*. Retrieved May 27, 2022 (https://www.cnn.com/2016/04/07/health/vegan-eggs-diet/index.html).

59. ^ Erbentraut, Joseph. 2016. "'Seagan' Diet Suggests It's Not a Crazy Idea for Vegans to Eat Seafood." *HuffPost*. Retrieved May 27, 2022 (https://www.huffpost.com/entry/seagan-diet-vegans-eating-seafood_n_57879151e4b08608d333169c).

60. ^ Ough, Tom. 2020. "Why I've Decided to Add Mussels and Oysters to My Vegan Diet." *The Telegraph*. Retrieved May 27, 2022 (https://www.telegraph.co.uk/food-and-drink/features/decided-add-mussels-oysters-vegan-diet/).

61. ^ Food deserts are typically defined as areas with few or no grocery markets and lack fresh and affordable food. For more information: Walker, Renee E.,

Christopher R. Keane, and Jessica G. Burke. 2010. "Disparities and Access to Healthy Food in the United States: A Review of Food Deserts Literature." *Health & Place* 16(5):876–84. doi: 10.1016/j.healthplace.2010.04.013.

62. ^ For a complete list of all the Vegan Society's newsletters since its first one in 1944, check out: https://issuu.com/vegan_society

63. ^ I write more about these confusions in a chapter I wrote for the upcoming book, *Expanding the Critical Animal Studies Imagination: Essays in Solidarity and Total Liberation* (date TBD; published by Peter Lang).

64. ^ An entire book about "ethical veganism": Casamitjana, Jordi. 2022. "Ethical Vegan: A Personal and Political Journey to Change the World." September Publishing. Retrieved May 30, 2022 (https://septemberpublishing.org/product/ethical-vegan/).

65. ^ One recent study found that, "Plant-based protein diets may be a cost-effective way to improve diet quality at all levels of income" (Aggarwal and Drewnowski 2019:451).

66. ^ Another study: Pais, Daniel Francisco, António Cardoso Marques, and José Alberto Fuinhas. 2022. "The Cost of Healthier and More Sustainable Food Choices: Do Plant-Based Consumers Spend More on Food?" *Agricultural and Food Economics* 10(1). doi: https://doi.org/10.1186/s40100-022-00224-9.

67. ^ Kimberlé Crenshaw used the concept of intersectionality to describe "the various ways in which race and gender interact to shape the multiple dimensions of Black women's employment experiences. My objective there was to illustrate that many of the experiences Black women face are subsumed within the traditional boundaries of race or gender discrimination as these boundaries are currently understood, and that the intersection of racism and sexism factors into Black women's lives in ways that cannot be captured wholly by looking at the race or gender dimensions of those experiences separately. I build on those observations here by exploring the various ways in which race and gender intersect in shaping structural, political, and representational aspects of violence against women of color. I should say at the outset that intersectionality is not being offered here as some new, totalizing theory of identity. Nor do I mean to suggest that violence against women of color can be explained only through the frameworks of race and gender considered here. Indeed, factors I address only in part or not at all, such as class or sexuality, are often as critical in shaping the experiences of women of color. My focus on the intersections of race and gender only highlights the need to account for multiple grounds of identity when considering how the social world is constructed." Source: Crenshaw, Kimberle. 1991. "Mapping the Margins: Intersectionality, Identity Politics, and Violence against Women of Color." *Stanford Law Review* 43(6):1241–99. Ahir Gopaldas makes the case that intersectionality has since expanded and that "newer definitions of intersectionality do not mention any particular group or social

identity structures...By not specifying particular social identity structures, these newer definitions expand the concept of intersectionality beyond race, class, and gender to include age, attractiveness, body type, caste, citizenship, education, ethnicity, height and weight assessments, immigration status, income, marital status, mental health status, nationality, occupation, physical ability, religion, sex, sexual orientation, socioeconomic status, and other naturalized—though not necessarily natural—ways of categorizing human populations." Source: Gopaldas, Ahir. 2013. "Intersectionality 101." *Journal of Public Policy & Marketing* 32(1_suppl):90–94. doi: 10.1509/jppm.12.044.

68. ^ Despite me standing in front of them, fully plant-based and very much alive.
69. ^ There is an informative commentary article that suggests physician should increase their knowledge about plant-based diets to help patients understand the importance of the links between diet and health: Stancic, Saray, Josh Cullimore, and Neal Barnard. 2022. "Six Applications of Plant Based Diets for Health Promotion." *American Journal of Lifestyle Medicine* 155982762211040. doi: 10.1177/15598276221104023.
70. ^ Brytek-Matera, Anna. 2019. "Vegetarian Diet and Orthorexia Nervosa: A Review of the Literature." *Eating and Weight Disorders - Studies on Anorexia, Bulimia and Obesity* 26(1):1–11. doi: 10.1007/s40519-019-00816-3.
71. ^ Şentürk, Erman, Begüm Güler Şentürk, Suat Erus, Bahadır Geniş, and Behcet Coşar. 2022. "Dietary Patterns and Eating Behaviors on the Border between Healthy and Pathological Orthorexia." *Eating and Weight Disorders - Studies on Anorexia, Bulimia and Obesity* 27(8):3279–88. doi: 10.1007/s40519-022-01457-9.
72. ^ This is also my reminder.
73. ^ Davis, Chana. 2018. "Busting the Myth of Incomplete Plant-Based Proteins." *Medium*. Retrieved June 1, 2022 (https://tenderly.medium.com/busting-the-myth-of-incomplete-plant-based-proteins-960428e7e91e).
74. ^ Langyan, Sapna, Pranjal Yadava, Fatima Nazish Khan, Zahoor A. Dar, Renu Singh, and Ashok Kumar. 2022. "Sustaining Protein Nutrition through Plant-Based Foods." *Frontiers in Nutrition* 8. doi: 10.3389/fnut.2021.772573.
75. ^ Messina, Ginny. 2021. "Plant Protein: A Vegan Nutrition Primer." *The Vegan RD*. Retrieved June 1, 2022 (https://www.theveganrd.com/vegan-nutrition-101/vegan-nutrition-primers/plant-protein-a-vegan-nutrition-primer/).
76. ^ I wish the nickname "The Johnald" would have caught on.
77. ^ Check out: Bündnis Marxismus und Tierbefreiung / Alliance for Marxism and Animal Liberation. 2018. *18 Theses on Marxism and Animal Liberation*. Retrieved November 24, 2022 (https://www.facebook.com/notes/750502818834215/).
78. ^ This section is adapted from an earlier essay I wrote and published on Medium: https://medium.com/@veganarchistmemes/debunking-the-

myths-around-vegans-and-quinoa-production-3cacbe440ae5. That essay can also be found at: https://theanarchistlibrary.org/library/john-tallent-dear-leftist-critics-of-veganism-veganism-is-not-ableist-or-classist.

79. ^ Former Staff Writer. 2019. "Veganism: A Cure for Climate Change? -." *The Brock Press*. Retrieved August 22, 2022 (https://www.brockpress.com/veganism-a-cure-for-climate-change/).
80. ^ MiNDFOOD. 2018. "MiNDFOOD." *MiNDFOOD*. Retrieved August 23, 2022 (https://www.mindfood.com/article/should-vegans-be-eating-honey/).
81. ^ Rokas Laurinavičius. 2018. "Beekeepers Sick of Vegan Diet Hypocrisy Shut Them down with Facts." *Bored Panda*. Retrieved August 23, 2022 (https://www.boredpanda.com/vegans-eating-agave-syrup-honey-beekeeper-response/?utm_source=google&utm_medium=organic&utm_campaign=organic).
82. ^ See: Food Empowerment Project. n.d. "Child Labor and Slavery in the Chocolate Industry." *FoodIsPower.org*. Retrieved February 11, 2023 (https://foodispower.org/human-labor-slavery/slavery-chocolate/).
83. ^ Catwoman. 2019. "Catwoman." *Tumblr.com*. Retrieved August 23, 2022 (https://vampiregirl2345.tumblr.com/post/173710439707/vegans-of-tumblr-listen-up-harvesting-agave-in).
84. ^ See: Fisher 2011:116.
85. ^ See: Robinson 2014:672.
86. ^ See: Womack 2013:12-13.
87. ^ Forest, Dylan. 2020. "Decolonizing Veganism: An Interview with Dr. Margaret Robinson." *ANIMAL PEOPLE FORUM*. Retrieved July 26, 2022 (https://animalpeopleforum.org/2020/09/23/decolonizing-veganism-an-interview-with-dr-margaret-robinson/).
88. ^ Kim, Claire Jean. 2020. "Makah Whaling and the (Non)Ecological Indian." Pp. 50–103 in *Colonialism and Animality*, edited by K. S. Montford and C. Taylor. London: Routledge. P. 82.
89. ^ See: Fisher, Linda 2011:111-12.
90. ^ See: Robinson, Margaret 2014:683, 685.
91. ^ See: Finkelstein, Norman 2023:23
92. ^ "Noble savage" refers to the stereotype of Indigenous people and cultures of the Americas, before and during the time of first contact by Europeans, as "primitives" living in states of "innocence" and "goodness." It is often believed to be an example of how humans existed alongside Nature before "civilization" (Whelan 1999). It has been extended to Indigenous peoples in other parts of the world as well, such as Indigenous Australians.
93. ^ See: Horsthemke 2018. This is a really good chapter that gets into a lot of the nuances of many types of standpoint theory. One important thing I bring up is how the author (wonderfully) speaks of the difference between "ways of

knowing" and "knowledge claims." I will quote the author at length because it is so important: "Once such a distinction is made between knowledge and knowledge claims, the tension between objectivity and subjectivity disappears, and considerations of social justice and privilege can be foregrounded without invoking a problematic constructivist or relativist view of knowledge. It is knowledge claims, but not knowledge as such, that may result from social relations and that are often ideologically biased. Knowledge claims may be mistaken, involve false beliefs, or be only minimally justified. And while it may be plausible to consider some points of view and knowledge claims privileged (for example, those of specialists and authorities within a particular discipline), they are not therefore infallible. If they are genuine claims to knowledge they must be checked against the facts or prove their mettle in the give-and-take of democratic deliberation and reasoned, scholarly argumentation. Some will survive such fact checking and disputation, and some will not" (209). Too often, various standpoints are given *absolute* authority to knowledge—so much so that sometimes the "ways of knowledge" notion looks at the scientific method as anywhere from "problematic" to "useless." Once we abandon a standard for evidence, every idea has the ability to be "correct" and that's a dangerous hill to die on.

94. ^ The ebook version that I have has no page numbers. This quote comes from Chapter 1, and it is the beginning of one of the paragraphs.
95. ^ See: Erickson-Schroth (2014). "[C]issexism and cisnormativity describe a systemic bias in favor of cisgender people that may ignore or exclude transgender people, and heterosexism and heteronormativity describe a systemic bias in favor of heterosexual relationships" (18). These concepts are related to other similar concepts, such as transphobia ("discrimination based on our status as transgender or gender nonconforming people"), homophobia ("discrimination against gay, lesbian, and bisexual people"), sexism ("discrimination based on our perceived sex"), misogyny ("hatred or dislike of women"), and trans-misogyny ("a form of misogyny directed at trans women") (17).
96. ^ See: Rothberg (2009:29).
97. ^ See: Davis (2004:11).
98. ^ Spiegel, Marjorie. [1989] 1996. *The Dreaded Comparison: Human and Animal Slavery*. 2nd ed. New York, NY: Mirror Books.
99. ^ See: https://www.youtube.com/watch?v=rVIzbOSPL5g
100. ^ See: Harper 2011b:76.
101. ^ This citation might be a little confusing because of the way Pellow numbered the "four pillars" and how I cited that as pages 5-6, possibly seeming to extend the "four pillars" to five and six pillars. Just to be clear, "(5-6)" refers back to the page numbers in the book where the quotes came from.
102. ^ There are many interpretations of this phrase, but any type of State or vanguard party that would subordinate people, temporarily or perpetually, is not

going to fly with most anarchists. The Kronstadt rebellion, the Gulag, Cheka, and others are still in anarchists' minds.
103. ^ See Chapter 3.
104. ^ As a reminder, domesecration is defined as 'is the systemic practice of violence in which social animals are enslaved and biologically manipulated, resulting in their objectification, subordination, and oppression. Through domesecration, many species of animals that lived on the earth for millions of years, including several species of large, sociable Eurasian mammals, came to be regarded as mere objects, their very existence recognized only in relation to their exploitation as "food animals" or similar socially constructed positions reflecting various forms of exploitation' (Nibert 2013:12).
105. ^ See: Harper (2011:77).
106. ^ Here's an article on some of Arpaio's rabid whiteness: Sterling, Terry Greene. 2021. "Joe Arpaio: Inside the Fallout of Trump's Pardon." *The Guardian*. Retrieved January 29, 2023 (https://www.theguardian.com/us-news/2021/apr/08/joe-arpaio-sheriff-arizona-donald-trump).
107. ^ See: Krásná (2022a).
108. ^ Race isn't real, but racism definitely is. See: Smedley and Smedley (2005).
109. ^ Check out these amazing remix videos: https://libcom.org/article/top-ten-richard-spencer-punch-remix-videos.
110. ^ Also sometimes known as "praxeology" or "theories of social practices."
111. ^See: McNeill (2022).
112. ^See: Brown (2020).
113. ^See: Schulman (2016).
114. ^See: Dixon and Piepzna-Samarasinha (2020).
115. ^See: Davis (2003).
116. ^See: Anderson (2021).
117. ^See: Guérin (2005).
118. ^ See: White (2017).
119. ^ See: Baker (2023).
120. ^See: Graeber (2010).
121. ^See: Shannon, Nocella, and Asimakopoulos (2012).
122. ^See: Mann (2013).
123. ^See: Press (2020).
124. ^See: Press (2021).

Bibliography

Abbatista, Guido. 2022. "Beyond the Human Zoos: Exoticism, Ethnic Exhibitions and the Power of the Gaze." *Beyond the Human Zoos: Exoticism, Ethnic Exhibitions and the Power of the Gaze* 207–17. doi: 10.1400/231668.

Adamczyk, Dominika, and Dominika Maison. 2022. "Vegan Stereotypes and Person Perception in a Job Application Situation – Differences Depending on the Type of Job and the Gender of the Candidate." *The Journal of Social Psychology* 1–13. doi: 10.1080/00224545.2022.2136564.

Adams, Carol J. 2017. *The Sexual Politics of Meat: A Feminist-Vegetarian Critical Theory*. New York, NY: Bloomsbury Academic.

AFROPUNK. 2017. "Vegans: You Should Be Worried about the Working Conditions of Farm Workers If You're Really against Cruelty - AFROPUNK." *AFROPUNK*. Retrieved July 8, 2022 (https://afropunk.com/2017/10/vegans-worried-working-conditions-farm-workers-youre-really-cruelty/).

Aggarwal, Anju, and Adam Drewnowski. 2019. "Plant- and Animal-Protein Diets in Relation to Sociodemographic Drivers, Quality, and Cost: Findings from the Seattle Obesity Study." *The American Journal of Clinical Nutrition* 110(2):451–60. doi: 10.1093/ajcn/nqz064.

Agrillo, Christian. 2014. "Numerical and Arithmetic Abilities in Non-Primate Species." in *The Oxford Handbook of Numerical Cognition*, edited by R. Cohen Kadosh and A. Dowker. Oxford University Press.

Ahronheim, Anna. 2018. "The Most Vegan Army in the World." *The Jerusalem Post | JPost.com*. Retrieved August 30, 2022 (https://www.jpost.com/Israel-News/The-most-vegan-army-in-the-world-568595).

Akers, Keith. n.d. "ANIMAL BROTHERS: Reflections on an Ethical Way of Life by Edgar Kupfer-Koberwitz." *Compassionate Spirit*. Retrieved November 20, 2022 (https://compassionatespirit.com/wpblog/books/animal-brothers/).

Akhtar, Aysha. 2018. "Suffering for Science and How Science Supports the End of Animal Experiments." Pp. 475–91 in *The Palgrave Handbook of Practical Animal Ethics*, edited by A. Linzey and C. Linzey. doi: 10.1057/978-1-137-36671-9_27.

Alandia, G., J. P. Rodriguez, S. -E . Jacobsen, D. Bazile, and B. Condori. 2020. "Global Expansion of Quinoa and Challenges for the Andean Region." *Global Food Security* 26:100429. doi: 10.1016/j.gfs.2020.100429.

Allen, Jenny A. 2019. "Community through Culture: From Insects to Whales." *BioEssays* 41(11):1900060. doi: 10.1002/bies.201900060.

Allenden, Nicole, Donald W. Hine, Belinda M. Craig, Annette L. Cowie, Paul D. McGreevy, and Amy D. Lykins. 2022. "What Should We Eat? Realistic Solutions for Reducing Our Food Footprint." *Sustainable Production and Consumption* 32:541–49. doi: 10.1016/j.spc.2022.05.008.

Alloun, Esther. 2017. "'That's the Beauty of It, It's Very Simple!' Animal Rights and Settler Colonialism in Palestine–Israel." *Settler Colonial Studies* 8(4):559–74. doi: 10.1080/2201473x.2017.1414138.

Alloun, Esther. 2020. "Veganwashing Israel's Dirty Laundry? Animal Politics and Nationalism in Palestine-Israel." *Journal of Intercultural Studies* 41(1):24–41. doi: 10/gnp47v.

Allport, G. W. 1985. "The Historical Background of Social Psychology." Pp. 1–46 in *Handbook of Social Psychology*. New York: Random House.

Almiron, Núria, and Marta Tafalla. 2019. "Rethinking the Ethical Challenge in the Climate Deadlock: Anthropocentrism, Ideological Denial and Animal Liberation." *Journal of Agricultural and Environmental Ethics* 32(2):255–67. doi: https://doi.org/10.1007/s10806-019-09772-5.

Alpi, Amedeo, Nikolaus Amrhein, Adam Bertl, Michael R. Blatt, Eduardo Blumwald, Felice Cervone, Jack Dainty, Maria Ida De Michelis, Emanuel Epstein, Arthur W. Galston, Mary Helen M. Goldsmith, Chris Hawes, Rüdiger Hell, Alistair Hetherington, Herman Hofte, Gerd Juergens, Chris J. Leaver, Anna Moroni, Angus Murphy, and Karl Oparka. 2007. "Plant Neurobiology: No Brain, No Gain?" *Trends in Plant Science* 12(4):135–36. doi: 10.1016/j.tplants.2007.03.002.

Alvarez, Linda. n.d. "Colonization, Food, and the Practice of Eating - Food Empowerment Project." *Food Empowerment Project*. Retrieved February 11, 2023 (https://foodispower.org/our-food-choices/colonization-food-and-the-practice-of-eating/).

Amara, Emira Ben. 2018. "Why Veganism Isn't Cruelty-Free - Affinity Magazine." *Affinity Magazine*. Retrieved July 8, 2022 (http://affinity-magazine.us/2018/04/05/why-veganism-isnt-cruelty-free/).

American Farm Bureau Federation. 2018. "Economic Impact of Immigration." *Fb.org*. Retrieved July 8, 2022 (https://www.fb.org/issues/

immigration-reform/agriculture-labor-reform/economic-impact-of-immigration).

American Psychological Association. 2014. "APA Dictionary of Psychology." *Apa.org*. Retrieved (https://dictionary.apa.org/psychology).

Amiot, Catherine E., and Brock Bastian. 2015. "Toward a Psychology of Human–Animal Relations." *Psychological Bulletin* 141(1):6–47. doi: 10/gfsp4h.

Anderson, William C. 2021. *The Nation on No Map: Black Anarchism and Abolition*. Chico, CA: AK Press.

Andrews, Kristin. 2022. "Does the Sentience Framework Imply All Animals Are Sentient?" *WBI Studies Repository*. Retrieved August 29, 2022 (https://www.wellbeingintlstudiesrepository.org/animsent/vol7/iss32/17/). doi: 10.51291/2377-7478.1737.

Angelella, G. M., C. T. McCullough, and M. E. O'Rourke. 2021. "Honey Bee Hives Decrease Wild Bee Abundance, Species Richness, and Fruit Count on Farms regardless of Wildflower Strips." *Scientific Reports* 11(1). doi: 10.1038/s41598-021-81967-1.

Angeli, Viktória, Pedro Miguel Silva, Danilo Crispim Massuela, Muhammad Waleed Khan, Alicia Hamar, Forough Khajehei, Simone Graeff-Hönninger, and Cinzia Piatti. 2020. "Quinoa (*Chenopodium quinoa* Willd.): An Overview of the Potentials of the 'Golden Grain' and Socio-Economic and Environmental Aspects of Its Cultivation and Marketization." *Foods* 9(2):216. doi: 10.3390/foods9020216.

Angier, Natalie. 2009. "Sorry, Vegans: Brussels Sprouts like to Live, Too." *The New York Times*, December 21.

Animal Ethics. 2021. "Snails and Bivalves: A Discussion of Indicators of Sentience — Animal Ethics." *Animal Ethics*. Retrieved June 2, 2022 (https://www.animal-ethics.org/snails-and-bivalves-a-discussion-of-possible-edge-cases-for-sentience/).

Anishchenko, Kseniya, Tracy Cushing, Celia Lenarz-Geisen, and Adane Wogu. 2022. "The Knowledge and Attitudes of Pediatricians Toward Plant-Based Diets." *Current Developments in Nutrition* 6(Supplement_1):421. doi: 10/gqkjc2.

Anthis, Kelly, and Jacy Reese Anthis. 2019. "Global Farmed & Factory Farmed Animals Estimates." *Sentience Institute*. Retrieved August 29, 2022 (https://www.sentienceinstitute.org/global-animal-farming-estimates).

Anthis, Jacy Reese. 2019. "US Factory Farming Estimates." *Sentience Institute*. Retrieved August 29, 2022 (https://www.sentienceinstitute.org/us-factory-farming-estimates).

Anthis, Jacy Reese, and Ali Ladak. 2021. "Animals, Food, and Technology (AFT) Survey: 2020 Update." *Sentience Institute*. Retrieved August 29, 2022 (https://www.sentienceinstitute.org/aft-survey-2020#2020-results).

Applegate, Catherine, Joe Rowles, Katherine Ranard, Sookyoung Jeon, and John Erdman. 2018. "Soy Consumption and the Risk of Prostate Cancer: An Updated Systematic Review and Meta-Analysis." *Nutrients* 10(1):40. doi: 10.3390/nu10010040.

April, Mackenzie L. 2019. "Readying the Rape Rack: Feminism and the Exploitation of Non-Human Reproductive Systems." *Dissenting Voices* 8(1).

Archer, Mike. 2014. "Ordering the Vegetarian Meal? There's More Animal Blood on Your Hands." *IFLScience*. Retrieved December 2, 2022 (https://www.iflscience.com/ordering-vegetarian-meal-there-s-more-animal-blood-your-hands-26212).

Aronson, Elliot, Timothy D. Wilson, Robin M. Akert, and Samuel R. Sommers. 2021. *Social Psychology, Global Edition*. 10th ed. S.L.: Pearson Education Limited.

Aslaug Sollund, Ragnhild. 2016. "Speciesism as Doxic Practice versus Valuing Difference and Plurality 1." *Eco-Global Crimes* 91–114. doi: 10.4324/9781315578651-6.

Aubrey, Allison. 2013. "Your Love of Quinoa Is Good News for Andean Farmers." *NPR*, July 17.

A Well-Fed World. 2021. "Farming Animals Is a Major Form of Food Waste." *A Well-Fed World*. Retrieved July 7, 2022 (https://awellfedworld.org/feed-ratios/).

Axelsson, Ratnakumar, Arendt, Maqbool, Webster, Perloski, Liberg, Arnemo, Hedhammar, and Lindblad-Toh. 2013. "The Genomic Signature of Dog Domestication Reveals Adaptation to a Starch-Rich Diet." *Nature* 495(7441):360–64. doi: 10.1038/nature11837.

Bahnmiller, Hannah. 2015. "The Intersections between Self-Deception and Inconsistency: An Examination of Bad Faith and Cognitive Dissonance." *Stance: An International Undergraduate Philosophy Journal* 8(1):71–80. doi: 10.33043/s.8.1.71-80.

Bakaloudi, Dimitra Rafailia, Afton Halloran, Holly L. Rippin, Artemis Christina Oikonomidou, Theodoros I. Dardavesis, Julianne Williams, Kremlin Wickramasinghe, Joao Breda, and Michail Chourdakis. 2021. "Intake and Adequacy of the Vegan Diet. A Systematic Review of the Evidence." *Clinical Nutrition* 40(5):3503–21. doi: 10.1016/j.clnu.2020.11.035.

Baker, Zoe. 2023. *Means and Ends: The Revolutionary Practice of Anarchism in Europe and the United States*. Edinburgh, Scotland: AK Press.

Bamyeh, Mohammed A. 2019. "The Two Anarchies: The Arab Uprisings and the Question of an Anarchist." Pp. 30–41 in *The Anarchist Imagination: Anarchism Encounters the Humanities and the Social Sciences*, edited by C. Levy and S. Newman. Routledge.

Baracchi, David, and Luigi Baciadonna. 2020. "Insect Sentience and the Rise of a New Inclusive Ethics." *Animal Sentience* 5(29). doi: 10.51291/2377-7478.1604.

Baran, Benjamin E., Steven G. Rogelberg, and Thomas Clausen. 2016. "Routinized Killing of Animals: Going beyond Dirty Work and Prestige to Understand the Well-Being of Slaughterhouse Workers." *Organization* 23(3):351–69. doi: 10.1177/1350508416629456.

Barańska, Agnieszka, Wiesław Kanadys, Magdalena Bogdan, Ewa Stępień, Bartłomiej Barczyński, Anna Kłak, Anna Augustynowicz, Marta Szajnik, and Urszula Religioni. 2022. "The Role of Soy Isoflavones in the Prevention of Bone Loss in Postmenopausal Women: A Systematic Review with Meta-Analysis of Randomized Controlled Trials." *Journal of Clinical Medicine* 11(16):4676. doi: 10.3390/jcm11164676.

Barr, W. Andrew, Briana Pobiner, John Rowan, Andrew Du, and J. Tyler Faith. 2022. "No Sustained Increase in Zooarchaeological Evidence for Carnivory after the Appearance of Homo Erectus." *Proceedings of the National Academy of Sciences* 119(5). doi: 10.1073/pnas.2115540119.

Bartholomew, Aaron, and James A. Bohnsack. 2005. "A Review of Catch-and-Release Angling Mortality with Implications for No-Take Reserves." *Reviews in Fish Biology and Fisheries* 15(1–2):129–54. doi: 10.1007/s11160-005-2175-1.

Barthels, Friederike, Saskia Poerschke, Romina Müller, and Reinhard Pietrowsky. 2020. "Orthorexic Eating Behavior in Vegans Is Linked to Health, Not to Animal Welfare." *Eating and Weight Disorders - Studies on Anorexia, Bulimia and Obesity* 25(3):817–20. doi: 10/gkmqtg.

Bastian, Brock, Steve Loughnan, Nick Haslam, and Helena R. M. Radke. 2011a. "Don't Mind Meat? The Denial of Mind to Animals Used for Human Consumption." *Personality and Social Psychology Bulletin* 38(2):247–56. doi: 10.1177/0146167211424291.

Bastian, Brock, Kimberly Costello, Steve Loughnan, and Gordon Hodson. 2011. "When Closing the Human–Animal Divide Expands Moral Concern." *Social Psychological and Personality Science* 3(4):421–29. doi: 10.1177/1948550611425106.

Bastian, Brock, and Steve Loughnan. 2016. "Resolving the Meat-Paradox: A Motivational Account of Morally Troublesome Behavior and Its Maintenance." *Personality and Social Psychology Review* 21(3):278–99. doi: 10.1177/1088868316647562.

Battaglia Richi, Evelyne, Beatrice Baumer, Beatrice Conrad, Roger Darioli, Alexandra Schmid, and Ulrich Keller. 2015. "Health Risks Associated with Meat Consumption: A Review of Epidemiological Studies." *International Journal for Vitamin and Nutrition Research* 85(1-2):70–78. doi: 10.1024/0300-9831/a000224.

Beef Board. 2021. "Dairy's Contribution to the Beef Industry | Beef Checkoff." *Beef Checkoff*. Retrieved October 29, 2022 (https://www.beefboard.org/2021/12/13/dairys-contribution-to-the-beef-industry/).

Bègue, Laurent. 2020. "Explaining Animal Abuse Among Adolescents: The Role of Speciesism." *Journal of Interpersonal Violence* 088626052095964. doi: 10/gps8q2.

Bekoff, Marc. 2008. *The Emotional Lives of Animals: A Leading Scientist Explores Animal Joy, Sorrow, and Empathy - and Why They Matter*. Novato, Calif.: New World Library.

Belcourt, Billy-Ray. 2014. "Animal Bodies, Colonial Subjects: (Re)Locating Animality in Decolonial Thought." *Societies* 5(1):1–11. doi: 10.3390/soc5010001.

Bellemare, Marc F., Johanna Fajardo-Gonzalez, and Seth R. Gitter. 2018. "Foods and Fads: The Welfare Impacts of Rising Quinoa Prices in Peru." *World Development* 112:163–79.

Bennett, Lauren Katie. 2021. "The Legal, Ethical and Welfare Implications of Feeding Vegan Diets to Dogs and Cats." *The Veterinary Nurse* 12(3):108–14. doi: 10.12968/vetn.2021.12.3.108.

Beran, Michael J., Bonnie M. Perdue, and Theodore A. Evans. 2014. "Monkey Mathematical Abilities." in *The Oxford Handbook of Numerical Cognition*, edited by R. Cohen Kadosh and A. Dowker. Oxford University Press.

Berners-Lee, M., C. Hoolohan, H. Cammack, and C. N. Hewitt. 2012. "The Relative Greenhouse Gas Impacts of Realistic Dietary Choices." *Energy Policy* 43:184–90. doi: 10.1016/j.enpol.2011.12.054.

Best, Steven. 2016. *Politics of Total Liberation: Revolution for the 21st Century*. New York: Palgrave Macmillan.

Bilewicz, Michal, Roland Imhoff, and Marek Drogosz. 2011. "The Humanity of What We Eat: Conceptions of Human Uniqueness among Vegetarians and Omnivores." *European Journal of Social Psychology* 41(2):201–9. doi: 10.1002/ejsp.766.

Biocyclic Vegan International. 2022. "Home" *Biocyclic-Vegan.org*. Retrieved August 18, 2022 (https://www.biocyclic-vegan.org/).

Birch, Jonathan. 2017. "Animal Sentience and the Precautionary Principle." *Animal Sentience* 2(16). doi: 10.51291/2377-7478.1200.

Birch, Jonathan, Charlotte Burn, Alexandra Schnell, Heather Browning, and Andrew Crump. 2021. *Review of the Evidence of Sentience in Cephalopod Molluscs and Decapod Crustaceans*. London: LSE Consulting.

Birkett, Lucy P., and Nicholas E. Newton-Fisher. 2011. "How Abnormal Is the Behaviour of Captive, Zoo-Living Chimpanzees?" edited by S. Gursky-Doyen. *PLoS ONE* 6(6):e20101. doi: 10.1371/journal.pone.0020101.

Blake, Imogen. 2018. "How a Vegan Lifestyle Isn't as Cruelty Free as People Might Think." *Daily Mail Online*. Retrieved July 8, 2022 (https://www.dailymail.co.uk/femail/food/article-5624979/How-vegan-lifestyle-isnt-cruelty-free-people-think.html).

Blakemore, Erin. 2016. "Don't Worry: Eating Quinoa Doesn't Hurt Peruvian Farmers." *Smithsonian Magazine*. Retrieved September 3, 2021 (https://www.smithsonianmag.com/smart-news/dont-worry-eating-quinoa-helps-peruvian-farmers-180958639/).

Blythman, Joanna. 2013. "Can Vegans Stomach the Unpalatable Truth about Quinoa?" *The Guardian*, January 16.

Bomb, Flower. 2020. "An Obituary for Identity Politics." *The Anarchist Library*. Retrieved August 19, 2023 (https://theanarchistlibrary.org/library/flower-bomb-an-obituary-for-identity-politics).

Bonifacio, Alejandro, Genaro Aroni, Milton Villca, and Jeffery W. Bentley. 2022. "Recovering from Quinoa: Regenerative Agricultural Research in Bolivia." *Journal of Crop Improvement* 1–22. doi: 10.1080/15427528.2022.2135155.

Bonnet, Céline, Zohra Bouamra-Mechemache, Vincent Réquillart, and Nicolas Treich. 2020. "Viewpoint: Regulating Meat Consumption to Improve Health, the Environment and Animal Welfare." *Food Policy* 97:101847. doi: 10.1016/j.foodpol.2020.101847.

Bourdieu, Pierre. 1977. *Outline of a Theory of Practice*. Cambridge: Cambridge University Press.

Bouvard, Véronique, Dana Loomis, Kathryn Z. Guyton, Yann Grosse, Fatiha El Ghissassi, Lamia Benbrahim-Tallaa, Neela Guha, Heidi Mattock, and Kurt Straif. 2015. "Carcinogenicity of Consumption of Red and Processed Meat." *The Lancet Oncology* 16(16):1599–1600. doi: 10.1016/s1470-2045(15)00444-1.

Branch, Glenn, and Craig A. Foster. 2018. "Yes, Flat-Earthers Really Do Exist." *Scientific American Blog Network*. Retrieved May 11, 2022 (https://blogs.scientificamerican.com/observations/yes-flat-earthers-really-do-exist/).

Braithwaite-Read, Victoria Ann and F. A. Huntingford. 2004. "Fish and Welfare: Do Fish Have the Capacity for Pain Perception and Suffering?" *Animal Welfare* 13(SUPPL.).

Braun, Sebastian F. 2007. "Ecological and Un-ecological Indians: The (Non)Portrayal of Plains Indians in the Buffalo Commons Literature." Pp. 192–208 in *Native Americans and the Environment: Perspectives on the Ecological Indian*, edited by M. E. Harkin and D. R. Lewis. London: University of Nebraska Press.

Braunsberger, Karin, and Richard O. Flamm. 2019. "The Case of the Ethical Vegan: Motivations Matter When Researching Dietary and Lifestyle Choices." *Journal of Managerial Issues* 31(3):228–45.

Briske, David D., Andrew J. Ash, Justin D. Derner, and Lynn Huntsinger. 2014. "Commentary: A Critical Assessment of the Policy Endorsement for Holistic Management." *Agricultural Systems* 125:50–53. doi: 10.1016/j.agsy.2013.12.001.

Briske, David D., Brandon T. Bestelmeyer, Joel R. Brown, Samuel D. Fuhlendorf, and H. Wayne Polley. 2013. "The Savory Method Can Not Green Deserts or Reverse Climate Change." *Rangelands* 35(5):72–74. doi: 10.2111/rangelands-d-13-00044.1.

Brown, Adrienne Maree. 2020. *We Will Not Cancel Us: And Other Dreams of Transformative Justice*. Chico, CA: AK Press.

Brown, Anna. 2022. "Deep Partisan Divide on Whether Greater Acceptance of Transgender People Is Good for Society." *Pew Research Center*. Retrieved May 11, 2022 (https://www.pewresearch.org/fact-tank/2022/02/11/deep-partisan-divide-on-whether-greater-acceptance-of-transgender-people-is-good-for-society/).

Brown, Gabe. 2018. *Dirt to Soil: One Family's Journey into Regenerative Agriculture*. White River Junction, VT: Chelsea Green Publishing.

Bruers, Stijn. 2021. "Speciesism, Arbitrariness and Moral Illusions." *Philosophia* 49(3):957–75. doi: 10/gpkvbr.

Brugnoli, Federico. 2012. *Life Cycle Assessment, Carbon Footprint in Leather Processing (Review of Methodologies and Recommendations for Harmonization)*. Shanghai, China: United Nations Industrial Development Organization - Leather and Leather Products Industry Panel.

Brulle, Robert J., Jason Carmichael, and J. Craig Jenkins. 2012. "Shifting Public Opinion on Climate Change: An Empirical Assessment of Factors Influencing Concern over Climate Change in the U.S., 2002–2010." *Climatic Change* 114(2):169–88. doi: 10.1007/s10584-012-0403-y.

Bryant, Christopher J. 2022. "Plant-Based Animal Product Alternatives Are Healthier and More Environmentally Sustainable than Animal Products." *Future Foods* 6:100174. doi: 10.1016/j.fufo.2022.100174.

Burkeman, Oliver. 2003. "Memo Exposes Bush's New Green Strategy." *The Guardian*. Retrieved September 1, 2022 (https://www.theguardian.com/environment/2003/mar/04/usnews.climatechange).

Butler, Judith. 1990. *Gender Trouble: Feminism and the Subversion of Identity*. London: Routledge.

Byrne, Sahara, and Philip Solomon Hart. 2009. "The Boomerang Effect a Synthesis of Findings and a Preliminary Theoretical Framework." *Annals of the International Communication Association* 33(1):3–37. doi: 10.1080/23808985.2009.11679083.

Cardwell, Hamish. 2022. "Climate Change: 'Global Veganisation Is Now a Survival Imperative' - IPCC Expert Reviewer." *RNZ*. Retrieved August 23, 2022 (https://www.rnz.co.nz/news/national/468715/climate-change-global-veganisation-is-now-a-survival-imperative-ipcc-expert-reviewer).

Carrington, Damian. 2018. "Avoiding Meat and Dairy Is 'Single Biggest Way' to Reduce Your Impact on Earth." *The Guardian*. Retrieved June 12, 2022 (https://www.theguardian.com/environment/2018/may/31/avoiding-meat-and-dairy-is-single-biggest-way-to-reduce-your-impact-on-earth).

Carter, John, Allison Jones, Mary O'Brien, Jonathan Ratner, and George Wuerthner. 2014. "Holistic Management: Misinformation on the Science of Grazed Ecosystems." *International Journal of Biodiversity* 2014:1–10. doi: 10.1155/2014/163431.

Carter, Nicholas, and Tushar Mehta. 2021. "Another Industry Attempt to Greenwash Beef: A Review of Regenerative Grazing | Medium." *Medium*. Retrieved August 18, 2022 (https://plantbaseddata.medium.com/the-failed-attempt-to-greenwash-beef-7dfca9d74333).

Casamitjana, Jordi. 2020. "The Foundations of Ethical Veganism." The Vegan Society. Retrieved May 30, 2022 (https://www.vegansociety.com/news/blog/foundations-ethical-veganism).

Cassidy, Emily S., Paul C. West, James S. Gerber, and Jonathan A. Foley. 2013. "Redefining Agricultural Yields: From Tonnes to People Nourished per Hectare." *Environmental Research Letters* 8(3):034015. doi: 10.1088/1748-9326/8/3/034015.

Caviola, Lucius, Jim A. C. Everett, and Nadira S. Faber. 2019. "The Moral Standing of Animals: Towards a Psychology of Speciesism." *Journal of Personality and Social Psychology* 116(6):1011–29. doi: 10/gdcf5m.

Caviola, Lucius, Stefan Schubert, Guy Kahane, and Nadira S. Faber. 2022. "Humans First: Why People Value Animals Less than Humans." *Cognition* 225:105139. doi: 10.1016/j.cognition.2022.105139.

CDC. n.d. "Tuskegee Study - Timeline - CDC - NCHHSTP." *Centers for Disease Control and Prevention*. Retrieved (https://www.cdc.gov/tuskegee/timeline.htm).

Charles, Dan. 2018. "Honeybees Help Farmers, but They Don't Help the Environment." *NPR.org*. Retrieved September 15, 2022 (https://www.npr.org/sections/thesalt/2018/01/27/581007165/honey-bees-help-farmers-but-they-dont-help-the-environment).

Çiçekoğlu, Pınar, and Güzin Yasemin Tunçay. 2018. "A Comparison of Eating Attitudes between Vegans/Vegetarians and Nonvegans/Nonvegetarians in Terms of Orthorexia Nervosa." *Archives of Psychiatric Nursing* 32(2):200–205. doi: 10.1016/j.apnu.2017.11.002.

Clark, Michael, and David Tilman. 2017. "Comparative Analysis of Environmental Impacts of Agricultural Production Systems, Agricultural Input Efficiency, and Food Choice." *Environmental Research Letters* 12(6):064016. doi: 10.1088/1748-9326/aa6cd5.

Clay, Anne Safiya, and Ingrid J. Visseren-Hamakers. 2022. "Individuals Matter: Dilemmas and Solutions in Conservation and Animal Welfare Practices in Zoos." *Animals* 12(3):1–22. doi: 10.3390/ani12030398.

Clifford-Clarke, Megan Marie, Katherine Whitehouse-Tedd, and Clare Frances Ellis. 2021. "Conservation Education Impacts of Animal Ambassadors in Zoos." *Journal of Zoological and Botanical Gardens* 3(1):1–18. doi: 10.3390/jzbg3010001.

Clonan, Angie, Paul Wilson, Judy A. Swift, Didier G. Leibovici, and Michelle Holdsworth. 2015. "Red and Processed Meat Consumption and Purchasing Behaviours and Attitudes: Impacts for Human Health, Animal Welfare and Environmental Sustainability." *Public Health Nutrition* 18(13):2446–56. doi: 10.1017/s1368980015000567.

Coffey, Alice, Robert Lillywhite, and Oyinlola Oyebode. 2022. "P24 Meat vs Meat Alternatives: Which Is Better for the Environment and Health? A Nutritional and Environmental Analysis of Animal-Based Products Compared with Their Plant-Based Alternatives." *J Epidemiol Community Health* 76(Suppl 1):A58–59. doi: 10.1136/jech-2022-SSMabstracts.121.

Cole, Matthew. 2011. "From 'Animal Machines' to 'Happy Meat'? Foucault's Ideas of Disciplinary and Pastoral Power Applied to 'Animal-Centred' Welfare Discourse." *Animals* 1(1):83–101. doi: 10.3390/ani1010083.

Cole, Matthew. 2013. "Asceticism and Hedonism in Research Discourses of Veg*Anism | Emerald Insight." *British Food Journal* 110(7):706–16. doi: 10.1108\/bfj.

Cole, Matthew, and Karen Morgan. 2011. "Vegaphobia: Derogatory Discourses of Veganism and the Reproduction of Speciesism in UK National Newspapers." *The British Journal of Sociology* 62(1):134–53. doi: 10/cfns2r.

Colla, Sheila R. 2022. "The Potential Consequences of 'Bee Washing' on Wild Bee Health and Conservation." *International Journal for Parasitology: Parasites and Wildlife* 18:30–32. doi: 10.1016/j.ijppaw.2022.03.011.

Collier, Elizabeth S., Kathryn L. Harris, Marcus Bendtsen, Cecilia Norman, and Jun Niimi. 2023. "Just a Matter of Taste? Understanding Rationalizations for Dairy Consumption and Their Associations with Sensory Expectations of Plant-Based Milk Alternatives." *Food Quality and Preference* 104:104745. doi: 10.1016/j.foodqual.2022.104745.

Colling, Sarat. 2020. *Animal Resistance in the Global Capitalist Era*. East Lansing, MI: Michigan State University Press.

Contreras, Russell. 2022. "Antisemitic Hate Crimes Appear up in Major Cities This Year." *Axios*. Retrieved (https://www.axios.com/2022/12/17/antisemitic-hate-crimes-rise-in-major-cities).

Craib, Ian. 2011. *Anthony Giddens (Routledge Revivals) [E-book version]*. Routledge.

Craig, Winston J. 2009. "Health Effects of Vegan Diets." *The American Journal of Clinical Nutrition* 89(5):1627S1633S. doi: 10.3945/ajcn.2009.26736n.

Craig, Winston J., Ann Reed Mangels, Ujué Fresán, Kate Marsh, Fayth L. Miles, Angela V. Saunders, Ella H. Haddad, Celine E. Heskey, Patricia Johnston, Enette Larson-Meyer, and Michael Orlich. 2021. "The Safe and Effective Use of Plant-Based Diets with Guidelines for Health Professionals." *Nutrients* 13(11):4144. doi: 10.3390/nu13114144.

Crenshaw, Kimberlé. 1991. "Mapping the Margins: Intersectionality, Identity Politics, and Violence against Women of Color." *Stanford Law Review* 43(6):1241–99.

Cross, Leslie. 1951. "History of Vegetarianism - IVU History." *International Vegetarian Union*. Retrieved September 30, 2021 (https://www.ivu.org/history/world-forum/1951vegan.html).

Crowley, Jennifer, Lauren Ball, and Gerrit Jan Hiddink. 2019. "Nutrition in Medical Education: A Systematic Review." *The Lancet. Planetary Health* 3(9):e379–89. doi: 10.1016/S2542-5196(19)30171-8.

Cudworth, Erika. 2015. "Killing Animals: Sociology, Species Relations and Institutionalized Violence." *The Sociological Review* 63(1):1–18. doi: 10/f64bwb.

Cui, Chendi, Rahel L. Birru, Beth E. Snitz, Masafumi Ihara, Chikage Kakuta, Brian J. Lopresti, Howard J. Aizenstein, Oscar L. Lopez, Chester A. Mathis, Yoshihiro Miyamoto, Lewis H. Kuller, and Akira Sekikawa. 2019. "Effects of Soy Isoflavones on Cognitive Function: A Systematic Review and Meta-Analysis of Randomized Controlled Trials." *Nutrition Reviews* 78(2):134–44. doi: 10.1093/nutrit/nuz050.

Cushing, Simon. 2003. "Against 'Humanism': Speciesism, Personhood, and Preference." *Journal of Social Philosophy* 34(4):556–71. doi: 10.1111/1467-9833.00201.

Cusworth, George, Jamie Lorimer, Jeremy Brice, and Tara Garnett. 2022. "Green Rebranding: Regenerative Agriculture, Future-Pasts, and the Naturalisation of Livestock." *Transactions of the Institute of British Geographers*. doi: 10.1111/tran.12555.

Daley, Jason. 2018. "Study Suggests Dolphins and Some Whales Grieve Their Dead." *Smithsonian Magazine*. Retrieved June 10, 2022 (https://www.smithsonianmag.com/smart-news/study-suggests-dolphins-and-some-whales-grieve-their-dead-180969414/).

D'Amelio, Enrico, Bernardina Gentile, Florigio Lista, and Raffaele D'Amelio. 2015. "Historical Evolution of Human Anthrax from Occupational Disease to Potentially Global Threat as Bioweapon." *Environment International* 85:133–46. doi: 10.1016/j.envint.2015.09.009.

Davis, Angela Y. 2003. *Are Prisons Obsolete?* New York: Seven Stories Press.

Davis, Angela, and Elizabeth Martínez. 1993. "Coalition Building among People of Color." *Center for Cultural Studies, University of California at Santa Cruz*.

Davis, Karen. 2004. "A Tale of Two Holocausts." *Animal Liberation Philosophy and Policy Journal* 2(2):1–20.

Deckha, Maneesha. 2018. "Postcolonial." in *Critical Terms for Animal Studies*, edited by L. Gruen. Chicago: Chicago the University of Chicago Press.

Deckha, Maneesha. 2020. "Veganism, Dairy, and Decolonization." *Journal of Human Rights and the Environment* 11(2):244–67. doi: https://doi.org/10.4337/jhre.2020.02.05.

Deckha, Maneesha. 2021. *Animals as Legal Beings: Contesting Anthropocentric Legal Orders*. Toronto: University of Toronto Press.

Dehghan, Saeed Kamali. 2019. "Are Mexican Avocados the World's New Conflict Commodity?" *The Guardian*, December 30.

DeGrazia, David. 2020. "Sentience and Consciousness as Bases for Attributing Interests and Moral Status: Considering the Evidence and Speculating Slightly Beyond." *Neuroethics and Nonhuman Animals* 17–31. doi: 10.1007/978-3-030-31011-0_2.

De Groeve, Ben, and Daniel L. Rosenfeld. 2022. "Morally Admirable or Moralistically Deplorable? A Theoretical Framework for Understanding Character Judgments of Vegan Advocates." *Appetite* 168:105693. doi: 10/gpkvb2.

De Groeve, Ben, Daniel L. Rosenfeld, Brent Bleys, and Liselot Hudders. 2022. "Moralistic Stereotyping of Vegans: The Role of Dietary Motivation and Advocacy Status." *Appetite* 174:106006. doi: 10.1016/j.appet.2022.106006.

De Groeve, Ben, Liselot Hudders, and Brent Bleys. 2021. "Moral Rebels and Dietary Deviants: How Moral Minority Stereotypes Predict the Social Attractiveness of Veg*Ns." *Appetite* 164:105284. doi: 10.1016/j.appet.2021.105284.

De Maria, M., Robinson, E. J. Z., Kangile, J. R., Kadigi, R., Dreoni, I., Couto, M., Howai, N., Peci, J., Fiennes, S. 2020: "Global Soybean Trade. The Geopolitics of a Bean." *UK Research and Innovation Global Challenges Research Fund (UKRI GCRF) Trade, Development and the Environment Hub*. doi: 10.34892/7yn1-k494.

Derrida, Jacques. 2004. "The Animal That Therefore I Am (More to Follow)." Pp. 113–28 in *Animal Philosophy: Essential Readings in Continental Thought*, edited by P. Atterton and M. Calarco. Continuum.

de Vere, Amber J., and Stan A. Kuczaj. 2016. "Where Are We in the Study of Animal Emotions?" *Wiley Interdisciplinary Reviews: Cognitive Science* 7(5):354–62. doi: 10.1002/wcs.1399.

Devries, Stephen, Arthur Agatston, Monica Aggarwal, Karen E. Aspry, Caldwell B. Esselstyn, Penny Kris-Etherton, Michael Miller, James H. O'Keefe, Emilio Ros, Anne K. Rzeszut, Beth A. White, Kim A. Williams, and Andrew M. Freeman. 2017. "A Deficiency of Nutrition Education and Practice in Cardiology." *The American Journal of Medicine* 130(11):1298–1305. doi: 10.1016/j.amjmed.2017.04.043.

de Waal, Frans. 2020. *Mama's Last Hug: Animal Emotions and What They Tell Us about Ourselves*. New York, Ny: W.W. Norton & Company.

de Waal, Frans B. M. 1999. "Anthropomorphism and Anthropodenial: Consistency in Our Thinking about Humans and Other Animals." *Philosophical Topics* 27(1):255–80. doi: https://doi.org/10.5840/philtopics199927122.

de Waal, Frans B. M., and Kristin Andrews. 2022. "The Question of Animal Emotions." *Science* 375(6587):1351–52. doi: 10/gpr25q.

Dias, Natália Fonseca, Adriana Seára Tirloni, Diogo Cunha dos Reis, and Antônio Renato Pereira Moro. 2020. "Risk of Slaughterhouse Workers Developing Work-Related Musculoskeletal Disorders in Different Organizational Working Conditions." *International Journal of Industrial Ergonomics* 76:102929. doi: 10.1016/j.ergon.2020.102929.

Dicks, Lynn V., Tom D. Breeze, Hien T. Ngo, Deepa Senapathi, Jiandong An, Marcelo A. Aizen, Parthiba Basu, Damayanti Buchori, Leonardo Galetto, Lucas A. Garibaldi, Barbara Gemmill-Herren, Brad G. Howlett, Vera L. Imperatriz-Fonseca, Steven D. Johnson, Anikó Kovács-Hostyánszki, Yong Jung Kwon, H. Michael G. Lattorff, Thingreipi Lungharwo, Colleen L. Seymour, and Adam J. Vanbergen. 2021. "A Global-Scale Expert Assessment of Drivers and Risks Associated with

Pollinator Decline." *Nature Ecology & Evolution* 5(10):1453–61. doi: 10.1038/s41559-021-01534-9.

Dinu, Monica, Rosanna Abbate, Gian Franco Gensini, Alessandro Casini, and Francesco Sofi. 2016. "Vegetarian, Vegan Diets and Multiple Health Outcomes: A Systematic Review with Meta-Analysis of Observational Studies." *Critical Reviews in Food Science and Nutrition* 57(17):3640–49. doi: 10.1080/10408398.2016.1138447.

Dixit, Sumita, Ashish Yadav, Premendra D. Dwivedi, and Mukul Das. 2015. "Toxic Hazards of Leather Industry and Technologies to Combat Threat: A Review." *Journal of Cleaner Production* 87:39–49. doi: 10.1016/j.jclepro.2014.10.017.

Dhont, Kristof, Gordon Hodson, and Ana C. Leite. 2016. "Common Ideological Roots of Speciesism and Generalized Ethnic Prejudice: The Social Dominance Human–Animal Relations Model (SD-HARM)." *European Journal of Personality* 30(6):507–22. doi: 10.1002/per.2069.

Dixon, Ejeris, and Lean Lakshmi Piepzna-Samarasinha, eds. 2020. *Beyond Survival: Strategies and Stories from the Transformative Justice Movement.* Chico, CA: AK Press.

Dodd, Sarah, Deep Khosa, Cate Dewey, and Adronie Verbrugghe. 2022. "Owner Perception of Health of North American Dogs Fed Meat- or Plant-Based Diets." *Research in Veterinary Science* 149:36–46. doi: 10/gqkjc5.

Doke, Sonali K., and Shashikant C. Dhawale. 2015. "Alternatives to Animal Testing: A Review." *Saudi Pharmaceutical Journal* 23(3):223–29. doi: 10.1016/j.jsps.2013.11.002.

Domínguez-Oliva, Adriana, Daniel Mota-Rojas, Ines Semendric, and Alexandra L. Whittaker. 2023. "The Impact of Vegan Diets on Indicators of Health in Dogs and Cats: A Systematic Review." *Veterinary Sciences* 10(1):52. doi: https://doi.org/10.3390/vetsci10010052.

Donovan, Josephine. 2006. "Feminism and the Treatment of Animals: From Care to Dialogue." *Signs: Journal of Women in Culture and Society* 31(2):305–29. doi: 10.1086/491750.

Dorning, Mike. 2019. "Trump's $28 Billion Trade War Bailout Is Overpaying Farmers." *Bloomberg.com*. Retrieved August 29, 2022 (https://www.bloomberg.com/news/articles/2019-12-04/trump-s-28-billion-trade-war-bailout-is-overpaying-many-farmers#xj4y7vzkg).

Draguhn, Andreas, Jon M. Mallatt, and David G. Robinson. 2021. "Anesthetics and Plants: No Pain, No Brain, and Therefore No Consciousness." *Protoplasma* 258(2):239–48. doi: 10/gzv3.

Drews, Debbie. 2016. "Like a Fish Out of Water." *Outside Bozeman*. Retrieved November 1, 2022 (https://outsidebozeman.com/activities/fishing/fish-out-water).

Dutkiewicz, Jan., and Gabriel N. Rosenberg. 2021. "The Myth of Regenerative Ranching." *The New Republic*. Retrieved August 18, 2022 (https://newrepublic.com/article/163735/myth-regenerative-ranching).

Driscoll, Janis Wiley. 1995. "Attitudes toward Animals: Species Ratings." *Society & Animals* 3(2):139–50. doi: 10.1163/156853095x00125.

Earle, Megan, and Gordon Hodson. 2017. "What's Your Beef with Vegetarians? Predicting Anti-Vegetarian Prejudice from Pro-Beef Attitudes across Cultures." *Personality and Individual Differences* 119:52–55. doi: 10.1016/j.paid.2017.06.034.

Edelblutte, Émilie, Roopa Krithivasan, and Matthew Nassif Hayek. 2022. "Animal Agency in Wildlife Conservation and Management." *Conservation Biology*. doi: 10.1111/cobi.13853.

Eldridge, David J., Alistair G. B. Poore, Marta Ruiz-Colmenero, Mike Letnic, and Santiago Soliveres. 2016. "Ecosystem Structure, Function, and Composition in Rangelands Are Negatively Affected by Livestock Grazing." *Ecological Applications* 26(4):1273–83. doi: 10.1890/15-1234.

Elgin, Ben. 2021. "Beef Industry Tries to Erase Its Emissions with Fuzzy Methane Math." *Bloomberg.com*. Retrieved November 5, 2022 (https://www.bloomberg.com/news/features/2021-10-19/beef-industry-falsely-claims-low-cow-carbon-footprint).

Ellingson, Ter. 2001. *The Myth of the Noble Savage*. Berkeley: University of California Press.

Emmerman, Karen S. 2019. "Moral Arguments against Zoos." Pp. 381–93 in *The Routledge Handbook on Animal Ethics*, edited by B. Fischer. New York, NY: Routledge.

Ergin Zengin, Sezen. 2019. "Normalizing Human-Animal Power Relations through Media: Zoo Discourses in Turkey." *Galatasaray Üniversitesi İleti-ş-Im Dergisi* (31):9–33. doi: 10.16878/gsuilet.580339.

Erickson-Schroth, Laura. 2014. *Trans Bodies, Trans Selves: A Resource for the Transgender Community*. New York: Oxford University Press.

European Food Safety Authority. 2012. "Scientific Opinion on the Safety and Efficacy of Taurine as a Feed Additive for All Animal Species." *EFSA Journal* 10(6). doi: 10.2903/j.efsa.2012.2736.

Fang, Janet. 2014. "Plants Can Hear Themselves Being Eaten." *IFLScience*. Retrieved June 2, 2022 (https://www.iflscience.com/plants-and-animals/plants-can-hear-themselves-being-eaten/).

FAO. n.d. "Dashboard-Old | Global Livestock Environmental Assessment Model (GLEAM) | Food and Agriculture Organization of the United

Nations." *Fao.org*. Retrieved October 29, 2022 (https://www.fao.org/gleam/dashboard-old/en/).

Fears, Darryl, and Emily Guskin. 2021. "The Strong Winds of Climate Change Have Failed to Move the Opinions of Many Americans." *Washington Post*. Retrieved May 11, 2022 (https://www.washingtonpost.com/climate-environment/2021/11/12/strong-winds-climate-change-have-failed-move-opinions-many-americans/).

Festinger, Leon. 1962. "Cognitive Dissonance." *Scientific American* 207(4):93–106. doi: 10.1038/scientificamerican1062-93.

Ficek, Rosa E. 2019. "Cattle, Capital, Colonization: Tracking Creatures of the Anthropocene in and out of Human Projects." *Current Anthropology* 60(S20):S260–71. doi: https://doi.org/10.1086/702788.

Finkelstein, Norman. 2023. *I'll Burn That Bridge When I Get to It!* Sublation Media.

Filazzola, Alessandro, Charlotte Brown, Margarete A. Dettlaff, Amgaa Batbaatar, Jessica Grenke, Tan Bao, Isaac Peetoom Heida, and James F. Cahill. 2020. "The Effects of Livestock Grazing on Biodiversity Are Multi-Trophic: A Meta-Analysis", edited by E. Seabloom. *Ecology Letters* 23(8):1298–1309. doi: 10.1111/ele.13527.

Fischer, Bob, and Andy Lamey. 2018. "Field Deaths in Plant Agriculture." *Journal of Agricultural and Environmental Ethics* 31(4):409–28. doi: 10.1007/s10806-018-9733-8.

Fishcount.co.uk. 2019. "Fish Count Estimates | Fishcount.org.uk." *Fishcount.org.uk*. Retrieved September 14, 2022 (http://fishcount.org.uk/fish-count-estimates-2).

Fisher, Linda. 2011. "Freeing Feathered Spirits." Pp. 110–16 in *Sister Species: Women, Animals and Social Justice*, edited by L. Kimmerer. Urbana, Chicago, And Springfield: University of Illinois Press.

Foley, Jonathan. 2014. "Feeding 9 Billion - National Geographic." *National Geographic Magazine*. Retrieved August 29, 2022 (https://www.nationalgeographic.com/foodfeatures/feeding-9-billion/).

Food Empowerment Project. 2013. "Child Labor and Slavery in the Chocolate Industry — Food Empowerment Project." *Foodispower.Org*. Retrieved September 3, 2021 (https://foodispower.org/human-labor-slavery/slavery-chocolate/).

Food Empowerment Project. 2022. "Produce Workers - Food Empowerment Project." *Foodispower.Org*. Retrieved July 8, 2022 (https://foodispower.org/human-labor-slavery/produce-workers/).

Forest, Dylan. 2020. "Decolonizing Veganism: An Interview with Dr. Margaret Robinson." *ANIMAL PEOPLE FORUM*. Retrieved December

1, 2022 (https://animalpeopleforum.org/2020/09/23/decolonizing-veganism-an-interview-with-dr-margaret-robinson/).

Francione, Gary L. 1996. *Rain without Thunder: The Ideology of the Animal Rights Movement*. Philadelphia, Pa.: Temple University Press.

Francione, Gary L. [2000] 2007. *Introduction to Animal Rights: Your Child or the Dog?* Philadelphia: Temple University Press.

Francione, Gary L. 2007a. "Francione: We're All Michael Vick." *Inquirer*. Retrieved November 25, 2022 (https://www.inquirer.com/philly/opinion/20070822_Were_all_Michael_Vick.html).

Francione, Gary L. 2007b. "Reflections on 'Animals, Property, and the Law' and 'Rain without Thunder.'" *Law and Contemporary Problems* 70(1):9–57.

Francione, Gary L. 2009. "'Happy Meat:' Making Humans Feel Better About Eating Animals – Animal Rights: The Abolitionist Approach." *Animal Rights: The Abolitionist Approach*. Retrieved November 2, 2022 (https://www.abolitionistapproach.com/happy-meat-making-humans-feel-better-about-eating-animals/).

Francione, Gary L. 2012a. "Sentience – Animal Rights the Abolitionist Approach." *Abolitionistapproach.com*. Retrieved September 15, 2022 (https://www.abolitionistapproach.com/sentience/).

Francione, Gary L. 2012b. "Animal Welfare, Happy Meat, and Veganism as the Moral Baseline." Pp. 169–89 in *The Philosophy of Food*. University of California Press.

Francione, Gary L. 2014. "On Capitalism and Animal Exploitation - Gary L. Francione: The Abolitionist Approach to Animal Rights." *Facebook.com*. Retrieved September 7, 2022 (https://web.archive.org/web/20220703093738/https://www.facebook.com/abolitionistapproach/posts/840379032648519).

Francione, Gary L. 2022. "Prof. Gary L. Francione on Instagram." *Instagram*. Retrieved September 8, 2022 (https://www.instagram.com/p/CYMfjmyr5bN/).

Fremstad, Shawn, Hye Jin Rho, and Hayley Brown. 2020. "Meatpacking Workers Are a Diverse Group Who Need Better Protections." *Center for Economic and Policy Research*. Retrieved January 14, 2023 (https://cepr.net/meatpacking-workers-are-a-diverse-group-who-need-better-protections/).

Funk, Cary, and Meg Hefferon. 2018. "Most Americans Accept Genetic Engineering of Animals That Benefits Human Health, but Many Oppose Other Uses." *Pew Research Center Science & Society*. Retrieved December 7, 2022 (https://www.pewresearch.org/science/2018/08/16/most-americans-accept-genetic-engineering-of-animals-that-benefits-human-health-but-many-oppose-other-uses/).

Fürst, M. A., D. P. McMahon, J. L. Osborne, R. J. Paxton, and M. J. F. Brown. 2014. "Disease Associations between Honeybees and Bumblebees as a Threat to Wild Pollinators." *Nature* 506(7488):364–66. doi: 10.1038/nature12977.

FWD.us. 2021. "Immigrant Farmworkers and America's Food Production - 5 Things to Know." *FWD.us*. Retrieved July 8, 2022 (https://www.fwd.us/news/immigrant-farmworkers-and-americas-food-production-5-things-to-know/).

Fremstad, Shawn, Hye Jin Rho, and Hayley Brown. 2020. "Meatpacking Workers Are a Diverse Group Who Need Better Protections - Center for Economic and Policy Research." *Center for Economic and Policy Research*. Retrieved July 9, 2022 (https://cepr.net/meatpacking-workers-are-a-diverse-group-who-need-better-protections/).

Funke, Franziska, Linus Mattauch, Inge van den Bijgaart, H. Charles J. Godfray, Cameron Hepburn, David Klenert, Marco Springmann, and Nicolas Treich. 2022. "Toward Optimal Meat Pricing: Is It Time to Tax Meat Consumption?" *Review of Environmental Economics and Policy* 16(2):219–40. doi: 10.1086/721078.

Gamboa, Cindybell, Carlos Ricardo Bojacá, Eddie Schrevens, and Miet Maertens. 2020. "Sustainability of Smallholder Quinoa Production in the Peruvian Andes." *Journal of Cleaner Production* 264:121657. doi: 10.1016/j.jclepro.2020.121657.

Garibaldi, L. A., I. Steffan-Dewenter, R. Winfree, M. A. Aizen, R. Bommarco, S. A. Cunningham, C. Kremen, L. G. Carvalheiro, L. D. Harder, O. Afik, I. Bartomeus, F. Benjamin, V. Boreux, D. Cariveau, N. P. Chacoff, J. H. Dudenhoffer, B. M. Freitas, J. Ghazoul, S. Greenleaf, and J. Hipolito. 2013. "Wild Pollinators Enhance Fruit Set of Crops regardless of Honey Bee Abundance." *Science* 339(6127):1608–11. doi: 10.1126/science.1230200.

Garnett, T., Godde, C., Muller, A., Röös, E., Smith, P., de Boer, I.J.M., zu Ermgassen, E., Herrero, M., van Middelaar, C., Schader, C. and van Zanten, H. 2017. *Grazed and Confused? Ruminating on cattle, grazing systems, methane, nitrous oxide, the soil carbon sequestration question – and what it all means for greenhouse gas emissions.* Food Climate Research Network, FCRN. University of Oxford.

Gecewicz, Claire. 2018. "'New Age' Beliefs Common among Both Religious and Nonreligious Americans." Pew Research Center. Retrieved May 11, 2022 (https://www.pewresearch.org/fact-tank/2018/10/01/new-age-beliefs-common-among-both-religious-and-nonreligious-americans/).

Geldmann, Jonas, and Juan P. González-Varo. 2018. "Conserving Honey Bees Does Not Help Wildlife." *Science* 359(6374):392–93. doi: 10.1126/science.aar2269.

Gerber, Pierre J., Anne Mottet, Carolyn I. Opio, Alessandra Falcucci, and Félix Teillard. 2015. "Environmental Impacts of Beef Production: Review of Challenges and Perspectives for Durability." *Meat Science* 109:2–12. doi: 10.1016/j.meatsci.2015.05.013.

Gerber, P.J., Steinfeld, H., Henderson, B., Mottet, A., Opio, C., Dijkman, J., Falcucci, A. & Tempio, G. 2013. *Tackling climate change through livestock – A global assessment of emissions and mitigation opportunities*. Food and Agriculture Organization of the United Nations (FAO). Rome.

Gibbons, Matilda, Andrew Crump, Meghan Barrett, Sajedeh Sarlak, Jonathan Birch, and Lars Chittka. 2022a. "Can Insects Feel Pain? A Review of the Neural and Behavioural Evidence." *Advances in Insect Physiology*. doi: 10.1016/bs.aiip.2022.10.001.

Gibbons, Matilda, Elisabetta Versace, Andrew Crump, Bartosz Baran, and Lars Chittka. 2022b. "Motivational Trade-Offs and Modulation of Nociception in Bumblebees." *Proceedings of the National Academy of Sciences* 119(31). doi: 10.1073/pnas.2205821119.

Gibbs, Beverley J. 2017. "Structuration Theory | Sociology." *Encyclopædia Britannica*.

Giddens, Anthony. 1984. *The Constitution of Society: Outline of the Theory of Structuration*. Cambridge: Polity Press.

Gillard, Thomas L., and Benjamin P. Oldroyd. 2020. "Controlled Reproduction in the Honey Bee (Apis Mellifera) via Artificial Insemination." *Advances in Insect Physiology* 1–42. doi: 10.1016/bs.aiip.2020.08.001.

Giller, Ken E., Renske Hijbeek, Jens A. Andersson, and James Sumberg. 2021. "Regenerative Agriculture: An Agronomic Perspective." *Outlook on Agriculture* 50(1):13–25. doi: 10.1177/0030727021998063.

Gillespie, Kathryn. 2011. "How Happy Is Your Meat? Confronting (Dis)Connectedness in the 'Alternative' Meat Industry." *The Brock Review* 12(1):100–128. doi: 10.26522/br.v12i1.326.

Gilliland, Gene. 1997. *Evaluation of Procedures to Reduce Delayed Mortality of Black Bass Following Summer Tournaments - Final Report*. OK: Oklahoma Department of Wildlife Conservation. Retrieved November 1, 2022 (https://web.archive.org/web/20200727083341/http://www.nes-portsman.com/articles/catch_release_studies/oklahoma_large-mouth.html).

Ginsburg, S., and E. Jablonka. 2021. "Sentience in Plants: A Green Red Herring?: Ingenta Connect." *Ingentaconnect.com*. Retrieved June 3, 2022 (https://www.ingentaconnect.com/content/imp/jcs/2021/00000028/f0020001/art00002).

Glick-Bauer, Marian, and Ming-Chin Yeh. 2014. "The Health Advantage of a Vegan Diet: Exploring the Gut Microbiota Connection." *Nutrients* 6(11):4822–38. doi: 10.3390/nu6114822.

Godfray, H. Charles J., Paul Aveyard, Tara Garnett, Jim W. Hall, Timothy J. Key, Jamie Lorimer, Ray T. Pierrehumbert, Peter Scarborough, Marco Springmann, and Susan A. Jebb. 2018. "Meat Consumption, Health, and the Environment." *Science* 361(6399). doi: 10.1126/science.aam5324.

Gold, Mark. 1995. *Animal Rights: Extending the Circle of Compassion*. Oxford England: Jon Carpenter.

González-Montaña, Jose-Ramiro, Francisco Escalera-Valente, Angel J. Alonso, Juan M. Lomillos, Roberto Robles, and Marta E. Alonso. 2020. "Relationship between Vitamin B12 and Cobalt Metabolism in Domestic Ruminant: An Update." *Animals* 10(10):1855. doi: 10.3390/ani10101855.

González-Montemayor, Ángela-Mariela, Adriana C. Flores-Gallegos, Lilia E. Serrato-Villegas, Xóchitl Ruelas-Chacón, Mercedes G. López, and Raúl Rodríguez-Herrera. 2020. "Processing Temperature Effect on the Chemical Content of Concentrated Aguamiel Syrups Obtained from Two Different Agave Species." *Journal of Food Measurement and Characterization* 14(3):1733–43. doi: 10.1007/s11694-020-00421-4.

Gopaldas, Ahir. 2013. "Intersectionality 101." *Journal of Public Policy & Marketing* 32(1_suppl):90–94. doi: 10.1509/jppm.12.044.

Graça, João, Maria Manuela Calheiros, Abílio Oliveira, and Taciano L. Milfont. 2018. "Why Are Women Less Likely to Support Animal Exploitation than Men? The Mediating Roles of Social Dominance Orientation and Empathy." *Personality and Individual Differences* 129:66–69. doi: 10.1016/j.paid.2018.03.007.

Graeber, David. 2010. *Direct Action: An Ethnography*. Edinburgh: AK Press.

Graeber, David, and David Wengrow. 2021. *The Dawn of Everything: A New History of Humanity*. New York Farrar, Straus and Giroux.

Grande, Sandy Marie Anglás. 1999. "Beyond the Ecologically Noble Savage: Deconstructing the White Man's Indian." *Environmental Ethics* 21(3):307–20. doi: 10.5840/enviroethics199921320.

Grand View Research. 2021. "Leather Goods Market Size, Share & Growth Report, 2030." *Grand View Research*. Retrieved November 3, 2022 (https://www.grandviewresearch.com/industry-analysis/leather-goods-market).

Gray, Joe. 2022. "Sentience in invertebrates: A report on a two-part webinar." *The Ecological Citizen* 5(2): 201–9.

Greenebaum, Jessica, and Brandon Dexter. 2018. "Vegan Men and Hybrid Masculinity." *Journal of Gender Studies* 27(6):637–48. doi: 10/ghnf6x.

Grenfell, Michael James, ed. 2012. *Pierre Bourdieu: Key Concepts*. 2nd ed. Durham, England: Acumen Publishing.

Grizzle, Gary. 2017. "Anarchist Sociology and the Legacy of Peter Kropotkin." *Theory in Action* 10(1):65–87. doi: 10.3798/tia.1937-0237.1704.

Gross, Aeyal. 2013. "Vegans for (and Against) the Occupation - Opinion." *Haaretz.com*. Retrieved August 30, 2022 (https://www.haaretz.com/opinion/2013-11-14/ty-article/.premium/vegan-while-occupying/0000017f-dbc2-df62-a9ff-dfd7db420000).

Gruen, Lori, and Robert C. Jones. 2015. "Veganism as an Aspiration." Pp. 153–71 in *The Moral Complexities of Eating Meat*, edited by B. Bramble and B. Fischer. Oxford University Press.

Guérin, Daniel. 2005. *No Gods, No Masters: Complete Unabridged*. AK Press.

Halteman, Matthew C. 2011. "Varieties of Harm to Animals in Industrial Farming." *Journal of Animal Ethics* 1(2):122–31. doi: 10.5406/janimalethics.1.2.0122.

Hamilton, Carrie. 2016. "Sex, Work, Meat: The Feminist Politics of Veganism." *Feminist Review* 114(1):112–29. doi: 10/f93qjg.

Hamilton, Lawrence. 2022. "Conspiracy vs. Science: A Survey of U.S. Public Beliefs." *Carsey School of Public Policy | UNH*. Retrieved (https://carsey.unh.edu/publication/conspiracy-vs-science-a-survey-of-us-public-beliefs).

Hanras, Eva, Sasha Mathieu, Basilie Chevrier, Emilie Boujut, and Géraldine Dorard. 2022. "Vegans, Strict Vegetarians, Partial Vegetarians, Omnivores: Do They Differ in Food Choice Motives, Coping, and Quality of Life?" *La Presse Médicale Open* 3:100033. doi: 10.1016/j.lpmope.2022.100033.

Hansen, Éverton, Patrice Monteiro de Aquim, and Mariliz Gutterres. 2021. "Environmental Assessment of Water, Chemicals and Effluents in Leather Post-Tanning Process: A Review." *Environmental Impact Assessment Review* 89:106597. doi: 10.1016/j.eiar.2021.106597.

Harper, A. Breeze. 2010. *Sistah Vegan: Black Female Vegans Speak on Food, Identity, Health, and Society*. New York: Lantern Books.

Harper, A. Breeze. 2011b. "Connections: Speciesism, Racism, and Whiteness as the Norm." Pp. 72–78 in *Sister Species: Women, Animals and Social Justice*, edited by L. Kemmerer. Urbana, Chicago, And Springfield: University of Illinois Press.

Hartmann, Christina, Patricia Furtwaengler, and Michael Siegrist. 2022. "Consumers' Evaluation of the Environmental Friendliness, Healthiness and Naturalness of Meat, Meat Substitutes, and Other Protein-Rich Foods." *Food Quality and Preference* 97:104486. doi: 10.1016/j.foodqual.2021.104486.

Haslam, Nick, Louis Rothschild, and Donald Ernst. 2000. "Essentialist Beliefs about Social Categories." *British Journal of Social Psychology* 39(1):113–27. doi: 10.1348/014466600164363.

Haslam, Michael, Tiago Falótico, and Lydia Luncz. 2018. "Recognizing Culture in Wild Primate Tool Use." *Evolution of Primate Social Cognition* 199–209. doi: 10.1007/978-3-319-93776-2_13.

Hayek, Matthew N., and Rachael D. Garrett. 2018. "Nationwide Shift to Grass-Fed Beef Requires Larger Cattle Population." *Environmental Research Letters* 13(8):084005. doi: 10.1088/1748-9326/aad401.

Hayek, Matthew N., Helen Harwatt, William J. Ripple, and Nathaniel D. Mueller. 2020. "The Carbon Opportunity Cost of Animal-Sourced Food Production on Land." *Nature Sustainability* 4(1):21–24. doi: 10.1038/s41893-020-00603-4.

Hecht, Susanna B. 2011. "From Eco-Catastrophe to Zero Deforestation? Interdisciplinarities, Politics, Environmentalisms and Reduced Clearing in Amazonia." Environmental Conservation 39(1):4–19. doi: 10.1017/s0376892911000452.

Herbst, Diane. 2022. "Fact Check: Was Dr. Oz Responsible for Cruelly Experimenting on Dogs?" *PEOPLE*, October 4.

Heiss, Sydney, Jaime A. Coffino, and Julia M. Hormes. 2017. "Eating and Health Behaviors in Vegans Compared to Omnivores: Dispelling Common Myths." *Appetite* 118:129–35. doi: 10.1016/j.appet.2017.08.001.

Herpich, Catrin, Ursula Müller-Werdan, and Kristina Norman. 2022. "Role of Plant-Based Diets in Promoting Health and Longevity." *Maturitas* 165:47–51. doi: 10/gqkjbj.

Tabios Hillebrecht, Anna Leah. 2017. "Disrobing Rights: The Privilege of Being Human in the Rights of Nature Discourse." Pp. 15-20 in *Can Nature Have Rights? Legal and Political Insights* (6), edited by Anna Leah Tabios Hillebrecht and María Valeria Berros, *RCC Perspectives: Transformations in Environment and Society*. doi: 10.5282/rcc/8210.

Hinrichs, Kim, John Hoeks, Lúcia Campos, David Guedes, Cristina Godinho, Marta Matos, and João Graça. 2022. "Why so Defensive? Negative Affect and Gender Differences in Defensiveness toward Plant-Based Diets." *Food Quality and Preference* 102:104662. doi: 10/gqkjcz.

Hodson, Gordon, and Megan Earle. 2018. "Conservatism Predicts Lapses from Vegetarian/Vegan Diets to Meat Consumption (through Lower

Social Justice Concerns and Social Support)." *Appetite* 120:75–81. doi: 10.1016/j.appet.2017.08.027.

Hoffman, Sarah R., Sarah F. Stallings, Raymond C. Bessinger, and Gary T. Brooks. 2013. "Differences between Health and Ethical Vegetarians. Strength of Conviction, Nutrition Knowledge, Dietary Restriction, and Duration of Adherence." *Appetite* 65:139–44. doi: 10.1016/j.appet.2013.02.009.

Holmberg, Mollie. 2021. "Constructing Captive Ecology at the Aquarium: Hierarchy, Care, Violence, and the Limits of Control." *Environment and Planning E: Nature and Space* 5(2):861–80. doi: 10.1177/25148486211014508.

Holmes, Seth M. 2013. *Fresh Fruit, Broken Bodies Migrant Farmworkers in the United States*. Berkeley, CA, USA: University of California Press.

Hooper, Beki, Delphine De Moor, and Erin Siracusa. 2022. "Animal Friendships Are Surprisingly like Our Own." *The Conversation*. Retrieved October 30, 2022 (https://theconversation.com/animal-friendships-are-surprisingly-like-our-own-188120).

Horsthemke, Kai. 2018. "Critical Animal Studies and Animal Standpoint Theory." Pp. 197–216 in *Animal Rights Education*. Cham, Switzerland: Palgrave Macmillan.

Huang, Jiaqi, Linda M. Liao, Stephanie J. Weinstein, Rashmi Sinha, Barry I. Graubard, and Demetrius Albanes. 2020. "Association between Plant and Animal Protein Intake and Overall and Cause-Specific Mortality." *JAMA Internal Medicine* 180(9):1173. doi: 10.1001/jamainternmed.2020.2790.

Hughes, Sara Salazar, Stepha Velednitsky, and Amelia Arden Green. 2022. "Greenwashing in Palestine/Israel: Settler Colonialism and Environmental Injustice in the Age of Climate Catastrophe." *Environment and Planning E: Nature and Space* 25148486211069896. doi: 10/gqdt3b.

Humane Society International. 2019. "The Fur Trade - Humane Society International." *Humane Society International*. Retrieved September 14, 2022 (https://www.hsi.org/news-media/fur-trade/).

Hussain, Grace. 2022. "What Are the Environmental Impacts of Dairy Farming?" *Sentient Media*. Retrieved July 27, 2023 (https://sentientmedia.org/the-dairy-industry-environment/).

Hutchinson, Isobel, Carla Owen, and Jarrod Bailey. 2022. "Modernizing Medical Research to Benefit People and Animals." *Animals* 12(9):1173. doi: 10.3390/ani12091173.

IPCC. 2023. "AR6 Synthesis Report: Climate Change 2023." *Ipcc.ch*. Retrieved May 11, 2022 (https://www.ipcc.ch/report/ar6/sry/).

Jablonka, Eva, and Simona Ginsburg. 2022. "Learning and the Evolution of Conscious Agents." *Biosemiotics* 15(3):401–37. doi: 10.1007/s12304-022-09501-y.

Jaeggi, Rahel. 2016. "What (If Anything) Is Wrong with Capitalism? Dysfunctionality, Exploitation and Alienation: Three Approaches to the Critique of Capitalism." *The Southern Journal of Philosophy* 54:44–65. doi: 10.1111/sjp.12188.

Jarmakowski-Kostrzanowski, Tomasz, and Piotr Radkiewicz. 2021. "Social Dominance Orientation Predicts Lower Moral Condemnation of Causing Harm to Animals." *Current Issues in Personality Psychology* 9(3):229–36. doi: 10.5114/cipp.2021.105732.

Jarmul, Stephanie, Alan D. Dangour, Rosemary Green, Zara Liew, Andy Haines, and Pauline FD Scheelbeek. 2020. "Climate Change Mitigation through Dietary Change: A Systematic Review of Empirical and Modelling Studies on the Environmental Footprints and Health Effects of 'Sustainable Diets.'" *Environmental Research Letters* 15(12):123014. doi: 10.1088/1748-9326/abc2f7.

Iwasaki, Jay M., and Katja Hogendoorn. 2021. "How Protection of Honey Bees Can Help and Hinder Bee Conservation." *Current Opinion in Insect Science* 46:112–18. doi: 10.1016/j.cois.2021.05.005.

Iwasaki, Jay M., and Katja Hogendoorn. 2022. "Mounting Evidence That Managed and Introduced Bees Have Negative Impacts on Wild Bees: An Updated Review." *Current Research in Insect Science* 2:100043. doi: 10.1016/j.cris.2022.100043.

Jackson, Jon. 2021. "Old PETA Campaign Claiming Links between Milk and Autism Resurfaces on Twitter." *Newsweek*. Retrieved January 29, 2023 (https://www.newsweek.com/peta-autism-twitter-ad-1559104).

Jaquet, François. 2021. "Speciesism and Tribalism: Embarrassing Origins." *Philosophical Studies*. doi: 10/gk9j5c.

Jenkins, Becky. 2018. "Who Pays for Our Cheap Meat? The Impact of Modern Meat Production on Slaughterhouse Workers: Considerations for Tourists." Pp. 42–57 in *Tourism Experiences and Animal Consumption: Contested Values, Morality, and Ethics*, edited by C. Kline. New York, NY: Routledge.

Jenkins, David J. A., Sonia Blanco Mejia, Laura Chiavaroli, Effie Viguiliouk, Siying S. Li, Cyril W. C. Kendall, Vladmir Vuksan, and John L. Sievenpiper. 2019. "Cumulative Meta-Analysis of the Soy Effect over Time." *Journal of the American Heart Association* 8(13). doi: 10.1161/jaha.119.012458.

Johnston, Genevieve, and Matthew S. Johnston. 2017. "'We Fight for All Living Things': Countering Misconceptions about the Radical Animal

Liberation Movement." *Social Movement Studies* 16(6):735–51. doi: 10.1080/14742837.2017.1319268.

Jones, Robert C. 2016. "Veganisms." Pp. 15–39 in *Critical Perspectives on Veganism*, edited by J. Castricano and R. R. Simonsen. Palgrave Macmillan Cham.

Joy, Melanie. 2011. Why We Love Dogs, Eat Pigs and Wear Cows: An Introduction to Carnism - the Belief System That Enables Us to Eat Some Animals and Not Others. San Francisco: Canari Press.

Kaldewaij, Frederike. 2006. "Animals and the Harm of Death." Pp. 528–32 in *Ethics and the Politics of Food*, edited by M. Kaiser and M. E. Lien. The Netherlands: Wageningen Academic Publishers.

Karcz, Karolina, and Barbara Królak-Olejnik. 2020. "Vegan or Vegetarian Diet and Breast Milk Composition – a Systematic Review." *Critical Reviews in Food Science and Nutrition* 61(7):1081–98. doi: 10.1080/10408398.2020.1753650.

Katy. 2019. "Queen Bees and Clipped Wings." *Bee Mission*. Retrieved September 15, 2022 (https://beemission.com/blogs/news/queen-bees-and-clipped-wings).

Kauffman, J. Boone, Robert L. Beschta, Peter M. Lacy, and Marc Liverman. 2022. "Livestock Use on Public Lands in the Western USA Exacerbates Climate Change: Implications for Climate Change Mitigation and Adaptation." *Environmental Management* 69(6):1137–52. doi: 10.1007/s00267-022-01633-8.

Kendrick, Heather M. N. 2018. "Autonomy, Slavery, and Companion Animals," *Between the Species* 22(1):236-59.

Kessler, Dana. 2012. "Israel Goes Vegan." *Tablet Magazine*. Retrieved August 30, 2022 (https://www.tabletmag.com/sections/food/articles/israel-goes-vegan).

Kim, Claire Jean. 2007. "MULTICULTURALISM GOES IMPERIAL: Immigrants, Animals, and the Suppression of Moral Dialogue." *Du Bois Review: Social Science Research on Race* 4(1):233–49. doi: 10/fhw6xh.

Kim, Claire Jean. 2011. "Moral Extensionism or Racist Exploitation? The Use of Holocaust and Slavery Analogies in the Animal Liberation Movement." *New Political Science* 33(3):311–33. doi: 10/fjdfgf.

Kim, Claire Jean. 2017. "Murder and Mattering in Harambe's House." *Politics and Animals* 3:1–15.

Kim, Claire Jean. 2020. "Makah Whaling and the (Non)Ecological Indian." Pp. 50–103 in *Colonialism and Animality: Anti- Colonial Perspectives in Critical Animal Studies*, edited by K. S. Montford and C. Taylor. London: Routledge.

Kim, Claire Jean. 2022. "Michael Vick, Race, and Animality." Pp. 197–212 in *Ecofeminism: Feminist Intersections with Other Animals and the Earth*, edited by C. J. Adams and L. Gruen. New York, NY: Bloomsbury Academic.

Kim, Hyunju, Laura E. Caulfield, and Casey M. Rebholz. 2018. "Healthy Plant-Based Diets Are Associated with Lower Risk of All-Cause Mortality in US Adults." *The Journal of Nutrition* 148(4):624–31. doi: 10.1093/jn/nxy019.

Kim, Jihye, Carol J. Boushey, Lynne R. Wilkens, Christopher A. Haiman, Loïc Le Marchand, and Song-Yi Park. 2022. "Plant-Based Dietary Patterns Defined by a Priori Indices and Colorectal Cancer Risk by Sex and Race/Ethnicity: The Multiethnic Cohort Study." *BMC Medicine* 20(1). doi: 10.1186/s12916-022-02623-7.

Kimmerer, Lisa. 2004a. "Hunting Tradition: Treaties, Law, and Subsistence Killing." *Animal Liberation Philosophy and Policy Journal* 2(2):26–44.

Kemmerer, Lisa. 2004b. "Killing Traditions: Consistency in Applied Moral Philosophy." *Ethics, Place & Environment* 7(3):151–71. doi: 10.1080/1366879042000332952.

Kirby, Steve. 2003. "Telling Lies? An Exploration of Self-Deception and Bad Faith." *European Journal of Psychotherapy & Counselling* 6(2):99–110. doi: 10.1081/13642530410001724179.

Klein, JoAnna. 2018. "Sedate a Plant, and It Seems to Lose Consciousness. Is It Conscious?" *The New York Times*, February 2.

Klopatek, Sarah C., Elias Marvinney, Toni Duarte, Alissa Kendall, Xiang (Crystal) Yang, and James W. Oltjen. 2021. "Grass-Fed vs. Grain-Fed Beef Systems: Performance, Economic, and Environmental Trade-Offs." *Journal of Animal Science* 100(2). doi: 10.1093/jas/skab374.

Knight, Andrew. 2008. "Systematic Reviews of Animal Experiments Demonstrate Poor Contributions toward Human Healthcare." *Reviews on Recent Clinical Trials* 3(2):89–96. doi: 10.2174/157488708784223844.

Knight, Andrew, and Madelaine Leitsberger. 2016. "Vegetarian versus Meat-Based Diets for Companion Animals." *Animals* 6(9):57. doi: 10.3390/ani6090057.

Knight, Sarah, Aldert Vrij, Julie Cherryman, and Karl Nunkoosing. 2004. "Attitudes towards Animal Use and Belief in Animal Mind." *Anthrozoös* 17(1):43–62. doi: 10.2752/089279304786991945.

Ko, Syl. 2013. "A Commentary on Non-Humans First - Vegan Feminist Network." *Vegan Feminist Network*. Retrieved May 31, 2022 (https://veganfeministnetwork.com/acommentaryonnon-humansfirst/).

Ko, Aph, and Syl Ko. 2018. *Aphro-Ism: Essays on Pop Culture, Feminism, and Black Veganism from Two Sisters*. New York: Lantern Books.

Ko, Aph. 2019. *Racism as Zoological Witchcraft: A Guide for Getting Out*. Brooklyn, Ny: Lantern Books.

Ko, Syl. 2017. "Addressing Racism Requires Addressing the Situation of Animals." Pp. 44–49 in *Aphro-ism: Essays on Pop Culture, Feminism, and Black Veganism from Two Sisters*. New York: Lantern Books.

Koch, Alexander, Chris Brierley, Mark M. Maslin, and Simon L. Lewis. 2019. "Earth System Impacts of the European Arrival and Great Dying in the Americas after 1492." *Quaternary Science Reviews* 207:13–36. doi: 10.1016/j.quascirev.2018.12.004.

Koeder, Christian, and Federico J. A. Perez-Cueto. 2022. "Vegan Nutrition: A Preliminary Guide for Health Professionals." *Critical Reviews in Food Science and Nutrition* 1–38. doi: 10.1080/10408398.2022.2107997.

Komarek, Adam M., Shahnila Dunston, Dolapo Enahoro, H. Charles J. Godfray, Mario Herrero, Daniel Mason-D'Croz, Karl M. Rich, Peter Scarborough, Marco Springmann, Timothy B. Sulser, Keith Wiebe, and Dirk Willenbockel. 2021. "Income, Consumer Preferences, and the Future of Livestock-Derived Food Demand." *Global Environmental Change* 70:102343. doi: 10.1016/j.gloenvcha.2021.102343.

Konar, Megan, and Landon Marston. 2020. "The Water Footprint of the United States." *Water* 12(11):3286. doi: 10/gqkjc8.

Krásná, Denisa. 2022a. "Animal Colonialism in North America: Milk Colonialism, Environmental Racism, and Indigenous Veganism." *Acta Universitatis Carolinae – Studia Territorialia* 22(1):61–90. doi: https://doi.org/10.14712/23363231.2022.9.

Kret, Mariska E., Jorg J. M. Massen, and Frans B. M. de Waal. 2022. "My Fear Is Not, and Never Will Be, Your Fear: On Emotions and Feelings in Animals." *Affective Science* 3(1):182–89. doi: 10/gqkjfq.

Lambert, Helen, Amelia Cornish, Angie Elwin, and Neil D'Cruze. 2022. "A Kettle of Fish: A Review of the Scientific Literature for Evidence of Fish Sentience." *Animals* 12(9):1182. doi: 10.3390/ani12091182.

Lambert, Helen, Angie Elwin, and Neil D'Cruze. 2021. "Wouldn't Hurt a Fly? A Review of Insect Cognition and Sentience in Relation to Their Use as Food and Feed." *Applied Animal Behaviour Science* 243:105432. doi: 10.1016/j.applanim.2021.105432.

Lambert, Helen, Angie Elwin, and Neil D'Cruze. 2022. "Frog in the Well: A Review of the Scientific Literature for Evidence of Amphibian Sentience." *Applied Animal Behaviour Science* 247:105559. doi: 10.1016/j.applanim.2022.105559.

Lambert, Helen, Gemma Carder, and Neil D'Cruze. 2019. "Given the Cold Shoulder: A Review of the Scientific Literature for Evidence of Reptile Sentience." *Animals* 9(10):821. doi: 10/ghvbm6.

Lanese, Nicoletta. 2019. "Plants 'Scream' in the Face of Stress." *Livescience.com*. Retrieved June 2, 2022 (https://www.livescience.com/plants-squeal-when-stressed.html).

Langyan, Sapna, Pranjal Yadava, Fatima Nazish Khan, Zahoor A. Dar, Renu Singh, and Ashok Kumar. 2022. "Sustaining Protein Nutrition through Plant-Based Foods." *Frontiers in Nutrition* 8. doi: 10.3389/fnut.2021.772573.

Latombe, Guillaume, Bernd Lenzner, Anna Schertler, Stefan Dullinger, Michael Glaser, Ivan Jarić, Aníbal Pauchard, John R. U. Wilson, and Franz Essl. 2022. "What Is Valued in Conservation? A Framework to Compare Ethical Perspectives." *NeoBiota* 72:45–80. doi: 10/gqk4jn.

Layne, Jodie. 2015. "Fat Positive Vegans Take to Twitter to Remind PETA That Vegans Come in All Sizes (so Stop the Fat Shaming)." *Bustle*. Retrieved January 29, 2023 (https://www.bustle.com/articles/90666-fat-positive-vegans-take-to-twitter-to-remind-peta-that-vegans-come-in-all-sizes-so).

Lazarus, Oliver, Sonali McDermid, and Jennifer Jacquet. 2021. "The Climate Responsibilities of Industrial Meat and Dairy Producers." *Climatic Change* 165(1–2). doi: 10.1007/s10584-021-03047-7.

Leach, Stefan, Robbie M. Sutton, Kristof Dhont, Karen M. Douglas, and Zara M. Bergström. 2023. "Changing Minds about Minds: Evidence That People Are Too Sceptical about Animal Sentience." *Cognition* 230:105263. doi: https://doi.org/10.1016/j.cognition.2022.105263.

Lederer, Ann-Kathrin, and Roman Huber. 2022. "The Relation of Diet and Health: You Are What You Eat." *International Journal of Environmental Research and Public Health* 19(13):7774. doi: 10/gqkx7c.

Lee, Courtney G. 2022. "Racist Animal Agriculture." *CUNY Academic Works*. Retrieved January 15, 2023 (https://academicworks.cuny.edu/clr/vol25/iss2/2/).

Legge, Melissa Marie, and Rasha Taha. 2017. "'Fake Vegans': Indigenous Solidarity and Animal Liberation Activism." *Journal of Indigenous Social Development* 6(1):63–81.

Levy, Aharon, and Yossi Maaravi. 2017. "The Boomerang Effect of Psychological Interventions." *Social Influence* 13(1):39–51. doi: 10.1080/15534510.2017.1421571.

Lewis, Edward. 2022. "New Left Project | Ethics and the Left." *New Left Project*. Retrieved September 7, 2022 (https://web.archive.org/web/20181028225703/http://www.newleftproject.org/index.php/site/article_comments/ethics_and_the_left/).

Leyens, Jacques-Philippe, Armando Rodriguez-Perez, Ramon Rodriguez-Torres, Ruth Gaunt, Maria-Paola Paladino, Jeroen Vaes, and Stéphanie

Demoulin. 2001. "Psychological Essentialism and the Differential Attribution of Uniquely Human Emotions to Ingroups and Outgroups." *European Journal of Social Psychology* 31(4):395–411. doi: 10.1002/ejsp.50.

Lindroth, Marjo, and Heidi Sinevaara-Niskanen. 2013. "At the Crossroads of Autonomy and Essentialism: Indigenous Peoples in International Environmental Politics." *International Political Sociology* 7(3):275–93. doi: 10.1111/ips.12023.

Li, Ni, Xiaoting Wu, Wen Zhuang, Lin Xia, Yi Chen, Rui Zhao, Mengshi Yi, Qianyi Wan, Liang Du, and Yong Zhou. 2019. "Soy and Isoflavone Consumption and Multiple Health Outcomes: Umbrella Review of Systematic Reviews and Meta-Analyses of Observational Studies and Randomized Trials in Humans." *Molecular Nutrition & Food Research* 64(4):1900751. doi: 10.1002/mnfr.201900751.

Lifton, Robert Jay. 2014. *Thought Reform and the Psychology of Totalism: A Study of "Brainwashing" in China*. Mansfield Centre, Ct: Martino Publishing.

Lindsay, Sarah May. 2022. "The 'Problem' of Multispecies Families: Speciesism in Emergency Intimate Partner Violence (IPV) Shelters." *Social Sciences* 11(6):242. doi: 10/gqkx7d.

LIVEKINDLY. 2018. "The Number of Vegans in the Israeli Army Has Grown 1900% in 3 Years." *LIVEKINDLY*. Retrieved August 30, 2022 (https://www.livekindly.com/vegans-israeli-army/).

Livingstone, Grace. 2018. "How Quinoa Is Changing Farmers' Lives in Peru." *BBC*, August 18.

Livingstone, Margaret S. 2022. "Triggers for Mother Love." *Proceedings of the National Academy of Sciences* 119(39). doi: 10.1073/pnas.2212224119.

Loeb, Josh. 2020. "The Trouble with Vegan Cats and Dogs." *Veterinary Record* 186(7):197–97. doi: 10.1136/vr.m663.

Logical Fallacies. 2022. "Logical Fallacies - List of Logical Fallacies with Examples." *Logicalfallacies.org*. Retrieved September 9, 2022 (https://www.logicalfallacies.org/).

Lombrozo, Tania. 2016. "Humans Are Animals, Too." *NPR.org*. Retrieved June 16, 2022 (https://www.npr.org/sections/13.7/2016/05/16/478189744/humans-are-animals-too).

Loughnan, Steve, Nick Haslam, and Brock Bastian. 2010. "The Role of Meat Consumption in the Denial of Moral Status and Mind to Meat Animals." *Appetite* 55(1):156–59. doi: 10/fp3qgs.

Low, Philip. 2012. "The Cambridge Declaration on Consciousness." in *Francis Crick Memorial Conference on Consciousness in Human and Non-Human Animals*, edited by J. Panksepp, D. Reiss, D. Edelman, B. Van Swinderen, P. Low, and C. Koch.

Luke, Brian. 1997. "A Critical Analysis of Hunters' Ethics." *Environmental Ethics* 19(1):25–44. doi: 10/f2cgq8.

Lusk, Jayson L., and F. Bailey Norwood. 2016. "Some Vegetarians Spend Less Money on Food, Others Don't." *Ecological Economics* 130:232–42. doi: 10.1016/j.ecolecon.2016.07.005.

Machovina, Brian, Kenneth J. Feeley, and William J. Ripple. 2015. "Biodiversity Conservation: The Key Is Reducing Meat Consumption." *Science of the Total Environment* 536:419–31. doi: 10/gf6376.

MacInnis, Cara C., and Gordon Hodson. 2015. "It Ain't Easy Eating Greens: Evidence of Bias toward Vegetarians and Vegans from Both Source and Target." *Group Processes & Intergroup Relations* 20(6):721–44. doi: 10.1177/1368430215618253.

Maggio, Rodolfo. 2018. *Pierre Bourdieu's Outline of a Theory of Practice*. CRC Press.

Malamud, Randy, Ron Broglio, Lori Marino, Scott O. Lilienfeld, and Nathan Nobis. 2010. "Do Zoos and Aquariums Promote Attitude Change in Visitors? A Critical Evaluation of the American Zoo and Aquarium Study." *Society & Animals* 18(2):126–38. doi: 10.1163/156853010x491980.

Mallatt, Jon, Michael R. Blatt, Andreas Draguhn, David G. Robinson, and Lincoln Taiz. 2021a. "Debunking a Myth: Plant Consciousness." *Protoplasma* 258(3):459–76. doi: 10/ghsrcj.

Mallatt, Jon, Lincoln Taiz, Andreas Draguhn, Michael R. Blatt, and David G. Robinson. 2021b. "Integrated Information Theory Does Not Make Plant Consciousness More Convincing." *Biochemical and Biophysical Research Communications* 564:166–69. doi: 10/gpkvc7.

Mallinger, Rachel E., Hannah R. Gaines-Day, and Claudio Gratton. 2017. "Do Managed Bees Have Negative Effects on Wild Bees?: A Systematic Review of the Literature" edited by N. E. Raine. *PLOS ONE* 12(12):e0189268. doi: 10.1371/journal.pone.0189268.

Malone, Benny. 2021. *How to Argue with Vegans: an Analysis of Anti-Vegan Arguments*. Benny Malone.

Malone, Benny. 2022a. "Defining Veganism." *Força Vegan Magazine*, February 22, 20–31.

Malone, Benny. 2022b. "There's No Ethical Consumption under Capitalism." *Força Vegan Magazine*, June 21, 125-39.

Mann, Geoff. 2013. *Disassembly Required: A Field Guide to Actually Existing Capitalism*. Edinburgh ; Oakland, CA: AK Press.

Mann, Stefan. 2020. "Could We Stop Killing?—Exploring a Post-Lethal Vegan or Vegetarian Agriculture." *World* 1(2):124–34. doi: 10/gpkvc9.

Markowski, Kelly L. 2022. "Identity Processes and Food Choice: Predictors of Dietary Lapses among Ethical and Health Vegans." *The Journal of Social Psychology* 1–17. doi: 10.1080/00224545.2022.2105194.

Marmer, William N. 1996. "Preservation and Tanning of Animal Hides." *ACS Symposium Series* 647:60–73. doi: 10.1021/bk-1996-0647.ch005.

Marx, Karl. 1852. "18th Brumaire of Louis Bonaparte. Karl Marx 1852." *Marxists.org*. Retrieved November 23, 2022 (https://www.marxists.org/archive/marx/works/1852/18th-brumaire/ch01.htm).

Massey, Gerald J. and Deborah A. Boyle. 1999. "Descartes's Tests for (Animal) Mind." *Philosophical Topics* 27(1):87–146. doi: 10.5840/philtopics199927119.

Maurizi, Marco. 2021. *Beyond Nature: Animal Liberation, Marxism, and Critical Theory*. Leiden: Brill.

Mbow, C., C. Rosenzweig, L.G. Barioni, T.G. Benton, M. Herrero, M. Krishnapillai, E. Liwenga, P. Pradhan, M.G. Rivera-Ferre, T. Sapkota, F.N. Tubiello, Y. Xu. 2019. "Food Security" in: *Climate Change and Land: an IPCC special report on climate change, desertification, land degradation, sustainable land management, food security, and greenhouse gas fluxes in terrestrial ecosystems*. Ipcc.ch. P.R. Shukla, J. Skea, E. Calvo Buendia, V. Masson-Delmotte, H.-O. Pörtner, D.C. Roberts, P. Zhai, R. Slade, S. Connors, R. van Diemen, M. Ferrat, E. Haughey, S. Luz, S. Neogi, M. Pathak, J. Petzold, J. Portugal Pereira, P. Vyas, E. Huntley, K. Kissick, M. Belkacemi, J. Malley, eds.

McKeever, Amy, and National Geographic Staff. 2022. "How Overfishing Threatens the World's Oceans—and Why It Could End in Catastrophe." *National Geographic*, February 7.

Monbiot, George. 2022. "The Most Damaging Farm Products? Organic, Pasture-Fed Beef and Lamb." *The Guardian*. Retrieved August 17, 2022 (https://www.theguardian.com/environment/2022/aug/16/most-damaging-farm-products-organic-pasture-fed-beef-lamb).

Marcet Rius, Míriam, Patrick Pageat, Cécile Bienboire-Frosini, Eva Teruel, Philippe Monneret, Julien Leclercq, Céline Lafont-Lecuelle, and Alessandro Cozzi. 2018. "Tail and Ear Movements as Possible Indicators of Emotions in Pigs." *Applied Animal Behaviour Science* 205:14–18. doi: 10.1016/j.applanim.2018.05.012.

Mariotti, François, and Christopher D. Gardner. 2019. "Dietary Protein and Amino Acids in Vegetarian Diets-A Review." *Nutrients* 11(11):E2661. doi: 10.3390/nu11112661.

Marlow, Harold J., William K. Hayes, Samuel Soret, Ronald L. Carter, Ernest R. Schwab, and Joan Sabaté. 2009. "Diet and the Environment: Does

What You Eat Matter?" *The American Journal of Clinical Nutrition* 89(5):1699S-1703S. doi: 10/dpzxm3.

Marrone, Giulia, Cristina Guerriero, Daniela Palazzetti, Paolo Lido, Alessandro Marolla, Francesca Di Daniele, and Annalisa Noce. 2021. "Vegan Diet Health Benefits in Metabolic Syndrome." *Nutrients* 13(3):817. doi: 10.3390/nu13030817.

Mason, G. J., and J. M. Lavery. 2022. "What Is It like to Be a Bass? Red Herrings, Fish Pain and the Study of Animal Sentience." *Frontiers in Veterinary Science* 9. doi: 10.3389/fvets.2022.788289.

Maust-Mohl, Maria, John Fraser, and Rachel Morrison. 2012. "Wild Minds: What People Think about Animal Thinking." *Anthrozoös* 25(2):133–47. doi: 10.2752/175303712x13316289505224.

McLean, Courtney P., Jayashri Kulkarni, and Gemma Sharp. 2022. "Disordered Eating and the Meat-Avoidance Spectrum: A Systematic Review and Clinical Implications." *Eating and Weight Disorders - Studies on Anorexia, Bulimia and Obesity* 27:2347–2375. doi: https://doi.org/10.1007/s40519-022-01428-0.

McGuire, Luke, Sally B. Palmer, and Nadira S. Faber. 2022. "The Development of Speciesism: Age-Related Differences in the Moral View of Animals." *Social Psychological and Personality Science* 14(2):228–37. doi: https://doi.org/10.1177/19485506221086182.

McKay, Becky. 2011. "Honey." *Journal of Agricultural & Food Information* 12(2):130–40. doi: 10.1080/10496505.2011.564522.

McNeill, Z. Zane, ed. 2022. *Vegan Entanglements: Dismantling Racial and Carceral Veganism*. Brooklyn, NY: Lantern Publishing & Media.

Medawar, Evelyn, Sebastian Huhn, Arno Villringer, and A. Veronica Witte. 2019. "The Effects of Plant-Based Diets on the Body and the Brain: A Systematic Review." *Translational Psychiatry* 9(1). doi: 10.1038/s41398-019-0552-0.

Meigs, Lucy. 2018. "Animal Testing and Its Alternatives – the Most Important Omics Is Economics." *ALTEX* 35(3):275–305. doi: 10.14573/altex.1807041.

Melina, Vesanto, Winston Craig, and Susan Levin. 2016. "Position of the Academy of Nutrition and Dietetics: Vegetarian Diets." *Journal of the Academy of Nutrition and Dietetics* 116(12):1970–80. doi: 10.1016/j.jand.2016.09.025.

Merriam-Webster. n.d. "Definition of VEGANISM." *Merriam-Webster.com*. Retrieved May 28, 2022 (https://www.merriam-webster.com/dictionary/veganism).

Merrill, Dave and Lauren Leatherby. 2018. "Bloomberg." *Bloomberg.com*. Retrieved June 12, 2022 (https://www.bloomberg.com/graphics/2018-us-land-use/).

Merskin, Debra. 2022. "She, He, Not It: Language, Personal Pronouns, and Animal Advocacy." *Journal of World Languages*. doi: 10/gqkjbt.

Messina, Mark. 2010. "Soybean Isoflavone Exposure Does Not Have Feminizing Effects on Men: A Critical Examination of the Clinical Evidence." *Fertility and Sterility* 93(7):2095–2104. doi: 10/dkjqkb.

Messina, Mark, John L. Sievenpiper, Patricia Williamson, Jessica Kiel, and John W. Erdman. 2022. "Perspective: Soy-Based Meat and Dairy Alternatives, despite Classification as Ultra-Processed Foods, Deliver High-Quality Nutrition on Par with Unprocessed or Minimally Processed Animal-Based Counterparts." *Advances in Nutrition* 13(3):726–38. doi: 10.1093/advances/nmac026.

Mikhalevich, Irina, and Russell Powell. 2020. "Minds without Spines: Evolutionarily Inclusive Animal Ethics." *Animal Sentience* 5(29). doi: 10.51291/2377-7478.1527.

Miller, Franklin G. 2013. "The Stateville Penitentiary Malaria Experiments: A Case Study in Retrospective Ethical Assessment." *Perspectives in Biology and Medicine* 56(4):548–67. doi: 10.1353/pbm.2013.0035.

Miller, Jon D., Eugenie C. Scott, Mark S. Ackerman, Belén Laspra, Glenn Branch, Carmelo Polino, and Jordan S. Huffaker. 2021. "Public Acceptance of Evolution in the United States, 1985–2020." *Public Understanding of Science* 31(2):223–38. doi: 10.1177/09636625211035919.

Minson, Julia A., and Benoît Monin. 2011. "Do-Gooder Derogation." *Social Psychological and Personality Science* 3(2):200–207. doi: 10.1177/1948550611415695.

Mirfakhraie, Amir. 2019. *A Critical Introduction to Sociology: Modernity, Colonialism, Nation-Building, and Post-Modernity*. 2nd ed. USA: Kendall Hunt Publishing Company.

Mitra, Filip Ramesh. 2018. "Lobbying for Captivity: Discourse and the Legitimisation of Zoos and Aquaria." MA Thesis, *Universitat Pompeu Fabra Digital Repository*. Retrieved September 17, 2022 (http://hdl.handle.net/10230/36077).

Mohr, Kylie. 2022. "There Are Millions of Acres of 'Failing' Rangelands, Data Shows." *High Country News*. Retrieved August 17, 2022 (https://www.hcn.org/issues/54.5/north-bureau-of-land-management-there-are-millions-of-acres-of-failing-rangelands-data-shows).

Montford, Kelly Struthers. 2016. "Dehumanized Denizens, Displayed Animals: Prison Tourism and the Discourse of the Zoo." *PhiloSOPHIA* 6(1):73–91. doi: 10.1353/phi.2016.0017.

Montford, Kelly Struthers and Tessa Wotherspoon. 2021. "The Contagion of Slow Violence: The Slaughterhouse and COVID-19." *Research Online*. Retrieved July 9, 2022 (https://ro.uow.edu.au/asj/vol10/iss1/7/). doi: 10.14453/asj.v10i1.6.

Morell, Virginia. 2015. "Meat-Eaters May Speed Worldwide Species Extinction, Study Warns." *Science (New York, N.Y.)*. doi: 10.1126/science.aad1607.

Mueller, Katharina F., Matthias Briel, Daniel Strech, Joerg J. Meerpohl, Britta Lang, Edith Motschall, Viktoria Gloy, Francois Lamontagne, and Dirk Bassler. 2014. "Dissemination Bias in Systematic Reviews of Animal Research: A Systematic Review" edited by L. Manzoli. *PLoS ONE* 9(12):e116016. doi: 10.1371/journal.pone.0116016.

Mycek, Mari Kate. 2018. "Meatless Meals and Masculinity: How Veg* Men Explain Their Plant-Based Diets." *Food and Foodways* 26(3):223–45. doi: 10.1080/07409710.2017.1420355.

Myers, Ransom A., and Boris Worm. 2003. "Rapid Worldwide Depletion of Predatory Fish Communities." *Nature* 423(6937):280–83. doi: 10.1038/nature01610.

Nachvak, Seyed Mostafa, Shima Moradi, Javad Anjom-shoae, Jamal Rahmani, Morteza Nasiri, Vahid Maleki, and Omid Sadeghi. 2019. "Soy, Soy Isoflavones, and Protein Intake in Relation to Mortality from All Causes, Cancers, and Cardiovascular Diseases: A Systematic Review and Dose–Response Meta-Analysis of Prospective Cohort Studies." *Journal of the Academy of Nutrition and Dietetics* 119(9):1483-1500.e17. doi: 10/gpkvdh.

Naghshi, Sina, Omid Sadeghi, Walter C. Willett, and Ahmad Esmaillzadeh. 2020. "Dietary Intake of Total, Animal, and Plant Proteins and Risk of All Cause, Cardiovascular, and Cancer Mortality: Systematic Review and Dose-Response Meta-Analysis of Prospective Cohort Studies." *BMJ* m2412. doi: 10.1136/bmj.m2412.

Nario-Redmond, Michelle R. 2020. *Ableism: The Causes and Consequences of Disability Prejudice*. Hoboken Wiley Blackwell.

NASA. 2022. "Scientific Consensus: Earth's Climate Is Warming." *Climate Change: Vital Signs of the Planet*. Retrieved May 11, 2022 (https://climate.nasa.gov/scientific-consensus/).

National Honey Board. 2022. "Honey Trivia." *National Honey Board*. Retrieved September 15, 2022 (https://honey.com/newsroom/presskit/honey-trivia).

Neal, Dave, Ed Boraas, Gary Elkin, and Iain McKay, eds. 2020. "An Anarchist FAQ: The Anarchist FAQ Editorial Collective, Version 15.4." *The*

Anarchist Library. Retrieved (https://theanarchistlibrary.org/library/the-anarchist-faq-editorial-collective-an-anarchist-faq-full).

Neldner, Karri, and Matti Wilks. 2022. "How Do Children Value Animals? A Developmental Review." *Psychology of Human-Animal Intergroup Relations* 1:1–22. doi: 10.5964/phair.9907.

Nelson, Miriam E., Michael W. Hamm, Frank B. Hu, Steven A. Abrams, and Timothy S. Griffin. 2016. "Alignment of Healthy Dietary Patterns and Environmental Sustainability: A Systematic Review." *Advances in Nutrition: An International Review Journal* 7(6):1005–25. doi: 10.3945/an.116.012567.

Neufingerl, Nicole, and Ans Eilander. 2021. "Nutrient Intake and Status in Adults Consuming Plant-Based Diets Compared to Meat-Eaters: A Systematic Review." *Nutrients* 14(1):29. doi: 10.3390/nu14010029.

Newall, Mallory. 2020. "More than 1 in 3 Americans Believe a 'Deep State' Is Working to Undermine Trump." *Ipsos*. Retrieved May 11, 2022 (https://www.ipsos.com/en-us/news-polls/npr-misinformation-123020).

Newkirk, Ingrid. 2010. "Temple Grandin: Helping the Animals We Can't Save." *PETA*. Retrieved December 1, 2022 (https://www.peta.org/blog/temple-grandin-helping-animals-cant-save/).

Newkirk, Ingrid. 2013. "PETA to Arizona Prisons Chief: Do like Sheriff Joe and Ditch Meat | PETA." *PETA*. Retrieved January 29, 2023 (https://www.peta.org/media/news-releases/peta-arizona-prisons-chief-like-sheriff-joe-ditch-meat/).

Nibert, David. 2002. *Animal Rights/Human Rights: Entanglements of Oppression and Liberation*. Lanham, Md.: Rowman & Littlefield.

Nibert, David. 2013. *Animal Oppression and Human Violence: Domesecration, Capitalism, and Global Conflict*. New York: Columbia University Press.

Nicholls, Allison A., Graham Bryant Epstein, and Sheila R. Colla. 2020. "Understanding Public and Stakeholder Attitudes in Pollinator Conservation Policy Development." *Environmental Science & Policy* 111:27–34. doi: 10.1016/j.envsci.2020.05.011.

Nickerson, Raymond S. 1998. "Confirmation Bias: A Ubiquitous Phenomenon in Many Guises." *Review of General Psychology* 2(2):175–220. doi: 10.1037/1089-2680.2.2.175.

Nijdam, Durk, Trudy Rood, and Henk Westhoek. 2012. "The Price of Protein: Review of Land Use and Carbon Footprints from Life Cycle Assessments of Animal Food Products and Their Substitutes." *Food Policy* 37(6):760–70. doi: 10.1016/j.foodpol.2012.08.002.

Niklewicz, Ali, A. David Smith, Alison Smith, Andre Holzer, Andrew Klein, Andrew McCaddon, Anne M. Molloy, Bruce H. R. Wolffenbuttel, Ebba

Nexo, Helene McNulty, Helga Refsum, Jean-Louis Gueant, Marie-Joe Dib, Mary Ward, Michelle Murphy, Ralph Green, Kourosh R. Ahmadi, Luciana Hannibal, Martin J. Warren, and P. Julian Owen. 2022. "The Importance of Vitamin B12 for Individuals Choosing Plant-Based Diets." *European Journal of Nutrition*. doi: 10.1007/s00394-022-03025-4.

Nixon, Rob. 2011. *Slow Violence and the Environmentalism of the Poor*. Cambridge, Massachusetts: Harvard University Press.

Nobari, Nassim. 2021. "17 - Social Movements in the Transformation of Food and Agriculture Systems." Pp. 371–97 in *Rethinking Food and Agriculture*, Woodhead Publishing Series in Food Science, Technology and Nutrition, edited by A. Kassam and L. Kassam. Woodhead Publishing.

Norman, Kristina, and Susanne Klaus. 2020. "Veganism, Aging and Longevity." *Current Opinion in Clinical Nutrition and Metabolic Care* 23(2):145–50. doi: 10.1097/mco.0000000000000625.

Núñez, Magali Flores. 2019. "Environmental Racism and Latino Farmworker Health in the San Joaquin Valley, California." *Harvard Kennedy School Journal of Hispanic Policy* 31:9–14.

Nuwer, Rachel. 2012. "Is This Mother Giraffe Mourning Her Dead Baby?" *Smithsonian Magazine*. Retrieved June 10, 2022 (https://www.smithsonianmag.com/smart-news/is-this-mother-giraffe-mourning-her-dead-baby-29645135/).

NYU News. 2021. "News Release: Meat and Dairy Companies Slow to Commit to Net-Zero Emissions, New Analysis Finds." *Nyu.edu*. Retrieved July 20, 2022 (https://www.nyu.edu/about/news-publications/news/2021/march/meat-and-dairy-companies-slow-to-commit-to-net-zero-emissions--n.html).

Ognyanova, K. et al. 2021. "The COVID States Project #60: COVID-19 Vaccine Misinformation: From Uncertainty to Resistance". Retrieved (osf.io/xtjad). doi:10.31219/osf.io/xtjad.

Oliver, Catherine. 2021. "Mock Meat, Masculinity, and Redemption Narratives: Vegan Men's Negotiations and Performances of Gender and Eating." *Social Movement Studies* 1–18. doi: 10.1080/14742837.2021.1989293.

Omer, Atalia. 2019. *Days of Awe: Reimagining Jewishness in Solidarity with Palestinians*. Chicago and London: The University of Chicago Press.

OpenSecrets. 2020a. "Livestock | OpenSecrets." *Opensecrets.org*. Retrieved July 20, 2022 (https://www.opensecrets.org/industries/indus.php?ind=A06&cycle=2020).

OpenSecrets. 2020b. "Dairy | OpenSecrets." *Opensecrets.org*. Retrieved July 20, 2022 (https://www.opensecrets.org/industries/indus.php?ind=A04&cycle=2020).

OpenSecrets. 2020c. "Meat processing & products | OpenSecrets." *Opensecrets.org*. Retrieved July 20, 2022 (https://www.opensecrets.org/industries/indus.php?ind=G2300&cycle=2020).

OpenSecrets. 2020d. "Poultry & eggs | OpenSecrets." *Opensecrets.org*. Retrieved July 20, 2022 (https://www.opensecrets.org/industries/indus.php?ind=A05&cycle=2020).

Orth, Taylor. 2022. "One in Four Americans Say They Believe in Astrology." *Yougov.com*. Retrieved May 11, 2022 (https://today.yougov.com/topics/entertainment/articles-reports/2022/04/26/one-four-americans-say-they-believe-astrology).

Otun, Jemiliat, Amirhossein Sahebkar, Linda Östlundh, Stephen L. Atkin, and Thozhukat Sathyapalan. 2019. "Systematic Review and Meta-Analysis on the Effect of Soy on Thyroid Function." *Scientific Reports* 9(1). doi: 10.1038/s41598-019-40647-x.

Our World in Data. 2018. "Aquaculture Production." *Our World in Data*. Retrieved September 14, 2022 (https://ourworldindata.org/grapher/aquaculture-farmed-fish-production).

Our World in Data. 2020. *Yearly Number of Animals Slaughtered for Meat, World, 1961 to 2020*.

Pacheco, P., Mo, K., Dudley, N., Shapiro, A., Aguilar-Amuchastegui, N., Ling, P.Y., Anderson, C. and Marx, A. 2021. "Deforestation fronts: Drivers and responses in a changing world." *WWF*. Gland, Switzerland.

Pais, Daniel Francisco, António Cardoso Marques, and José Alberto Fuinhas. 2022. "The Cost of Healthier and More Sustainable Food Choices: Do Plant-Based Consumers Spend More on Food?" *Agricultural and Food Economics* 10(1):18. doi: 10/gqkjbg.

Palumbo-Liu, David. 2015. "'It's Ugly, It's Vicious, It's Brutal': Cornel West on Israel in Palestine — and Why Gaza Is 'the Hood on Steroids.'" *Salon*. Retrieved November 6, 2022 (https://www.salon.com/2015/02/25/its_ugly_it%E2%80%99s_vicious_it%E2%80%99s_brutal_cornel_west_on_israel_in_palestine_%E2%80%94_and_why_gaza_is_the_hood_on_steroids/).

Pape, Olive. 2018. "Why There Is No 'Ethical Consumption' under Capitalism." *Fightback*. Retrieved July 4, 2022 (https://marxist.ca/article/why-there-is-no-ethical-consumption-under-capitalism).

Patterson, Charles. 2002. *Eternal Treblinka: Our Treatment of Animals and the Holocaust*. New York: Lantern Books.

Pedrinelli, Vivian, Rafael Vessecchi Amorim Zafalon, Roberta Bueno Ayres Rodrigues, Mariana Pamplona Perini, Renata Maria Consentino Conti, Júlio Cesar de Carvalho Balieiro, and Márcio Antonio Brunetto. 2021. "Influence of Number of Ingredients, Use of Supplement and Vegetarian or Vegan Preparation on the Composition of Homemade Diets for Dogs and Cats." *BMC Veterinary Research* 17(1). doi: 10.1186/s12917-021-03068-5.

Peggs, Kay. 2009. "A Hostile World for Nonhuman Animals: Human Identification and the Oppression of Nonhuman Animals for Human Good." *Sociology* 43(1):85–102. doi: 10/dmwp97.

Peggs, Kay. 2012. *Animals and Sociology*. Houndmills, Basingstoke, Hampshire; New York: Palgrave Macmillan.

Pellow, David Naguib. 2014. *Total Liberation: The Power and Promise of Animal Rights and the Radical Earth Movement*. University of Minnesota Press.

Physicians Committee for Responsible Medicine. 2013. "Soy and Health." *Physicians Committee for Responsible Medicine*. Retrieved June 1, 2022 (https://www.pcrm.org/good-nutrition/nutrition-information/soy-and-health).

Piazza, Jared, Matthew B. Ruby, Steve Loughnan, Mischel Luong, Juliana Kulik, Hanne M. Watkins, and Mirra Seigerman. 2015. "Rationalizing Meat Consumption. The 4Ns." *Appetite* 91:114–28. doi: 10/gf6375.

Piazza, Jared, and Steve Loughnan. 2016. "When Meat Gets Personal, Animals' Minds Matter Less." *Social Psychological and Personality Science* 7(8):867–74. doi: 10.1177/1948550616660159.

Picon, Natalie. 2020. "Sexual Violence in the Animal Industry." MA Thesis, Department of Philosophy, Fordham University. ProQuest, 27737543.

Pickett, Susana. 2021. "Veganism, Moral Motivation and False Consciousness." *Journal of Agricultural and Environmental Ethics* 34(3). doi: 10.1007/s10806-021-09857-0.

Pierce, Jessica. 2018. "What the Grieving Mother Orca Tells Us about How Animals Experience Death." *The Conversation*. Retrieved June 10, 2022 (https://theconversation.com/what-the-grieving-mother-orca-tells-us-about-how-animals-experience-death-101230).

Pleasants, Nigel. 2010. "Moral Argument Is Not Enough: The Persistence of Slavery and the Emergence of Abolition." *Philosophical Topics* 38(1):159–80. doi: https://doi.org/10.5840/philtopics20103818.

Pollakova, Daniela, Aikaterini Andreadi, Francesca Pacifici, David Della-Morte, Davide Lauro, and Claudio Tubili. 2021. "The Impact of Vegan Diet in the Prevention and Treatment of Type 2 Diabetes: A Systematic Review." *Nutrients* 13(6):2123. doi: 10.3390/nu13062123.

Pollan, Michael. 2007. *The Omnivore's Dilemma: A Natural History of Four Meals*. New York, NY: Penguin Books.

Poore, J., and T. Nemecek. 2018. "Reducing Food's Environmental Impacts through Producers and Consumers." *Science* 360(6392):987–92. doi: 10/gdm4z3.

Post, S. G. 1991. "The Echo of Nuremberg: Nazi Data and Ethics." *Journal of Medical Ethics* 17(1):42–44. doi: 10.1136/jme.17.1.42.

Potts, Simon G., Jacobus C. Biesmeijer, Claire Kremen, Peter Neumann, Oliver Schweiger, and William E. Kunin. 2010. "Global Pollinator Declines: Trends, Impacts and Drivers." *Trends in Ecology & Evolution* 25(6):345–53. doi: 10.1016/j.tree.2010.01.007.

Pratto, Felicia, Jim Sidanius, Lisa M. Stallworth, and Bertram F. Malle. 1994. "Social Dominance Orientation: A Personality Variable Predicting Social and Political Attitudes." *Journal of Personality and Social Psychology* 67(4):741–63. doi: 10.1037/0022-3514.67.4.741.

Press, Alex N. 2020. "Workers at No Evil Foods Say the Vegan, Progressive Company Busted Their Union Drive." *Jacobin*. Retrieved November 5, 2022 (https://jacobin.com/2020/06/no-evil-foods-unionizing-workers-organizing).

Press, Alex N. 2021. "Capitalists Exploit Workers — Even When They're 'Socialists.'" *Jacobin*. Retrieved November 5, 2022 (https://jacobin.com/2021/05/no-evil-foods-union-busting-nlrb-vegan).

Prisner-Levyne, Yann. 2020. "Trophy Hunting, Canned Hunting, Tiger Farming, and the Questionable Relevance of the Conservation Narrative Grounding International Wildlife Law." *Journal of International Wildlife Law & Policy* 23(4):239–85. doi: 10/gqhnkm.

Probyn-Rapsey, Fiona. 2018. "Anthropocentrism." Pp. 47–63 in *Critical Terms for Animal Studies*. University of Chicago Press.

Proctor, Helen, Gemma Carder, and Amelia Cornish. 2013. "Searching for Animal Sentience: A Systematic Review of the Scientific Literature." *Animals* 3(3):882–906. doi: 10.3390/ani3030882.

PRRI-IFYC. 2022. "Understanding QAnon's Connection to American Politics, Religion, and Media Consumption - PRRI." *PRRI*. Retrieved May 11, 2022 (https://www.prri.org/research/qanon-conspiracy-american-politics-report/).

Psychology Today. n.d. "Anthropomorphism." *Psychology Today*. Retrieved December 1, 2022 (https://www.psychologytoday.com/us/basics/anthropomorphism).

Purina Institute. n.d. "Hot Topics." *PurinaInstitute.com*. Retrieved August 19, 2022 (https://www.purinainstitute.com/hot-topics).

Purkis, Jonathan. 2004. "Towards an Anarchist Sociology." Pp. 39–54 in *Changing Anarchism: Anarchist Theory and Practice in a Global Age*, edited by J. Purkis and J. Bowen. Manchester University Press.

Putnam, Walter. 2012. "'Please Don't Feed the Natives': Human Zoos, Colonial Desire, and Bodies on Display." Pp. 55–68 in *The Environment in French and Francophone Literature and Film*, edited by J. Percsels. Brill.

Ramp, Daniel, and Marc Bekoff. 2015. "Compassion as a Practical and Evolved Ethic for Conservation." *BioScience* 65(3):323–27. doi: 10.1093/biosci/biu223.

Ranganathan, Janet, Richard Waite, Tim Searchinger, and Jessica Zionts. 2020. "Regenerative Agriculture: Good for Soil Health, but Limited Potential to Mitigate Climate Change." *World Resources Institute*. Retrieved August 31, 2022 (https://www.wri.org/insights/regenerative-agriculture-good-soil-health-limited-potential-mitigate-climate-change).

Raz-Chaimovich, Michal. 2019. "Veganism Goes Viral." *Globes.co.il*. Retrieved August 30, 2022 (https://en.globes.co.il/en/article-veganism-goes-viral-1001298773).

Reed, Katharine E., Juliana Camargo, Jill Hamilton-Reeves, Mindy Kurzer, and Mark Messina. 2021. "Neither Soy nor Isoflavone Intake Affects Male Reproductive Hormones: An Expanded and Updated Meta-Analysis of Clinical Studies." *Reproductive Toxicology* 100:60–67. doi: 10.1016/j.reprotox.2020.12.019.

Regan, Tom. 1983. *The Case for Animal Rights*. Berkeley: University of California Press.

Regan, Tom. 2004. *The Case for Animal Rights*. Berkeley: University of California Press.

Regan, Tom. 2005. *Empty Cages: Facing the Challenge of Animal Rights*.

Reiley, Laura. 2020. "The Fastest-Growing Vegan Demographic Is African Americans. Wu-Tang Clan and Other Hip-Hop Acts Paved the Way." *Washington Post*. Retrieved May 31, 2022 (https://www.washingtonpost.com/business/2020/01/24/fastest-growing-vegan-demographic-is-african-americans-wu-tang-clan-other-hip-hop-acts-paved-way/).

Ripple, William J., Christopher Wolf, Thomas M. Newsome, Matthew G. Betts, Gerardo Ceballos, Franck Courchamp, Matt W. Hayward, Blaire Valkenburgh, Arian D. Wallach, and Boris Worm. 2019. "Are We Eating the World's Megafauna to Extinction?" *Conservation Letters* 12(3). doi: 10.1111/conl.12627.

Ritchie, Hannah. 2020a. "Less Meat Is Nearly Always Better than Sustainable Meat, to Reduce Your Carbon Footprint." *Our World in Data*. Retrieved July 7, 2022 (https://ourworldindata.org/less-meat-or-sustainable-meat).

Ritchie, Hannah. 2020b. "The Carbon Footprint of Foods: Are Differences Explained by the Impacts of Methane?" *Our World in Data*. Retrieved (https://ourworldindata.org/carbon-footprint-food-methane).

Ritchie, Hannah. 2020c. "You Want to Reduce the Carbon Footprint of Your Food? Focus on What You Eat, Not Whether Your Food Is Local." *Our World in Data*. Retrieved July 7, 2022 (https://ourworldindata.org/food-choice-vs-eating-local).

Ritchie, Hannah, and Max Roser. 2021. "Forests and Deforestation." *Our World in Data*. Retrieved July 7, 2022 (https://ourworldindata.org/soy).

Robinson, David G., Andreas Draguhn, and Lincoln Taiz. 2020. "Plant 'Intelligence' Changes Nothing." *EMBO Reports* 21(5). doi: 10/gpz8v8.

Robinson, David G., and Andreas Draguhn. 2021. "Plants Have Neither Synapses nor a Nervous System." *Journal of Plant Physiology* 263:153467. doi: 10/gpkvdt.

Robinson, Margaret. 2014. "Animal Personhood in Mi'kmaq Perspective." *Societies* 4(4):672–88. doi: 10.3390/soc4040672.

Robinson, N. Bryce, Katherine Krieger, Faiza M. Khan, William Huffman, Michelle Chang, Ajita Naik, Ruan Yongle, Irbaz Hameed, Karl Krieger, Leonard N. Girardi, and Mario Gaudino. 2019. "The Current State of Animal Models in Research: A Review." *International Journal of Surgery* 72:9–13. doi: 10.1016/j.ijsu.2019.10.015.

Rogerson, David. 2017. "Vegan Diets: Practical Advice for Athletes and Exercisers." *Journal of the International Society of Sports Nutrition* 14(1). doi: 10.1186/s12970-017-0192-9.

Rohrmann, Sabine, Kim Overvad, H. Bas Bueno-de-Mesquita, Marianne U. Jakobsen, Rikke Egeberg, Anne Tjønneland, Laura Nailler, Marie-Christine Boutron-Ruault, Françoise Clavel-Chapelon, Vittorio Krogh, Domenico Palli, Salvatore Panico, Rosario Tumino, Fulvio Ricceri, Manuela M. Bergmann, Heiner Boeing, Kuanrong Li, Rudolf Kaaks, Kay-Tee Khaw, and Nicholas J. Wareham. 2013. "Meat Consumption and Mortality - Results from the European Prospective Investigation into Cancer and Nutrition." *BMC Medicine* 11(1). doi: 10.1186/1741-7015-11-63.

Romero, Simon, and Sara Shahriari. 2011. "Quinoa's Global Success Creates Quandary at Home." *The New York Times*, March 19.

Rosenfeld, Daniel L. 2019. "Ethical Motivation and Vegetarian Dieting: The Underlying Role of Anti-Speciesist Attitudes." *Anthrozoös* 32(6):785–96. doi: 10/gqknft.

Rothberg, Michael. 2009. *Multidirectional Memory: Remembering the Holocaust in the Age of Decolonization*. Stanford, Calif.: Stanford University Press.

Rothberg, Michael. 2014. "Multidirectional Memory." *Témoigner. Entre Histoire et Mémoire* 119(2014):176. doi: 10.4000/temoigner.1494.

Rothgerber, Hank. 2019. "Meat-Related Cognitive Dissonance: A Conceptual Framework for Understanding How Meat Eaters Reduce Negative Arousal from Eating Animals." *Appetite* 146(104511):104511. doi: 10.1016/j.appet.2019.104511.

Rowland, M. J. 2004. "Return of the 'Noble Savage': Misrepresenting the Past, Present and Future." *Australian Aboriginal Studies* 2004(2):2–14.

Rowlands, Mark. 2020. "The Moral Animal." Pp. 83–91 in *The Routledge Handbook of Animal Ethics*, edited by B. Fischer. New York, Ny: Routledge.

Rowntree, Jason E., Paige L. Stanley, Isabella C. F. Maciel, Mariko Thorbecke, Steven T. Rosenzweig, Dennis W. Hancock, Aidee Guzman, and Matt R. Raven. 2020. "Ecosystem Impacts and Productive Capacity of a Multi-Species Pastured Livestock System." *Frontiers in Sustainable Food Systems* 4. doi: 10.3389/fsufs.2020.544984.

Ruby, Matthew B., and Steven J. Heine. 2011. "Meat, Morals, and Masculinity." *Appetite* 56(2):447–50. doi: 10.1016/j.appet.2011.01.018.

Ruch, Jeff, and Chandra Rosenthal. 2022. "Interior Has Bad Case of Climate 'Cow Blindness': Failure to Address Commercial Livestock Climate Impacts Invites Lawsuits." *PEER.org*. Retrieved August 17, 2022 (https://peer.org/interior-has-bad-case-of-climate-cow-blindness/).

Ruehlman, Linda S., and Paul Karoly. 2022. "Adherence versus Striving to Adhere to Vegan, Vegetarian, or Pescatarian Diets: Applying a Goal-Centered, Self-Regulatory Framework." *Journal of Health Psychology* 27(9):2236–46. doi: 10.1177/13591053221111976.

Russo, Laura, Charlotte W. de Keyzer, Alexandra N. Harmon-Threatt, Kathryn A. LeCroy, and James Scott MacIvor. 2021. "The Managed-To-Invasive Species Continuum in Social and Solitary Bees and Impacts on Native Bee Conservation." *Current Opinion in Insect Science* 46:43–49. doi: 10.1016/j.cois.2021.01.001.

Sabaté, Joan, and Sam Soret. 2014. "Sustainability of Plant-Based Diets: Back to the Future." *The American Journal of Clinical Nutrition* 100(suppl_1):476S-482S. doi: 10/f573nc.

Salinas, Carmen Martín. 2019. "Is Vegan Feeding Advisable in First Childhood?" *OA Journal of Food and Nutrition* 1(001). doi: 10.33118/oaj.food.2019.01.001.

Samuel, Sigal. 2021. "Big Meat Spends Millions to Block Climate Policy — Just like Big Oil." *Vox*. Retrieved July 20, 2022 (https://www.vox.com/future-perfect/22379909/big-meat-companies-spend-millions-lobbying-climate).

Sanbonmatsu, John. 2014. "The Animal of Bad Faith: Speciesism as an Existential Project." Pp. 29–45 in *Critical Animal Studies: Thinking the Unthinkable*, edited by J. Sorenson. Toronto: Canadian Scholars' Press Inc.

Sánchez-Gómez, Luis A. 2013. "Human Zoos or Ethnic Shows? Essence and Contingency in Living Ethnological Exhibitions." *Culture & History Digital Journal* 2(2):1–25. doi: 10.3989/chdj.2013.022.

Santiago-Ávila, Francisco J., and William S. Lynn. 2020. "Bridging Compassion and Justice in Conservation Ethics." *Biological Conservation* 248:108648. doi: 10.1016/j.biocon.2020.108648.

Sartre, Jean-Paul. [1943] 2018. *Being and Nothingness: An Essay in Phenomenological Ontology*. Abingdon, Oxon, UK: Routledge.

Schatzki, Theodore. 2012. "A Primer on Practices." Pp. 13–26 in *Practice-Based Education: Perspectives and Strategies*, edited by J. Higgs, R. Barnett, S. Billett, M. Hutchings, and F. Trede. Brill.

Schatzki, Theodore. 2016. "Practice Theory as Flat Ontology." Pp. 28–42 in *Practice Theory and Research: Exploring the Dynamics of Social Life*, edited by G. Spaargaren, D. Weenink, and M. Lamers. London and New York: Routledge.

Schieltz, Jennifer M., and Daniel I. Rubenstein. 2016. "Evidence Based Review: Positive versus Negative Effects of Livestock Grazing on Wildlife. What Do We Really Know?" *Environmental Research Letters* 11(11):113003. doi: 10.1088/1748-9326/11/11/113003.

Schreefel, L., R. P. O. Schulte, I. J. M. de Boer, A. Pas Schrijver, and H. H. E. van Zanten. 2020. "Regenerative Agriculture – the Soil Is the Base." *Global Food Security* 26:100404. doi: 10.1016/j.gfs.2020.100404.

Schulman, Sarah. 2016. *Conflict Is Not Abuse: Overstating Harm, Community Responsibility, and the Duty of Repair*. Vancouver: Arsenal Pulp Press.

Schuppli, Caroline, and Carel P. van Schaik. 2019. "Animal Cultures: How We've Only Seen the Tip of the Iceberg." *Evolutionary Human Sciences* 1. doi: 10.1017/ehs.2019.1.

Scott, Evon, Giorgos Kallis, and Christos Zografos. 2019. "Why Environmentalists Eat Meat." *PLOS ONE* 14(7). doi: 10.1371/journal.pone.0219607.

Searchinger, Timothy D., Stefan Wirsenius, Tim Beringer, and Patrice Dumas. 2018. "Assessing the Efficiency of Changes in Land Use for Mitigating Climate Change." *Nature* 564(7735):249–53. doi: 10.1038/s41586-018-0757-z.

Sebastian, Christopher. 2021. "What Do Veganism and Conspiracy Theories Have in Common?" *Euronews*. Retrieved January 29, 2023 (https://www.euronews.com/green/2021/04/12/what-do-veganism-and-conspiracy-theories-have-in-common).

Sebastiani, Giorgia, Ana Herranz Barbero, Cristina Borrás-Novell, Miguel Alsina Casanova, Victoria Aldecoa-Bilbao, Vicente Andreu-Fernández, Mireia Pascual Tutusaus, Silvia Ferrero Martínez, María Gómez Roig, and Oscar García-Algar. 2019. "The Effects of Vegetarian and Vegan Diet during Pregnancy on the Health of Mothers and Offspring." *Nutrients* 11(3):557. doi: 10.3390/nu11030557.

Seed, Amanda, and Richard Byrne. 2010. "Animal Tool-Use." *Current Biology* 20(23):R1032–39. doi: 10.1016/j.cub.2010.09.042.

Selinger, Eliška, Manuela Neuenschwander, Alina Koller, Jan Gojda, Tilman Kühn, Lukas Schwingshackl, Janett Barbaresko, and Sabrina Schlesinger. 2022. "Evidence of a Vegan Diet for Health Benefits and Risks – an Umbrella Review of Meta-Analyses of Observational and Clinical Studies." *Critical Reviews in Food Science and Nutrition* 1–11. doi: 10.1080/10408398.2022.2075311.

Shannon, Deric, Anthony J. Nocella, and John Asimakopoulos. 2012. *The Accumulation of Freedom: Writings on Anarchist Economics*. Oakland, CA: AK Press.

ShareScore.com. 2022. "Check Social Share Counts for Any URL [Social URL Analytics]." *Shareaholic*. Retrieved August 23, 2022 (https://www.sharescore.com/?url=https://www.boredpanda.com/vegans-eating-agave-syrup-honey-beekeeper-response/).

Shepon, A., G. Eshel, E. Noor, and R. Milo. 2016. "Energy and Protein Feed-To-Food Conversion Efficiencies in the US and Potential Food Security Gains from Dietary Changes." *Environmental Research Letters* 11(10):105002. doi: 10.1088/1748-9326/11/10/105002.

Shields, Randy. 2017. "Tom Regan: The Life of the Animal Rights Party." *CounterPunch.org*. Retrieved September 7, 2022 (https://www.counterpunch.org/2017/02/24/tom-regan-the-life-of-the-animal-rights-party/).

Shove, Elizabeth, Mika Pantzar, and Matt Watson. 2012. *The Dynamics of Social Practice: Everyday Life and How It Changes*. SAGE.

Shukla, P.R., J. Skea, R. Slade, A. Al Khourdajie, R. van Diemen, D. McCollum, M. Pathak, S. Some, P. Vyas, R. Fradera, M. Belkacemi, A. Hasija, G. Lisboa, S. Luz, J. Malley, eds. 2022. "Climate Change 2022: Mitigation of Climate Change. Contribution of Working Group III to the Sixth Assessment Report of the Intergovernmental Panel on Climate Change." *IPCC*. Cambridge University Press, Cambridge, UK and New York, NY, USA. doi: 10.1017/9781009157926.

Silvério, Divino V., Paulo M. Brando, Marcia N. Macedo, Pieter S. A. Beck, Mercedes Bustamante, and Michael T. Coe. 2015. "Agricultural Expansion Dominates Climate Changes in Southeastern Amazonia: The Overlooked

Non-GHG Forcing." *Environmental Research Letters* 10(10):104015. doi: 10.1088/1748-9326/10/10/104015.

Singer, Peter. 2009. *Animal Liberation: The Definitive Classic of the Animal Movement*. New York, N.Y. Harper Collins.

Singer, Peter. [1975] 2015. *Animal Liberation: The Definitive Classic of the Animal Movement*. New York, NY: Open Road Media.

Singh, Julietta. 2018. *Unthinking Mastery: Dehumanism and Decolonial Entanglements*. Durham: Duke University Press.

Singleton, Benedict E., Maris Boyd Gillette, Anders Burman, and Carina Green. 2021. "Toward Productive Complicity: Applying 'Traditional Ecological Knowledge' in Environmental Science." *The Anthropocene Review* 205301962110570. doi: 10.1177/20530196211057026.

Sivaram, N. M., and Debabrata Barik. 2019. "Toxic Waste from Leather Industries." *Energy from Toxic Organic Waste for Heat and Power Generation* 55–67. doi: 10.1016/b978-0-08-102528-4.00005-5.

Skitolsky, Lissa. 2013. "Recollecting Violence: Michael Rothberg's *Multidirectional Memory*." *POSTMODERN CULTURE: Journal of Interdisciplinary Thought on Contemporary Cultures* 20(2). doi: http://dx.doi.org/10.1353/pmc.2010.0007.

Slade, Jessica, and Emma Alleyne. 2021. "The Psychological Impact of Slaughterhouse Employment: A Systematic Literature Review." *Trauma, Violence, & Abuse* 152483802110302. doi: 10.1177/15248380211030243.

Smedley, Audrey, and Brian D. Smedley. 2005. "Race as Biology Is Fiction, Racism as a Social Problem Is Real: Anthropological and Historical Perspectives on the Social Construction of Race." *American Psychologist* 60(1):16–26. doi: https://doi.org/10.1037/0003-066x.60.1.16.

Smith, P. 2022. "Leather Goods Market Value Worldwide 2016-2021." *Statista*. Retrieved November 3, 2022 (https://www.statista.com/statistics/861562/leather-goods-market-value-worldwide/).

Smith, Trevor J. 2019. "Corn, Cows, and Climate Change: How Federal Agricultural Subsidies Enable Factory Farming and Exacerbate U.S. Greenhouse Gas Emissions." *Washington Journal of Environmental Law & Policy* 9(1): 26–55. Retrieved August 28, 2022 (https://digitalcommons.law.uw.edu/wjelp/vol9/iss1/3).

Sneddon, Lynne U., David C. C. Wolfenden, Matthew C. Leach, Ana M. Valentim, Peter J. Steenbergen, Nabila Bardine, Donald M. Broom, and Culum Brown. 2018. "Ample Evidence for Fish Sentience and Pain." *Animal Sentience* 3(21). doi: 10.51291/2377-7478.1375.

Sneddon, Lynne U., Javier Lopez-Luna, David C. C. Wolfenden, Matthew C. Leach, Ana M. Valentim, Peter J. Steenbergen, Nabila Bardine, Amanda D. Currie, Donald M. Broom, and Culum Brown. 2018. "Fish Sentience

Denial: Muddying the Waters." *Animal Sentience* 3(21). doi: 10.51291/2377-7478.1317.

Solomon, Adrian. 2017. "One Face of Dehumanization: Animalization." *Synergy* 13(1):40–51. Retrieved on November 9, 2022 (http://www.synergy.ase.ro/issues/2017-vol13-no-1/6-solomon.pdf).

Sones, Mordechai. 2018. "IDF Most Vegan Army in World." *Israel National News*. Retrieved August 30, 2022 (https://www.israelnationalnews.com/news/252681).

Springer, Simon. 2022. "Check Your Anthroprivilege! Situated Knowledge and Geographical Imagination as an Antidote to Environmental Speciesism, Anthroparchy, and Human Fragility." in *Vegan Geographies: Spaces beyond Violence, Ethics beyond Speciesism*, edited by P. Hodge, A. McGregor, S. Springer, O. Véron, and R. J. White. Brooklyn, NY: Lantern Publishing & Media.

Springmann, Marco, H. Charles J. Godfray, Mike Rayner, and Peter Scarborough. 2016. "Analysis and Valuation of the Health and Climate Change Cobenefits of Dietary Change." *Proceedings of the National Academy of Sciences* 113(15):4146–51. doi: 10.1073/pnas.1523119113.

Staff, Arutz Sheva. 2014. "Israel Is the 'Most Vegan Country in the World.'" *Israel National News*. Retrieved August 30, 2022 (https://www.israelnationalnews.com/news/186427).

Stanescu, Vasile. 2019. "'Cowgate': Meat Eating and Climate Change." Pp. 178–94 in *Climate Change Denial and Public Relations: Strategic Communication and Interest Groups in Climate Inaction*, edited by N. Almiron and J. Xifra. London: Routledge.

Stanley, Eric A., and Nat Smith. 2015. *Captive Genders: Trans Embodiment and the Prison Industrial Complex*. 2nd ed. Oakland, CA, USA; Edinburgh, Scotland: AK Press.

Starostinetskaya, Anna. 2017. "Israeli Army Introduces Vegan Combat Rations." *VegNews.com*. Retrieved August 30, 2022 (https://vegnews.com/2017/4/israeli-army-introduces-vegan-combat-rations).

Staus, Nancy. 2019. "The Educational Value of Zoos: An Empirical Perspective." Pp. 367–80 in *The Routledge Handbook of Animal Ethics*, edited by B. Fischer. New York, NY: Routledge.

Steiner, Gary. 2011. "The Differences between Singer, Regan, and Francione." *Scribd*. Retrieved September 7, 2022 (https://www.scribd.com/document/340038729/The-Differences-Between-Singer-Regan-And-Francione).

Stern, Robert. 2004. "Does 'Ought' Imply 'Can'? And Did Kant Think It Does?" *Utilitas* 16(1):42–61. doi: 10.1017/s0953820803001055.

Stevens, Andrew W. 2017. "Quinoa Quandary: Cultural Tastes and Nutrition in Peru." *Food Policy* 71:132–42.

Stewart, Hayden, Jeffrey Hyman, Diansheng Dong, and Andrea Carlson. 2020. "The More That Households Prioritise Healthy Eating, the Better They Can Afford to Consume a Sufficient Quantity and Variety of Fruits and Vegetables." *Public Health Nutrition* 24(7):1841–50. doi: 10.1017/s1368980020004929.

Stewart, Kate, and Matthew Cole. 2009. "The Conceptual Separation of Food and Animals in Childhood." *Food, Culture & Society* 12(4):457–76. doi: 10.2752/175174409x456746.

Stoll-Kleemann, Susanne, and Uta Johanna Schmidt. 2016. "Reducing Meat Consumption in Developed and Transition Countries to Counter Climate Change and Biodiversity Loss: A Review of Influence Factors." *Regional Environmental Change* 17(5):1261–77. doi: 10.1007/s10113-016-1057-5.

Stucki, Saskia. 2020. "(Certified) Humane Violence? Animal Production, the Ambivalence of Humanizing the Inhumane, and What International Humanitarian Law Has to Do with It." Pp. 121–31 in *Studies in Global Animal Law*, edited by A. Peters. Springer Open.

Su, Ruijun, Wenfei Dai, Yulian Yang, Xuelin Wang, Rui Gao, Mengying He, Chuan Zhao, and Junpeng Mu. 2022. "Introduced Honey Bees Increase Host Plant Abundance but Decrease Native Bumble Bee Species Richness and Abundance." *Ecosphere* 13(6). doi: 10.1002/ecs2.4085.

Sullivan, Katherine. 2021. "Israel Becomes First Country in the World to Ban Fur | PETA." *PETA*. Retrieved August 30, 2022 (https://www.peta.org/blog/israel-bans-fur/).

Sutter, Daniel Olivier, and Nicole Bender. 2021. "Nutrient Status and Growth in Vegan Children." *Nutrition Research* 91:13–25. doi: 10.1016/j.nutres.2021.04.005.

Sztybel, David. 2006. "Can the Treatment of Animals Be Compared to the Holocaust?" *Ethics & the Environment* 11(1):97–132. doi: https://doi.org/10.1353/een.2006.0007.

Tabor, Ronald D. 2013. *The Tyranny of Theory: A Contribution to the Anarchist Critique of Marxism*. Black Cat Press.

Taft, Molly. 2022. "The Beef Industry Is Trying to Sell Us Bullshit." *Gizmodo*. Retrieved October 30, 2022 (https://gizmodo.com/beef-industry-spin-climate-change-1849629519).

Takacs, Berill, Julia A. Stegemann, Anastasia Z. Kalea, and Aiduan Borrion. 2022. "Comparison of Environmental Impacts of Individual Meals - Does It Really Make a Difference to Choose Plant-Based Meals instead of Meat-Based Ones?" *Journal of Cleaner Production* 379:134782. doi: 10.1016/j.jclepro.2022.134782.

TallBear, Kimberly. 2001. "Racialising Tribal Identity and the Implications for Political and Cultural Development." Pp. 1–9 in *The Indigenous Peoples and Racism Conference*. Sydney, Australia.

Tasca, Andrea Luca, and Monica Puccini. 2019. "Leather Tanning: Life Cycle Assessment of Retanning, Fatliquoring and Dyeing." *Journal of Cleaner Production* 226:720–29. doi: 10.1016/j.jclepro.2019.03.335.

Tawinikay. 2018. "Autonomously and with Conviction: A Métis Refusal of State-Led Reconciliation." *The Anarchist Library*. Retrieved November 16, 2022 (https://theanarchistlibrary.org/library/tawinikay-autonomously-and-with-conviction).

Taylor, Katy, and Laura Rego Alvarez. 2020. "An Estimate of the Number of Animals Used for Scientific Purposes Worldwide in 2015." *Alternatives to Laboratory Animals* 47(5-6):196–213. doi: 10.1177/0261192919899853.

Taylor, Katy, Nicky Gordon, Gill Langley, and Wendy Higgins. 2008. "Estimates for Worldwide Laboratory Animal Use in 2005." *Alternatives to Laboratory Animals* 36(3):327–42. doi: 10.1177/026119290803600310.

Taylor Phillips, L., and Brian S. Lowery. 2015. "The Hard-Knock Life? Whites Claim Hardships in Response to Racial Inequity." *Journal of Experimental Social Psychology* 61:12–18. doi: 10.1016/j.jesp.2015.06.008.

Taylor, Sunaura. 2017. *Beasts of Burden: Animal and Disability Liberation*. New York: New Press.

The Vegan Society. 2022. "The Vegan Society's Grow Green Campaign: Solutions for the Farm of the Future." *The Vegan Society*. Retrieved August 18, 2022 (https://www.vegansociety.com/take-action/campaigns/grow-green).

The Vegan Society. n.d.a. "History." *The Vegan Society*. Retrieved March 22, 2022 (https://www.vegansociety.com/about-us/history).

The Vegan Society. n.d.b. "Definition of Veganism." *The Vegan Society*. Retrieved December 14, 2022 (https://www.vegansociety.com/go-vegan/definition-veganism).

Thomas, Margaret A. 2016a. "Are Vegans the Same as Vegetarians? The Effect of Diet on Perceptions of Masculinity." *Appetite* 97:79–86. doi: 10.1016/j.appet.2015.11.021.

Thomas, Margaret A. 2016b. "Are Vegans the Same as Vegetarians? The Effect of Diet on Perceptions of Masculinity." *Appetite* 97:79–86. doi: 10.1016/j.appet.2015.11.021.

Thomson, Diane M. 2016. "Local Bumble Bee Decline Linked to Recovery of Honey Bees, Drought Effects on Floral Resources" edited by R. Irwin. *Ecology Letters* 19(10):1247–55. doi: 10.1111/ele.12659.

Thorning, Tanja Kongerslev, Anne Raben, Tine Tholstrup, Sabita S. Soedamah-Muthu, Ian Givens, and Arne Astrup. 2016. "Milk and Dairy Products: Good or Bad for Human Health? An Assessment of the Totality of Scientific Evidence." *Food & Nutrition Research* 60(1):32527. doi: 10.3402/fnr.v60.32527.

Thürmer, J. Lukas, Juliane Stadler, and Sean M. McCrea. 2022. "Intergroup Sensitivity and Promoting Sustainable Consumption: Meat Eaters Reject Vegans' Call for a Plant-Based Diet." *Sustainability* 14(3):1741. doi: 10/gqkjfm.

Tian, Saiqi. 2020. "Recent Advances in Functional Polyurethane and Its Application in Leather Manufacture: A Review." *Polymers* 12(9). doi: 10.3390/polym12091996.

Trejo-Salazar, Roberto-Emiliano, Luis E. Eguiarte, David Suro-Piñera, and Rodrigo A. Medellin. 2016. "Save Our Bats, Save Our Tequila: Industry and Science Join Forces to Help Bats and Agaves." *Natural Areas Journal* 36(4):523–30. doi: 10.3375/043.036.0417.

Trenkova, Lilia. 2016. "The Womyn's Club: Vegan Feminism and Transphobia." *Collectively Free*. Retrieved August 24, 2022 (https://www.collectivelyfree.org/the-womyns-club-and-transphobia/).

Treves, A., F. J. Santiago-Ávila, and W. S. Lynn. 2019. "Just Preservation." *WBI Studies Repository*. Retrieved August 21, 2022 (https://www.wellbeingintlstudiesrepository.org/antpdec/9/).

Trupp, Alexander. 2015. "Exhibiting the 'Other' Then and Now: 'Human Zoos' in Southern China and Thailand." *Advances in Southeast Asian Studies* 4(1):139–49. doi: 10.14764/10.ASEAS-4.1-8.

Tucker, Robert C., ed. 1978. *The Marx-Engels Reader*. 2nd ed. New York: Norton.

Tuite, Eileen K., Simon A. Moss, Clive J. Phillips, and Samantha J. Ward. 2022. "Why Are Enrichment Practices in Zoos Difficult to Implement Effectively?" *Animals* 12(5):554. doi: 10.3390/ani12050554.

Twine, Richard. 2010. "Intersectional Disgust? Animals and (Eco)Feminism." *Feminism & Psychology* 20(3):397–406. doi: 10.1177/0959353510368284.

Twine, Richard. 2017. "A Practice Theory Framework for Understanding Vegan Transition." *Animal Studies Journal* 6(2):192-224. Retrieved November 24, 2022 (https://ro.uow.edu.au/asj/vol6/iss2/12).

Twine, Richard. 2020. "Where Are the Nonhuman Animals in the Sociology of Climate Change?" *Society & Animals* 1–26. doi: 10/gpkvfc.

Tyson, Elizabeth. 2018. "Speciesism and Zoos: Shifting the Paradigm, Maintaining the Prejudice." Pp. 165–79 in *The Palgrave Handbook of*

Practical Animal Ethics, edited by A. Linzey and C. Linzey. London: Macmillan Publishers Ltd.

Ulaby, Neda. 2017. "Bats and Tequila: A Once Boo-Tiful Relationship Cursed by Growing Demands." *NPR.org*. Retrieved August 22, 2022 (https://www.npr.org/sections/thesalt/2017/10/29/560292442/bats-and-tequila-a-once-boo-tiful-relationship-cursed-by-growing-demands).

Ecker, Ullrich K. H., Caitlin X. M. Sharkey, and Briony Swire-Thompson. 2023. "Correcting Vaccine Misinformation: A Failure to Replicate Familiarity or Fear-Driven Backfire Effects." *PloS One* 18(4):e0281140. doi: 10.1371/journal.pone.0281140.

UMass Lowell Center for Public Opinion. 2020. "American Opinions on Race, Policing, Systemic Racism | Center for Public Opinion | Research." *Uml.edu*. Retrieved May 11, 2022 (https://www.uml.edu/Research/public-opinion/polls/2020/Race-Policing.aspx).

UN News. 2022. "Climate Change Impacts 'Heading into Uncharted Territory', Warns UN Chief." *UN News*. Retrieved (https://news.un.org/en/story/2022/09/1126511).

United States Department of Agriculture. 2019. "FoodData Central." *Usda.gov*. Retrieved August 22, 2022 (https://fdc.nal.usda.gov/fdc-app.html#/food-details/170277/nutrients).

United States Environmental Protection Agency. 2022. "Global Greenhouse Gas Emissions Data | US EPA." *US EPA*. Retrieved August 28, 2022 (https://www.epa.gov/ghgemissions/global-greenhouse-gas-emissions-data).

United States Geological Survey. n.d. "Eutrophication | U.S. Geological Survey." *Usgs.gov*. Retrieved June 12, 2022 (https://www.usgs.gov/centers/wetland-and-aquatic-research-center/science/science-topics/eutrophication).

University of Cambridge. 2014. "Changing Global Diets Is Vital to Reducing Climate Change, Researchers Say." *ScienceDaily*. Retrieved March 27, 2023 (http://www.sciencedaily.com/releases/2014/08/140831150209.htm).

University of Cambridge. 2018. "Think of Honeybees as 'Livestock' Not Wildlife, Argue Experts." *University of Cambridge: Research*. Retrieved (https://www.cam.ac.uk/research/news/think-of-honeybees-as-livestock-not-wildlife-argue-experts).

Ursachi, Claudiu Ștefan, Florentina-Daniela Munteanu, and Gabriela Cioca. 2021. "The Safety of Slaughterhouse Workers during the Pandemic Crisis." *International Journal of Environmental Research and Public Health* 18(5):2633. doi: 10.3390/ijerph18052633.

USDA APHIS (United States Department of Agriculture, Animal and Plant Health Inspection Service. 2022. "USDA APHIS | Animal Welfare Act." *Usda.gov*. Retrieved August 25, 2022 (https://www.aphis.usda.gov/aphis/ourfocus/animalwelfare/sa_awa).

Valido, Alfredo, María C. Rodríguez-Rodríguez, and Pedro Jordano. 2019. "Honeybees Disrupt the Structure and Functionality of Plant-Pollinator Networks." *Scientific Reports* 9(1). doi: 10.1038/s41598-019-41271-5.

van Casteren, Adam, David S. Strait, Michael V. Swain, Shaji Michael, Lidia A. Thai, Swapna M. Philip, Sreeja Saji, Khaled Al-Fadhalah, Abdulwahab S. Almusallam, Ali Shekeban, W. Scott McGraw, Erin E. Kane, Barth W. Wright, and Peter W. Lucas. 2020. "Hard Plant Tissues Do Not Contribute Meaningfully to Dental Microwear: Evolutionary Implications." *Scientific Reports* 10(1). doi: 10.1038/s41598-019-57403-w.

van den Heuvel, Ellen G. H. M., and Jan M. J. M. Steijns. 2018. "Dairy Products and Bone Health: How Strong Is the Scientific Evidence?" *Nutrition Research Reviews* 31(2):164–78. doi: 10.1017/s095442241800001x.

Vanham, D., M. M. Mekonnen, and A. Y. Hoekstra. 2013. "The Water Footprint of the EU for Different Diets." *Ecological Indicators* 32:1–8. doi: 10.1016/j.ecolind.2013.02.020.

Van Norman, Gail A. 2019. "Limitations of Animal Studies for Predicting Toxicity in Clinical Trials." *JACC: Basic to Translational Science* 4(7):845–54. doi: 10.1016/j.jacbts.2019.10.008.

Veganic Agriculture Network. 2022. "Veganic Agriculture Network" *Veganic Agriculture Network*. Retrieved August 18, 2022 (https://www.goveganic.net/).

Vegan Organic Network. 2022. "Vegan Organic Network – Vegan Organic (Stockfree) Growing for People, Animals and the Environment." *Veganorganic.net*. Retrieved August 18, 2022 (https://veganorganic.net/).

Vegan Sidekick. 2022. "Vegan Sidekick: Photo." *Tumblr.com*. Retrieved June 5, 2022 (https://vegansidekick.tumblr.com/image/85009745145).

Ventura, B. A., M. A. G. von Keyserlingk, C. A. Schuppli, and D. M. Weary. 2013. "Views on Contentious Practices in Dairy Farming: The Case of Early Cow-Calf Separation." *Journal of Dairy Science* 96(9):6105–16. doi: 10.3168/jds.2012-6040.

Vettori, Virginia, Chiara Lorini, Bianca Bronzi, and Guglielmo Bonaccorsi. 2022. "Water Global Health Benefit: The Water Footprint of the Dietary Patterns and the Acceptability of a 100% Plant-Based Diet." *Medical Sciences Forum* 4(1):33. doi: 10/gqkjc7.

Visalberghi, E., Sabbatini, G., Taylor, A. H., & Hunt, G. R. 2017. "Cognitive insights from tool use in nonhuman animals." In J. Call, G. M. Burghardt,

I. M. Pepperberg, C. T. Snowdon, & T. Zentall, eds., *APA Handbook of Comparative Psychology: Perception, Learning, and Cognition* 673–701. American Psychological Association. https://doi.org/10.1037/0000012-030.

Volcano, Abbey. 2012. "Police at the Borders." Pp. 33–42 in *Queering Anarchism: Addressing and Undressing Power and Desire*, edited by C. B. Daring, J. Rogue, D. Shannon, and A. Volcano. Oakland, CA: AK Press.

Waldron, David, and Janice Newton. 2012. "Rethinking Appropriation of the Indigenous." *Nova Religio* 16(2):64–85. doi: 10.1525/nr.2012.16.2.64.

Wallach, Arian D., Marc Bekoff, Michael Paul Nelson, and Daniel Ramp. 2015. "Promoting Predators and Compassionate Conservation." *Conservation Biology* 29(5):1481–84. doi: 10.1111/cobi.12525.

Wallach, Arian D., Marc Bekoff, Chelsea Batavia, Michael Paul Nelson, and Daniel Ramp. 2018. "Summoning Compassion to Address the Challenges of Conservation." *Conservation Biology* 32(6):1255–65. doi: 10.1111/cobi.13126.

Wallach, Arian D., Erick Lundgren, Chelsea Batavia, Michael Paul Nelson, Esty Yanco, Wayne L. Linklater, Scott P. Carroll, Danielle Celermajer, Kate J. Brandis, Jamie Steer, and Daniel Ramp. 2020. "When All Life Counts in Conservation." *Conservation Biology* 34(4):997–1007. doi: 10.1111/cobi.13447.

Ward, Eric. 2018. "Think of Honeybees as 'Livestock' Not Wildlife, Argue Experts." *University of Cambridge*. Retrieved September 15, 2022 (https://www.cam.ac.uk/research/news/think-of-honeybees-as-livestock-not-wildlife-argue-experts).

Worsham, Lynn. 2013. "Toward an Understanding of Human Violence: Cultural Studies, Animal Studies, and the Promise of Posthumanism." *Review of Education, Pedagogy, and Cultural Studies* 35(1):51–76. doi: https://doi.org/10.1080/10714413.2013.752697.

Watanabe, Fumio, Yukinori Yabuta, Tomohiro Bito, and Fei Teng. 2014. "Vitamin B12-Containing Plant Food Sources for Vegetarians." *Nutrients* 6(5):1861–73. doi: 10.3390/nu6051861.

Weaver, James R., John S. Ascher, and Rachel E. Mallinger. 2022. "Effects of Short-Term Managed Honey Bee Deployment in a Native Ecosystem on Wild Bee Foraging and Plant–Pollinator Networks." *Insect Conservation and Diversity* 15(5):634–44. doi: 10.1111/icad.12594.

Weber, Magdalena, and Marlene Kollmayer. 2022. "Psychological Processes Underlying an Omnivorous, Vegetarian, or Vegan Diet: Gender Role Self-Concept, Human Supremacy Beliefs, and Moral Disengagement from Meat." *Sustainability* 14(14):8276. doi: 10.3390/su14148276.

Weekers, Timothy, Leon Marshall, Nicolas Leclercq, Thomas James Wood, Diego Cejas, Bianca Drepper, Louise Hutchinson, Denis Michez, Jean-Marc Molenberg, Guy Smagghe, Peter Vandamme, and Nicolas J. Vereecken. 2022. "Dominance of Honey Bees Is Negatively Associated with Wild Bee Diversity in Commercial Apple Orchards regardless of Management Practices." *Agriculture, Ecosystems & Environment* 323:107697. doi: 10.1016/j.agee.2021.107697.

Wehrmaker, Ariane Maike, Nynke Draijer, Guido Bosch, and Atze Jan van der Goot. 2022. "Evaluation of Plant-Based Recipes Meeting Nutritional Requirements for Dog Food: The Effect of Fractionation and Ingredient Constraints." *Animal Feed Science and Technology* 290:115345. doi: 10/gqkjfh.

Weiss, Erica. 2016. "'There Are No Chickens in Suicide Vests': The Decoupling of Human Rights and Animal Rights in Israel." *Journal of the Royal Anthropological Institute* 22(3):688–706. doi: 10.1111/1467-9655.12453.

Wei, Yuxia, Jun Lv, Yu Guo, Zheng Bian, Meng Gao, Huaidong Du, Ling Yang, Yiping Chen, Xi Zhang, Tao Wang, Junshi Chen, Zhengming Chen, Canqing Yu, Dezheng Huo, and Liming Li. 2019. "Soy Intake and Breast Cancer Risk: A Prospective Study of 300,000 Chinese Women and a Dose–Response Meta-Analysis." *European Journal of Epidemiology* 35(6):567–78. doi: 10.1007/s10654-019-00585-4.

White, Courtney. 2020. "Why Regenerative Agriculture?" *The American Journal of Economics and Sociology* 79(3):799–812. doi: 10/gqkdjs.

White, Richard J. 2017. "Capitalism and the Commodification of Animals: The Need for Critical Vegan Praxis, Animated by Anarchism!" Pp. 270–93 in *Animal Oppression and Capitalism*, edited by D. Nibert. Santa Barbara, California: Praeger.

Whiten, Andrew. 2021. "The Burgeoning Reach of Animal Culture." *Science* 372(6537). doi: 10.1126/science.abe6514.

Wilkins, Abbie M., Lucy S. McCrae, and E. Anne McBride. 2015. "Factors Affecting the Human Attribution of Emotions toward Animals." *Anthrozoös* 28(3):357–69. doi: 10.1080/08927936.2015.1052270.

Wilks, Matti, Lucius Caviola, Guy Kahane, and Paul Bloom. 2021. "Children Prioritize Humans Over Animals Less Than Adults Do." *Psychological Science* 32(1):27–38. doi: 10/ghqn35.

Willett, Walter, Johan Rockström, Brent Loken, Marco Springmann, Tim Lang, Sonja Vermeulen, Tara Garnett, David Tilman, Fabrice DeClerck, Amanda Wood, Malin Jonell, Michael Clark, Line J. Gordon, Jessica Fanzo, Corinna Hawkes, Rami Zurayk, Juan A. Rivera, Wim De Vries, Lindiwe Majele Sibanda, Ashkan Afshin, Abhishek Chaudhary, Mario

Herrero, Rina Agustina, Francesco Branca, Anna Lartey, Shenggen Fan, Beatrice Crona, Elizabeth Fox, Victoria Bignet, Max Troell, Therese Lindahl, Sudhvir Singh, Sarah E. Cornell, K. Srinath Reddy, Sunita Narain, Sania Nishtar, and Christopher J. L. Murray. 2019. "Food in the Anthropocene: The EAT–Lancet Commission on Healthy Diets from Sustainable Food Systems." *The Lancet* 393(10170):447–92. doi: 10/gft25h.

Williams, Sage. 2020. "Vegan Statistics — New Data Investigation for 2021." *Futurekind.Com*. Retrieved August 26, 2021 (https://www.futurekind.com/blogs/vegan/vegan-statistics).

Winders, Delcianna J., and Elan Abrell. 2021. "Slaughterhouse Workers, Animals, and the Environment: The Need for a Rights-Centered Regulatory Framework in the United States That Recognizes Interconnected Interests." *Health and Human Rights* 23(2):21–33.

Winebarger, Lisa. 2012. "Standing behind Beastly Emissions: The U.S. Subsidization of Animal Agriculture Violates the United Nations Framework Convention on Climate Change." *American University International Law Review* 27(4): 991-1035. Retrieved August 29, 2022 (https://digitalcommons.wcl.american.edu/auilr/vol27/iss4/14/).

Winstead, Amanda. 2021. "Why Vegans Should Focus on Farmworkers' Rights | NationofChange." *Nationofchange.org*. Retrieved July 8, 2022 (https://www.nationofchange.org/2021/06/14/why-vegans-should-focus-on-farmworkers-rights/).

Wirnitzer, Katharina C. 2020. "Vegan Diet in Sports and Exercise – Health Benefits and Advantages to Athletes and Physically Active People: A Narrative Review." *International Journal of Sports and Exercise Medicine* 6(3). doi: 10.23937/2469-5718/1510165.

Wise, Steven M. 1998. "Hardly a Revolution-The Eligibility of Nonhuman Animals for Dignity-Rights in a Liberal Democracy." *Vermont Law Review* 22:793-915.

Wise, Steven M. 2005. *Though the Heavens May Fall: The Landmark Trial That Led to the End of Human Slavery*. Cambridge, Mass.: Da Capo Press.

Wise, Steven M. 2010. "LEGAL PERSONHOOD AND THE NONHUMAN RIGHTS PROJECT." *Animal Law Review* 17(1, Fall 2010):1–11. Retrieved June 19, 2022 (https://www.animallaw.info/article/legal-personhood-and-nonhuman-rights-project).

Womack, Craig. 2013. "There Is No Respectful Way to Kill an Animal." *Studies in American Indian Literatures* 25(4):11. doi: 10/gpkvbz.

Woodward, Natalie. 2019. "Eternal Mirroring: Charles Patterson's Treatment of Animals and the Holocaust." *Journal of Animal Ethics* 9(2):158–69. doi: 10/gps8qw.

Worsham, Lynn. 2013. "Toward an Understanding of Human Violence: Cultural Studies, Animal Studies, and the Promise of Posthumanism." *Review of Education, Pedagogy, and Cultural Studies* 35(1):51–76. doi: https://doi.org/10.1080/10714413.2013.752697.

Wrenn, Corey. 2018. "How to Help When It Hurts? Think Systemic." *Animal Studies Journal* 7(1):149-179. Retrieved May 13, 2022 (https://ro.uow.edu.au/asj/vol7/iss1/8).

Wright, James, ed. 2015. *International Encyclopedia of the Social & Behavioural Sciences.* Vol. 20. 2nd ed. Amsterdam: Elsevier.

Wright, L. 2015. "Men, Meat, and Hegan Identity: Veganism and the Discourse of Masculinity." Pp. 107–129 in *The Vegan Studies Project: Food, Animals, and Gender in the Age of Terror.* University of Georgia Press. http://www.jstor.org/stable/j.ctt183q3vb.11.

WWF. n.d. "Soy | Industries | WWF." *World Wildlife Fund.* Retrieved August 8, 2022 (https://www.worldwildlife.org/industries/soy).

Xu, Jingwen, Yanting Shen, Yi Zheng, Gordon Smith, Xiuzhi Susan Sun, Donghai Wang, Yong Zhao, Wei Zhang, and Yonghui Li. 2021. "Duckweed (Lemnaceae) for Potentially Nutritious Human Food: A Review." *Food Reviews International* 1–15. doi: 10.1080/87559129.2021.2012800.

Zafalon, Rafael Vessecchi Amorim, Larissa Wünsche Risolia, Thiago Henrique Annibale Vendramini, Roberta Bueno Ayres Rodrigues, Vivian Pedrinelli, Fabio Alves Teixeira, Mariana Fragoso Rentas, Mariana Pamplona Perini, Isabella Corsato Alvarenga, and Marcio Antonio Brunetto. 2020. "Nutritional Inadequacies in Commercial Vegan Foods for Dogs and Cats" edited by N. Righini. *PLOS ONE* 15(1):e0227046. doi: 10.1371/journal.pone.0227046.

Milton Keynes UK
Ingram Content Group UK Ltd.
UKHW022104021023
429821UK00004B/27